Japanese
Women
Poets

Japanese Women Poets
An Anthology

Translated and with an Introduction by

Hiroaki Sato

An East Gate Book

M.E.Sharpe
Armonk, New York
London, England

An East Gate Book

Library of Congress Cataloging-in-Publication Data

Japanese women poets : an anthology / translator and editor Hiroaki Sato.
   p. cm.—(Japan in the modern world)
 Includes bibliographical references and index.
 ISBN: 978-0-7656-1783-5 (cloth : alk. paper)
 1. Japanese poetry—Translations into English. 2. Japanese poetry—Women authors—
Translations into English. I. Sato, Hiroaki, 1942–

PL872.E3J379 2007
895.6′1089287—dc22   2006019874

Printed in the United States of America

The paper used in this publication meets the minimum requirements of
American National Standard for Information Sciences
Permanence of Paper for Printed Library Materials,
ANSI Z 39.48-1984.

BM (c)   10   9   8   7   6   5   4   3   2   1

To Nancy

I sent a poem to a man I was in love with as fleetingly as dew:

White dew, dreams, this world, illusions: all these last for eternities in comparison.

—Izumi Shikibu

Brief Contents

Detailed Contents

The Age of Haikai and Kanshi

Interludes

The Modern Age

Note and Acknowledgments

All Japanese names in this anthology are given the Japanese way, family name first. Following Japanese custom, poets are sometimes identified by personal name or penname, sometimes by family name. Unless otherwise noted, all translations are mine. Several *Kojiki* and *Nihon Shoki* translations originally appeared in *From the Country of Eight Islands: An Anthology of Japanese Poetry* (Doubleday, 1981; Columbia University Press, 1986); a passage from *Mumyōshū* quoted in the introduction, a passage from the *Masu-Kagami* in the Kunai-kyo section, as well as all the poems of Princess Shikishi, in *String of Beads: Complete Poems of Princess Shikishi* (University of Hawaii Press, 1993); "Record of an Autumn Wind," complete and fully annotated, in *Monumenta Nipponica*, vol. 55, no. 1 (Spring 2000); all the poems of Ema Saikō, in *Breeze Through Bamboo: Kanshi of Ema Saikō* (Columbia University Press, 1997); Yosano Akiko's "Cochineal Purple" (from *Midaregami*), "May It Not Come to Pass that You Die," "The Woman," "In Praise of May," and "Auguste's Single Strike" in *The University of California Book of Romantic and Post-Romantic Poetry;* some of Nagase Kiyoko's poems, in *Poetry Kanto 2006*; many of Fujiki Kiyoko's haiku, in *ant ant ant ant ant* (Fall 2003); some of Ishigaki Rin's poems, in *From the Country of Eight Islands* and *Poetry Kanto 2006*; Takarabe Toriko's "Talk of Horses" in *Circumference* (Fall 2003), several in online magazine *Fascicle* (Summer 2005), and several in *Poetry Kanto 2006*; all of Shinkawa Kazue's poems, in *Not a Metaphor: Poems of Shinkawa Kazue* (P.S., A Press, 1999); many of Tada Chimako's poems, in *Anthology of World Poetry of the 20th Century*, Volume II (Green Integer); all of Tomioka Taeko's poems, in *See You Soon: Poems of Taeko Tomioka* (Chicago Review Press, 1979); some of Koyanagi Reiko's poems, in *Rabbit of the Nether World* (Red Moon Press, 1999); all of Kimura Nobuko's poems, in *The Village Beyond: Poems of Nobuko Kimura* (P.S., A Press, 2002); one of her poems, "Over There," also in the Asia special issue of *Atlanta Review* (Spring/Summer 2002); all of Nagashima Minako's poems, in *The Girl Who Turned into Tea: Poems of Minako Nagashima* (P.S., A Press, 2000); fifteen of Kamakura Sayumi's haiku in *Modern Haiku* (Fall 2000); Abe Hinako's "Garden Party" and "The Future Belongs to Olenka" in online magazine *Fascicle* (Summer 2005) and Nagami Atsuko's poem, "Descending to 'Hell Valley' in the Nippara Stalactite Cave," in the *Tin House* magazine (Summer 2003, Vol. 4, No. 4) and some others, in *Bomb* (Spring 2004); all of Park Kyong-Mi in online magazine *The Green Integer Review*, No. 2 (March–April 2006); Hirata Toshiko's "Recent Photos" and "A Woman's Life or Nakayama Atsuko" and Koike Masayo's "The Most Sensuous Room" in online magazine *How2* (2005); most of "A Brief Survey of Haiku by Women," in *Modern Haiku* (Autumn 2002) and most of "A Brief

Survey of Senryū by Women," in *Modern Haiku* (Winter–Spring 2003); "Twelve Months" in *Modern Haiku* (Winter–Spring 2006); and some of the other modern haiku, in *Blythe Spirit* and *Frogpond*.

My relatives and friends helped collect books for this anthology: Hirata Takako, Kamei Haruko, and Yano Sumiko among my relatives; Abe Hinako, Ishii Tatsuhiko, Kakizaki Shōko, Takagaki Chihiro, Ueda Akira, and Yajima Mieko among my friends. Many poets gave me their books. Abe Hinako, Bessho Makiko, Ishii Tatsuhiko, Koike Masayo, Takagaki Chihiro, and Yajima Mieko obtained bibliographic and other information for me. Taira Sōsei helped me with women's senryū. Louise E. Virgin helped prepare some of the illustrations.

Doris Bargen, Kathleen Dooley, Jim Kacian, Leza Lowitz, Douglas Messerli, Grace Ogawa-Preuss, Linda Peevey, and Ursula Smith read and commented on some of the translations. Kate Wildman Nakai, editor, and Lynne E. Riggs, managing editor, of *Monumenta Nipponica*, edited "Record of an Autumn Wind" with professional dedication. My erudite friend Kyoko Iriye Selden helped me in countless ways. Among other things, she transcribed on the computer for me the handwritten manuscript *Kurehatori*, a collection of tanka by Sakuma (née Hiroe) Tachieko. The painter Makie Hino drew the portrait of Yatabe Ryōkichi (p. xxxi) from an old photograph.

My primary readers were, as always, Robert Fagan, Lenore Parker, and Nancy Rossiter.

This book would not have been possible without the patience and generosity of everyone.

Hiroaki Sato

Chronology

Nara Period (710–784)
  712: *Kojiki (Record of Ancient Matters)*
  720: *Nihon Shoki (History of Japan)*
  751: *Kaifūsō (Fond Recollections of Poetry)*, anthology of kanshi
  Late in the century: *Man'yōshū (Collection of Ten Thousand Leaves)*
    Beowulf

Heian Period (794–1185)
  814–827: three imperial anthologies of kanshi
  905: *Kokinshū (Collection of Ancient and Modern Poems)*, first imperial
    anthology of Japanese poems
  Early 11th century: *Genji Monogatari (The Tale of Genji)*

Kamakura Period (1192–1333)
  1205: *Shin-Kokinshū (New Collection of Ancient and Modern Poems)*, eighth
    imperial anthology of Japanese poems
  late 13th century: *Yoru no Tsuru (The Night Crane)*, Abutsu's treatise on poetics

Muromachi Period (1331–1573)
  1357: *Tsukubashū (Tsukuba Collection)*, semi-imperial renga anthology
    Christine de Pizan (1364–1430)
  1439: *Shin-Zoku-Kokinshū (New Sequel to the Collection of Ancient and
    Modern Poems)*, 21st and last imperial anthology of Japanese poems
From the latter half of the 15th century to the late 16th century: Japan's Age of
    Warring States
    Isabella d'Este (1474–1539)
    Louise Labé (1520?–66)
    1557: *Tottel's Miscellany*

Edo Period (1600–1868)
    Ann Bradstreet (1612?–72)
    Aphra Behn (1640–89)
    Juana Ines de la Cruz (1648–95)
  1684: *Kokin Haikai Onna Kasen (Thirty-Six Ancient and Modern Women
    Haikai Poets)*, collection of 36 women haikai poets compiled by Ihara
    Saikaku; first such anthology
  1702: *Mikawa Komachi (Mikawa Beauties)*, second half devoted to women
    haikai poets, compiled by Ōta Hakusetsu

1747: *Tamamoshū (Coralline Collection)*, collection of women haikai poets compiled by Yosa Buson

1789: *Umiyama (Sea and Mountain)*, anthology with a substantial collection of haibun by a woman
Elizabeth Barrett Browning (1806–61)
Emily Dickinson (1830–86)
Christina Rossetti (1830–94)

Modern Period (since 1868)
1868: Tokugawa shogunate replaced by monarchism
Amy Lowell (1874–1925)
Edith Sitwell (1887–1964)
1882: *Shintai-shi Shō (New-Style Poetry)*, first attempt to introduce Western-style verse
1901: *Midaregami (Hair in Disorder)*, collection of tanka by Yosano Akiko
1904–05: Russo-Japanese War
1911: Hiratsuka Raichō starts a women's magazine, *Seitō (Bluestockings)*
1941: Japan assaults Pearl Harbor
1945: Japan surrenders

Twelve Months

Until it adopted the solar calendar in the early 1870s, Japan used the lunar calendar. In the lunar calendar, a month consists of twenty-nine or thirty days. To make up for the obvious shortfall, seven intercalary months are inserted every nineteen years. Lunar months are about forty days behind those of the solar calendar, though an intercalary month sometimes throws this off. Unlike the solar calendar, in which spring begins in March, in the lunar calendar spring begins in First Month.

The basic Japanese names for the twelve months, lunar and solar, are numerical: *ichi-gatsu,* "First Month," for January, *ni-gatsu,* "Second Month," for February, and so on. But each lunar month also has a variety of names, some originating in China, some in Japan. A list of the most common alternative names for the twelve lunar months, along with their etymological explanations or conjectures, is given below, each illustrated with a haiku by a woman. Much of the information comes from Muzuhara Shūōshi, Katō Shūson, and Yamakoto Kenkichi, eds., *Nihon Dai-Saijiki* (Kōdansha, 1983), a massive compendium of fifteen thousand *kigo,* "seasonal words," each seasonal indicator accompanied by haiku—sometimes dozens of them. I have also consulted the four-volume *Haikai Saijiki* (Shinchōsha, 1950–1968) and the five-volume *Haiku Saijiki* (Kadokawa Shoten, 1955–1980).

Intimate Month *(Mutsuki)* for First Month. The name is said to reflect the tendency of people to get together and become *mutsumaji,* "intimate," during the New Year festivities. Kusamura Motoko (1919–1974) wrote, referring to the pine decorations for the New Year known as *kadomatsu,* "gate pines":

> *Matsu torete nochi no Mutsuki no kakeashi ni*
> After the pines taken off Intimate Month trots away

Clothes Doubled *(Kisaragi)* for Second Month. With the word consisting of ki (clothes) and saragi (wearing more), it tells you that the lingering cold can sometimes force you to wear more clothes. Hosomi Ayako (1907–1987) wrote:

> *Kisaragi ga mayu no atari ni kuru gotoshi*
> As though Clothes Doubled came near my eyebrows

More Growth *(Yayoi)* for Third Month. The name is thought to derive from *iyaoi,* "irrepressible growth," in reference to the time of year when the growth of plants becomes ever more pronounced. Ichiriki Tamiko (dates uncertain) wrote:

Hoshimono o sukoshi yoru hosu Yayoi-zuki
I put up some clothes to dry at night under the More Growth moon

Deutzia Month *(Uzuki)* for Fourth Month. The shrub with white flowers called *unohana* or *utsugi (Deutzia crenata* or *scabra)* flourishes during this month. Some regret the infelicitous sound of the English and Latin names of the plant and substitute deutzia with "mock orange" or "saxifrage"; both English and Latin names come from Jean Deutz, mayor of Amsterdam and patron of botany. *Unohana* is prized for the bright white clusters its flowers make, which in classical poetry are often compared to snow or crystal. Chiyo-jo (1703?–1775) captures that aspect of this flowering shrub in her hokku:

Unohana wa hi o mochinagara kumorikeri
Deutzia flowers hold forth their light on a cloudy day

Seedling Month *(Satsuki)* for Fifth Month. Some say *satsuki* is an abbreviation of *sanaetsuki*, "rice-seedling month," and some that it is that of *samidare-tsuki*, "rainy-season month," although, for that matter, *sa* in *samidare* itself is said to mean Fifth Month, *midare* meaning "water-dripping." Yamazaki Tomiko (dates uncertain) uses one of the non-abbreviated names of *satsuki* in the following haiku in which *ni*, "load," suggests a basket filled with rice seedlings:

Shimabito no mina ni o ou ya Sanaetsuki
The island people all carry a load: Rice-seedling Month

Waterless Month *(Minazuki)* for Sixth Month. Japan's rainy season *(tsuyu)*, which lasts for about thirty days, is followed by hot, sun-drenched days during this month, hence the name. In the following haiku of Hasegawa Kanajo (1887–1969), the water in the rice paddies still hasn't evaporated:

Minazuki no tagoto ni sagi o tenjikeri
In Waterless Month each paddy's dotted with herons

Letter Month *(Fumizuki)* for Seventh Month. *Fumi* means "letter," "writing," "book," etc. The seventh day of Seventh Month is Tanabata, Japan's star festival when the once-a-year meeting is allowed to take place between Princess Weaver (Vega) and the Oxherd (Altair) across the River of Heaven (the Milky Way). As U. A. Casal describes it in *The Five Sacred Festivals in Ancient Japan* (Sophia University, 1967), on this day freshly cut bamboo is "adorned with numerous pieces of gaily colored paper: neat strips which twirl on a thread, and which, closer inspection will show, are covered with inscriptions, poems in fact." The name of the month comes, some say, from the act of opening anthologies for children to copy appropriate poems on those gaily colored strips of paper. In

Hasegawa Kanajo's piece on the month, sasafuri, "bamboo leaves falling," is a summer kigo, which may onomatopoeically suggest rain, and the word *hana,* "flowers," points to the colorful strips of paper. Rain on Tanabata prevents the two lovers from having their annual tryst. Some haiku practitioners argue you can't use two kigo in a single piece.

Sasafuri ya Fumizuki no hana ochi nagashi
Bamboo leaves falling Letter Month flowers drop and flow

Leaf Month *(Hazuki)* for Eighth Month. The tanka poet Fujiwara no Kiyosuke (1104–1177) says in his treatise on poetics, *Ōgishō,* that the name derives from the fact that during the month tree leaves turn color and fall. The renga master Matsumura Jōha (1524–1602) argues in *Shihōshō,* a treatise on poetics he prepared for the warlord Toyotomi Hideyoshi, that the Chinese characters to be used for *hazuki* should be those that mean "first" and "month" because it is in this month that geese, coming from the north, first appear in Japan. In the following haiku by Kashiwamura Sadako (born 1916), Otoko-yama most likely refers to a hill south of Kyoto which has atop it the famous shrine for the deity of war, Iwashimizu Hachiman-gū:

Otoko-yama kudarite Hazuki no te o nurasu
Coming down Mount Male I wet my Leaf Month hands

Long Month *(Nagatsuki)* for Ninth Month. Nights become longer during the month, hence the name, some say. Shibata Hakuyōjo (1906–1984) has:

Nagatsuki no ichiju katamuku hoshi-akari
In Long Month a single tree tilts in the star light

Godless Month (*Kannazuki*) for Tenth Month. Yoshida Kenkō (1283–1351?) devotes Section 202 of his *Tsurezuregusa* (*Essays in Idleness*) to a discussion of the striking name: "There is nothing that says that, Tenth Month being called Godless Month, we should avoid deity-related services [during this month]. There is no authoritative source on this, either. However, the name may derive from the fact that there is no shrine festival this month. There is a theory that in this month all the thousands of deities gather at the Grand Shrine [of Ise, where the presiding deity is Sun Goddess Amaterasu-ō-mi-kami], but there is no authority on this. In the event, Ise should make it a particularly festive month, but it does no such thing. In Tenth Month, there are a number of imperial visits to various shrines, but many are inauspicious." In other words, according to Kenkō, why this month is called "godless" is not known. In more recent accounts, all the deities are said to gather at the Grand Shrine of Izumo, where the chief deity Ōkuninushi-no-mikoto is male, perhaps for a fall banquet, and because they vacate their own shrines to congregate in one, the month, it is explained, is "godless." Katsura Nobuko (1914–2004) has written a mystifying piece:

Hashigo yori hito no nioi ya Kannazuki
From a ladder comes someone's smell this Godless Month

Frost Month (*Shimotsuki*) for Eleventh Month. The name is understood to reflect the meteorological phenomenon of the month. Watanabe Kazuko (dates uncertain) wrote:

Shimotsuki ya chashibu shimitaru fukin hosu
Frost Month: I dry a napkin soaked with tea puckeriness

Priests' Run *(Shiwasu)* for Twelfth Month. So called because during the last month of the year even monks and priests, who are supposed to maintain transcendental calm, are forced to run about to take care of unfinished business and chores. Conversely, some say the name derives from *shihatsu,* "month in which to finish doing things." Matate Masayo (dates uncertain) has:

Machi Shiwasu ten ni mukaite ashiba kumu
Town in Priests' Run: toward heaven scaffolds build

Introduction

Something held women back when it came to the writing of poetry, and since whatever it was that held them back failed to hold women back from writing novels, we must suppose that the inhibition had something, at least, to do with the antiquity and prestige of the art.

—James Fenton[1]

Japanese poetry, which dates from the seventh century or earlier, has two distinct features: the sizable presence of women poets from the outset and a verse structure based on simple syllabic patterns.

Japan's oldest extant book, the *Kojiki* (*Record of Ancient Matters*), compiled in 712, and the more elaborate retelling of the same mythological and semi-mythological imperial lineage, the *Nihon Shoki* (*History of Japan*), compiled in 720, together contain a total of 190 distinct songs, and 58 of them, or 30 percent, are attributed to women. The figure falls to 12 percent for the *Man'yōshū* (*Collection of Ten Thousand Leaves*), the great anthology of about 4,550 poems that took shape in the late eighth century. In "the twenty-one imperial anthologies," compiled from the early tenth century to 1439,[2] the number of women included sometimes becomes very small, but they are always present. In the case of the fourth imperial anthology, the *Go-Shūishū* (*Collection of Later Gleanings*), compiled in 1087, 104 of the total of 329 poets are women, as are the three best represented: Izumi Shikibu (born late 970s), Sagami (991?–1061?), and Akazome Emon (957?–1041?).[3] This came about, explained the poet and ethnological student of Japanese literature Orikuchi Shinobu (Shaku Chōkū; 1887–1953),

---

1. James Fenton, *The Strength of Poetry: Oxford Lectures* (Farrar, Straus and Giroux, 2001), 103.

2. The idea of compiling verse anthologies by the order of the emperor apparently came from China, but China never pursued the matter in earnest. Japan, in any case, is almost certainly the only country in the world that produced so many anthologies at the behest of the head of state. See Maruya Saiichi's short history of Japanese literature, *Nihon Bungaku Hayawakari* (Kōdansha, 1984), 7–8.

3. The "real" names of women poets in early periods are often unknown. The names we know are usually "court (nick)names," and the naming can be capricious. Izumi Shikibu was so called because her husband, Tachibana no Michisada, once served as governor of Izumi Province, and her father, Ōe no Masamune, was an officer in the Shikibu-shō, Ministry of Ceremonial. Sagami, who had nothing that might correspond to the second part of a "full name," was so called because her husband, Ōe no Kimiyori, once served as governor of Sagami Province. Akazome Emon was so called because her father, Akazome Tokimochi, was an *emon*, a palace guard. She was also called Masahira Emon because her husband was Ōe no Masahira.

because of Japan's "historical habit of recognizing women's poetry as the same as men's in rank."[4]

In contrast, women's presence in Western poetry until recent centuries is so meager as to tempt James Fenton to make the kind of assertion cited at the outset of this introduction. Or, as Burton Watson once put it, explaining how the situation is different in Japan, "Try writing 'Sappho' on a sheet of paper and listing under it all the other famous women poets in Western literature down to the middle of the [nineteenth] century and you will see what I mean."[5] In England, for example, *Tottel's Miscellany,* the first anthology of English verse, published in 1557, does not seem to include a single woman, even among the "uncertain authors."

In certain of the later periods—in particular, from the late fourteenth century to the early seventeenth century, when the court was overshadowed by the military government and the whole country was in a state of constant warfare—women poets may not have done as well as their forebears, but they were never completely eclipsed. When it comes to the past one hundred years or so, several books of poems by women have created national sensations. Among them are *Midaregami* (*Hair in Disorder*), in 1901, by Yosano Akiko (1878–1942), who sang in romantic delirium of a young woman's desires and fantasies; *Chibusa Sōshitsu* (*My Breasts Lost*), in 1954, by Nakajō Fumiko (1922–1954), who chronicled the effects of a breast cancer that eventually killed her; *Sarada Kinenbi* (*Salad Anniversary*), in 1987, by Tawara Machi (born 1962), who described youthful love affairs with the sort of lightheartedness that was thought to characterize a generation known by the sobriquet *shin-jinrui,* "new mankind"; and *B-men no Natsu* (*Summer on Side B*), in 1994, by Mayuzumi Madoka (born 1962), who depicted an illicit love affair in a book-length sequence of haiku. One might add *Yorikakarazu* (*Relying on Nothing*), a 1999 book by Ibaraki Noriko (born 1926), which, because a popular column of a major daily mentioned it, sold 300,000 copies.

Anthologies are always arbitrary in their selections to a greater or lesser extent, but two recent ones seem to set new standards for tanka poets in modern times. In Takano Kimihiko's *Gendai no Tanka* (Kōdansha, 1991), 38 out of the 105 poets selected for the period since the late nineteenth century are women. In Okai Takashi's *Gendai Hyakunin Isshu* (Asahi Shimbunsha, 1996), 34 of the 100 poets selected for the period since the end of the Second World War are women.

The title of Okai's book, incidentally, comes from the most famous mini-anthology ever compiled in Japan: the *Hyakunin Isshu* (*One Hundred Poems by One Hundred Poets*). In that canonical selection, prepared in the thirteenth century by Fujiwara no Teika (1162–1241), 21 of the 100 poets are women.

---

4. Orikuchi Shinobu, *Josei Tanka-shi* (*History of Tanka by Women*), vol. 11, *Zenshū,* 4th rev. ed. (Chūō Kōron Sha, 1984), 48.
5. Burton Watson, Introduction, in *See You Soon: Poems of Taeko Tomioka,* trans. Hiroaki Sato (Chicago Review Press, 1979), 11.

Women Assessing Their Own Position

This is not to say that Japanese women poets have been mostly content with their lot. *Mumyō Sōshi (Nameless Book)*, a remarkable work of literary criticism that is attributed to the poet known as Lord Shunzei's Daughter (1171?–1252?)—actually a grandchild of Fujiwara no Shunzei (1114–1204), who adopted her—creates a setting in which an old nun listens to a group of young women discuss women's literary achievements: There is *Genji Monogatari (The Tale of Genji)*, one of the women says, "a rarity that couldn't have been born of the forces of this world alone." There is, says another, *Sagoromo Monogatari (The Tale of Sagoromo)*, "second only to *Genji* in popularity." And there is *Yoru no Nezame (Awaking at Night)*, whose focus on one woman's suffering "touches you deeply." (*Sagoromo Monogatari* is attributed to Minamoto no Yorikuni's Daughter, also known as Rokujō Saiin Senji [died 1092]. The author of *Yoru no Nezame* is unknown but is assumed to be female.)

Among the writers and poets, the women go on to say, Ono no Komachi, judging from her poetry, "must have been exquisite in every way—in her appearance, her conduct, her heart." Sei Shōnagon may not be "as good a poet as you might expect" but has "fully expressed her heart in *Makura no Sōshi* [*The Pillow Book*], detailing all the wonderful, pitiful, exquisite, and felicitous things in it." There are, in addition, Koshikibu no Naishi and her mother, Izumi Shikibu, as well as their employer, Empress Teishi, not to mention Murasaki Shikibu and her employer, Empress Shōshi, also known by her Buddhist name, Jōtōmon'in.[6]

As it happens, this discussion is touched off when one of the group laments the "mortifying" (*kuchioshi*) state in which women find themselves. Anthologists—such as Shunzei, who, at Retired Emperor Goshirakawa's command, edited a few years earlier the seventh imperial anthology of Japanese poetry, the *Senzaishū*—often end up including mediocre pieces of those of higher status as a mark of deference, the young woman notes. "That must be humiliating, don't you think?" she asks. "Yes, it must be," she responds to her own question before continuing: "But nothing is more mortifying than being a woman. Since long ago many of us have fine-tuned our sensibilities and studied the Way of Poetry but not one has been asked to edit an imperial anthology. Isn't that mortifying?"

The young woman ends her complaint saying that aspiring poets must try to "imitate" superior poets of the past and the present, "even those who are only slightly better" than they, imitation being *de rigueur* in writing poetry. To this, another person, perhaps the old nun or Lord Shunzei's Daughter herself, says: "You know

---

6. *Mumyō Sōshi* is thought to have been written around 1200. A century earlier, the scholar of Chinese classics Ōe no Masafusa (1041–1111) assessed the situation differently. He cited Izumi Shikubu and Akazome Emon as representative poets but mentioned neither Murasaki Shikibu nor Sei Shōnagon, apparently because he did not regard the ability to write prose in the indigenous Japanese language as worth noting.

mimicking is something you shouldn't do. If you do it, you'll fall into an abyss!" With that, "everyone laughs."

Here, Lord Shunzei's Daughter may have been self-consciously joking. She was skilled at *honkadori*—the art, which was then being codified by poets such as Shunzei's son, Teika, of incorporating into a poem a word or phrase found in someone else's poem. And this brings us to versification.

Development of Verse Forms

When poetic forms first took shape in Japan, there were at least five, all based on units of five and seven syllables. Two of them were dominant: the 5-7-5-7-7-syllable *tanka*, "short song," and the *chōka* or *nagauta*, "long song," which repeats the 5-7-syllable combination three times or more, usually ending with an extra seven and often followed by an envoi of one or more tanka. (*Ka* is a sinified pronunciation of the Chinese character for the Japanese word *uta*, "song.") As the early English student of Japanese literature W.G. Aston (1841–1911) wrote, in 1899, the chōka was "an instrument not unfitted . . . for the production of narrative, elegiac, and other poems." But that verse form began to be neglected early on, so that a mere 5 of the 1,111 poems in the *Kokinshū* (*Collection of Ancient and Modern Poems*) were chōka; virtually all the others were composed in the tanka form. Subsequently, the tanka became the almost exclusive poetic vehicle for those writing in Japanese—a development Aston pondered as "a question which it is more easy to ask than to answer."[7]

I say "writing in Japanese" because Japanese poets also wrote verse in classical Chinese, called *kanshi* (*hanshi* in Chinese). In fact, the first three "imperial anthologies" were of poems the Japanese wrote in Chinese: *Ryōunshū* (*Cloud-Borne Collection*), in 814, *Bunka Shūreishū* (*Collection of Literary Masterpieces*), in 818, both compiled by order of Emperor Saga (786–842), and *Keikokushū* (*Collection for the Ordering of the State*), in 827, compiled by order of Emperor Junna (786–840). Included in the *Keikokushū* is Princess Uchiko (aka Uchishi; 807–847), Saga's daughter with a member of the Korean royalty, whose kanshi has been described as among the very best written by the Japanese. It was a period of what Mishima Yukio (1925–1970) called "intoxication with a culture from abroad."[8] The statesman-scholar-poet Sugawara no Michizane (845–903), for one, took the remarkable step of writing a seven-character, four-line kanshi for each tanka he selected for his "newly

---

7. W.G. Aston, *A History of Japanese Literature* (Heinemann, 1899; repr., Charles E. Tuttle, 1972), 59. Inexplicably, the reprint edition drops part of the preface in which Aston discusses the eternally insoluble difficulty a translator faces in conveying the literary connotations of certain plant names and philosophical or aesthetic concepts.

8. Mishima Yukio, *Nihon Bungaku Shōshi* (*A Short History of Japanese Literature*), vol. 35, *Mishima Yukio Zenshū* (Shinchōsha, 2003), 577.

selected *Man'yōshū*," in 893—whether he did so to explain to a Chinese or a Korean, should one happen to come by, what the Japanese verse was trying to say, or to demonstrate that Japanese verse also had some poetic value, we don't know. Here is an anonymous tanka in the *Kokinshū* (no. 215, attributed to the imaginary poet Sarumaru Dayū when included in the *Hyakunin Isshu*), followed by Michizane's kanshi:

> *Okuyama ni momiji fumiwake naku shika no koe kiku toki zo aki wa kanashiki*

> When I hear deep in the mountains the call of a deer picking its way
>   through crimson leaves, the autumn makes me full of sorrow

> *qiu shan ji ji xie ling ling*
> *mi lu ming yin shu chu ling*
> *shen di xin lai you yang chu*
> *wu peng wu jiu yi you leng*

> The autumn mountain hushed, hushed, the leaves falling, falling,
> Antlered deer are heard calling in many places.
> In a place where a winning view is sought for a picnic
> I have no friend, no sake, and my heart grows even more cold.[9]

We notice at once that the kanshi with its twenty-eight syllables manages to say a great deal more than the tanka with its thirty-one.

Trying to write like Chinese poets such as Po Chu-i (772–846) and Yuan Zhen (779–831) and doing so in a foreign linguistic medium, Japanese poets inevitably gained a number of ideas from them, including that of composing poems on given topics (and about paintings) and categorizing them accordingly. In this process, one fateful turn of events was the failure of the Japanese poets to follow their models in addressing political and social issues in poetry—what the great scholar of Chinese classics Yoshikawa Kōjirō (1904–1980) summed up as "the urge for *kōgai*" or lamentation, "a sensibility for human destiny with social solidarity at its center."[10] In his massive history of Japanese literature, Konishi Jin'ichi has called that failure "a bizarre phenomenon from the viewpoint of common sense in the world."[11] Writing poems in Chinese, at any rate, became so dominant that verse in Japanese could hardly be shown "in public places," such verse having become

---

9. A selection from the *Shinsen Man'yōshū* is included in Kojima Noriyuki and Arai Eizō, ed., *Kokin Waka Shū* (Iwanami Shoten, 1989). This pair is cited on p. 368.

10. Yoshikawa Kōjirō, *"Zakkan," geppō* accompanying Kojima Noriyuki, ed., *Kaifūsō*, etc. (Iwanami Shoten, 1964), 7.

11. Konishi Jin'ichi, *Nihon Bungei Shi* (*History of Japanese Literary Arts*), vol. 2 (Kōdansha, 1985), 195. As he notes, Sugawara Michizane was an outstanding exception.

"partially a [learning] aid of ladies and could not be brought before gentlemen," as the Japanese foreword and the Chinese afterword of the *Kokinshū* memorably lamented when it was compiled in the early tenth century. And even after Japanese verse was officially recognized, kanshi continued to be written—until it quickly withered away in the early twentieth century.[12] In Japan and some other East Asian countries, Chinese played a role akin to Latin in European countries.

To go back to Japanese prosody: While chōka thrived, the 5-7-5-7-7-syllable tanka tended to break into 5-7, 5-7, and 7. But by the tenth century the form was more often breaking into 5-7-5 and 7-7. As that happened, and as the upper and lower hemistiches of the tanka began to be composed by different hands and then linked, the *renga,* "linked verse," was born. Initially a witty exchange made up of just the two units, it developed into a sequential group composition alternating 5-7-5- and 7-7-syllable units up to fifty times, to a total of one hundred long and short hemistiches. In that formation, the most important part was the opening unit, called the *hokku.* Required to indicate the time and place of composition, it had to be able to stand on its own. As a result, hokku began to be composed independently, probably in the sixteenth century, spawning what may be the world's shortest poetic form, haiku, although that name did not gain currency until early in the twentieth century.[13]

So, indigenous Japanese verse forms have grown in a simple genealogical line, from tanka to renga to hokku/haiku. It was a process of a brief form fragmenting, then further contracting, which amazed not only W.G. Aston, but also other early English students of Japanese literature, such as B.H. Chamberlain (1850–1935)[14] and Arthur Waley (1889–1966). These old forms survive to this day nonetheless, coexisting, for over a century now, with longer, much more flexible poems that came into being toward the end of the nineteenth century under Western influences. At first, "new-style" poems, as they were called initially, were composed in various combinations of the time-tested five- and seven-syllable units, as well as newly created ones with six and eight syllables. But soon the influence of *vers libre* swamped the land, and the use of syllabic patterns, both traditional and new, was washed away from the new genre. One book that exemplifies this transitional phase, with the strong hold of the "set forms" of tanka and hokku/haiku manifest, is *Uta Nikki (Verse Di-*

---

12. Burton Watson's two-volume *Japanese Literature in Chinese* (Columbia University Press, 1975–76) is the first major work in this genre. The translations of the titles of the three imperial anthologies are his.

13. For more detailed descriptions of the early prosodic development of Japanese verse, see Robert H. Brower's essay, "Japanese," in *Versification: Major Language Types*, ed. W. K. Wimsatt (New York University Press, 1972), 38–51, as well as Brower's earlier work with Earl Miner, *Japanese Court Poetry* (Stanford University Press, 1961), 56–78.

14. For Chamberlain's exasperation, see his *Things Japanese* (1905; the title later changed to *Japanese Things*; repr. Charles E. Tuttle, 1971), 376–77.

ary), a substantial collection of poems Mori Ōgai (1862–1922) wrote during the Russo-Japanese War.[15]

In Japan, as elsewhere, free verse was part of the movement to adopt colloquial language. In tanka and haiku, this led to the idea of *jiyūritsu,* "free rhythm," which ignored syllabic units and count.[16] In both genres, but in haiku in particular, remarkable poets have appeared, but neither the complete adherence to colloquial language nor free rhythm has become the mainstream.

Today the term *shi,* "poem" or "poetry," commonly refers to vers libre (though few use the French term or its Japanese equivalent now). This practice raises an immediate question: Aren't tanka, renga, and haiku also "poems"? They are, but they are seldom put in that category because of the strong sense of specialization in Japan. In a country where those who write tanka are called *kajin,* those who write haiku *haijin,* and those who write shi *shijin,* some haiku commentators even try to differentiate haiku from *ichigyō-shi,* "one-line poem"—a proposition possible only because of the assumption that the haiku, which, like the tanka, is regarded as a monolinear verse form by most haiku practitioners and commentators, functions in its own domain. In any case, poetry in Japan today, as in most other countries, is hard to define, except to say that it is "that which its own author considers to be poetry," in the words of the translator and anthologist Eliot Weinberger.[17]

One recent development to be noted is not prosodic but ethnic: a growing interest in the writings in Japanese, including poetry, by people of Korean descent. In 1910 Japan annexed Korea, then called *Taehanjeguk,* Great Han Empire. As a result, many Koreans migrated to Japan (just as many Japanese did to Korea) and learned Japanese and began writing in it (though not many Japanese are known to have reciprocated). With Japan's defeat in the Second World War, in 1945, Korea regained its independence, and many Koreans and people of Korean descent returned to Korea, but many stayed in Japan. For this anthology I have selected two poets from the postwar generation, Cheon Mihye (born 1955) and Park Kyong-Mi (born 1956), as representing two differing ethnic sensibilities.

Poetic Devices

The simple syllabic structures of classical verse forms do not mean that tanka, renga, and hokku are rhetorically simple. They employ a number of sophis-

15. A selection of these poems in my translation is included in J. Thomas Rimer, ed., *Not a Song Like Any Other: An Anthology of Writings by Mori Ōgai,* (University of Hawaii Press, 2004), 280–311.

16. One surprising development may be the popularity of free rhythm haiku among the Japanese immigrants on the West Coast of the United States. See Violet Kazue de Cristoforo, ed., *May Sky: There Is Always Tomorrow: An Anthology of Japanese American Concentration Camp Kaiko Haiku* (Sun and Moon, 1997).

17. Eliot Weinberger, *American Poetry Since 1950: Innovators and Outsiders (Marsilio,* 1993), xii.

ticated devices: *makura-kotoba, joshi, kakekotoba, mitate,* and *uta-makura,* among others.

The *makura-kotoba,* "pillow word," is an epithet consisting of five syllables or less, which conjures up the word that follows by sense or alliteration or both. Thus, *akane sasu,* "madder-illuminating"—"madder" here being a red dye extracted from the roots of the plant *akane* (*Rubia tinctorum*)—precedes or modifies *hi,* "light" or "day." *Saho-yama,* "Mount Saho," precedes *sao,* "pole," and *Kurabu-yama,* "Mount Kurabu," precedes *kurashi,* "dark."

The importance of makura-kotoba in early poetry was such that Fujiwara no Kintō (966–1041) observed in his treatise *Shinsen Zuinō* (*New Essential Poetics*): "Ancient people often put a makura-kotoba in the first part [of a poem], revealing the intended meaning in the second," adding that even though the practice became less prevalent during the *Kokinshū* days, "it was still regarded as bad form to reveal the thought at the outset." Much later, Orikuchi Shinobu expanded on the idea and speculated that ancient poets simply strung together images as they saw them until the words reached a requisite length, then added "a thought," almost an afterthought. His example is one of the three songs the first (mythological) emperor, Jimmu, is said to have sung in smiting the army led by his adversary, Prince Tomi:

> *Kamikaze no* (divine-wind-of)[18] *Ise no umi no* (Ise-of-sea-of) *ohishi ni*
> (boulder-on) *hai-motorofu* (crawl-go-around) *shitadami no* (periwinkle-of)
> *i-hai-motohori* (be-crawl-go-around) *uchiteshi-yamamu* (smite-and-stop)[19]

Here, the only "thought" is the last part, meaning "We shall stop only with the enemy smitten." (The phrase became one of Japan's military slogans during the Second World War.) The rest consists simply of things that he saw, from larger to smaller ones. This speculation is worth bringing up because some translators ignore pillow words as cumbersome. Cumbersome they certainly are, especially because the word order must usually be reversed in English. But I always retain them in my translation. (A poem that is comparable to Jimmu's song is the one that begins, "By the river of Yamashiro, of continuous peaks," on page 9, which is attributed to Princess Iwa, Emperor Nintoku's consort.)

The *joshi,* "introductory phrase," which consists of two or more opening syllabic units and therefore often takes up over half of the length of a tanka, functions like a makura-kotoba by bringing in a word by sense or alliteration. It also serves as a simile or metaphor.

The *kakekotoba,* "pivotal word," is a pun and comes naturally to Japanese, a language full of homonyms and homophones. As is often pointed out, puns are

---

18. Makura-kotoba.

19. Orikuchi's essay *Jokeika no Hassei* (*Origins of Poems Describing Landscape*), quoted in Yoshimoto Takaaki, *Kodai Kayō Ron* (Kawade Shobō Shinsha, 1977), 147–48. The song is "primitive" in that the syllabic units are not "regular": 5-6-4-6-5-7-7.

usually employed for comic effect in English today, but not necessarily so in classical Japanese poetry, and they were used routinely in "serious" verse. The *engo,* "associative word," which also relies on the homonymous and homophonic nature of Japanese, is a means of achieving unity in imagery.

Mitate, literally, "regarding one thing as something else," is a simile or metaphor. Minamoto no Toshiyori (1055–1129) calls it *nisemono,* "resembling thing," and elegantly cites examples in his treatise *Zuinō (Essential Poetics):* "To liken cherry flowers to white clouds; compare scattering flowers to snow; compare plum blossoms with the robe of one's lover; doubt if deutzia flowers are really not the waves breaking on Hedge Island; analogize crimson leaves to a brocade; wonder if the dewdrops on a grass bush are not uneven beads unstrung; regard them, as they spill in the wind, as tears on one's sleeves; compare the ice at water's edge to the surface of a mirror . . . ; and analogize the felicitous person to the pine or bamboo, or argue that he can easily compete with a crane or a tortoise in longevity."

Having said this, Toshiyori cast doubt on the modern validity of such "ancient things," adding, "Something has to be done about them." But he did not propose any remedy. In the many centuries that followed, poets continued to use the same similes and metaphors.

There are also *uta-makura,* "poetic pillows." Mainly place names, they are expected to evoke certain images and sentiments because they appeared in famous poems of the past. Poets—especially those during the Edo period—traveled long distances simply to "relive" the sentiments associated with those names. The foremost example in this anthology is Arii Shokyū (1711–1784), who attempted to trace parts of the route Matsuo Bashō (1644–1694) followed in his famous journey to the interior. I have already mentioned honkadori—the kind of allusion that, incidentally, would be treated as plagiarism today. The practice of *daiei,* composing a poem on a given topic, might also be included in the rhetorical devices of classical Japanese poetry. Daiei includes *byōbu-uta,* the practice of composing poems for screen paintings.

As an example in which some of these prosodic devices render their translation impractical, I might cite a tanka by Izumi Shikibu, "Poem 691" in the fourth imperial anthology *Go-Shūishū.* After Kintō praised it as Izumi's best, this poem generated a good deal of arcane debate. It is a "love poem" composed in response to a man who had, one headnote says, complained, unreasonably, that she wouldn't allow him to visit her to make love (*warinaku uramuru hito*).

> *Tsu no kuni no Koya tomo hito o iubeki ni hima koso nakere ashi no yaebuki*

Tsu no kuni (Province of Tsu, the area where today's Osaka and Hyōgo join) and Koya (the northwestern part of today's Itami City) are both makura-kotoba, with *tsu* also meaning "port" or "ferry." Much of the province at the time was under water or otherwise marshy, so *ashi,* "reeds," which grew profusely, is an engo. *Koya* also means "hut" and "come" (in the imperative mood). The upper hemistich forms a joshi. Moving on to the lower hemistich, *hima* means both "free time" and "space" or "gap"—with the phrase *hima-naku* (from *hima koso nakere,* in which *koso* is an emphatic) meaning both "so closely woven," in reference to the roof thatched with "reeds in eight layers" (*ashi no yaebuki*), and, by poetic convention, "with people watching me uninterruptedly." This hemistich also contains an inversion. So, the *meaning* that Izumi wishes to convey, ever cleverly, might be given as "I should tell him to come to my reed-thatched hut but too many people are watching," but that would only scratch the surface. Little wonder Ivan Morris (1931–1976) lamented, surely with some exaggeration: "There can be no literature in the world less suited to translation than classic Japanese Poetry."[20] Still, for all the punning and other rhetorical devices on display—to Arthur Waley "the least pleasing features of Japanese poetry"[21]—Orikuchi Shinobu, for one, admired the poem, saying it is "blunt," as it is "utterly different from the kind of women's poetry that tries to draw men's attention through sinuous feelings and clinging ways."[22]

Brevity and Context

The tanka—the mother of the renga and the grandmother of the hokku/haiku—is short. When puns and other overlaying devices are ignored, the tanka generally says, in English translation, about as much as a heroic couplet does. In 1882 Toyama Shōichi (1848–1900) famously pronounced that, when it came to the duration of "thought" it could express, the tanka was like the *senkō hanabi*, "fizzler," the most delicate of the fireworks. For that matter, Yatabe Ryōkichi (1851–1899) declared that for a Japanese to write kanshi was like someone trying to "swim in a room." They made these dismissals in compiling with another scholar, Inoue Tetsujirō (1855–1944)—none of them was a poet—the first principled attempt to introduce longer Western poems to Japan, the *Shintai-shi Shō* (*Selection of New-Style Verse*).[23] Brevity invites obscurity, as Aston said of the hokku of Bashō, citing Horace: *Brevis esse laborat, obscurus fit.*[24] To make up for this deficiency, some context was often provided—mainly in three ways: circumstantial, narrative,

---

20. Ivan Morris, trans., *The Pillow Book of Sei Shōnagon,* vol. 1 (Columbia University Press, 1967), xix. In this book Morris translated the 150-plus tanka mostly in three to five lines.

21. Arthur Waley, *Japanese Poetry: The "Uta"* (1919; repr. University Press of Hawaii, 1976), 11.

22. Orikuchi Shinobu, *Josei Tanka-shi,* 29–30.

23. Yano Hōjin, ed., *Meiji Shijin Shū* (*Anthology of Meiji Poets*; Chikuma Shobō, 1972), 1:4. For a complete English translation of *Shintai-shi Shō,* with citation of the originals of the poems translated, see *Literature: East & West,* vol. 19, *Toward a Modern Japanese Poetry,* 1–4, 7–33.

24. Aston, *A History,* 294. Despite the perennial adulation of the poet, Aston's observation more than a century ago remains true: "A very large proportion of Bashō's [poems] are so obscurely allusive as to transcend the comprehension of the uninitiated foreigner." He could easily have dropped "foreigner."

Portrait of Yatabe Ryōkichi (1851-1899):
One of the three compilers-translators of the
Shintai-shi Shō (*Selection of New-Style Verse*).

and, what for want of a better term, may be called formulaic.

First, as to circumstantial reinforcements, some scholars conjecture that *uta,* "songs," arose from ritualistic *mondō,* "inquiry and reply," which went on to become what were categorized as *sōmon,* "inquiring about each other," which then led to the custom of composing verse for *zōtō,* "exchange [of gifts]."[25] Mallarmé would later call similar productions *vers de circonstance.* It was natural, then, that the compiler of such pieces, be it a poet or an anthologist, should often add notes on the circumstances of composition, and such notes, even when they do not go beyond brief memos, help clarify the context.

Context-giving becomes central in *uta-monogatari,* "poetic tales," in which tanka are generally said to have come first, narratives second. The earliest extant collections of such tales are *Ise Monogatari* (*Tales from Ise*) and *Yamato Monogatari* (*Tales from Yamato*), both from the tenth century. The "tale" that graces the opening of *Yamato Monogatari* reads in its entirety:

When the Retired Emperor at the Teiji Mansion was about to abdicate, Lady Ise wrote on a wall of the Koki Palace:

I depart but the Inner Palace will think nothing of it. Why does not seeing it make me so sad?

When the Retired Emperor saw it, he wrote next to it:

I'm the only one who won't be here. You should all be able to return and see it, should you not?

---

25. Orikuchi Shinobu sought the origins of women's skills in verse composition in the ritual of *kakeai,* "give and take," in various festivals where men and women selected for one group competed to beat those selected for another group. In such contests wit and cleverness, not gender, played the primary role; *Josei Tanka-shi,* 15–20. This account almost exactly describes some of the improvisational public haiku contests popular in the United States today.

Here the Retired Emperor is Uda (867–931), who abdicated in Seventh Month, 897. Lady Ise (875?–939?), one of the attendants to his consort, Onshi, bore Uda a child about the time of his abdication. To the modern reader, the short, episodic "tale" may not make itself sparklingly clear even with such background information; but without the context the tale suggests, the two tanka cited will be hopelessly obscure.

The other side of this development, as may be expected, is the use of tanka in prose narratives, such as diaries and romances. For example, more than 250 tanka are sprinkled throughout the *Kagerō Nikki* (*Gossamer Diary*), the autobiography of Michitsuna's Mother (937?–995), in which the author describes prolonged difficulties with her husband Fujiwara no Kaneie (929–990). A ranking aristocrat who held the high posts of regent, chancellor, and prime minister, Kaneie was typical of men in polygamous Heian Japan and moved from one woman to another. In describing life with such a man, Michitsuna's Mother—so called because her son with Kaneie was named Michitsuna (955–1020), who attained the rank of major counselor—created a poem that has achieved immortality. Not long after she gave birth, Kaneie began paying attention to another woman.

> One evening he left home, saying, "I'll be too busy at the Palace to get away." I doubted his word and had a maid follow him. She came back and said, "He stayed at such-and-such a place in Machi no Kōji." That was what I had thought, and I was terribly depressed, but I did not know how to say it to him. A few days later, toward daybreak, someone knocked on the gate. I knew it was he, but I felt too depressed to have it opened. In the end he left in the direction of what I thought was the usual house. In the morning I decided not to let it go at that, wrote the following with far greater care than usual, and tied it to a withered chrysanthemum [and sent it to him]:

> The night when, aggrieved, you sleep alone, you know how long before the day breaks

This poem, included in the third imperial anthology *Shūishū* and, later, in the *Hyakunin Isshu,* is clear enough on its own, but the pain it describes becomes clearer when you learn the circumstances through the narrative.

As for formulaic compositions, they were inevitable. The oldest extant such effort by an individual poet, which happens to be the most extensive, is a set of 368 pieces by Sone no Yoshitada (923?–1003?): A total of 364 of them are tanka, with thirty for each month, plus four, each one preceded by a chōka that opens the section for each of the four seasons. A true sequence, the set is remarkable also as it includes many tanka composed before restrictive rules on poetic diction and other matters took over, some describing "love" with *Man'yō*-style immediacy. His chōka are notable as well; they do not follow the regular 5-7 pattern or the combination of 7-5 syllables that was becoming more popular.

It is subject to debate whether Yoshitada or Minamoto no Shigeyuki (923?–

1000?) was the first to compose what would later become the standard format called *hyakushu-uta,* "one hundred tanka." But by the early eleventh century, composing a set of one hundred had become common enough. In 1024 Sagami, whom we met earlier, dedicated to a shrine just such a set, complaining about her estranged husband, wishing for a baby, talking about her dreams, and so forth. To her amazement, no doubt, she received a response in the same format, in the name of the deity of the shrine. The following year, she dedicated another set in gratitude.

The hundred-piece set was formalized in 1105–1106, when sixteen poets agreed to work out one set each, with a topic specified for each of the hundred poems. The set, called the *Horikawa Hyakushu* because Emperor Horikawa (1079–1107) was the ruling monarch at the time, was made up of six major categories: spring (twenty pieces), summer (fifteen), autumn (twenty), and winter (fifteen), love (ten), and *zō,* "miscellany" (twenty). Temporal progression was incorporated into each category.

Versification as a Serious Undertaking

There were, in fact, two types of tanka: those composed informally, impromptu (*ke*)—for instance, as an aubade and a response to it—and those for official presentation (*hare*). For the latter, poetry contests (*uta-awase*) were frequently held, and poets were sometimes asked to submit a hundred-piece set. One or two poems might be chosen from such a set for inclusion in an imperial anthology.

Composing tanka for official presentation was a serious matter. How serious may be discerned from the portraits Kamo no Chōmei (1153–1212) drew of two women poets in his treatise on poetics, *Mumyōshō (Nameless Excerpts).* Of the two, Lord Shunzei's Daughter is already familiar to us. Kunai-kyō (1185?–1204?) is a young woman whom Retired Emperor Gotoba (1180–1239) asked to join the ranks of accomplished poets when he was thinking of preparing the eighth imperial anthology, the *Shin-Kokinshū:*

> In the present imperial reign, the person known as Lord Shunzei's Daughter and Kunai-kyō—these two are the most accomplished poets and need have felt no embarrassment among the ancient masters. Their methods of making poems are quite different. People tell me that Lord Shunzei's Daughter, when making poems for official presentation, begins days in advance to read various poetry collections over and over; when she has looked them over to her heart's content, she sets all of them aside, lights a lamp dimly in some isolated place, and works her poems out.
>
> Kunai-kyō would have books and scrolls spread in front of her from beginning to end and, with the light on a low lamp-holder set very close to her, write down bits and pieces, never neglecting the work night or day. She thought about poetry so hard that she would become ill, once almost dying. Her father, a lay priest, would warn her: "You can't do anything at all unless you are alive. Why do you work so hard at it that you become ill?"
>
> But she did not heed his warnings and in the end exhausted her life and died, probably because of all her worries.

The portrait of Lord Shunzei's Daughter, reminiscent of that of her grandfather Shunzei in the treatise on poetics *Kiribioke* (*Paulownia Brazier*), which is attributed to Teika, suggests the prevalence of a certain attitude expected in poetry composition: "On nights when the cold became extreme, my late father would turn a faint lamp away, put on a white, sooty priestly robe, tie its strings, pull a quilt over it, hug a paulownia brazier under the quilt, plant his elbows on the brazier, and, utterly alone in hushed quietude, on his bed, compose poems." Indeed, there was a reason verse composition was taken with gravity. In *Korai Fūtei Shō* (*Styles of Poetry since Ancient Times*), his treatise on poetics with a mini-anthology prepared for Princess Shikishi (died 1201), Shunzei argued: "Those who immerse their minds in the way of poetry [*kono michi*] . . . may, on account of the profound meaning of Japanese poetry [*Yamato uta*], understand the inexhaustibility of the Buddhist scriptures, gain the opportunity to go to Paradise after death, and enter the Bodhisattva Universal Virtue's Sea of Salvation."

With such a religious dedication, and with generations of poets focusing on such a short poetic form, the tanka—and, later, renga—became highly refined. But this also led to stultification, at least from today's perspective. The rules and constraints devised for the verse forms stifled innovation. To show how tanka writing was codified early on and how that approach influenced tanka poets for the many centuries that followed, I have translated *Yoru no Tsuru* (*The Night Crane*), a treatise on poetics by the nun Abutsu (1222?–1283).

Why, then, did men and women continue to write tanka? One answer is that their aim was not to be "original." Originality is a "modern cult," as Wendell Berry noted.[26] In the formulation the literary historian Konishi Jin'ichi posited, there were two contrasting notions that underlay any artistic and literary pursuit in Japan from the medieval period onward: *ga,* "elegance," "an effort to become part of eternity through achievement of perfection," and *zoku,* "earthiness," a decision to "remain in a natural state." So defined, ga is a form of classicism that stresses such things as professionalism, heritage, universality, and authority, but not, say, romantic or individualistic creativity. One product of the ga ideal in literature was the notion of *hon'i,* "essential meaning"—the conceit that every phenomenon should have a single true attribute, such that *harusame,* "spring rain," must fall quietly, even though in reality rains in spring may often be torrential; and *koi,* "love," must be a perpetual state of suffering, even though in reality someone in love may be deliriously happy. So, those who took up tanka—an embodiment of ga—did not at all mind turning out similar-sounding pieces; in fact, that was exactly what they expected to do.[27]

This is evident even with someone like Sakuma Tachieko (1814–1861), who com-

---

26. Wendell Berry, *Standing by Words* (North Point Press, 1983), 13.

27. Konishi made this his central argument in his small book *"Michi"—Chūsei no Rinen* (*"The Way"—The Medieval Principles*; Kōdansha, 1975) and later expanded on it in his five-volume history of Japanese "literary arts," *Nihon Bungei Shi* (Kōdansha, 1985–92), especially in volumes 3 and 4.

posed tanka in trying circumstances. It took Yosano Akiko to break out of the mold. Akiko's diction was not radically new, but the matters she chose to describe—narcissistic admiration of her own youthful body, for example—and the way she described them, were. To be liberated from convention, poets needed a stiff wind, which in Akiko's case was the Pre-Raphaelite romanticism and fin-de-siècle culture of the West.

"Earthy" Elements

So tanka stultified. After Eifukumon'in (1271–1342), who, along with her consort, Emperor Fushimi (1265–1317), is thought to represent the last glow of classical tanka, I have selected only two tanka poets before Akiko: Rikei (died 1616), because she described a military campaign and its aftermath, and the just-mentioned Tachieko, because she shows what tanka was like only a few decades before Akiko.

Fortunately, there was the zoku tradition. Parallel to the composition of classical tanka, attempts were made to explore new diction and subject matter. These were most successful in renga. Not long after this verse form came into being, it branched into two types: orthodox and unorthodox. The latter, which went on to predominate by the sixteenth century, was marked by the use of everyday language and mundane subject matter. The shackles of court dictates in poetry were such that change in language and subject matter alone was considered *haikai,* "humorous" or "entertaining," hence the name of the genre, *haikai no renga* or simply *haikai.* It was in this genre that Bashō worked. And as haikai—often used as an umbrella term for all activities related to the genre—spread among ordinary people, it became a "democratizing" force as well as an educational tool. In describing Igarashi Hamamo (1772?–1848), who traveled all over the land, initiated and presided over women-only haikai sessions, and compiled the records of eighteen of them in *Yae-yamabuki* (*Eightfold Globe Flower*) around 1810, the scholar-poet Bessho Makiko (born 1934) has written:

> There could have been no better method than haikai for home education. You could memorize rhythmical 5-7-5 [and 7-7] pieces as if singing them. You learned reading and writing. You came to know seasonal words, let your mind play with the changing of seasons, pay attention to grass, tree, insect, fish, bird, and beast, and know the traditions of snow, moon, and flower. It was an entrance to the classics, and you acquired the ability to make appropriate salutations.[28]

By "the changing of seasons," Bessho, herself a haikai practitioner, refers to the requirement of renga composition that things described in a sequence must shift in their seasonal suggestions from time to time, according to complex rules. The snow, the moon, and the flower have been representative of the winter, autumn, and spring ever since two lines from Po Chu-i became a celebrated favorite among Japanese poets: "Friends over lute, verse, and wine, you've all left me; / I think

---

28. Bessho Makiko, *"Kotoba" o Te ni shita Shinsei no Onna-tachi* (*Ordinary Women Who Got Hold of "Words"*) (Origin Shuppan Center, 1993), 99.

of you the most at the time of snow, moon, and flower." The writer of the opening unit, the hokku, had to refer to the occasion in a celebratory or self-deprecating way, hence "appropriate salutations."

What is typical of the haikai spirit? Since Bessho has argued that Bashō's democratic attitude helped popularize haikai among women,[29] let us cite as an example a hokku that Bashō praised in his letter to the poet:

> *Haru no no ya izure no kusa ni kaburekemu*
> In the spring field which grass gave me this rash?

The poet is Nozawa Ukō (died 1722?), and she composed it, a headnote tells us, when she went into the field to collect young herbs with her friends. The act of going out in a field to gather spring herbs was perfectly acceptable in orthodox tanka and renga, but not something as inelegant as *kabure,* "rash," hence the piece is haikai.[30]

Haikai spawned three distinct subgenres: *haibun, kana-shi* (also known as *washi*), and *senryū*. Haibun, which Bashō first identified as a genre, is a piece of prose imbued with the haikai spirit, however you may define it. Usually graced by a hokku or two, it is a direct offshoot of poetic tales. Kana-shi, "verse in Japanese script," refers to a group of often rhyming verses à la kanshi that the haikai poet Kagami Shikō (1665–1731) and his circle of poets created. One notable prosodic decision the group made was to regard fourteen syllables in Japanese as the equivalent of the seven-character line in kanshi.[31] Kana-shi were composed throughout the Edo period but never attracted a large body of practitioners. The reason may be that Japanese versifiers instinctively felt rhyming wasn't quite right in their polysyllabic language.

Senryū was born of the competitive game of *maeku-zuke,* "follow-up to the preceding unit," originally part of the practice for haikai no renga composition. Renga, in essence, was based on the art of linking two verses, called *tsukeai,* "joining together," and this in later periods turned into the competitive game of maeku-zuke. So, in a 1761 contest, a 7-7-syllable statement was offered:

> *mottomona koto mottomona koto*
> that's understandable, that's understandable

Among the winners with a 5-7-5-syllable response was someone identified as Sakuragi:

---

29. Most notably in her history of women in haikai, *Bashō ni hirakareta Haikai no Josei Shi* (*History of Women in Haikai Opened by Bashō*) (Origin Shuppan Center, 1989).

30. For Bashō's letter, see p. 164f.

31. More than two hundred years later, Nakamura Shin'ichirō (1918–1997), the poet and student of French literature who experimented in rhyming in Japanese, would determine that the seventeen-syllable haiku was the equivalent of the seven-character line in kanshi as well as the alexandrine in the amount of information that could be conveyed; Nakamura Shin'ichirō, *Edo Kanshi* (Iwanami Shoten, 1985), 83–85.

atsusō ni hotaru o tsukamu musume no ko
as if it were hot a young girl holds a firefly

In time the preceding units dropped away and the senryū, too, became independent. The genre name, meaning "river willow," though eponymous of the enormously popular maeku-zuke judge Karai Senryū (1718–1790), gained currency retroactively around 1900.

Finally, out of tanka—sometimes described as the oldest poetic form in continuous use—grew *kyōka*, "mad tanka," a 5-7-5-7-7-syllable verse composed for humorous or satirical effects, mainly through puns and allusions. Though the founder of the genre is traditionally Fujiwara no Tamemori (1265–1328), the genre reached its peak about the time senryū did, between the second half of the eighteenth and the early nineteenth centuries. Chie no Naiji (1745–1807), Kaneko Michi's pen name, meaning "wife with no wits," and Fushimatsu no Kaka (1745–1810), Yamazaki Matsu's pen name, meaning "knobby pine's old woman"—kyōka writers created jokey names for themselves—were counted among the best women poets in the genre. For example, Chie no Naiji has left us a piece with the headnote, "Because it rains on the fifteenth night," that is, the night of the full moon by the lunar calendar:

Meigetsu no kumoma ni hikaru kimi masade saenu amayo no monogatari kana

Without you who shine like a full moon between clouds, we tell stories this insipid rainy night

How is this composition humorous? The setup itself at once reminds the reader of Murasaki Shikibu and her *Tale of Genji,* in particular a scene in the "Hahakigi" chapter in which Genji and several of his male friends, rained in, discuss the women they have known. The reference to *kumo,* "cloud," suggests Murasaki's most famous poem, which begins with "We met again" (see p. 58), and the phrase *hikaru kimi,* here translated "you who shine," is a give-away: it can only refer to Genji the Shining Prince, the protagonist of the *Tale.* The word *ama* means both "rain" and "women." So the piece also says, "Absent the Shining Prince, we none-too-bright women talk about our experiences," obviously, of men.

Fushimatsu no Kaka has a kyōka on "Warrior's Love":

Mononofu no yatake-gokoro no hikaruru wa imo ga yanagi no mayumi narikeri

What draws the warrior's ferocious heart are the willow eyebrows of the one he loves

The humor of this piece, which is elegant and clever, comes from two punning words: *yatake,* which means both "ferocious" and "arrow-bamboo," and *mayumi,* "true bow," which includes the word *mayu,* "eyebrow." The word *hikaruru,* here given as "draw," is an engo, associated with the drawing of a bow.

Translation

The problems of verse translation are perennial. "The whole question as to the best equivalents for alien metres is a notoriously difficult one," B.H. Chamberlain observed in presenting a paper titled "Bashō and the Japanese Poetic Epigram" at the Asiatic Society of Japan in 1902.[32] By epigram, he referred to what the term meant "in its earlier acceptation, as denoting any little piece of verse that expresses a delicate or ingenious thought"—in this instance, "*Hokku* (also *Haiku* and *Haikai*)."[33] Chamberlain noted that "the Japanese epigram has exactly the same number of syllables (seventeen) as the hexameter, when the latter runs to its full length of five dactyls." Then he cast the "epigram" into a tetrameter couplet whenever he could. Here's his translation of a famous hokku by Kaga no Chiyo (1703?–1775):

> Where may he have gone off today—
> The hunter after dragonflies?[34]

The Victorian scholar also pointed to the two results translators of Japanese verse into English since then have confirmed time and again. Commenting on recent translations by his contemporary Lafcadio Hearn (1850–1904), he observed: "Some of the renderings are in the metre of the elegiac distich, which, owing to the far larger number of syllables of that form of verse, necessitates more or less expansion of the originals. Others, rendered literally, though less attractive as English—or Anglicised—poems, possess superior value for the scientific enquirer."[35] Here is Bashō's hokku rendered into an elegiac distich:

> Never an intimation in all those voices of *sémi* . . .
> How quickly the hush will come . . . how speedily all must die.[36]

---

32. B. H. Chamberlain, "Bashō and the Japanese Poetic Epigram," *Transactions of the Asiatic Society of Japan* 30, no. 2 (1902): 253.

33. Ibid., 243.

34. Ibid., 300. The original Chamberlain cites is a variant: *Tombo-tori / Kyō wa dokora ye / Itta yara.* The standard version is: *Tombotori kyō wa doko made itta yara.* See "Dragonfly-catcher," p. 150, for my translation.

35. Ibid., 362.

36. Lafcadio Hearn, *Japanese Lyrics* (Houghton Mifflin, 1915), cited in *The Classic Tradition of Haiku: An Anthology*, ed. Faubion Bowers (Dover, 1996), 17. Original: *Yagate shinu keshiki wa miezu semi no koe.* Hearn also rendered a number of tanka into elegiac distiches. In the glossary of *Historical Manual of English Prosody* (1910; repr. Schocken, 1966), George Saintsbury defines *distich* thus: "A synonym for 'couplet,' but of wider range, as there is no reason why the verses should be metrically similar. There is, however, in the practical use of the word, an understanding that there shall be a certain completeness and self-containedness of *sense*." The last part reminds us of one of the original requirements of the hokku.

And as an example "rendered literally," Chiyo's hokku cited above comes out, in Hearn's hand, as "Catching dragon-flies! . . . I wonder where *he* has gone to-day!"[37] The point, of course, is that "more or less expansion of the originals"—or amplification or embellishment—is inevitable when corresponding numbers of syllables are given in English translation, whether by according a "line" to each of the 5- and 7-syllable units, as Stephen Carter does in *Japanese Traditional Poetry* (Stanford University Press, 1991), or by treating as a line each of the 17-syllable upper hemistich and the 14-syllable lower hemistich, as Royall Tyler does in *The Tale of Genji* (Viking, 2001). This is simply because a syllable in Japanese, which is a polysyllabic language, has less value than in English, which is not.

In any event, I have chosen to follow more or less the second approach in the full knowledge that literal renditions, as I have shown, are seldom possible. I have done this even in the matter of verse forms. The prevailing view in Japan is that "the tanka is a one-line poem," to quote the opening sentence of the astonishingly multifaceted argument for "tanka as modern poetry" by the poet Ishii Tatsuhiko (born 1952).[38] In contrast, at least in American academia, the prevailing view is that the tanka is a five-line poem. One force behind this belief seems to be the sense that "a one-line poem—at least in Western languages—is willy-nilly at the same time a no-line poem . . . to speak of a 'one-line poem' is to speak of something that cannot exist,"[39] an assertion belied by fact and practice. To cite an esoteric example, Ralph Hodgson (1871–1962), who in the late 1930s helped a Japanese committee translate a substantial selection from the *Man'yōshū* into English, was, according to his fellow English poet James Kirkup (born 1923), "a pioneer among the type of modern poets who prefer the clarity and concision of the monostich."[40]

So I apply the "set form" of one line to tanka (except "ancient songs" and those in the *Man'yōshū*) and hokku/haiku unless the original manner of presentation shows otherwise.[41] I translate both classical (pre-mid-nineteenth century) and modern poetry, and I need to pay heed not only to medieval theories and practices such as scattered writing (*chirashigaki*) employed purely for aesthetic effects, sometimes in total disregard of syntax,[42] but to modern practices as well. The latter include lineation (*gyōwake*), the use of punctuation (*kutōten*), and the use of spacing

37. Lafcadio Hearn, *A Japanese Miscellany* (ICG Muse, 2001), 99.
38. Ishii Tatsuhiko, *Gendai-shi to shite no Tanka* (Shoshi Yamada, 1999), 15. The sentence in question reads: *tanka wa ichigyō no shi de aru.*
39. William R. LaFleur, "Marginalia: The Expanse and the Limits of a New Anthology," *Monumenta Nipponica* 38, no. 2 (Summer 1983): 199–200.
40. James Kirkup, *Eibungaku Saiken* (Daishūkan Shoten, 1980), 58.
41. I am by no means the first to translate hokku/haiku consistently in one line. In his tract "Issa's Life and Poetry," Asiatic Society of Japan, Second Series, vol. 9 (December 1932), Max Bickerton translated in one line all of the haiku he cited.
42. For samples, see illustrations in the following pages. Koizumi Yoshinaga devotes chapter 3 of his PhD dissertation, "The Calligraphic Model Textbooks for Women in the Edo Period" (1999) to the discussion of *chirashigaki*, finding its earliest extant example in the mid-tenth century. The dissertation is online.

within a line (*wakachigaki*). Lineated tanka, made famous by Ishikawa Takuboku (1886–1912), have tended to lose syllabic patterns, as may be seen in Orikuchi Shinobu's four-line poems and in the five-line tanka (*gogyō-ka*) that Kusakabe Enta (born 1938) has advocated. A liberal, imaginative use of punctuation and spacing is most typically found in the works of Ishii Tatsuhiko, who also argues that tanka can be most effective when sequentially composed. Among Japanese poets, after all, such differences, at least in modern times, continue to attract the kind of attention that the distinctions between Spenserian and Shakespearean sonnets once did among English poets.[43] I will bring up such matters as they become relevant in this anthology in introducing each poet, but for those tempted to object, I have a simple question: What would a believer in the tanka as a five-line poem do when confronted with a tanka actually written in five lines, such as those in an alliterative sequence by Koike Sumiyo (born 1955) in her book *Gazoku* (Roppō Shuppansha, 1991)?

Itsu kaeru	5
itsu ku itsu au	3-4
itsu wakaru	5
itsu yuku ware o	4-3
itsu wasururu ya	7

When will you go home
when will you come when will we meet
when shall we part
when will you forget me
when I go

Or with the prize-winning Imahashi Ai (born 1976), who, in her first book, *Ō-kyaku no Hiza* (Hokumeisha, 2003), casts her tanka in one to eight lines, sprinkles them with what appears to be arbitrary punctuation and in-line spacing, making some look like concrete poems, and often ignores syllabic count or blurs syllabic distinctions? In fact, if there is a single notable trend in recent tanka, it is not so much lineation as the nullification of syllabic patterns even when the total number of syllables approximates thirty-one.

---

43. For a detailed discussion of tanka lineation in Japanese, see my article "Lineation of Tanka in English Translation," *Monumenta Nipponica* 42, no. 3 (Autumn 1987): 347–56. I discuss how Hagiwara Sakutarō (1886–1942), regarded as the first "modern" Japanese poet, approached tanka lineation in *Howling at the Moon: Poems and Prose of Hagiwara Sakutarō* (Green Integer, 2002), 19–25. In "Forms Transformed: Japanese Verse in English Translation," included in Frank Stewart, ed., *The Poem Behind the Poem: Translating Asian Poetry* (Copper Canyon, 2004), 172–82, I look at the same question from a different angle.

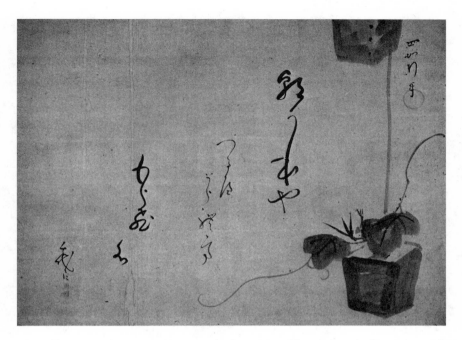

Chiyo-ni's painting of morning-glories and a bucket with a hokku which reads, from right to left:

Asagao ya / tsurube / torarete / moraihi / mizu

The well-bucket taken by morning-glories, water sought

Jogakusei no mure	8
tsubushitemo onaji yō ni yattekurukara	5-6-7
kanojora wa ari	7

Throngs of girl students
you squish them but since they keep coming the same way
they're ants

Keitai o wasureta gogo. wa	5-6-1
dare kara mo kata o tsukamareteinai kankaku	5-11-4

Afternoons I forget to bring my cell. Phone
no one's grabbing me by the shoulders is the sensation

All this is another way of saying that in translating poems, I try to remain faithful to the original poem to the best of my ability, and that includes the original line formations.

Chiyo-ni's landscape painting with a hokku which reads, from right to left:
Hatsukari ya / yama he / kubare / ba / no ni tarazu
First geese: if placed against the mountain, too few in the field

I should add a word on tanka, renga, and haiku written in English. Tanka in English are relatively new, and most poets regard the form as a five-line poem. I know only two poets who have written tanka in one line: Rachel Blau DuPlessis and Kimiko Hahn. Renga—or *renku*, to use the term retroactively applied—has recently become popular, at least among American poets.[44] Most write renga by alternating three- and two-line units, but some by alternating long and short lines.[45] Haiku are not new, and among haiku aficionados one-line writers are common, notable among them Janice Bostok, marlene mountain, and Chris Gordon. Among non-haiku poets, John Ashbery, in *A Wave,* Allen Ginsberg, in *Death & Fame,* and Michael O'Brien, in *The Floor and the Breath, Sills,* and *Six Poems,* have published one-line haiku—with Ginsberg and O'Brien deploying seventeen syllables as well.

Selection and Presentation

The selection of poets for this anthology follows to a great extent personal predilection. Some poets familiar to anyone with a cursory knowledge of Japanese

44. The most famous "Western" attempt in renga composition was made by Octavio Paz et al. in *Renga: A Chain of Poems*, originally published in France in 1971.

45. The rules range from nonexistent to complex, although even when they are complex, they seldom approach the complexity demanded in "traditional" renga, which is the way it should be, as I have argued.

literature may be missing, both in classical and modern periods, while some names unknown to even those who closely follow the genre may be present. Among modern tanka poets, to include Okamoto Kanoko (1889–1939), while ignoring such obvious luminaries as Gotō Miyoko (1915–1988), who taught Empress Michiko, and Baba Akiko (born 1928), for example, will, I know, raise some eyebrows. Also, even though I am highly selective with tanka poets, I have tried to be inclusive with haiku and senryū poets—itself an overstatement: A recent anthology of women haiku poets, *Joryū Haiku Shūsei* (Rippū Shobō, 1999), which covers eighty-one poets during the hundred-year period from the late nineteenth century onward, cites about fifteen thousand haiku.[46]

I have stressed kanshi, a genre mostly neglected until recently even in Japan. But I've been sparing with three genres of verse: renga, kana-shi, and kyōka. I have included only a few samplings of renga because of the complexity of its rules, which Chamberlain called, in the days when anthropological evenhandedness in cultural studies was unknown, "puerile."[47] Less dismissive, Konishi Jin'ichi once compared reading an old renga sequence to reading a musical score or a play whose performers ceased to exist long ago.[48] More important, though it would surely be instructive to translate, with detailed commentary, at least one of the eighteen sequences Hamamo composed with women in its entirety, there is as yet no fully annotated text, and I am far from familiar with all the intricate rules of renga.[49] I have not included kana-shi, because I was unable to find women among those who wrote them, and kyōka—except the two cited in this introduction—because, even though puns and allusions are not necessarily heavier than those deployed in orthodox tanka, the "fun" is lost when it is explained.

The anthology is chronologically arranged, by year of birth of the poet, when it is known, not by year of writing or publication of the poem. This overall scheme does not apply to three sections: "Haikai Poets as Eccentrics," "A Brief Survey of Senryū by Women," and "A Brief Survey of Haiku by Women." The first presents the Edo period's view of haikai and those who dabbled in it in summary form, even though all the poets in it appear later in their own sections. The two "surveys" cover poets who, in my opinion, do not have enough fasci-

---

46. For the modern period, there is a two-volume anthology: Leza Lowitz and Miyuki Aoyama, trans., *Other Side River: Free Verse* (Stone Bridge Press, 1995) and Leza Lowitz, Miyuki Aoyama, and Akemi Tomioka, trans., *Long Rainy Season: Haiku and Tanka* (Stone Bridge Press, 1994).

47. Chamberlain, "Bashō and the Japanese Poetic Epigram," 258.

48. Konishi Jin'ichi, *Sōgi* (Chikuma Shobō, 1971), 65–66. Konishi was writing before a recent renga revival, although it is doubtful that the crusty academician would recognize today's renga as such.

49. Konishi Jin'ichi recalled Yamada Yoshio, an orthodox renga master and a redoubtable scholar of Japanese literature, saying it would take at least twenty years of "practice" before one could compose a proper renga; ibid., 67.

nating work, along with those who appear later in regular chronological order. I have presented these sections as separate entities to provide a quick grasp of a particular perspective or genre.

Despite such omissions and other deficiencies, I hope I have covered enough material in this anthology to show the history, the variety, and the scope of Japanese women poets.

Ancient Songs

Songs from the *Kojiki*

The *Kojiki* (*Record of Ancient Matters*) is a history of Japan compiled in 712 on the basis of the accounts left by Hieda no Are, a young court attendant of exceptional brilliance who "could repeat whatever he read, memorize whatever he heard." At the time, Japan had not devised its own writing system out of Chinese characters, and the *Kojiki* displays a hybrid use of Chinese characters—sometimes Chinese as it was, sometimes for their meanings, sometimes for their sounds.

As its foreword says, the *Kojiki* "begins with the Opening of Heaven and Earth and ends with the Reign of Owarida," namely, Empress Suiko (554–628), by semi-mythological tradition the thirty-third ruler of Japan. It is a mixture of myths, legends, and facts and incorporates folk songs. Ōkuninushi-no-mikoto, "Great Land-Ruler Prince," a deity whose "song" is the first cited below, defeated his eighty siblings to found the nation, the account says. "Deity of Eight-Thousand Spears" is a translation of Yachihoko-no-kami, one of several names given him.

Prince Ōkuninushi and Princess Nunakawa

When the Deity of Eight Thousand Spears went to night-visit[1] Princess Nunakawa in the Country of Koshi,[2] he sang as he reached her house:

The Divine Prince of Eight Thousand Spears,
finding no wife to pillow in the Country of Eight Islands,
hearing there was a wise woman,
hearing there was a beautiful woman
far, far away, in the Country of Koshi,
set out to night-visit her,
came here to night-visit.
Sword thongs still untied,
pullover still untied,
at the wooden door where the maiden sleeps
I stand, pushing and shaking,[3]
I stand, pulling and shoving,

---

1. *Yobau*, "call to each other" or "crawl [into a lover's bedroom] at night." In his translation, *Kojiki* (Princeton University Press, 1969), p. 104, Donald Philippi gives the word "woo."
2. *Koshi no kuni*, "the land beyond": the northern region.
3. The switching of grammatical elements—here, speakers—in an apparently single speech is called enallage and occurs, for example, in The Song of Solomon, 1:2.

3

and on the green hills thrashers call;
birds of grass fields, pheasants resound;
birds of the garden, roosters call.
Don't I hate them, those calling birds!
Won't someone hit them and shut them up?
This is the way the story's told
by the low-running fisherman messenger.

Princess Nunakawa, not yet opening the door, sang from within:

Divine Prince of Eight Thousand Spears,
because I am a woman, a pliant grass blade,
my heart is a bird on an inlet.
For now I am my own bird,
but later I will be your bird.
Your life, do not let it die!
This is the way the story's told
by the low-running fisherman messenger.
When the sun hides behind the green hills,
night will come, black as black-lily seeds.
Then, like the morning sun, come, smiling radiantly!
These arms white as mulberry rope,
breasts youthful as soft snow,
hold them with your bare hands, caress them;
your arm and my arm crossed for pillows,
thighs outstretched, we'll sleep our sleep.
So do not speak with too much love,
Divine Prince of Eight Thousand Spears.
This is the way the story's told.

Accordingly, they did not meet that night but came together on the night of the following day.

Prince Ōkuninushi and Princess Suseri

Then the Deity's chief wife, the Divine Princess Suseri, became extremely jealous like a concubine. Her husband deity, at a loss, was about to leave Izumo for Yamato. When he had dressed and stood ready, he put one hand on his horse saddle, one foot in the stirrup, and sang:

When, having carefully put on
a robe black as black-lily seeds,
I look down at my chest like an offshore bird

and flap my wings, no, this won't do.
Like a shore wave, toss it back!
When, having carefully put on
a robe in kingfisher-green,
I look down at my chest like an offshore bird
and flap my wings, no, this too won't do.
Like a shore wave, toss it back!
When, having carefully put on
a robe dyed with the juice of a dye-tree,
indigo grown on the hill and pounded,
I look down at my chest like an offshore bird
and flap my wings, yes, this is good.
My dear love, my princess,
though I flock away like a flock of birds,
though I recede like birds receding,
you won't cry, you say,
but like a pampas grass stalk on the hill,
head dropping, that's how you'll cry,
like morning rain that rises in mist,
my young-grass wife, my princess.
This is the way the story's told.

    Here his wife fetched a great sake cup and, approaching, offered it to him, singing:

Divine Prince of Eight Thousand Spears,
    Greater Ruler of our Land,
because you are a man,
at every island point you go round,
at every shore point you row round, no exception,
you must have a young-grass wife.
But I, because I am a woman,
I have no man besides you,
I have no husband besides you.
Under fluffy painted curtains,
under downy silken covers,
under rustling mulberry covers,
my breasts youthful as soft snow,
arms white as mulberry rope,
hold them with your bare hands, caress them;
your arm and my arm crossed for pillows,
thighs outstretched, sleep your sleep.
Kindly have this superb sake.

She sang; then they were united through the cup and embraced each other. They remain so to this day.

The Maidservant from Mie and the Empress

Another time, Emperor [Yūryaku],[4] seated under a zelkova tree with a hundred branches, in Hatsuse, was holding a banquet, when a maidservant from Mie, of the Country of Ise, offered him a large sake cup, reverentially holding it high. A zelkova leaf fell and floated in it. But the maidservant, unaware that a fallen leaf was floating in the cup, continued to offer the sake. When he noticed the leaf, the Emperor struck her down, put his sword on her neck, and was about to cut her apart, when she said to him, "Please do not kill me, my lord." Then she sang:

The Hishiro Palace, in Makimuku,
is a palace where the morning sun shines,
a palace where the evening sun gleams,
a palace where bamboo roots grow amply,
a palace where tree roots crawl everywhere,
a palace of eight hundred weight of pounded earth.
By this Imperial Gate of cypress, the luxuriant tree,
by the Hall for Tasting the New Harvest,[5] grows
a zelkova tree with a hundred ample branches.
Its upper branches cover heaven,
its middle branches cover the East,
its lower branches cover the countryside.
From its upper branches, a leaf at the tip of the branches
falls and touches its middle branches;
from its middle branches, a leaf at the tip of the branches
falls and touches its lower branches;
from its lower branches, a leaf at the tip of the branches
falls into a beautiful cup held up
by a child of Mie, in a silk robe,
and immerses itself like floating fat,
the water curdling, curdling,[6]
how awe-inspiring all this,
Honored Child of the High-Shining Sun!
This is the way the story's told.

---

4. Twenty-first emperor.
5. The hall where the emperor ceremonially samples the autumn harvest.
6. Both "floating fat" and "curdling, curdling" refer to the beginning of the *Kojiki,* where the creation of the Japanese archipelago is described; they are, therefore, thought to be felicitous.

Because she offered this song, the Emperor forgave her for the crime. Thereupon the Empress sang. In her song she said:

On this high ground of Yamato,
the elevated gathering place,
by the hall for tasting the new harvest grows and stands
a broadleaf sacred true camellia tree.
Seated like its leaves spreading wide,
seated like its blossoms shining bright,
is the Honored Child of the High-Shining Sun.
To him kindly offer abundant sake.
This is the way the story's told.

Songs from the *Nihon Shoki*

The *Nihon Shoki* (or *Nihongi, History of Japan*) is a formal version of the *Kojiki* and was compiled in 720: written entirely in Chinese, in the manner of China's dynastic chronicles, and studded with borrowings from Chinese sources. It was, in short, "an attempt at an official national history which could be shown with pride, should the occasion demand, to any foreign embassy or court."[7] It, too, begins with the creation of Japan—"When Heaven and Earth were yet to be separated and Ying and Yang not divided"—but it ends with the forty-first ruler, Empress Jitō (645–702), transferring her power to a successor, Emperor Mommu, in 697. It includes folk songs and poems not found in the *Kojiki*.

Princess Iwa, Emperor Nintoku's Consort

In Intimate Month in the spring of the twenty-second year [of his reign], Emperor [Nintoku][8] talked to his Empress[9] and declared, "I'd like to bring in Princess Yata and make her my spouse." The Empress would not hear of it. Thereupon the Emperor begged her, singing:

This a nobleman's express word:
like a spare bowstring I'd be with her when you're away,
I wish to have you side by side.

The Empress sang in reply:

With robes, two layers may be fine.
You, who want two night-beds side by side,
you terrify me!

The Emperor sang again:

Like the parallel beaches
at the cape of sun-dominated Naniwa,
the child wanted me to put you side by side!

The Empress sang in reply:

---

7. Philippi, *Kojiki*, 16–17.
8. The sixteenth emperor. In *Shinwa kara Rekishi e (From Mythology to History)*, volume 1 of the twenty-six-volume history of Japan, *Nihon no Rekishi* (Chūō Kōron Sha, 1973), pp. 370–84, Inoue Mitsusada argues that with Emperor Nintoku's father, Ōjin, the Japanese imperial lineage ceased to be entirely mythological. If Ōjin did exist, he may be the Japanese ruler who appears in Chinese documents from around 420 to 430.
9. They were married for twenty-one years by then, and she had borne him four sons.

Like the robe of the summer worm, the silkworm,
to hide and lodge in two layers,
how could this be good?

The Emperor sang again:

The one taking the road, half weeping,
along the Hika slope of Morning Wife,[10]
would do best with a companion.

The Empress, determining not to approve of it, kept silent and would not reply again.

On the eleventh of Long Month in the autumn of the thirtieth year [of his reign], the Empress traveled to the Country of Ki; she collected trifoliate oak leaves at Cape Kumano and returned. The Emperor, taking advantage of her absence, summoned Princess Yata and installed her in the Palace. When she reached Naniwa Ferry, the Empress heard that the Emperor had wed Princess Yata, and she became greatly upset. She threw the trifoliate oak leaves into the sea and did not stay there. As a result, people of that time called the sea where she scattered the oak leaves Oak-Leaf Ferry. The Emperor, however, who did not know she had become angry and had not stayed, went to Ōtsu and, while waiting for her ship, sang:

Naniwa people, hold the bell-ship,
up to your waists in the water, hold the bell-ship,
hold that great ship!

But the Empress not only did not stay in Ōtsu; she turned back, went upriver, and, turning around Yamashiro, headed toward Yamato. The following day the Emperor dispatched Aide Mountain Bird[11] to make her return. He sang:

Catch up with her in Yamashiro, Mountain Bird,
catch up, catch up with her
and see my lovely wife!

The Empress would not return but kept on. When she reached the Yamashiro River, she sang:

By the river of Yamashiro, of continuous peaks,

---

10. *Asazuma*: The name of the place Princess Iwa came from.
11. *Toriyama*: Personal or family name suggesting a messenger.

I go upriver and, as I go up,
at the river bend there grows and stands
a tree with eighty leaves, less than a hundred,[12]
like the Great Lord.

> She then went over Nara Hill, where, as she saw Kazuraki in the distance, she sang:

By the river of Yamashiro, of continuous peaks,
I go up to the Palace and, as I go up,
I pass by Nara, where the blue clay is good,[13]
I pass by Yamato, of little shields.
The country I'd like to see
is Kazuraki, in Takamiya,
there where my home is.

> She then returned to Yamashiro and built her main house to the south of Tsutsuki Hill and resided there.
> In winter, on the first day of Godless Month, the Emperor dispatched Subject Mouth Held,[14] the ancestor of the Ikuwa Clan, to call back the Empress. When he reached the Tsutsuki Palace, Mouth Held was granted an audience with the Empress, but she kept silent and would not respond. He prostrated himself in front of the Empress's Great Chamber, remaining there night and day, wet with snow and rain, and would not leave. His sister, Princess Kuniyori, who served the Empress, happened to be in close attendance at the time. Seeing her older brother wet with rain, she shed tears and sang:

In Yamashiro, at Tsutsuki Palace,
I see my older brother trying to say something,
and tears come to my eyes.

The Empress said to Princess Kuniyori, "Why do you weep?" The princess replied, "The one prostrating himself in the courtyard, trying to say something, is my older brother. He's wet with rain but won't leave. He remains prostrate, trying to see you. I can only weep, Your Majesty." The Empress told her, "Tell your older brother to go back at once. I shall never return." Mouth Held returned in consequence and made his report to the Emperor.

---

12. *Momo tarazu*, here given as "less than a hundred," is a makura-kotoba for *yaso*, "eighty." Similar ways of counting exist in other languages. *Yaso* also means "many," "innumerable."

13. *Aoni yoshi*, here given as "where the blue clay is good," is a makura-kotoba for Nara. The reason, it is explained, is that the area produced blue clay used as paint.

14. Kuchimochi: Personal name suggesting a messenger. The clan Ikuwa included a powerful bowman who shot through an iron shield brought by visitors from Koguryo, Korea.

Princess Kage

... The Crown Prince[15] for the first time knew that Shibi (Tunny) had taken Princess Kage (Shadow) before he did and realized that neither the father, Minister Matori, nor the son, Shibi, had any respect for him. He became furious and his face reddened. That night he went swiftly to the mansion of Kanamura, of the Ōtomo Clan, and plotted to gather soldiers. The Ōtomo Clan, leading several thousand soldiers, blocked the road and killed Shibi on Mount Nara. [One account has it that Shibi, who was staying in Princess Kage's house, was killed that night.] Princess Kage hurried to the place where he was killed, and saw that he indeed was. Alarmed and terrified, she was utterly lost, tears of sorrow filling her eyes. Finally, she made a song, which went:

We pass by Furu, of Isonokami,
we pass by Takahashi, of the rush pillow,
we pass by Ōyake, of many things,
we pass by Kasuga, of the spring day,
we pass by Osaho, where wives hide.
We even load our bowl with rice,
we even load our cup with water,
Weeping, soaked with tears, she goes,
poor Princess Kage!

Princess Kage, having finished burying him, was about to go home, when she said, sobbing, "I'm so bitter that I've lost my dear husband today." Depressed and shedding tears, she sang:

In a valley of Nara, where blue clay is good,
he's hidden in a waterlogged place, like a beast.
Do not root up the water-spurting young Tunny,
baby wild boars.

The Older Prince of Nugari and Imperial Princess Kasuga

In Long Month, the Older Prince of Nugari[16] wedded Imperial Princess Kasuga on his own. One moonlit night, he talked and talked with her until, before he knew it, it was daybreak. Then his poetic thoughts quickly turned into words, which he sang himself:

---

15. The twenty-fifth emperor, Buretsu, who was partly mythical.
16. The twenty-seventh emperor, Ankan, who was partly mythical.

Finding no wife to pillow in the Country of Eight Islands,
hearing there was a beautiful woman,
hearing there was a good woman,
in the Country of Kasuga, of a spring day,
I push open and enter myself
the wooden door of cypress, the luxuriant tree,
tug at the hem toward her feet,
tug at the hem toward her pillow,
make my love's arm pillow me,
make my arm pillow my love,
arms holding each other, crossed like vines,
and we sleep our sleep well like boar on a skewer.
Birds of the garden, roosters have called,
birds of grass fields, pheasants resound.
That I love you I still haven't said,
yet the day has broken, my love.

The princess sang in response:

Down the Hatsuse River, of Komoriku,
bamboo flows toward us, woven bamboo, fresh bamboo.
I'll make a koto out of its trunk,
I'll make a flute out of its tip;
playing it, I climb up
Mount Mimoro, stand there, and look round:
In the pond of Iware, of luxuriant vines,
even the fish in the water come up to lament.
Our Sovereign familiar with the eight corners[17]
wears his sash of detailed design,
its knot hanging, head hanging, everyone's here to lament.[18]

---

17. *Yasumishishi*, here translated as "familiar with the eight corners," is a makura-kotoba that modifies *wago ōkimi*, "our Sovereign."

18. In this context this is an aubade expressing sorrow at the parting at dawn. Some suspect that this song is a misplaced imperial threnody.

Poems from the *Man'yōshū*

The *Man'yōshū* (*Collection of Ten Thousand Leaves*) is an anthology of 4,550 poems in twenty volumes, its coverage ranging from songs attributed to mythological figures to what may be called the "diary poems" of Ōtomo no Yakamochi (718–785). Yakamochi, in fact, played a major role in the last phase of its compilation and editing, which had apparently started some decades earlier: The last four of the twenty volumes give the impression of being his personal collection, and a total of 473 poems, or more than one tenth of the poems, included in the anthology are his. Yakamochi was of a distinguished military clan and in his last position was Commander-in-Chief to Subjugate the East. His political involvement at the time of his death is thought to have delayed bringing the *Man'yōshū* to light.

The songs and poems in the anthology were written down in the same way as in the *Kojiki* with a hybrid use of Chinese characters. This highly inventive, imaginative use of the Chinese writing system made the collection increasingly unintelligible, especially as the simplified writing systems of *hiragana* and *katakana* were devised and accepted, so that in 893 Sugawara no Michizane lamented about the *Man'yōshū*: "Its sentences and phrases are convoluted, these are neither verses nor odes, the writing system is random and warped. It is difficult to get into it and understand it." Finally, in 951, Emperor Murakami assigned five scholar-poets to decipher the anthology. Since those men worked in the female quarters of the palace, some say that the women's desire to understand the poems of bygone days was an impetus to the first systematic attempt to read the large collection.

Chronologically, the first woman poet to appear is Princess Iwa, whose poems top the "Love" (*Sōmon*) section of volume two. (For Princess Iwa, see also pp. 8–10). Her first poem here, whose beginning in my translation, "Since you went away, days have grown long" (*Kimi ga yuki ke nagaku narinu*), may remind some readers of the first line of "Autumn Leaves" by Johnny Mercer and Jacques Prévert, is attributed to Princess Sotōri, "See Through," a nickname of Princess Karu, in the section that immediately follows. However, the latter version is slightly different, suggesting that the poem or song was popular. Princess Karu had an incestuous relationship with her brother and was exiled—either along with him, according to one account, or alone, according to another. Her nickname came from her beauty, which, it is said, was so intense it glowed through her robe.

Princess Iwa, Emperor Nintoku's Consort

Four songs Princess Iwa made, longing for the Emperor:

Since you went away, days have grown long.
Seeking you in the mountains shall I come to meet you?
   Shall I just wait, and wait?

I'm so much in love with you.
A boulder on a high mountain as my pillow,
   I'd rather die.

Just as I am I'll wait for you
   until frost forms
on my sheer undulating black hair.

Morning haze lying mistily over the rice ears in autumn paddies,
where on earth will my longing cease?

   A song in another book says:

Staying awake I'll wait for you
   even if frost falls
on my black hair like black-lily seeds.

Empress Okamoto
(594–661)

The "original note"—an old annotation that has become part of the transmitted text—states that it is not clear whether the name Okamoto refers to Jomei (593–641) or Kōgyoku (594–661). Jomei (male) reigned from 629 to 641. Kōgyoku (female) reigned from 642 to 645 and from 655 to 661, the second time with the name Saimei. The latter engaged in large-scale construction works and died while in Kyūshū helping send reinforcement troops to Paekche, Korea.

Because they've kept being born since the age of deities,
people are innumerable, filling the land,
and like flocks of teals they come and go.
But because you whom I long for aren't among them,
during the day, until the day darkens,
during the night, until the night finally whitens,
I think of you, unable to sleep my sleep,
until I've let the night whiten, this long night.

    Envoi

Over the hill flocks of teals fly noisily
but I'm lonesome because you aren't among them.

Along the Ōmi Road, on Mount Toko, the Unknown River:
how many days will I go on longing?

Princess Nukata
(Born 638?)

Princess Nukata was first loved by Prince Ōama (later Emperor Tenmu, 631?–686) and then by his older brother, Emperor Tenchi (626–671). She probably wrote poems on behalf of other courtiers.

> When Emperor [Tenchi] issued an order to Minister of the Center Fujiwara [no Kamatari] to hold a contest to compare the glow of myriad cherry blossoms on spring mountains with the colors of a thousand leaves on autumn mountains, Princess Nukata declined [to participate] with a song:

When spring comes after holing up in winter,
birds that didn't sing come and sing,
blossoms that didn't bloom come into bloom.
But mountains luxuriant, we can't go there and take them,
grasses deep we can't take them and look at them.
When we look at the leaves on autumn mountains,
we take yellow leaves and admire them.
We leave the green ones alone and lament.
This I regret but I prefer autumn mountains.

> The song Princess Nukata made when she went down to the Country of Ōmi:

Mount Miwa, of tasteful sake,
until you hide behind the mountains
of Mount Nara, where the blue clay is good,
until the bends of the road accumulate,
I'd like to go to you to look closely;
you are a mountain I often turn to see.
So how could the clouds hide you heartlessly?

> Envoi

How can the clouds hide Mount Miwa so?
I wish they had some pity.
    How could they hide you?

The song Princess Nukata made when people leaving the Imperial Mausoleum in Yamashina[1] were dispersing:

Our Sovereign familiar with the eight corners:
serving His Majesty's awesome mausoleum
on Mount Mirror, of Yamashina,
during the night, throughout the night,
during the day, throughout the day,
crying, raising their voices,
now the people of the Palace of a hundred laid stones
are leaving, parting.

The song Princess Nukata made longing for the Emperor of Ōmi:[2]

As I wait for you, longing,
moving the blinds of my house,
   an autumn wind blows.

---

1. The mausoleum for Emperor Tenchi.
2. Emperor Tenchi.

Empress Naka
(7th Century)

Empress Naka may be the same person as Princess Hashihito. If so, Emperor Tenchi was her older brother and Emperor Tenmu her younger brother. She was the consort of Emperor Kōtoku, who was her uncle. She may have been the nominal ruling monarch from 665 to 668. Some suspect that she was Empress Saimei.

> When Emperor [Jomei] hunted in the Uchi field, Empress Naka had an old man of Hashimoto offer a song to His Majesty:

Our Sovereign familiar with the eight corners
takes it out and caresses it in the morning,
goes to it and stands by it in the evening,
the catalpa bow he uses.
I hear the sound of its fittings.
He must be setting out now for a morning hunt,
he must be setting out now for an evening hunt.
The catalpa bow he uses,
I hear the sound of its fittings.

Envoi

Horses lined up in *tamakiwaru*[3] Uchi's large field,
they must be morning-trampling
that grass-deep field!

---

3. *Makura-kotoba* whose meaning is unknown.

Empress Yamato
(7th Century)

Tenchi's consort, Empress Yamato may have been the ruler of the land for a while after her husband fell ill in 671.

When Emperor [Tenchi] passed away, Empress Yamato made a song:

Others, yes, may stop longing,
but his vine-crowned visage in my mind
   I can never forget.

Empress Yamato's song:

In the Sea of Ōmi, where whales are taken,[4]
leaving the offing a boat comes rowing,
close to the shore a boat comes rowing.
Paddle in the offing, do not splash hard,
paddle near the shore, do not splash hard:
The birds my young-grass husband loved
   may fly away.

---

4. *Isanatori*, here given as "where whales are taken," is a makura-kotoba that modifies *umi*, "sea." The Sea of Ōmi is Lake Biwa; it is Japan's largest lake, but it has no whales.

Anonymous Lady
(7th Century)

When Emperor [Tenchi] passed away, a lady made a song. Her name remains unknown.

Being of this world, unable to be near a deity,
I live apart, aggrieved over you in the morning,
I live away, longing for you, my lord.
If you were jewels, I'd carry you tied round my wrist,
if you were a robe, I'd never take you off.
I long for you, my lord; last night
    I saw you in my dreams.

Empress Jitō
(648–702)

Politically astute, Jitō, Tenmu's consort, was the ruling monarch from 689 to 695. She created the domicile system, improved the military, and began the construction of the Fujiwara Imperial Palace. Her frequent travels provided courtier poets such as Kakinomoto no Hitomaro with opportunities to compose poems. The chōka she is said to have memorized in her dream contains incoherent parts.

The Empress's song:

Spring past, summer must have come:
white-cloth robes are set out to dry, they say,
   on heavenly Mount Kagu.[5]

When Emperor [Tenmu] passed away, the Empress made a song:

Our Sovereign familiar with the eight corners,
come evening, must look at them,
as the day breaks, must ask about them,
those mountain maples on Deity Hill.
Today, too, will His Majesty ask about them,
tomorrow, too, will he look at them?
Turning back to look at the mountain,
come evening, I feel mysteriously sad,
as the day breaks, disconsolate, I live,
the sleeves of my rough-woven robe
   have no time to dry.

When the Emperor passed away, Her Majesty made a song:

The cloud lying on the north mountain,
the blue cloud, goes on leaving the stars,
   leaving the moon.

Eight years after Emperor [Tenmu] passed away, on the ninth of Ninth Month, on the night of the Imperial alms-giving ceremony, she memorized a song from a dream:

---

5. Selected for the *Hyakunin Isshu*.

In the Kiyomi Palace, in Asuka,
Your Majesty ruled under heaven,
Our Sovereign familiar with the eight corners,
child of the high-shining sun,
I do not know what you thought,
in the Province of Ise, of divine winds,
in the waves where offshore seaweed undulates,
in the province where the salt scent fills the air,
I miss you so much, so indescribably,
child of the high-shining sun.

Empress Jitō as imagined by Kanō Tan'yū
(1602–1674)

Imperial Princess Ōku
(661–701)

Born to Emperor Tenmu and Emperor Tenchi's daughter, Princess Ōku was appointed
vestal of the Grand Shrine of Ise when she was twelve. The nature of her involvement
with the alleged revolt of her brother, Prince Ōtsu (663–686), is not clear. Ōtsu, who
excelled in both literary and martial arts, was accused and executed. One theory holds
that Empress Jitō incited him to rebellion, which was doomed to fail, to promote her
own son, Prince Kusakabe (662–689).

> When Prince Ōtsu secretly came down to Ise Shrine and went up [to the
> Capital], Princess Ōku made two songs:

As I saw my beloved off to Yamato,
    the night grew late;
I stood soaked with daybreak dew.

The two of us going will find the autumn mountains hard-going;
how are you alone passing over them?

> After Prince Ōtsu passed away, Princess Ōku came up to the Capital and made
> two songs:

I'd rather be in the Province of Ise, of Divine Wind.
Why have I come here when you are no more?

When you, whom I want to see, are no more,
why have I come here, tiring my horse?

> When Prince Ōtsu's corpse was moved to Mount Futagami, in Kazuraki, and
> buried, Princess Ōku, aggrieved and hurt, made two songs:

I, being a human of this world,
    from tomorrow on,
will regard Mount Futagami as my younger brother.

I'd like to pluck some *ashibi*[6] growing on the bank,
though you, whom I ought to show them to, no longer exist.

> Original note: When we think of it now, this last song doesn't look like one for
> the transfer and burial [of the corpse]. We speculate that when she returned to the
> Capital from the Ise Shrine, she may have made this song, moved to sobbing, as
> she saw the flowers by the roadside.

6. *Andromeda japonica*: a shrub with clusters of small, white, pot-shaped flowers.

Imperial Princess Tajima
(Died 708)

One of Emperor Tenmu's six daughters, Imperial Princess Tajima, while married to one of his ten sons, Takechi (654–696), fell in love with another son, Hozumi (died 715). Whether that had anything to do with the fact that Takechi was the oldest but low in imperial rank because his mother was lowly in social status, while Hozumi was the fifth but high in rank because his mother was from the distinguished family of Soga, cannot be known.

> While living in Prince Takechi's palace, Imperial Princess Tajima made a song, longing for Prince Hozumi:

The rice ears in autumn paddies lean, lean to one side;
I wish I could lean to you,
    though people may talk badly.

> When the Emperor dispatched Prince Hozumi to the mountain temple in Shiga, Ōmi, Imperial Princess Tajima made a song:

Rather than stay behind and remain longing for you,
    I'd follow and catch up with you.
Tie string markers where the road bends, my love.

> While living in Prince Takechi's palace, Imperial Princess Tajima secretly made love to Prince Hozumi. When this became public, she made a song:

Because people talk a great deal, talk badly,
    I cross a morning river
which I haven't crossed in my whole life.

> Imperial Princess Tajima made a song:

Rather than live in a village where people talk a great deal,
    I should have gone along
with the geese that called this morning.

Ōtomo no Sakanoue no Iratsume
(First Half of the 8th Century)

Daughter of Ōtomo no Yasumaro (died 714) and mother-in-law of Ōtomo no Yakamochi, Sakanoue no Iratsume, with eighty-four poems, is the best represented woman poet in the *Man'yōshū*. She married Prince Hozumi in her teens and, after his death, married his half-brother Sukunamaro. After Sukunamaro's death, she went to the Dazaifu, in 728, to live with another half-brother, Tabito (665–731), the administrator-commander of the western headquarters and a noted poet. With Tabito's death, she became, basically, the head of the Ōtomo house. Her poems stylistically influenced Yakamochi.

> Ōtomo no Sakanoue no Iratsume, while performing a rite for a deity, made a song, along with a short song:

Our divine prince who has continued to live
since everlasting Heaven's Plain:
To a *sakaki*[7] branch from mountain depths,
I attach *shiraka*, I place and attach *yū*;[8]
I dig the earth and set down a sacred vase,
string bamboo rings amply and hang them.
Like a deer, knees bent, I prostrate myself,
like a pliant woman, covered with a robe,
so intensely I am praying to you,
 but shall I not meet you?

> Envoi

Holding a *yū tatami* in my hand,
so intensely I pray to you,
 but shall I not meet you?

> Original note: In Eleventh Month, in the winter of the fifth year of Tempyō [733], when they enshrined the deity of the Ōtomo Tribe, she made these extemporaneously. For this reason they are called "songs to enshrine a deity."

In the seventh year [of Tempyō: 735], Ōtomo no Sakanoue no Iratsume, grieving over the nun Rigan's death, made a song, along with a short song:

---

7. An evergreen glabrous tree with green branches (*Cleyera japonica*), whose branches are indispensable in Shinto rites.
8. *Shiraka* and *yū* are simple adornments made of strips of paper or cloth.

From the country of Silla, of mulberry rope,
hearing what people said was good,
you came, crossing over to a country
with no relatives or siblings to talk to.
This country where our Sovereign reigns
has innumerable villages and houses
that pack the Capital that the sun illuminates,
but, I do not know what you thought,
you sought us out, like a crying child,
near the friendless hills of Saho
and even built a house, of mulberry sheets.
And through a long string of *aratama*[9] years
you continued to live, as you did.
Still, there is no exception to the fact
that all living things must face death.
While all the people you depended on
were away traveling on grass pillows,
you morning-crossed the Saho River
and, looking at the Kasuga Field behind you,
headed toward the foot-wearying hills
in the evening darkness to hide yourself.
Not knowing what to say, what to do,
I walk about, all by myself,
my white-cloth sleeves never dry.
Grieved, I cry, and my tears,
turning into clouds over Mount Arima,
    must have fallen as rain.

    Envoi

Because life can't possibly be kept
you left your house, of mulberry sheets,
    and hid yourself in clouds.

> Original note: The nun of the Country of Silla in this account had the name Rigan. Deeply moved, albeit from a distance, by our Imperial virtues, she was naturalized in our Holy State. She stayed in the house of the Major Councilor and General, Lord Ōtomo [no Yasumaro], and several decades passed. In the seventh year of Tempyō, she sank into a terminal illness and swiftly went to the Nether World. The mistress, Lady Ishikawa, was away, visiting the hot springs of Arima for dietary and medicinal treatment, and could not attend her funeral. Only [Sakanoue no] Iratsume was at

---

9. *Aratama no* is a makura-kotoba that modifies *toshi*, "year," *tsuki*, "month," or *haru*, "spring." One scholar interprets it to mean "of new life" or "of renewed vitality."

home, and she saw to it that the coffin and the funeral were taken care of properly. She made this song and sent it to the mistress at the hot springs.

A song of resentment by Ōtomo no Sakanoue no Iratsume, along with a short song:

Like the sedge of sun-dominated Naniwa,
as deeply as its roots you spoke to me,
and said it would last for years and longer,
so my heart polished as a mirror
I yielded to you. From that very day
my heart did not sway this way or that
like seaweed moving in the waves,
counting on you as I would a great ship.
But a rock-smashing deity distanced you
or someone of this world prevented you:
you used to come but no longer do,
nor do I see a catalpa messenger.
As this happens, I don't know what to do.
During black-lily nights, throughout them,
during red-lit days, till darkness comes,
I cry, aggrieved, but to no avail.
I think of you but know of no recourse.
Feeble women, they say, and they're right,
like an infant I just weep and weep,
walking back and forth, impatiently
    waiting for your messenger.

    Envoi

If at the outset you hadn't said it would last long
    and made me count on you,
I wouldn't have met thoughts such as these.

From the Tomi Estate, Ōtomo no Sakanoue no Iratsume sent a song to her daughter, Ō Iratsume, along with a short song:

Although I wasn't going to the Distant World,
at our gate you appeared melancholy,
deep in thought, my child, mistress of the house.
Be it the black-lily night or day,
when I think of you, I lose weight;
I lament, and even my sleeves grow wet.

If I miss you so unreasonably,
I hardly can stay in the Old Capital
    for another month.

    Envoi

Thoughts as wild as morning hair,
you, my love, must miss me:
    you appeared in my dreams.

        Original note: These songs were given in response to Ō Iratsume's songs.

    A song sent from the Capital, along with a short song:

The Deity of the Ocean Sea, the divine prince,
keeps pearls in his comb box, I'm told,
and treasures them devoutly. More highly
than that I think of you. But, my child,
it's the rule of the human world,
you let yourself be pulled away by your man
toward Koshi, far beyond the slopes.
Since we parted, as crawling vines do,
your eyebrows arched like waves in the offing
appear in my mind unreasonably,
undulating, undulating like a great ship.
If I miss you like this, I, growing old,
    how can I bear myself?

    Envoi

Had I known I'd miss you like this,
I wouldn't have spent a day without seeing you
    like a mirror.

        Original note: Ōtomo no Sakanoue no Iratsume gave these two songs to her daughter,
        Ō Iratsume.

Kasa no Iratsume
(First Half of the 8th Century)

Nothing is known about Kasa no Iratsume except for a total of twenty-nine love poems she sent to Ōtomo no Yakamochi. The following twenty-four are clustered in one place in the *Man'yōshū*.

Twenty-four songs Kasa no Iratsume sent to Ōtomo no Sukune Yakamochi:

Look at my keepsake and think of me;
   I, too, will think of you
as long as a string of *aratama* years.

Like the pines on Mount Toba where white birds fly,
pining, longing,
   I spend these months.

As if not knowing I'm in clothes-fulling[10] Uchimi Village,
you do not come though I wait for you.

"A string of *aratama* years has passed, and now,"
never think that, my love, and divulge my name.

Is it because I let you know my thoughts?
I opened up my lovely comb box
   or so I dreamed.

A crane calling in the dark night:
will I only keep hearing you,
   never meeting you?

Longing for you, not knowing what to do,
under a small pine on Mount Nara,
   I stand, grieving.

White dew on the twilight grass of my house,
I almost fade,
   thinking of you.

---

10. *Koromode no*, here given as "clothes-fulling," is a makura-kotoba that modifies clothes-related words such as Uchimi, in which *uchi* means "to full," "to beat."

As long as my life lasts, how can I forget you?
even if day by day
   my thoughts may intensify.

Even the grains of sand on the eight-hundred-day beach
can't exceed my love, can they,
   offshore island guard?

The eyes of this world so many,
   I can only long for you
though you're stepping-stone close.

Of love some even die:
like a waterless river I grow thin beneath,
   by month, by day, different.

Though I glimpsed you vaguely as in morning mist,
I keep longing for you,
   as if I'm about to die.

Waves roar in onto the beach of the Ise Sea:
you are as awesome yet I long for you.

Truth to tell, I never thought
   I'd long for you so
when no mountain or river separates us.

Come evening my thought intensifies
   with the image of
when I saw you, how you spoke.

If of thoughts of love we were to die,
I'd have repeated death a thousand times!

I took a sword and held it by my side,
   so I dreamed.
What sign save that I'll see you?

Without the reasoning of deities of heaven and earth
I'd die without seeing you, whom I love.

I think of you. You, too, do not forget me.
May this be ceaseless as the wind across the bay.

The bell is struck to tell people to go to sleep,
but because I think of you I cannot sleep.

To think of someone who doesn't think of you
is like groveling in a large temple,
     to a preta's ass.[11]

Truth to tell, I never thought
     that once again
I'd be back in my hometown.

When close, I can get by without seeing you;
if you moved any farther away
     I'd be unable to exist.

> Original note: The last two are the ones she sent after they parted.

---

11. *Gaki*, "preta," is a "hungry ghost," someone greedy condemned to eternal starvation after death. The images of pretas were placed in large temples as a warning about greed.

Maidservant
(First Half of the 8th Century)

All we know about this maidservant is this song and the account given in the original note, below. Prince Sai, whom the note mentions, died in 737. This is the shortest chōka in the *Man'yōshū*.

A song expressing longing for a husband:

I eat rice but it doesn't taste good.
I sleep but can't feel peace.
Madder-illumined you, your heart,
    I'm unable to forget.

> Original note: As legend has it, there was a maidservant attending Prince Sai. For some time she was on night duty and unable to see her husband. She became depressed, and her longing for him deepened. One night she saw him in a dream. Startled awake, she groped to hold him, but her hands touched nothing. So she sobbed, choking, and sang this song aloud. Hearing it, the prince took pity and exempted her from night duty forever, they say.

The Wife of Lord Isonokami no Otomaro
(First Half of the 8th Century)

Isonokami no Otomaro, who died in 750, was exiled in 739 as a result of his adulterous liaison with a widow; he was pardoned a few years later. He held a round of government posts; he also excelled in writing kanshi and kambun, "prose in Chinese." Little is known about Otomaro's wife, to whom the following poems are attributed. The third poem, along with its envoi, is apparently composed in the role of the exiled husband.

The three songs that follow, along with a short song, were made when Lord Isonokami no Otomaro was exiled to Tosa Province:

The prince of Furu, of Isonokami,
misled by a woman, of feeble arms,
tied with a rope like a horse,
surrounded with bow and arrow like a deer,
accepting Our Sovereign's order,
recedes into a borderland, far under heaven.
From Mount Matsuchi, of old clothes,
    will he ever return?

* * *

Accepting Our Sovereign's order,
to the Province of Tosa, next to ours,
he sets out, departing, my dear husband.
Human-figured Deity, of Suminoe,
too awesome, too fearsome to mention,
kindly settle yourself on his ship's bow,
lest he come upon rough waves and winds
at any point of an island he arrives at,
at any point of a beach he stops at,
so he may return with speed,
without incident, without illness
    to the province where he belongs.

* * *

To my venerable father I am his loveliest child.
To my mother, the mistress, I am her loveliest child.

At the Kashiko Slope where offerings are made
by people of eighty clans going up,
I reverently offer paper strips and go
      toward the distant Tosa Road.

Envoi

Though the small beach of the Ōzaki Deity is narrow,
a hundred boatmen don't just pass by, they say.[12]

---

12. Unstated: But I am compelled to pass by without paying my respects because I am
in a hurry.

The Kurumamochi Clan's Daughter
(Dates Unknown)

A song expressing longing for her dear husband, along with short songs:

Because words from you, you of ruddy cheeks,
no messenger of beautiful catalpa brings to me,
I've brooded, have taken ill, all alone.
Do not blame it on a rock-smashing deity.
Do not bring a diviner to have a turtle burned.
Because of longing my body aches, yes.
Clearly it has pierced me through and through,
and my heart, among the innards, has shattered.
The end of my life is imminent.
And now, is it you, calling to me?
Or is it my dear mother, of sagging breasts,
at the crossroad of eighty, less than a hundred,
who is evening-divining, questioning a diviner,
    when I'm about to die?

Envoi

Questioning a diviner
or evening-divining at the crossroad of eighty
    I know no way of seeing you.

I think nothing of my life;
only because of you, you of ruddy cheeks,
    I wanted it to last long.

> Original note: As legend has it, there once was a young woman. Her family name was Kurumamochi. For a long time her husband did not even send her a letter. As a result, her heart ached with longings until she sank into illness. She grew thinner by the day and in no time faced the road to the Nether World. Thereupon a messenger was sent to summon her husband. Then sobbing and shedding tears, she recited these songs aloud and passed away, they say.

Empress Kōken
(718–770)

This poet served as ruling monarch twice: first as Kōken, from 749 to 757, then as Shōtoku, from 760 to 770. The ambassador mentioned in the headnote, Fujiwara no Kiyokawa (706–778), led an embassy to China in 752 and had an audience with Emperor Huan Tsung. On his way back he was shipwrecked off Vietnam, but he made it back to Changan, where he became an official of high rank in the Tang court. He died there.

> A song, along with a short song, that Her Majesty made when she sent Koma no Ason Fukushin, Junior Fourth Rank, Upper Grade, to Naniwa to present sake and other things to the Ambassador to the Tang Court, Fujiwara no Ason Kiyokawa, and others:

The nation of sky-filling Yamato
is a nation Great Deities protect,
where going by water is like going by land,
being aboard is like being seated on a bed.
Your four ships, bows side by side,
will quickly cross and return, in peace,
so you may read your report. That day
we shall drink this sake together,
    this beautiful sake.

> Envoi

So your four ships may return soon,
    gray-hair strips attached
to the hem of my robe, purified, I shall wait.

A Border Guard's Wife
(Dates Unknown)

The system of *sakimori*, border guards (literally, cape guards), dates at least from the early seventh century, with its earliest mention in a legal code that appeared in 664. By a 701 decree, the length of service was set at three years. Most soldiers were taken from eastern provinces and placed in the islands closest to the continent: Tsushima, Oki, and Kyūshū (or its northern areas). It is a singular credit to Ōtomo no Yakamochi that he decided to collect poems by *sakimori* and their relatives. He probably did so because while serving as major general in the Ministry of Military Affairs, he was put in charge of them as they passed through Naniwa, today's Osaka, in Second Month of 755. During that month he wrote a number of poems, among them four chōka, expressing sympathy with those people. The following chōka is attributed to a border guard's wife.

This month you're sure to come, I thought,
and, counting on it as I might a great ship,
I was waiting, wondering when it might be.
But you passed away like a yellow leaf,
a messenger of beautiful catalpa said.
I heard the news as vaguely as a firefly.
The ground I trod on felt aflame.
Now standing or seated I do not know where I am,
like morning mist I am confused;
with sighs as long as eight feet, I lament
and while lamenting I see no sign.
Where on earth are you? Wondering,
I wish to drift away like heaven's cloud,
drift and die like a wounded deer.
This is my wish but I do not know the road.
So seated all alone, longing for you,
    I only weep aloud.

    Envoi

Each time I see geese flying over a reedy shore,
their wings remind me of the javelins you carried.

Mother of a Member of an Embassy to the Tang Court
(First Half of the 8th Century)

In the fifth year of Tempyō [733], when the ships of an embassy to the Tang Court were about to leave Naniwa and enter the sea, a mother [of a member of the embassy] gave him a song, along with a short song:

The deer that spouse-visits[13] autumn bush clovers
has only one child, just one for progeny, they say.
Just like the deer, I have only one child,
and he sets out on a grass-pillow journey.
So I string bamboo rings closely and hang them,
I take out and hang paper strips on a ritual pot,
and, performing the rite, I think of my child:
　　May he be safe and sound.

　　Envoi

If frost forms in a field where travelers lodge,
protect my child with your wings,
　　heaven's flock of cranes!

---

13. Literal translation of *tsuma-dou*, "woo." There was a belief that stags regarded bush clovers as their wives.

The Age of Tanka

The first imperial anthology of Japanese verse, *Kokinshū*, compiled in 905, proclaimed in its preface—a declaration that would define the nature of Japanese poetry for the next thousand years:

> Japanese poetry takes the human heart as its seed and grows into myriad leaves that are words. The people of this world, filled as they are with things to do, speak out what they think in their hearts whenever they see something, hear something. Listen to a bush-warbler singing in the flowers or to the voice of a frog living in the water: Who among the living things, all living things, does not make poetry? What moves heaven and earth without exertion of force, makes even the invisible demons and deities feel pity, softens the relations between man and woman, and soothes the hearts of ferocious warriors is poetry. . . .

The far-reaching influence of the *Kokinshū* was not limited to what to be sung of. Because twenty anthologies compiled by order of the emperor followed the *Kokinshū* and because the 5-7-5-7-7-syllable tanka was used almost exclusively in these "twenty-one imperial anthologies," it became the official verse form in court poetry. That lasted for half a millennium. The next dominant forms, the renga, "linked verse," and the hokku/haiku, were the direct outgrowths of the tanka form, and these more plebeian forms predominated for the next five hundred years.

The other salient feature of the imperial anthologies was categorization of verse into the four seasons, love, and miscellany. This practice encouraged composing verse with specific topics in mind, an approach that grew ever more fine-tuned with the importance of the contest called *uta'awase*, "poetry matches," where precedents and other details were argued and judged. Renga and hokku/haiku poets followed suit, though in a far less strict way.

Two enduring effects of the *Kokinshū* preface may be given. Because of its mention there, the unassuming bird *uguisu*, "bush-warbler" (*Cettia diphone*), became the avian harbinger of spring, and the idea that when it comes to the frog you are to supposed to think of its "voice" became so fixed that when Matsuo Bashō (1644–1694) spoke of the sound of a frog leaping into the water in his hokku, the act was thought anti-traditional and, therefore, "humorous."

We begin this section with three kanshi poets.

Princess Uchiko
(806–847)

The third daughter of Emperor Saga (786–842), with a mother who was a natural-ized member of the Korean royal family, Uchiko (also Uchishi) familiarized herself with Chinese literature at an early age. The custom of choosing the *saiin*, the vestal of the Kamo Shrines, began in 818, when Saga created the post and appointed Uchiko to it. She composed the first of the poems selected here, in 823, when her father came to visit her with a retinue of courtiers and gave a banquet. The topic that Saga suggested for his more literarily disposed subjects was "mountain residence on a spring day," each verse to use four designated characters for rhyme. Uchiko's poem so impressed Saga that he presented her with "Third (Imperial) Rank" on the spot.

Mountain Residence on a Spring Day

My quiet, dark abode stands behind water and trees.
But once the Airy Palanquin descends on the bank of the pond,
the lone bird in the woods learns the riches of spring,
the cold flower hiding in the vale sees the light of the sun.
A waterfall nearby starts like year's first rolling thunder,
the mountain hues clear to the top above a line of evening shower.
All this makes me realize again the depth of your kind heart.
How can I repay your sky-wide generosity during my life?

In Response to His Majesty's Poem:
"Year's Last Night"

Outside the world, uneventful, left to time and fate,
I am unaware of the vain passage of years and months.
The daybreak lamp remains, but the stars are gone,
a cold blossom blooming alone in the snow's light.
In the dawning woods, haze warm, birds sing forth;
in the dark vale ice melts, a waterfall sounds desultory.
I try my spring clothes in the old trunk all night long,
expecting to see, come morning, willow branches bud.

In Response to His Majesty's Poem:
"Mount Wu Is High" [1]

Mount Wu is high and rugged.
Look at it: How tall is it?
Piling green faces an azure sea;
a waterfall flies down a purple sky.
Mornings dark clouds obscure,
evenings long rains fall fluttering.
At times a daybreak macaque screams,
a chilly voice on an aged tree branch.

In Response to His Majesty's Poem:
"Moon Above Barrier Mountains"

White and lucid the moon above Barrier Mountains,
the flow of its light shines on ten thousand li away.
Leaves with bead-like dew are clean;
frost flowers coldly face the fan, the moon.
Cold geese long gone in the clear sky,
a solitary monkey calls out before dawn.
How can I bear it in my empty bed,
thinking of you, disconsolate?

---

1. Mount Wu is a mountain in China famous for a legend about King Xiang, who, when he visited a high place near Lake Dongting, dreamed he made love to the goddess of Mount Wu. When she left him, she said she lived at a high place south of Mount Wu and turned into a cloud in the morning and a rain in the evening.

Member of the Korenaga Family

Nothing is known about this poet except that she probably served Emperor Saga. The following poem, made in response to Saga's, deals with one of the favorite topics in Chinese poetry: fulling clothes in preparation for the winter. The fuller is usually a lonely woman, often a wife left behind by her husband on a military expedition.

In Response to His Majesty's Poem:
"Fulling Clothes"

Late autumn, the entrance to our bedroom's cold,
the wind swish-swish, the dew round-round.
I think of you far away and am pained by the border guard;
on the expedition you must suffer, clothes unlined.
My mirror left in the box, I no longer use makeup;
on the loom the shuttle moves no more, and I tear the fabric left.
I ask, "Which is the good place to full the clothes?"
"Below the window of the southern tower, the moonlight's plentiful."
The mallet a lotus flower, the block a brocade stone,
they are from Huaying, from Fenglin.
I full white silk, I full glossed silk
until the Galaxy turns west and I'm tired out.
My gossamer sleeves flutter in the wind, fragrant,
up and down in the clear moon, hands cold.
The intermittent rhythm wandering around Changxin,
its clear sounds cut the air to enter Zhaoyang.
By lamplight, in my room,
with scissors and measure I mark the lengths,
put a thread through a needle's eye, weeping, and make a knot;
resentful, I sew clothes for you ten thousand li away.
Be not suspicious because I've made the waist different from the past.
Last night you entered my dream, face emaciated.

Princess from the Ōtomo Family

This poet was probably a lady-in-waiting who served in Emperor Saga's court.

Late Autumn Reflection

The season in desolation, the year past its prime,
near my chamber entrance it's hushed, autumn sun cold.
In the clouds are distant geese, their voices familiar;
in the eaves-trees late cicadas, their tunes about to die.
Chrysanthemums by the water laden with dew, flowers left chilly,
lotuses in the inlet frosty, their old cups out of shape.
In stillness, alone, this hurt, driven by the four seasons,
I cannot bear to look at the falling leaves that flutter, flutter.

Ono no Komachi

(fl. 833–858)

"Ono no Komachi is in the tradition of Princess Sotōri of ancient days," said the editors of the *Kokinshū*, referring to the semimythological beauty and poet. "She touches your heart but does not overpower you. She is like a noblewoman with some ailments." She was one of six poets the editors chose for similar assessment; as a result, she came to be counted among the Six Poetic Saints. Later, Fujiwara no Kintō selected Komachi as one of the Thirty-Six Poetic Saints.

The color of the flower has faded, as vainly as my life and world have passed in these long rains[2]

Because I fell asleep thinking of him I saw him. Had I known it was a dream I wouldn't have woken[3]

Ever since I saw someone I love while dozing I've been depending on what are called dreams

When I miss him desperately I wear my leopard-seed[4] nightclothes turned inside out[5]

In the real world all right perhaps: Seeing you watching for others' eyes in a dream desolates me[6]

Following my endless thoughts[7] I'll come by night; if it's a dreampath, no one should notice me

---

2. Included in *Hyakunin Isshu*. It employs two puns: *furu*, here given as "pass," also means "grow old" and "fall" (as rain); and *nagame*, here given as "long rains," also means "watch," "gaze."

3. This and the two poems that follow top the "Love: II" section of the *Kokinshū*.

4. *Mubatama no*, here given as "leopard-seed," is a pillow word that modifies "night." The leopard flower produces black seeds.

5. There was a folk belief that you could meet someone you loved if you wore your clothes in this manner.

6. A love affair must be conducted in secrecy. In a dream one can be free. The fact that you don't appear in my dreams suggests you don't really love me. This and the two that follow form a sequence of sorts in "Love: III" of the *Kokinshū*.

7. *Omohi*, here given as "thoughts," includes an orthographic pun meaning "fire," so the suggestion is made that the poet follows the light of her burning thought.

By the dreampath I commute without resting my legs; but this is nothing like an actual glimpse

What changes with its color invisible is surely the flower of the human heart[8] of this world

When Fun'ya no Yasuhide[9] became third secretary for Mikawa and sent me word, "Why don't you come along to see my prefecture?" I made a poem in reply:

Living alone I'm a floating weed; if my root severs and the water pulls I think I'll come along

This moonless[10] night I can't meet him, I think, awake, fire crackling on my chest burning my heart

Because it appeared that the man finally began not to care for me:

Having started to ride a melancholy[11] boat on my own not a day passes without waves soaking me wet

In the days when I had no man I had set my mind on but had matters to brood about:

On the bay where the fisherman lives, the rowboat oarless crosses the world sea, I in sorrow

When I paid my respects at a temple called Isonokami,[12] the night fell. I decided to come home at the break of day and stayed. Someone told me, "Henjō[13] resides at this temple." So I sent in word to see how he would react:

---

8. In a Buddhist metaphor, a human heart compared to a flower is a calm, clear heart.

9. One of the six poets discussed in the introduction to the *Kokinshū*: "His language is skillful but it does not fit the content. He is like a merchant wearing fine clothes."

10. *Tsuki*, here given as "moon," also has the sense of "means," so the opening part of this poem also says: "On this night I have no means of meeting him."

11. *Uki*, here given as "melancholy," also means "floating."

12. The temple used to be in Tenri, Nara. The name means "on the rock."

13. Abbot Henjō (815–890), one of the six poets discussed in the introduction to the *Kokinshū*; like everyone else, he is criticized: "He understands the poetic form but his poems have little truth in them. If we were to make a comparison, it would be like looking at a woman painted in a picture and yearning vainly for her."

Traveling I sleep on a rock and it's so cold; I wish you would lend me your robe
of moss[14]

In reply Henjō wrote:

Having turned against the world I have just one robe of moss but can't *not* lend it.
Let's sleep together![15]

"I hope to blend into the clouds like a crane," someone said and died. Remembering him with sadness:[16]

In everlasting[17] sky, adrift,
a cloud floats, myself afloat;
my life of dew, the day lily
not yet faded, things to brood on
increase like round small sedge.
Years and months pass, raw gems;[18]
on spring days the scent of flowers,
on summer days the breeze through trees,
on autumn nights the light of the moon,
on winter nights the sound of a shower,
in this world loves and heartbreaks,
melancholy things and pains I've known.
Myself in particular, heart-pierced,
my sleeve's lining has no time to dry.
How pitiful, things always like this,
so thinking I, as in Live Pine Grove,[19]

---

14. Sacerdotal robe.

15. In Section 168 of *Tales of Yamato*, Henjō appears under his lay name, Yoshimine no
Munesada. In the story, Munesada initially is a handsome, brilliant poet who is popular among
women and has three wives. But upon the death of Emperor Ninmyō (810–850), he decides
to "abandon the world" to become a monk. The poetic encounter occurs at Kiyomizu Temple,
in Kyoto. At the time, Munesada is still a mendicant monk wearing only a miserable straw
coat. When Komachi, having elicited his response, tries to talk to him further, he bolts.

16. This chōka is in the collection of thirty-six poets as designated by Fujiwara no Kintō
but not in any of the imperial anthologies.

17. *Hisakata no*, here given as "everlasting," is a pillow word that modifies heavenly
phenomena such as "sky" and "light."

18. *Aratama no*, a pillow word here given as "raw gems," is known to modify "year,"
"month," "spring," but its meaning is uncertain. Some suggest it means "new soul."

19. Iki no Matsubara, a pine wood lining Hakata Bay, where the mythological Empress
Jingū is said to have stopped on her way to conquer Silla, on the Korean Peninsula. Iki is a
place name that means "live" or "go" or both. Uta-makura, "poetic pillow."

I've lived, like the Nagara Bridge[20]
life prolonged, a crane in the shallows
crying, a boat rowing on a bay
getting wet, for some time afloat[21]
a water plant, just like myself.
Away from all this one day I hope
to see the one on the cloud I love,
and have nothing more to worry
 of this world.

---

20. Nagara no Hashi, a bridge built over the Yodo River, in Naniwa. It is used to alliteratively modify a word beginning with naga, "long"—here, nagaraeba, "life prolonged." During Komachi's days the bridge was known to need frequent repair.

21. Ukimi, here given as "afloat," also means "melancholy self."

Ise
(875?–939?)

Born to Fujiwara no Tsugikage (dates unknown), this poet is known as Ise because her father was once governor of Ise Province. While serving Onshi (Yoshiko; 872–907), the consort of Emperor Uda, she bore Uda a child. She also fell in love with two of Onshi's brothers, Fujiwara no Nakahira (875–945), who became Minister of the Right, and Tokihira (871–909), who became Prime Minister. When she was about forty, she bore a child to Uda's son, Prince Atsuyoshi (887–930), who was famed for his amorous prowess. The collection of Ise's poems contains nearly four hundred pieces, many composed for screen paintings. Here I have selected two pieces that describe Onshi's death—one a tanka with a substantial headnote, and the other a chōka.

> This Empress was gravely ill for a long time until she eventually passed away, on the eighth of Sixth Month. Those who had served her were terribly, deeply saddened and, gathering together, wept. Gradually, however, the time came for making preparations for services for her afterlife. On a day when it was raining particularly hard, the one who said she was distressed[22] was in her private room. Those who had served the Empress in her chambers were gathered and were weaving plaited threads for a service. The one in her room sent word to ask, "Have you finished the weaving?" and "What are you doing now?" They said to one another, "We are just watching the rain," and sent back a reply: "We finished weaving the threads. Now we are weaving our voices together, weeping." The one in her room said:

Weaving the crying voices together into a thread, I wish you'd string my tears together with it[23]

> After the Empress of Seventh Avenue passed away:

Like the waves in the offing
it's growing wilder in the Palace, and I,
Ise fisherwoman who has lived there for years,
feel as though I've lost my boat in the tides,
sad that I've no place to stay overnight.
Our tears, their color crimson,
fell like a shower among us

---

22. Ise. This roundabout way of telling a story suggests some attempt to objectify the setup of the anthology, which is evident in its early section.

23. Murasaki Shikibu refers to this poem in the "Agemaki" chapter of *The Tale of Genji*.

and, like autumn maples, people
have scattered away, departing.
Now there's no more shade to rest under,
with what's left flowering pampas grass
growing in the garden with you no more.
When I call out to the sky, the first geese
fly past, crying,
    looking at this place as foreign.

Akazome Emon
(957?–1041?)

Murasaki Shikibu wrote of Akazome Emon: "The wife of the Governor of Tamba is called Masahira Emon in and around aristocratic mansions and the Palace. Her poems may not be particularly outstanding but they are truly dignified. She doesn't compose poems on everything simply because she is a poet, but as far as those that I know are concerned, they deal with even fleeting occasions in a way that puts you to shame."

Masahira is Ōe no Masahira (952–1012), a renowned scholar of Chinese classics, as well as a poet. Akazome's naming was as arbitrary as any, but the fact that sometimes her husband's name crowned her name suggests, some say, that the two served the Imperial Palace as a loving, close couple, though, when younger, she had several liaisons and created amorous complications. For much of her long life she was such a literary force at court that she is thought to be the author of the first half of the court history *Eiga Monogatari*, which covers the period from Emperor Uda's reign (887–897) to 1092.

Akazome Emon is featured in several near contemporary accounts. So here, instead of translating a selection of her poems, of which she has left us about six hundred, I will translate some of those accounts to give a glimpse of court life and the use of poetry. *Fukuro Zōshi* is a treatise on poetics that Fujiwara no Kiyosuke (1104–1177) prepared for Emperor Nijō (1143–1165). The *Konjaku Monogatari* is a large, anonymous compendium of often homiletic tales, which is thought to have taken its present shape in the first half of the twelfth century. The *Gōki*, which Kiyosuke cites in a couple of his accounts, is a diary of Ōe no Masafusa (1041–1111), Masahira's great grandson.

In the following translation certain information is added without comment.

Fukuro Zōshi, Episode 57

The judgment of waka differs from one person to another. Fujiwara no Sadayori once asked his father, Kintō, Major Counselor of Shijō, "Who is the superior poet, Izumi Shikibu or Akazome Emon?" Kintō replied, "You can't answer that in one word. Izumi is a poet who made *koya tomo hito o iubeki ni* [I should let you come to my hut]."[24] Sadayori said, "Among Izumi's poems, most people say *harukani terase yamano ha no tsuki* [shine on me into the distance, moon at the rim of hills] is the best. What do you think of that, sir?" Kintō replied, "That's because they're misguided. *Kuraki yori kuraki michi* [from darkness to a dark path] is a phrase from the Lotus Sutra. You don't even have to contemplate how she thought of it. *Harukani terase* [shine on me into the distance] in the second half is something that the sutra phrase simply pulled out. On the other hand, to start out by saying *koya tomo hito*

---

24. For a full citation and exegesis of this poem, see pp. xxix–xxx of the introduction.

o [I should let you come] and to go on to say *hima koso nakere* [because there's no space] is not something an ordinary person can think of."

The *Gōki* tells us that Ryōzen said, "Both Izumi and Akazome are poetic saints. But of the twelve poems Akazome composed for the screens for Fujiwara no Michinaga's wife, Lady Rinshi, of the Takatsukasa Palace, ten are excellent. Also, during the poetry match at Fujiwara no Yorimichi's Kayano-in Mansion, she composed many an excellent piece. When it comes to screen poems, Izumi didn't even come close to her."

In my view, you can believe with respect what the Major Counselor said, but you can't accept whatever Ryōzen may have said. Even so, in poetry matches, Akazome certainly was a natural. Izumi's poems seldom made it into poetry matches. Hers did that only in the so-called Retired Emperor Kazan's Poetry Match and Chōgen Poetry Match.

Fukuro Zōshi, Episode 93

During the reign of Emperor Ichijō, in the second year of Kankō (1005), Fujiwara no Kintō, then Middle Counselor, submitted a letter of resignation. Chamberlain Middle Controller of the Right Fujiwara no Tsuneyori conveyed the imperial will and returned the letter according to form. The word was that His Majesty would promote Kintō by one rank. The Counselor had not come to work for months. His letter was written especially well.

About this letter, the Counselor had said to Masahira, "I want to submit a letter of resignation. I had the outstanding scholars Ki no Tadana and Ōe no Mochitoki competitively prepare a draft, but neither has come up with one that fully expresses my sentiments. Only you can write them out."

Masahira, having unthinkingly accepted the task, looked troubled when he came home. Akazome asked, "What's the matter?" Masahira told her what had happened, adding, "Both Tadana and Mochitoki are far superior in talent and erudition. It would be difficult indeed for me to do better than either in writing out the Counselor's sentiments. I don't know what to do."

After thinking awhile, Akazome said, "The Counselor is a man who thinks exceedingly highly of himself. Could it be that neither Tadana nor Mochitoki wrote to suggest that the Counselor is depressed because he has not attained the kind of high rank his ancestors achieved? What do you think? Shouldn't that be written in the letter?"

Masahira said, "I've seen the drafts and, you are quite right, neither has mentioned that." So he began his draft by saying, "I am a legitimate fifth-generation descendent of Prime Minister Ōe no Yoshifusa," and listed the men that followed one by one, in the end suggesting that his rank remains low. He took it to the Counselor. The Counselor was touched and happy, and adopted it.

Thus Akazome Emon not only had high ideals, but she was also wise in the way of letters.

Fukuro Zōshi, Episode 101

When Middle Chancellor Fujiwara no Michitaka was still a minor captain of the Inner Palace Guards, Left Division,[25] he became intimate with Akazome Emon's sister. He then forgot about her, and she, for her part, started longing for him. Come evening she would brood, with the blinds facing south lifted.

One evening someone in a court cloak came by enveloped in an abundance of scent. It was him. She was happy, and they made love. After that he came night after night. But neither in the morning nor in the evening was there a sound of a carriage or a horse moving. Wondering, she put a long thread through a needle and attached the needle to a sleeve of the man's cloak. The next morning the thread was found hanging from a tree in the garden to the south. After that the man stopped coming. He must have been the spirit of the garden tree. By then she was pregnant. But when the time for childbirth came, only the placenta came out. When she opened it, there was plenty of blood in it but nothing else. This is what the *Gōki* tells us.

Akazome Emon wrote a poem:[26]

> Unhesitatingly I should have gone to bed, but watched the moon till late into the night, until it inclined

The *Gōki* says, "Akazome Emon is Akazome Tokimochi's daughter. Because he served in the fourth- and third-grade positions in the U-emon, the Outer Palace Guards, Right Division, she is called Akazome Emon. In fact, she is Taira no Kanemori's daughter. After separating from her mother, Kanemori learned that she had had a baby girl and visited her to take the baby. But her mother, who did not want to lose her, argued that the baby was not his, and a quarrel ensued. She brought a suit through Tokimochi, at the time an Imperial Police officer. She had already had a liaison with him. She insisted that the daughter was not Kanemori's but Tokimochi's. Kanemori requested an interview with the daughter," and so forth.

---

25. "Middle Chancellor," *naka no kampaku*, is not a title; Michitaka (953–995), who became Chancellor, was so called because he was a son of Kane'ie (929–990) and an older brother of Michinaga (966–1027). Both Kane'ie and Michinaga became Chancellor, and Michitaka came between the two.

26. The *Go-Shūishū* includes the poem with the following headnote: "When the Middle Chancellor was a minor captain of the Left Division, he courted [Akazome Emon's] sister. But after indicating he would visit her, he did not. So the next morning [Akazome] made a poem on her behalf." This poem is included in the *Hyakunin Isshu*.

Konjaku Monogatari, Volume 24, Episode 51

At a time now past, Ōe no Masahira's wife was a daughter of a man called Akazome Tokimochi. She gave birth to Takachika. When he grew up, Takachika excelled as a man of letters. In public service, he finally became Governor of Izumi. When he went down to the assigned province, he took his mother along. Unexpectedly, though, Takachika fell ill. He suffered for days until his illness took a turn for the worse. His mother, Akazome Emon, much aggrieved, dedicated to Sumiyoshi Shrine a sacred staff with a poem written on one of its paper strips:

> Having no regard for my life I'd give up for him, I'm still sad to be separated from him

That night Takachika recovered completely.

Also, when Takachika wished to have a government position, Akazome composed the following poem and took it the Lady of the Takatsukasa Palace:[27]

> Consider, Lady: brushing the snow off my head before it melts, I'm in such a hurried state

Her husband was deeply touched by this, and that's how Takachika was made Governor of Izumi.

Also, when her husband, Masahira, talked a shrine priest's daughter into loving him and did not come home to her for a long time, Akazome made the following poem and sent it to the priest's house while he was there:

> In my house the pine awaits no sign; if it were a cypress grove you might come to visit[28]

Masahira must have been embarrassed to see this. He went back to Akazome to live with her and stopped visiting the priest's daughter, or so goes the story.

---

27. In Akazome Emon's personal anthology, the headnote says she took this poem to Jōtōmon'in in the first month when governors were appointed. Jōtōmon'in is Shōshi, daughter of Michinaga and Rinshi and Emperor Ichijō's consort.

28. A shrine is usually surrounded by a stand of ancient cedars.

Murasaki Shikibu
(973?–1014?)

Murasaki Shikibu is the famous author of the preeminent work of Japanese literature, *The Tale of Genji*, but little is known about her. Even her name is unusual; though Shikibu derives from her father's court rank, Murasaki, which means "purple," is a sort of thing seldom found among the names of other ladies-in-waiting. What we know is that she was the second daughter of Fujiwara no Tametoki and accompanied her father when he was appointed Governor of Echizen, in 996, and governor of Echigo, in 1011. She married Fujiwara no Nobutaka, who was nearly twenty years her senior, perhaps in 998. They had a daughter, Kenshi, later known as Daini no Sanmi, an accomplished poet. Nobutaka died in 1001. In 1005 Murasaki was summoned to serve Empress Shōshi (988–1074). It was during her court service that she composed *The Tale of Genji*. She is also identified as Tō Shikibu. (Shōshi became Empress Dowager upon her husband Ichijō's death, in 1011. In poetry anthologies she is usually identified by her Buddhist name, Jōtōmon'in.)

In addition to *The Tale of Genji*, she has left a *nikki*, "diary"—a miscellany of observations and reflections, including what appear to be letters, written between 1008 and 1010—and a collection of 128 poems, of which 89 are her own. These numbers compare with almost 800 poems she wove into her *Genji*. The following selection is made from the collection. Some headnotes are taken from other sources or changed in consideration of them. The asterisks indicate a passage not translated.

Someone who has been a friend since childhood—I came across her after an interval of several years, briefly, around the tenth of Seventh Month, before she left as if racing with the moon:

We met again but before I could tell I saw you, you hid yourself in clouds, midnight moon![29]

She[30] was to go to a distant place. She came on the day Autumn ended; the following daybreak, insects' voices were piteous:

The insect in the hedge too is crying feebly, sad at autumn parting that cannot be stayed

---

29. Selected for the *Hyakunin Isshu*.

30. This seems to refer to the person described in the preceding poem. Regardless, the poem probably describes a daughter of a governor or someone appointed governor in a distant province.

Someone sent word, "May I borrow your thirteen-string koto?" adding, "I'd like to come over and study it with you, if I may." My reply was:

The sound of the insect in dew-laden sagebrush being faint, who would want to visit her?

※

Someone who came to stay with us because he needed to change directions[31] behaved in rather ambiguous fashion and went home. Early the next morning I sent him a morning glory:

Uncertain, I could not tell it was you or what at predawn, feigning, the morning glory

He must not have recognized my handwriting. In reply, he said:

Which color I can hardly tell: the morning glory has wilted so it barely exists, desolately[32]

※

A daughter of someone going to Tsukushi wrote to me:

When I imagine the seas to the west and look at the moon I can only cry; such are these days

In reply:

By way of the moon going west I shall never cease writing letters, clouds for their path

※

Someone troubled wrote to complain. In reply, around Frost Month:

Frost and ice are frozen so solid I cannot use my brush to write, or such is the way I feel

---

31. Yin-yang rules required avoiding certain directions on certain days. Someone planning to go to a destination lying in an unlucky direction had to stay in someone's house overnight so he might then choose a lucky direction to reach his destination.

32. Some speculate that this exchange may have been between Murasaki and her future husband, Nobutaka, after their first sexual encounter, which wasn't consummated.

In reply:

Even if you can't please write so I may wash away the frost and ice, along with
    my thoughts

✻

My older sister died, and someone lost one of her younger sisters. When we saw
each other, we decided to regard each other as the one each had lost. So, in letters,
I called her My Older Sister, and she called me My Middle One. When we had
to part, each going to a distant place, we regretted our parting, though quietly:

Entrust wings of geese going north with your letters, not ceasing to write for the
    clouds[33]

The response came from the one on the Seas to the West:

Going round, all return over mountains to the City, though, if you ask just when,
    it is far away[34]

✻

On the Lake of Ōmi,[35] at a place called the Cape of Mio, I saw people drag-
    ging in a net:

At the Sea of Mio I see folks dragging in a net, busy at work, I myself longing
    for the City

Also, on the beach of some inlet, cranes called severally:

Hidden in an inlet, feeling the same, cranes call. Who are the ones you've remem-
    bered?

Someone said, "Here comes the evening shower!" To be sure, the sky darkened
    and lightning flashed:

---

33. Alludes to the legend that the Former Han military commander Su Wu (140–60 B.C.E.),
while in captivity, sent his letters to his king by tying them to the legs of geese.

34. The original incorporates the names of two places that were in the direction Murasaki
was headed: Kaeru Yama, "Mount Return," and Itsuhata, "just when."

35. Japan's largest lake, Biwa. The three poems that follow were apparently composed
on the road between Kyoto and Echizen, where Murasaki was with her father.

Sudden clouds, in the evening shower the waves grow rough, disquieting our floating boat

＊

The next year, someone who had said, "I'm going to come to see the Chinese people,"[36] sent word: "How may I persuade you that in spring everything melts?" So:

Though spring, the snow on White Peak keeps accumulating and it's hard to tell when it will melt

Someone who I heard was in love with a daughter of the Governor of Ōmi constantly sent word to me, saying, "I'm not of two minds." Annoyed:

Plover calling to your mates across the lake, I hope your voice won't die in those eighty ports[37]

To someone who dripped vermilion on his letter and sent it to me, saying, "This is the color of my tears,"[38] I sent a reply:

Crimson tears are something I cannot stand, the changing heart visible in their color[39]

After all he was a person who had taken young women.[40]

When I heard that he was showing my letters to others, I sent him a simple verbal message: "Put together all my existing letters and return them to me; otherwise, I won't write you another reply." "I'll return them all," he said, but with bitter protests. That was around the tenth of First Month:

The thin ice frozen above melting, do you want the mountain stream below to cease?

Reconciled, he returned the letters to me after it became very dark:

---

36. In Ninth Month of 995, the seventy-odd Chinese who had been shipwrecked in Wakasa, north of Kyoto, were moved northeast to Echizen. Here, "someone" is thought to be Nobutaka, who wanted to use that as a pretext to see her to obtain a vow to marry him.

37. Lake Biwa was known for its many ports, and each port was a base for prostitution.

38. Tears shed in extreme grief are said to be "tears of blood."

39. The crimson extracted from safflower fades easily.

40. Nobutaka is known to have had a couple of other wives.

Ready to melt in the easterly, let the water over stones cease, bottom visible, if
    it must

"Now I won't say a word to you," he said angrily. Amused, I replied:

If you stop speaking to me, fine with me; why in the world should I bank on Anger
    Pond[41]?

    Around midnight, again:

Not strong willed, nor to be counted among men, I, boiling, stand by Anger Pond
    to no avail

Someone who had been away in a distant place died. When her parents and
siblings returned to the Capital and wrote me the sad news, I sent this:

If I knew which cloudpath, I would visit you where you are, goose who fell from
    the line

In a picture scroll there was a drawing of an ugly, spirit-possessed woman,
and behind it a drawing of a lowly monk who bound up another woman, who
was dead and had turned into a demon. Her husband was reciting a sutra to
exorcise the spirit. When I saw it:[42]

The one who died he's blaming as a pretext, troubled, his heart having grown
    demonic

    In reply:

Yes indeed! Because your heart is in darkness, a demon's shadow is what you
    clearly see

---

41. *Mihara no Ike*. Its identity is uncertain. Here it is used as a pun.
42. The exchange is thought to be between Murasaki and a female friend after Nobutaka's
death. Normally, as here, a possessing spirit is of someone dead, rather than someone alive. And
the soul of someone dead is called a "demon." In reference to the picture, Murasaki is evincing
an unusually critical stance, casting into doubt the reality of spirit possession. Her poem can
also be interpreted as self-reflection; in that case, "the one who died" refers to her husband,
and the translation would become: "The one who died I'm blaming as a pretext, troubled, my
heart having grown demonic." The person who replies to her observation says, in effect: Yes,
you can see such things clearly because you are troubled by your husband's death.

While aggrieved about the transience of life, I was looking at a picture scroll of famous places in Michinoku Province:

Since the evening someone close turned into smoke, I've felt intimate with the name Salt Oven Bay[43]

While my world was in turmoil, by way of sending someone morning glories:

I know, I know, we race with dew on morning glories while we last, and I'm so aggrieved

The grief that matters did not turn out the way I had expected in time became routine, and I reflected how preoccupied about it I once was:

Negligible, I cannot leave my body to my heart, but what follows my body is my heart

In what circumstances can my heart follow itself? I know it can't, but can't reconcile myself to it

When I looked at the Palace for the first time, everything was so sad:

Melancholy thoughts having followed me in my heart, now the Nine-fold[44] confuses me

About the time of More Growth, my senior friend at the Court, Miya no Ben, by way of writing to me, inquired, "When are you going to come back to work with us?":[45]

Since that trouble disturbed your thoughts like willow branches, so much time has passed!

In reply:

Idly I watch the long rains these days, as ever disturbed like willow branches in the rain

---

43 Shiogama no Ura: a salt-producing site in Matsushima, in today's Miyagi, it is known in poetic tradition for its haunting beauty. The smoke from burning seaweed is associated with the smoke from cremations.

44. *Kokonoe*: another name for the Palace.

45. Perhaps Murasaki temporarily withdrew from the court on account of the jealous, slanderous remarks that her fellow ladies-in-waiting made about her. Murasaki is known to have tutored Empress Shōshi on Chinese classics.

When I was troubled like that and was feeling I might collapse, I heard some people say, "She's so supercilious, I can't stand her":

Unreasonably people say I'm not like any other, but how can I throw my own self away?

❋

At the Tsuchimikado Palace, the Fifth Volume for the Thirty Sermons fell on the fifth day of Fifth Month. When I thought of the Devadatta Chapter that would come today, it occurred to me that the Buddha must have picked nuts for this lord, rather than for Asita:[46]

Exquisite! Today being the fifth day of Fifth Month, the Law also comes in Volume Five!

The pond was so close to the building that the bonfires, with the holy lights added, rendered the water clearer than it was during the day. As I looked at it, I could not help thinking how the occasion would fascinate me if I had fewer troublesome thoughts, and tears sprang to my eyes:

Bonfires undisturbed in the pond, the Light of the Law will be clear for thousands of years

So I hid my sentiments under the cover of the public event. As it happened, the person who was seated facing me was someone who, to go by her face, figure, and age, seemed highly unlikely to be troubled by various thoughts. Yet she was deeply troubled and made a poem:

The bonfires illuminating the pond to its bottom dazzle me when I'm such a melancholy soul

---

46. After she became pregnant, Empress Shōshi sometimes lived in her father Michinaga's palace, the Tsuchimikado. To pray for the safe delivery of her baby, a series of thirty sermons based on the Lotus Sutra, usually one a day, was offered from the 23rd of Fourth Month to the 22nd of Fifth Month. The fifth volume of the Lotus Sutra contains chapter 12, "Devadatta," which says women and evil people can also attain Buddhahood. Devadatta, while he was known as Asita, was a sage who taught the Law to the Buddha, and while he did so, the Buddha performed a disciple's chores, such as picking nuts, for him. Later he regarded the Buddha as a mortal rival and did a number of demonic things. The "lord" here is Michinaga.

When day finally began to break, I went out to the covered passage between the buildings and, my hands on the railing, watched for a while the water flowing out from under my room. It was the time of year when the sky appears as attractive as when it is suffused with spring haze or veiled in autumn mist. I knocked on Ko Shōshō's shutters in one corner, and she unbarred and lowered them. Together we stepped down onto the verandah and looked out:

Looking at my reflection, melancholy, my tears fall, so plaintive the sound of the waterfall

In reply:

Alone, full of tears, on the water, melancholy alongside, whose reflection could that be?

❋

I remembered someone who hadn't come to see me for a long time:

Forgetting is the way of this world, I realize, but I lament having no way of dealing with myself

❋

On the evening of the day the year's first snow fell, someone wrote:[47]

Missing you, living on, the first snow that has fallen may have faded, I begin to think

In reply:

Falling, only melancholy intensifies, but unawares, first snow accumulates in the wild garden

Not knowing how to deal with myself, though I think it's all melancholy I simply live on

---

47. The following exchange is thought to have occurred between a lady-in-waiting and Murasaki after Murasaki withdrew from the court, temporarily or otherwise.

❋

On the twenty-ninth of Priests' Run[48] I returned to the Palace. It was on the same night, I thought, that I had arrived there for the first time. As I recalled how confused I was at the time, as if on a dreampath, I realized how well I'd accustomed myself to it all, and I loathed myself for this. It grew very late. Since Her Majesty was in confinement for purification, I did not go to see her but lay down in a forlorn state of mind. "Here the atmosphere is very different, isn't it? Back home, we'd be asleep by now, but listen, how busy those noisy shoes[49] are!" the people in front of me were saying, obviously aroused. I couldn't help telling myself:

The year ends and my world grows old in the sound of winds, the inside of my heart desolate

---

48. Twelfth Month. The year was 1009.
49. Of the men visiting their ladies in their quarters.

Izumi Shikibu
(Born Late 970s)

Murasaki Shikibu, Izumi's colleague at the court, famously said of her: "As for Izumi Shikibu, I corresponded with her in a fascinating sort of way. Yes, Izumi was someone exceptionable in conduct, but when she became intimate with you and dashed off a letter, she was the talented one; you could detect elegance even in her casual words. Her poetry is extremely good. In learning, in poetic theory, she may not have been a true poet. But when she said whatever came to her mind, she'd make a poem that invariably had something unique that caught your eye."

Murasaki called Izumi "someone exceptionable in conduct" (*keshikaranu kata*) because even in a time when rules for sexual relations were lax, to put it mildly, Izumi's behavior was thought scandalous. While married to her first husband, Tachibana no Michisada, she had consecutive affairs with Emperor Reizei's third and fourth sons, Tametaka (977–1002) and Atsumichi (981–1007). The affair with Tametaka led to her separation from Michisada. In 1010 she remarried, to Fujiwara no Yasumasa, but her extramarital liaisons continued.

Despite Murasaki's praise for Izumi's impromptu compositions, Izumi, unlike most of her contemporaries, also composed acrostic and other sequences. We begin with a set of twelve poems, the first sound units of which form a phrase. Izumi is believed to have composed the set after Michisada sued for separation when her liaison with Tametaka came to light. It is followed by a set of fifty consisting of five parts, which Izumi is believed to have composed after Atsumichi's death. We will end with a selection from imperial anthologies.

After a Marital Breakdown

> Against my wishes something unsettling came to pass: I had to leave my usual place of residence, and I was aggrieved. I heard that my parents were also extremely aggrieved. So I sent them the following. The first characters [of the poems] form an old saying:[50]

In my previous life did I criticize someone in love? I feel as if punished by some retribution

Had you only let me fade like fleeting dew! Instead, you've turned me into a jewel to no avail

---

50. *I-ha-ho-no-na-ka-ni-su-ma-ha-ka-ha*, "I wish I lived inside a rock." Part of a tanka in the *Kokinshū*, no. 952.

*Ho*me elsewhere can things still be as bad? I'd like to know by changing my residence

No what's the use of staying on? I would throw away my body with my decayed sleeves

*Na*turally both tears and waves soak my sleeves now that I know we are on separate boats

*Ka*rma, this: not only is your child sad in her own world, but you are also made to suffer

*Ni*ghted, muddy bay: If you heard I live at its bottom, you might not miss me any longer

*Su*llen at the past, thinking of the months and days I spent, light and dark, looking at you

*Ma*de to doze, I should regard this sad world as a dream, but for some reason I cannot sleep

Ha! I don't even live at the bottom of a flowerless valley; why am I lost in deep thought?

Can be like this, like this I'll cease to be; my mother will surely miss me, my previous life

*Ha*rd to see: each time I note spring rain falling the melancholy of this world affects me so

Mourning for Prince Atsumichi

In endless idle loneliness, I wrote my thoughts down and assembled them, and they ended up looking like poems. I grouped them into "Longing during the Day," "Looking Out at Dusk," "Thoughts in the Evening," "Awaking at Midnight," and "Love at Daybreak."

Longing during the Day

Longing during the day, if it weren't like this, I wouldn't be thinking of you after so many days

Life is limited and I don't know when mine will end, pity me, how long will I long for you

Not seeing you, pity me, how many days have passed I wonder, the drops of my tears numberless

This self wandering in darkness, my ink-dyed sleeves don't know how to dry during the day[51]

Not going along with you, this is day,[52] yes, but what can I do with my self that did not die?

Days have passed but I can't forget you, my heart turning into seeds of "longing grass"

My heart that thinks of you isn't dew, no, but each time it's exposed to the sun it almost fades

With you gone, "Will you be back alive,"[53] I've wondered but not even with a shadow seen the days pass

Had I known it would be like this I would have died the death, so sad is this parting just once

Looking Out at Dusk

Looking at the sun setting at the rim of a mountain, I recollect, tears flow, and life darkens

This moment I wish were forsaken forever lest I grieve at dusk tomorrow as I do today

What kind of hour is the twilight? Even the sound of a wind unseen by the eye stirs pity

What's incomparably sorrowful is looking out at dusk, giving it up finally and not waiting

As the sun sets, birds fly, each to her mate, but where could I possibly go to look for you?

---

51. In the original both "dry" and "day" are implied in *hiru*.

52. *Hiru*, here given as "day," is supposed to pun on "rocambole," an important medicinal herb at the time, but how the pun works hasn't been puzzled out.

53. *Ikuka*, here given as "Will you be back alive," also means "How many days."

In twilight the path you took for me is covered by webs spiders make, all to my silky grief

Even while grieving as if it were my daily task, what's desolate above all else is the twilight

If you haven't forgotten, think of me: how harrowing the distant hill[54] seen at evening dusk

At evening dusk, when I look at the way the clouds are, the thought of not gazing takes shape

Thoughts in the Evening

Others must see the moon as limpid this evening; in my eyes it's shadowed, clouded with tears

My body, which isn't Fuji's peak but is aflame,[55] should be called a night-fire every evening[56]

More desolate than waiting for one who won't come is staying up in the evening aggrieved

Tears of those aggrieved every evening must be the thousands of dewdrops that form on grass

Hating to live, depressed that I can't fade away, I envy the evening light before the wind

Only the moon could soothe my aggrieved heart; what I don't want to see is the evening sky

Unknown to anyone, what pitifully reaches my ears: the sound of a bell at evening while I mourn

---

54. Perhaps the hill where Prince Atsumichi is buried.

55. Mount Fuji, which erupted last in 1707, was more active during the Heian period. In *Sarashina Diary,* Fujiwara Takasue's Daughter describes her travels through the region in 1020: "In the province where I had grown up, it's a mountain whose west side we saw. Its appearance is something you'll see nowhere else in the world. This incomparably shaped mountain looks as though painted with indigo, but because the snow remains [at the top] without fading all the year round, it appears as if it wore a white shoulder coat on a dark-hued robe. From the mountaintop, which is a little flattened, smoke climbs up. In the evening we saw fire rise."

56. In the original both "night-fire" and "evening" are implied in the word *yoi,* which is repeated.

Sorrow is: while life is no more than an evening dream, I think of things so painfully

To soothe me, you[57] should appear in a flash of light, in evening lightning that's seen, unseen

For someone staying up aggrieved, the *nuru* in the evening[58] can speak only of her sleeves

Awaking at Midnight

My sleeves, when I awake in the dark of night and search, they are surely soaking wet

On my bed where, thinking, thinking, I lie awake, my own arm for pillow is there to no avail

In love with you I would weep myself to sleep, unable to see you again except in a dream

How you turned into a cloud[59] I'd like to learn in one word when at midnight things are like this

I should be able to see you in a dream if only someone mourning could have any sleep

Awake, and a wind moves through my body, its sound in the past I heard outside my ears

Haven't dozed, and now it's daybreak; would someone asleep could see me in her dream with pity

If I could sleep I wouldn't be brooding during the night; being continually awake is so painful

Unable to soothe myself I turned my Chinese robe inside out,[60] only to be even more awake

---

57. Prince Atsumichi as a phantom.
58. *Nuru* means both "fall asleep" and "wet." "I would have gone to bed in the evening if I'd known you'd never come" is a jilted lover's standard remonstration.
59. Died. Because of cremation, "turn into smoke" and "turn into a cloud" mean "die."
60. Based on the folk belief that one can see someone one loves by wearing a night robe inside out.

Love at Daybreak

When I look out at the moon at daybreak over Sumiyoshi,[61] I miss one who has receded so far

Is someone longing a different thing? When was it? I used to be startled by birds calling

Longing at daybreak after having not seen you even in a dream must be the ultimate longing

All through the night I long for you, daybreak comes, and before the crow I begin to cry

When will the time come for my heart to clear? I listen to snipes beating their wings,[62] crying

When enclosed in beautiful blinds we used to sleep, did I ever feel satiated at the break of day?[63]

Now at daybreak I, too, know: longings are what drive the woodcutters to hurry home[64]

"It's already dawn," and now I look at it, though the daybreak sky isn't the one I long for

Even if the one I long for appears, what can I do? Things uncertain in the dark daybreak sky

Poems from Imperial Anthologies

The first imperial anthology in which Izumi appears is the third, the *Shūishū*, where she is represented by a single poem, though it went on to become one of

---

61. Uta-makura: A bay in Settsu (today's Osaka). Associated with "forgetful grass." Also includes a pun, "clear and good."

62. *Shigi*, "snipes," live in flocks and are known to bestir themselves at dawn by flapping their wings and calling.

63. In the original, "satiation" and "daybreak" are implied in *aku*. Alludes to the lines in Po Chu-i's "Song of Everlasting Regret": "Inside the lotus-flower blinds it was warm as the spring night went by. / The spring night was so short it was painful. He rose only when the sun was high."

64. The poem is based on a tenuous pun on *ki*, which means both "wood" and "heart" or "longings."

her most famous. In the fourth, the *Go-Shūishū*, she is the best-represented poet, with sixty-seven pieces. The following selection includes poems that appear in the third through eighth imperial anthologies.

From the Shūishū (1005 or 1006)

I made a poem and sent it to the Holy Man Shōku:

From darkness to a dark path I'm to enter: Shine on me into the distance, moon at the rim of hills[65]

From the Go-Shūishū (1086)

Because many cherry blossoms had fallen in my garden, I made a poem:

If winds don't blow them off, I'll view the blossoms fallen in the garden while spring lasts[66]

I'm downcast, feel only melancholy; it must be because autumn mist has risen in my heart

On the last day of Eighth Month I attached a poem to a bush clover branch and sent it to him:

Our love, never to last forever, must have faded; kindly visit at least the dewy bush clover

On morning glories:

Even while alive we can't count on life: what tells us about this world are the morning glories

---

65. Allusion to a phrase in chapter 7, "The Parable of the Phantom City," in the Lotus Sutra: "from darkness they enter into darkness, / to the end never hearing the Buddha's name" (Burton Watson, trans., *The Lotus Sutra* [Columbia University Press, 1993], 121). For a discussion of this poem, see p. 54. According to a story cited in *Mumyō Sōshi,* Shōku "sent her a sacerdotal habit instead of a poem in reply. It was by wearing it that she passed away." The author of the literary commentary adds: "However sinful Izumi Shikibu may have been, it is wonderful to hear that people since have been succored" by this poem.

66. Usually cherry blossoms are sung of while they are abloom or scattering. This is one of the few poems that speak of fallen blossoms positively.

While staying at a mountain temple, I happened to see someone being cremated and made a poem:

Each time smoke rises I can't help wondering: When, when, will people see me in that state?

After Koshikubu no Naishi[67] died, I saw my grandchildren playing together and made a poem:

Having left us, who does she think of? She must think more of her children; I think more of mine[68]

When I was thinking of becoming a nun,[69] I made a poem:

The mere thought of discarding myself saddens me: I think of my body once so used to you

On the last night of Twelfth Month, I made a poem:

This the night dead people visit, I'm told, but you aren't here, in my house, this soulless village

On behalf of a man who wanted to send a poem to a woman for the first time, I composed a poem:

Do not pretend: Every night you must be seeing someone in your dreams—it is me

Like the grass in the snow that fades underneath, even by chance, I'd like to see the one I love

To someone who promised to come but did not, I sent a poem in the morning:

I've ended the night all awake, though I'm not frost on the feathers of a duck sleeping alone

Because someone who had not come to visit for a long time did, but then stopped coming again, I made a poem:

If it all had ended while I was depressed, if it had, I'm certain I could have forgotten you

---

67. Izumi's daughter. She died in 1025.
68. A Japanese critic has called this poem an example of Izumi's *colloque sentimental.*
69. After Prince Atsumichi's death.

Unaware of my black hair in disorder I lay, when, first, he parted it; he's the one
I so miss

After I was abandoned by a man,[70] I wrapped his dresses and sent them to him,
tying a poem to his leather sash:

Unable to bear the tears I wept and shed we ended it all; now I feel like a light
indigo sash[71]

When I was feeling unusually poor, I sent someone a poem:

I'll no longer be; for a memento outside this world, I wish I could see you just
one more time[72]

Although in this world there's no color called love, it surely seeps deeply into
the body

Longing for you, my heart shattered into a thousand pieces, but not one piece has
been lost

My body has been traded for love; it's just that you couldn't see it clearly like a
summer bug

I sent a poem to a man I was in love with as fleetingly as dew:

White dew, dreams, this world, illusions: all these last for eternities in comparison

A man came to visit late at night but, hearing that I'd gone to sleep, went
home. Early the next morning he sent a message to explain what had happened. In reply:

Sound asleep I was but you could have made a sound on a bamboo flute though
late at night

A man came to visit in the evening but soon went home. And so:

Some don't think anything of a closed wooden door though I close mine with
hesitation

---

70. Perhaps her first husband, Tachibana no Michisada, who left her because of her
liaisons.
71. A metaphor for separation on account of a Saibara song.
72. Selected for the *Hyakunin Isshu*.

When I had to be someplace, I made sure to send a man a poem:

I'd be happy to tell you where I'm going if only I knew you were the kind who would ask

A man who secretly made love to me came to visit one rainy night. After going home he sent word that he had gotten wet:

In such secrecy, all this rain:[73] should someone ask, with what shall I say my sleeves are wet?

In reply to a complaint I sent to a man who was writing letters to someone else, he sent me a word of protest denying it, and so:

With your heart like a spider up in the air, how on earth shall I live through another day?

A man said he'd never again go to see a woman he was seeing. But later, I heard he did go to see her one fiercely raining night. So I sent him a poem:

Like Mount Three Hats you put her away you said; then how dare you, on a rainy night?

Someone went away saying my gate took time to open, so I sent a poem:

Long but the day also breaks for the autumn night; I wish you'd waited at my wooden door

In Tango Province, the night before the day Yasumasa wanted to hunt, I heard a deer cry and made a poem:

Understandable: How can the deer not cry? He knows this to be the last night of his life

A man who talks with me asked me to write a poem he wanted to send to a woman, so I first made a poem expressing my own thoughts:

Speaking to me, you at times soothe me, but you must have forgotten me, involved in love

After I was abandoned by a man,[74] I went to Kibune to offer prayers; when I saw fireflies flying over the stream of ablutions, I made a poem:

73. Rain means tears.
74. Believed to be her second husband, Fujiwara no Yasumasa.

Brooding, the many fireflies may be my soul, I think, that has gone out of my
body, yearning

In reply:

Rapids in mountain depths that boil and fall: do not brood so lest your soul shatter
like them[75]

From the Kin'yōshū (1126–27)

Even after Koshikibu no Naishi passed away, Jōtōmon'in[76] kept up her annual gift of silk fabric. When I saw "For Koshikibu" written on one such gift,
I made a poem:

Without rotting under the moss with you, I am sorrowed to see your unburied
name

From the Shikashū (1151?)

When I was setting out for Tango Province to accompany Fujiwara no Yasumasa, I sent a poem to a man who was having a secret affair with me:

Is it that I alone will be thinking of you? Tasteless: You don't even know where
I'm going[77]

One night when the moon was bright, a man came to see me but left without
coming into my bed. The following morning I sent him a poem:

In tears I kept looking where you walked out, and watched the moon with nothing
in my heart

While I was waiting impatiently for a man I was counting on, I heard sleet
falling on bamboo leaves out front, so made a poem:

Sleet falling on bamboo leaves swish-swishing, sleeping by myself is far from
my mind

---

75. This poem has a note woven into the text, which says: "Legend has it that this was a
response from the Deity of Kibune and that Izumi Shikibu heard it as a male voice."
76. Annotated earlier, Empress Shōshi's title after she took Buddhist vows, in 1026.
77. Unstated is Izumi's complaint that her lover, after learning she was leaving the Capital,
didn't bother to ask her where she was going.

A man who, like me, had to keep the matter secret complained that I didn't see him the moment he wanted me to, so I made a poem:

You yourself cannot follow what your heart wants: remember that and you know how things are

A man who came to see me secretly pushed aside his rustling robe saying it was too noisy, so I made a poem:

Having no rustling around you can be painful; here's someone who doesn't like it close by

From the Senzaishū (1188)

When a man separated from me was about to go to a distant place, someone asked how I felt.[78] So I sent a poem:

If he were in the same Capital, though separated, I wouldn't feel the way I do this time around

To someone who unexpectedly deceived me into making love:[79]

This lovemaking is all predetermined, I know, yet just thinking of it is harrowing enough

Prince Atsumichi, Commander of Dazai, had stopped coming to see me, but in the fall he remembered to visit, so I made a poem:

Even if I'd waited it wouldn't have been like this; all so unexpected this autumn evening

Untitled:

Time passes, he will forget, and the matter will end; yet I'm counting on the vow he made

He looked at the daybreak moon, loved it, got up, and left: the memory of it all that I saw

---

78. The man here is Izumi's first husband, Tachibana no Michisada, and the inquirer, Akazome Emon. The poem was made when Michisada was appointed governor of Mutsu, in 1004.
79. Headnote supplied from Izumi's "personal collection."

INCORPORATING NAMES:[80] ON *SAMIDARE*:[81]

By night he must have dropped by: Night Chamber rush-mat this morning water-stained

From the Shin-Kokinshū (1205)

At year end, lamenting my old age, I made a poem:

I count them and few days remain for the year; nothing is as sorrowful as growing old

Koshikibu no Naishi used to wear a Chinese outer robe with a design of bush clover with dew forming on it. After she passed away, Jōtōmon'in kindly inquired about it.[82] I gratefully made a poem to send to her:

The dew I saw form has remained; to what shall I compare the one who fleetingly vanished?

Jōtōmon'in, in reply:

Had we expected this: to look at the dew fleetingly forming on her sleeve as her keepsake

After Koshikibu no Naishi passed away, I donated a hand-box she used to keep around for sutra chanting, and made a poem:

Hear if you can that I miss you, desolate; the bell tolls, and I can't forget you even for a moment

Untitled:[83]

My pillow won't say things unknown: Do not talk of the spring night's dream that you saw

---

80. A category of poems that weave a name into a sentence. In the example here, it would be like saying the word "hem" is woven into part of a speech, "*he m*ust."

81. Means both "May rains" and "in disorder"—translation can't reflect the pun.

82. According to Izumi's personal collection, Jōtōmon'in asked if she could have Koshikibu's robe to make a cover for a sutra out of it.

83. Composed as a direct response to Ise's poem: "If as a dream do not talk; even pillows know they say, so we did not use pillows but our arms"—which comes with a headnote: "In bed with someone who secretly came to see me" (*Shin-Kokinshū,* no. 1159).

Around the time of More Growth, someone just talked all night and went home. He then sent word to me, "This morning I feel terribly depressed." I responded:

This morning lament: you, uselessly, did not even try to dream a spring night just one night

One night when the moon was bright, someone sent me fireflies wrapped in paper.[84] When it was raining, I sent him a poem:

If you felt love you'd have visited in tonight's sky; what I saw must have been the light of the moon

No shadow of the one who inhabited my house only the daybreak moon night after night

Untitled:

While alive they can witness the end of my life but no one, sadly, will remember me[85]

When I thought of becoming a nun, someone dissuaded me:

If I were to endure such melancholy and live longer, I would think of things even worse

---

84. Symbol of undeclared love.

85. One poem in an acrostic sequence of forty-three verses incorporating two lines from a kanshi, read in Japanese, which says: "Look at our body, and it's a grass uprooted from a beachhead; discuss our life, and it's a boat unmoored from a riverbank."

Sagami
(991?–1061?)

Sagami, known by that name because her husband, Ōe no Kimiyori (Kin'yori), served as governor of Sagami Province, may have been an illegitimate child. Her father remained unidentified, even though her mother was married to the illustrious warrior-commander Minamoto no Raikō (948–1021)—the first nonaristocrat to be admitted to court—and her maternal relatives produced some outstanding scholars. As a story of the time has it, Kimiyori, himself a poet, was deeply enamored of her as a poet, so much so that when he applied for a certain government post, he was turned down on account of that infatuation. Still, he was already married when he succeeded in wooing her, and, after marrying her, he had other women. Sagami herself seems to have had a liaison with the poet Fujiwara no Sadayori (995–1045).

Of the approximately six hundred poems assembled in Sagami's various anthologies, half consist of three one-hundred-piece sequences, which were set off by a sequence she dedicated to Hashiriyu (also Sōtō) Shrine on Mount Izu, in Sagami, in First Month 1024. The sequence described some of the anxieties that were plaguing her at the time, estrangement from her husband, among others. Also, though she had followed her husband to the province that was to become her namesake, perhaps in 1021, she had done so reluctantly, because she was in love with Sadayori, her mother had just been widowed, and she, being a city girl, didn't want to go to such a rustic, even barbarous, place.

To her utter surprise, she received a response from the shrine in the same format three months later. Since such dedicatory pieces were put in tubes and buried in the shrine compound and no one was supposed to know of their existence, Sagami was touched but did not think of writing a response. At the end of the year, though, the governor's mansion burned down and Kimiyori blamed her, saying it was the consequence of her dedicating such personal complaints to a shrine. So she changed her mind and wrote and dedicated another one-hundred-piece sequence to the shrine the following spring.

Translated below is her preface to the initial sequence and a small selection from it.

At a time when I had more vexing thoughts than usual, and against my wishes, I went down east. Still, I thought to take advantage of the occasion to see some historical places. So, in the first month of my third year there, I paid my respects at Hashiriyu, in Hakone. Because I felt I wouldn't be able to say all the things I wanted to say [while praying at the shrine], I made a small booklet out of dedicatory paper while rained in and idling in a lodge on my way there and wrote in it my inner thoughts just as they were. All the hundred pieces looked antiquated, but I thought it wouldn't do to make a small selection and be suggestive, even though there were too many that were too clever for my liking. Because it was all so sudden, I had them buried under the shrine. During my purification, I had Buddhist meals.

Frozen beneath, the ice is still far from melting; I wish to leave it to the wind over spring hills

For many years I have cultivated it, but our old mid-mountain paddy has gone to seed

To sow rice so it will grow, may the Deity supply rice-seedling water to the mountain paddy

In the spring field where he has sealed me, a young herb, do not let him pick other violets

Even a pheasant in a spring field,[86] even if hunted, won't think himself as much at risk as I do

If only I could go to the muddy fields[87] of water-oats to make the pastured stud feel close to me

Aware how even tears can't extinguish my thoughts, I only pity the fireflies of the marsh[88]

The plant fence of my house is woven so carelessly the flower of the pink[89] is laden with dew

Thinking my hope may come true, I almost let myself cry out with abandon as the cricket does

When looked at in comparison with this world,[90] the morning glory flowers for eternity

In a winter river how are wood ducks[91] afloat asleep? Even the usual bed is cold this frosty night

---

86. Because of its sharp calls and long tail, the pheasant in the mating season was thought to offer a ready target to a hunter.

87. *Yodo-no*, "muddy fields," can also be read *yo-dono*, "night chamber," "bedroom." The place name Yodo, which means "stagnant," refers to the marsh area where the three rivers of Kamo, Katsura, and Uji converged.

88. The firefly is a metaphor for burning love.

89. *Tokonatsu*, the name given here to the pink, puns on *toko*, "bed."

90. *Yononaka*, "the world," is a metaphor for transience in general and the transience of the relationship between man and woman in particular.

91. *Oshi* or *oshidori*, also called mandarin ducks—following Chinese literary tradition, a symbol of uxorious love.

A banked fire my body is not, but this winter night I'm awake, an ember burning underneath

Wishing for a Child

I only wish to be endowed with an incense child,[92] living by myself as I am, feeling helpless

While my breast-sagging parent is alive, I hope to let her know, with her child's child, she's lived long

Though nothing in my life happens the way I want it to, I want this treasure above all else

Would that I could have a shining, jewel-like boy so I might caress him so as to make him grow

There are examples of pines growing on boulders: pregnant lady,[93] would you lend me some seeds

What follows is a chōka Sagami composed when Kimiyori, not long after leaving for Tōtōmi as governor, this time with another woman, came back to Kyoto to bring a dancer for the court festivities but neglected to visit her. Toward the end of the poem, Sagami wonders if her affair with Sadayori, now long past, was the reason for Kimiyori's utter estrangement. The incident she describes is thought to have occurred around 1031.

The poem comes with a headnote whose indirect tone suggests an attempt to turn the account into one that appeared to be written by a third party. The poem itself is covered with layers of meanings conveyed through puns, allusions, and metaphors. To give a few examples: *aki*, "autumn," also means "to become tired of [one's lover]"; *shigure*, "shower," stands for tears; *tōyama*, "distant mountain," echoes Tōtōmi, which means "distant bay"; "sleeves decaying" means crying all the time; and *kuchiba*, "as [something] decays," also suggests "leaf," as well as "poem," because, by orthographic convention, *ba* is interchangeable with *ha*.

92. *Takimono no*, "of incense," is a pillow word, which modifies *ko*, which means "basket," as well as "child."

93. According to a history of Hashiriyu Shrine, its female deity had "a figure like a heavenly maiden." She was worshipped as a goddess of childbirth.

Someone who had been assigned to a distant place toward the end of autumn came up [to Kyoto] to bring a dancer for the Five-Movement Dances.[94] But [Sagami] must have had something to be angry about:

The autumn started and passed. After that,
in Godless Month, there were only showers.
I gazed, far beyond the clouds,
at the distant mountain,
                    remembering.
My sleeves decaying, for what reason,
          I wrote poems, gathered them,
and left them to a stormy wind,
which dropped them everywhere.
          As I heard this
the frost withered, discolored things
on a hedge with no place for me,
a dewdrop, congealed into
an icicle on a bamboo-grass leaf.
Fading, not fading, I waited.
The Mourning Robe dyed with wild indigo
you wore, that I heard. And yet,
with the Imperial Fence parting us,
the Fertile Light was unknown to me.
Uncertain how you were, I grieved.
          That was natural.
Nevertheless, my pain intensified.
How could I redirect the dream
          this time around?

In nothing am I strong.
          As I wept,
my bed, my bay, had no time to dry.
As tides came in, myself a boat afloat,
burning, not knowing whereto,
          was how I felt.
Now there was little chance for me
to be able to see you, if only briefly,

----

94. *Gosechi*, "Five-Movement," is a female-only dance performed in the Imperial Palace in Eleventh Month. It consisted of two parts, one requiring four virgin dancers, the other five. For both, two dancers had to be from the provinces and governors were responsible for selecting and bringing them to the Capital. The dance was the culminating part of the annual ritual called *Toyo no Akari [Bountiful Light] no Sechie*, in which the emperor ritually sampled newly harvested rice and distributed some to his subjects. Murasaki Shikibu has a description of the Gosechi in her diary.

to have a glimpse of you, on this beach.
        A forgetful clam
you had picked for my sake.
The Ise fisherman has little time,
        with that as an excuse,
making no noise, you went away.

Writing down my painful yearnings,
drips soaking me, sincerely
I reflect, and it mystifies me:
we were as friendly as pond wood ducks,
but we weren't linked underneath.
I happened to say, unthinking,
"I saw him," and at those words,
like the water in the field excessively
covered with waterweeds, we were cut.
That may be so, but like Iwashiro's
tied pine was our relationship.
Not that I wish to resort to that bond.
The root I pulled outside the rope,
now totally withered, I, the gromwell,
am distressed more than the camellia
turned into ashes. I'm shattered.

Princess Shikishi
(Died 1201)

The third daughter of the seventy-seventh emperor, Goshirakawa, Shikishi (also Shokushi, Noriko) served as *saiin*, vestal of the Kamo Shrines, for ten years when young. Despite her exalted position, and though recognized as an outstanding poet by her contemporaries, she was so retiring, even eremitic, that not much is known about her. About four hundred of her poems survive, three hundred of them in three one-hundred-poem sets, known as *hyakushu-uta*. The set selected here is the one she probably wrote not long before her death—of which Fujiwara no Teika said, "All of the pieces are divine." Teika and five other editors chose forty-nine of her poems for the eighth imperial anthology, *Shin-Kokinshū*, making her the fifth-best represented poet in it. Teika also chose one of the forty-nine to represent her in his selection of one hundred poets, which, later named *Hyakunin Isshu*, would be regarded as canonical. The poem, on the topic of "love to be endured," reads:

> String of beads, if you must break, break; if you last longer, my endurance is sure to weaken

Here, "string of beads" is a metaphor for life.

The one-hundred-poem set is followed by a rare sequential exchange known to us. The exchange took place when Teika's father, Shunzei (1114–1204), wrote a group of nine poems mourning his dead wife and sent it to Shikishi.

One Hundred Poems

Spring: Twenty Poems

Peaks' snow of the past year still in the sky, it's hazy on one side in spring's path[95]

Mountain deep, pine door is unaware of spring: on it, intermittently dripping, snow's water beads[96]

The snow faded, and unfamiliar first grass: its glimpse suggests spring in the field

Sea of Grebes: a rowing boat's full sail in the haze also makes such a spring scape[97]

---

95. *Kasumi*, "haze," is a sign of spring.

96. The poem uses a common but unobtrusive pun, *matsu*, which means "pine tree" and "to wait."

97. Nio no Umi, the Sea of Grebes, is another name for Lake Biwa, Japan's largest lake, which lies east of Kyoto.

Princess Shikishi as imagined by Kanō Tan'yū (1602–1674)

The rim of a foot-wearying mountain hazy at dawn, just out of the valley a bird's
    single call[98]

I look to the end of the haze: mountains with shelves of white clouds in the dawn-
    ing sky

As plum blossoms from the fence visit my sleeves, dreams in my light sleep fade
    on my pillow

___

98. The bird here is likely to be the bush-warbler, the avian harbinger of spring.

Even when my watching you today becomes the past, plum near the eaves, do not forget me[99]

Now the cherry seems to have bloomed; it's cloudy, hazy with spring, the way the world appears

Flowers have bloomed in my mind while I awaited them: at last to Yoshino I've transplanted them[100]

Buried by clouds on the peaks and snow on the slopes, where are the blossoms in Yoshino Village?[101]

When I visit the cherries on Takasago Peak, layers of them lie hazily west of the City

Visitors, go home without breaking off branches: even a warbler's wingwind cruel to my cherry

White clouds on hazy Mount Takama: are they or aren't they blossoms? Travelers going home

When in dreams winds blow on fading blossoms restless is my light sleep in spring

As I look this morning winds pass the treetops of my house with countless layers of unknown snow[102]

Now not to speak of winds: Would there were a weir in Yoshino River for the blossoms going over the rocks

Flowers have fallen; as I look out for no special color, in the empty sky spring rain falls

---

99. Alludes to a famous poem of Sugawara no Michizane, composed when he was leaving his house for exile: "When east winds blow, / send out your fragrance, / plum flowers— / though masterless, / do not forget the spring!" (Burton Watson, trans., *Japanese Literature in Chinese*, Vol. 1 [Columbia University Press, 1975], p. 129).

100. Yoshino, a cluster of mountains in Nara, became famous for its snow, then for its cherry blossoms.

101. To the poetic conceit of confusing white clouds with cherry flowers is added the conceit that the snow, at least of Yoshino, can also be confused with cherry blossoms.

102. "Unknown snow" is cherry flowers—unknown to the sky because it is not the usual snow.

Wild geese leave no brush traces, fading away as they are over the waves and clouds

Unable to stop them with cries, resenting spring: this a warbler's tear, clinging to a twig[103]

Summer: Fifteen Poems

As I part again with my cherry-colored robe, waves of wisteria at my house retain spring

Is he telling me in which village he'll wait? Under flowering deutzia a cuckoo whispers[104]

The cloud where a cuckoo has called now a reminder, soon I gaze at the dawning sky

Only your call, cuckoo sobbing in the cloudpath: have you shed tears? This evening rain

A cuckoo, near the hilltop where wisps of clouds blur, is still talking to the daybreak moon

Among dark water rocks summer insects flit, with no bonfire, till the break of day

Chaotic May rain clouds having closed into one, water beads from the roof, unstrung, chaotic

When I leave my past to a flowering orange, a wind wafts to the ferns under my eaves

Thinking to have the past that does not return I sleep: to my dream pillow comes an orange scent

Kudzu field's bay winds grow close to summer nights: as autumn rises a cicada's wing-robe

---

103. The warbler resents the spring because it has allowed the cherry blossoms to scatter away even while he has been crying hard to stop them.

104. *U no hana*, "deutzia," a shrub with white or pinkish flowers, is a floral harbinger, and the *hototogisu*, "cuckoo," an avian harbinger, of summer. The combination of the two sometimes suggests a love affair.

Saying, "It's cool," I sought the wind's message: wild lilies wavering near a clump
of grass

Night deep, the sound of water trickling among rocks lucid, it becomes cool where
I sleep light

Pond cold, dew sits on floating lotus leaves; the fields must have tinted beads laid
over them

The moon's color, too, says autumn's close; late at night will reeds near my hedge
startle me?

Is it to tell the geese of the autumn wind? Fireflies rising close to the evening
clouds[105]

Autumn: Twenty Poems

I sleep light toward morning: different on my sleeves, my old fan stirs autumn's
first wind

As I watch, through leaves moves the evening moon, giving a hint of the autumnal
sky

Cicadas' voices exhausted on the hillside, when, again, the sunset bell
startles[106]

---

105. Alludes to an episode in *Ise Monogatari*, which reads in its entirety:

   Once, there was a man. A woman, whose father closely guarded her, wondered
how she could speak her mind to the man. But perhaps because it was difficult for her
to talk to him, she became ill and, when about to die, said, "I've been so in love with
him." When her parent learned about this, he went to the man and, weeping, told him.
In consternation the man came to visit, but she had already died.
   So he stayed in her place, mourning, in frustration. It was the last day of Waterless
Month, and it was very hot. In the evening he played some music [for the dead soul].
Late that night, there was some cool breeze. Fireflies flew up high. When the man saw
them while lying down [he made these poems]:

   Fireflies going away, if you get above the clouds, tell the geese that an autumn wind
   blows

   When I brood all this slow summer day long, I feel sad for no reason at all

106. The word translated here as "cicada" is not the generic *semi*, but *higurashi*, a species
of cicada prized for the limpidity of its chirping, to which Kenkyūsha's *Japanese-English
Dictionary* gives the name "clear-toned cicada." In the *Man'yōshū*, the characters applied
to *higurashi* mean "the day is in the twilight," evidently because it chirps most often in the
early morning and in the evening.

In my deserted garden, wrapped in sedge, in the depth of dew, a pine cricket's
voice

At my gate, startled by the wind across rice fields: there beyond the mist the first
voices of geese

Like waves rolling, dye flowers tumultuous as I print bush clover in the Bay of
Mano

Colored with white dew the trees are slow, yet bush clover's lower leaves know
autumn already

Told of autumn I think of things: at the rim of a hill clouds linger in the evening
sky

Flowering pampas grass again dew-soaked: I thought I would not be out and gaze
in autumn's prime

Their hunting robes must be chaotic, catalpa bows heaved amid bush clovers,
under dew

On bush clovers wild geese put their tears, the dew now frozen formed in the
moonlight

Gazing, lonely: Would there were an abode outside autumn! Over fields and hills
the moon clear

Night has deepened; near the hill the moon clear, and in Tōchi Village the sound
of fulling cloth[107]

In the old village my burdock eaves wither away, as the moon grows clearer night
by night

Frozen, sleepless, should my sleeves turn color, dew-forming, tree-searer over the
peaks?

---

107. Alludes to Po Chu-i's poem "Listening to a Mallet at Night":

Troubled wife at which house is it, beating cloth in autumn?
Moon bitterly cold, wind harsh, the mallet breaks my heart.
In Eighth Month, Ninth Month, the nights are truly long.
Beating a thousand times, ten thousand times, endlessly.
If I heard it till daybreak, my whole head would turn white,
because at each beating one strand of gray hair is added.

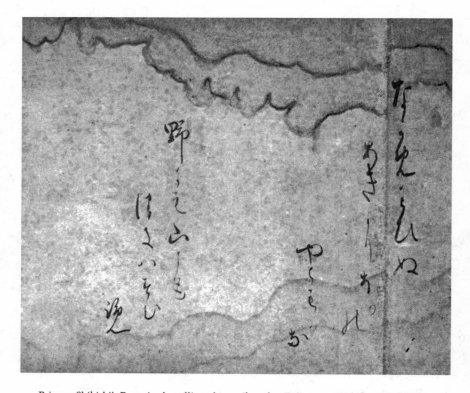

Princess Shikishi's Poem in the calligraphy attributed to Fujiwara no Yukifusa (died 1337).
The poem reads, from right to left:

nakame wabinu / aki yori hoka / no / yato mo / kana / no ni mo yama ni mo / tsuki ha sumu / ran

Gazing, lonely: Would there were an abode outside autumn! Over fields and hills the moon clear

Evident in my garden where sedge turns color: closeness of winter when people stay away

Though autumn hues grow remote on the hedge, moonlight's closer to my bedroom pillow

In the sedge field early frost forms; in the Long Month sky at dawn my thoughts dissolve

Coming through paulownia leaves now difficult, though I do not wait for someone necessarily

Think what I may, this is the last autumn dusk; as the sky darkens the clouds turn to showers

Winter: Fifteen Poems

Godless Month: as storms sweep down Mount Mimuro, Tatsuta River tie-dyes itself in crimson[108]

Left on treetops the brocade remains: from my garden, autumn's colors have taken leave

As I watched winter came: along the edge of a cove where ducks are, thin ice is forming

In the shower everywhere red leaves fell; now hailstones drop on garden leaves

Wild winter sky all day now suddenly turns cloudy, sleet slashing aslant as winds vie

On the frost the reed ducks are unable to brush off, thin ice falls shattering

Hail falling, in the roadside bamboo grass I hardly sleep, not seeing the City even in dreams

On the mat my midnight sleeves lucid, lucid, first snow white on the hillside pines

The sky as a flock rises grows snowy, lucid, dark; in my icy bedroom a wood duck cries

Body piercing: the garden fire rises lucidly, up to the frosty night stars in the dawn sky

Wind of heaven, the maidens cross ice this winter night, sleeves polished by the light of the moon[109]

Days accumulate; the snow intensifies the smoke from charcoal kilns, desolate in Ōhara Village

---

108. Alludes to a poem on autumn by Ariwara no Narihira (825–880): "Unheard of even in the age of rock-smashing gods: tie-dyeing the waters of Tatsuta River in Korean crimson" (*Kokinshū*, poem 294).

109. Alludes to a poem by Yoshimine no Munesada, also known as Abbot Henjō (815–890): "Made while looking at the dancing princesses of *Gosechi*": "Wind of heaven, blow shut the pathway of clouds, so the maidens may stay for some time." For *Gosechi*, see footnote 94, p. 84. Munesada's poem is based on the legend that the dance originated when Emperor Tenmu saw heavenly maidens dance on Mt. Yoshino.

Across the ocean, the winter must have grown deep; ice has tied up fishermen's boats

Even in the snow outside the City people do not visit, spring has come close, next door

Life prolonging itself, how many more times must I face old age and pity my-self?

Love: Ten Poems

Be a guide: this is a boat rowing in the traceless waves, not knowing where to, eightfold salt wind

Like the water-markers in a marsh fenced in by rocks, my sleeves remain unknown and decay[110]

In your dream, see the way my sleeves look during the night, as I grieve my way into sleep

No one knows of my love: do not let abroad the tears I'm holding back in bed, boxwood pillow

I'd let him know: I see him as infrequently as flowering flags in Sugata Pond, waves wilting me

"Waves nestle up to my wife's gemlike skirt," but he does not, and my sleeves never dry

Meeting remote as rock azaleas on a beach: without a word said, my tinged heart will decay

Will my sleeves dry for a moment, when evening dew is settling in safflower Asaha Field?

---

110. Alludes to a love poem attributed to Kakinomoto no Hitomaro (flourished in the late seventh century): "Water-hidden in mountain depths, in a marsh fenced in by rocks, I keep longing, with no way to meet you" (*Shūishū*, poem 661).

I meet you today: pine branch votive grass, do you know how many nights my sleeves have wilted?

How can I wait gazing, when you have just said, "Do not forget," in the daybreak moon[111]

Travels: Five Poems

Glimpsed sprouting out of the snow in the City: Grass I tie together in Nakayama tonight[112]

Sleeping on the seaweed bed of a rough beach, I, a skeleton shrimp, wet my sleeves

My City friends, like beach huts on an isle far off, have been far for long, waves between us

How many more nights before this ends? Near the miscanthus on Iwashiro Hill I tie a pillow

On pine roots of Ojima shore, night's pillow. Do not become badly wet, sleeves: no fisherman's[113]

Mountain Living: Five Poems

Near my abode only the tracks of woodcutters who, gathering brushwood, often come and go

Now I should find myself confined in a pine-beamed cedar hut, my sleeves thick with moss[114]

Mountain winds vying through leaves at the peak, down from the clouds a stag's voice

---

111. Alludes to a poem on love by Monk Sosei (dates uncertain), written in the role of a woman: "Because you said, 'I'll come now,' I've waited until the Long Month moon, at daybreak, has come out." Sosei's poem is included in the *Hyakunin Isshu*.
112. "Tying grass together" is a metaphor for sleeping while traveling.
113. Alludes to a love poem of Minamoto no Shigeyuki: "In Matsushima, fishermen working Ojima shore had sleeves that were indeed as wet as these!"
114. *Koke fukaki sode*, "sleeves thick with moss," is a metaphor for someone who has taken Buddhist vows.

No one visits this brushwood door; the moon rising from the foot-wearying hills
    sees it first

Mountain village: pine's voices ceaseless on hilltop, amid leaves I miss water in
    the valley below

Birds: Five Poems

At daybreak a tassel-adorned bird affects me as I think of the long sleep on my
    pillow[115]

What a crying crane thinks at heart I do not know, yet her voice at night pierces
    me[116]

Depressing thoughts shatter me, clouds lighten, in a rift in the mists, muffled, a
    snipe preens

Fleeting: like the grebe's floating nest on waves adrift in wind, how my life passes
    by

When they thrash the sedge in Ono for harvesting, at the end of growths of grass
    a quail rises

Felicitations: Five Poems

Adding to pine winds of the thousand years you will live, bamboos also attune
    themselves

Under heaven grasses and trees bud forth: Your Reign will know no bounds for
    generations

For years, thousands of generations, you will reign, and I await a friend of snow,
    moon, flowers[117]

---

115. *Yūtsuke-dori*, "tassel-adorned bird," is another name for the rooster. *Nagaki neburi*, "long sleep," is a Buddhist metaphor for the life of someone who remains troubled by thoughts of life and death and never becomes enlightened.

116. The poem is based on the old Chinese notion that a crane calling at night is doing so for its lost young. In a line of his poem "Playing the Five-String Lute," Po Chu-i says, "The night crane, thinking of her young, cries in her cage."

117. Alludes to Po Chu-i's lines: "Friends in music, poetry, and wine have all abandoned me. / In snow, the moon, and flowers I think of you the most."

Even the crane on the rock of Tortoise Tail is mindful: such is the color of water there

May you reign until a pebble in the Chikuma River turns into a boulder overgrown with moss[118]

An Exchange with Fujiwara no Shunzei

Shunzei wrote:

On the 23rd, Second Month, fourth year of Kenkyū [1193], the companion of my children for many years[119] hid herself.[120] "Since then months have passed fleetingly, and it's already the last day of Sixth Month now," I thought. As I looked at the sky in the evening dusk and kept remembering things from the past, I scribbled these:

To my remorse I had grown used to her forever; the parting was so deep, so sorrowful

How was our link linked in our previous lives, that I should be so deeply full of sorrow?

There are dreams I forget awhile; but startled awake, I feel the sorrow all the more

Be it at the top of a mountain or at the limit of sky, if only I had a magician who goes to tell[121]

---

118. Alludes to an anonymous poem on felicitations in the *Kokinshū* (poem 343): "May you live for a thousand, eight thousand generations, until a pebble becomes a boulder and overgrown with moss!" This poem was later adopted as the lyric for what eventually became Japan's national anthem. It is based on a Chinese legend about a stone that grew into a boulder.

119. His wife.

120. Died.

121. Alludes to a poem in the "Kiritsubo" chapter of *The Tale of Genji*: "If I had a magician who goes to seek, I might know by word of mouth where her soul lies!" The poem is by Emperor Kiritsubo in grief over his dead mistress, who gave birth to Genji. This portion of *Genji* heavily alludes to Po Chu-i's famous poem "Song of Everlasting Regret," in which a respected medium sends his disciple to another world to seek out Yang Kuei-fei, now dead, on behalf of her grief-stricken emperor lover. The word *maboroshi*, here given as "magician," is used in the more usual sense of "illusion" in Shikishi's first poem in response.

Grieving, spring's passed and summer's ending, but our parting has taken place I feel just today

Until when am I to gaze at the sky of this world, watching with pity the evening clouds?

   Also, at her grave at Hōshō Temple:

Desperate, I've come parting the field of grass, but my heart shatters, you under the moss[122]

Parting fields of grass my tears shatter, but you under the moss do not respond

Some souls stay under the moss they say; someone who's been there, tell me where

   When someone unexpectedly brought these poems to the Former Vestal's place of residence and showed them to her, she responded:

It has become a brief dream, an illusion, though I thought it was a link you'd grown used to forever

Sorrowed by the parting endlessly deep, your sleeves laden with thoughts have changed color

Now you are aggrieved over your sleepless sleep, meeting her only along the path of dreams

Ready to part the waves to clouds' limits to see the magician: your grief is that intense

That autumn has come I know from winds over the reeds, yet the parting in spring startles

Aggrieved and not knowing where she's gone: despite this sorrow, the clouds in the sky

Lie down, rise many years on the parting bed, waiting to see the dew on the same lotus flower

---

122. *Kusa no hara*, "field of grass," is a metaphor for a graveyard.

Just hearing about it saddens me: the grass field I haven't even parted with sleeves,
   spilling dew

The wordless parting carried so much sorrow even her portrait was, sadly, of no
   use[123]

Parting in different ways would give no consolation, even if you were told where
   she'd gone

   Again:

So pained, hearing of it I become dew-drenched, as autumn wind sweeps through
   the garden of parting

Shunzei, in reply:

In the autumn wind blowing off your deep-hued words, dew in the sagebrush
   garden scatters along

---

123. The passage in *Genji* immediately following the poem cited in note 121 begins with
the sentence: "The features of Yang Kuei-fei painted in a picture, even by a superior painter,
can't have much liveliness, because there are limits to what can be done with a brush."

Kenreimon'in Ukyō no Daibu
(Born 1157?)

Kenreimon'in Ukyō no Daibu—Ukyō no Daibu for short—is a court name that can be translated as Master of the Office of the Household of Lady Kenreimon. The Kenreimon'in part of it derives from the fact that she first served Tokushi (1155–1223?), consort of Emperor Takakura (1161–1181), whose retirement title was Kenreimon'in. The rest of the name may reflect the possibility that the poet's mother, the noted *shō* player Yūgiri, was once married to Fujiwara no Shunzei, and Shunzei held the post of Master of the Office of the Household when Yūgiri sent her daughter to serve the court.

Ukyō no Daibu is one poet whose writings show the grave effect of the five-year war between the rival military clans, Taira and Minamoto, from 1180 to 1185. One of her lovers was a commanding officer who chose to drown himself to escape capture in the final battle of the war. He was Taira no Sukemori (1161–1185), a grandson of the de facto ruler Kiyomori (1118–1181). His courtship and youthful death were central to Ukyō no Daibu's life.

Ukyō no Daibu had another, much older, lover, Fujiwara no Takanobu (1142–1205). Takanobu was accomplished as both poet and painter, although today he is far better known as a portrait artist. As Nakamura Shin'ichirō notes in his book on Ukyō no Daibu's work, André Malraux in his encyclopedic survey *The Voices of Silence* has called Takanobu's portrait of the leader of the Minamoto clan, Yoritomo (1147–1196), "one of the world's supreme works of art." Takanobu was substantive as a poet as well; his personal anthology contains about 960 poems. Many of the poems chronicle his affairs with a variety of women, Ukyō no Daibu among them.

Ukyō no Daibu prepared her collection when Fujiwara no Teika asked to see her poems, perhaps in 1232, for the imperial anthology he was compiling, the ninth *Shin-Chokusenshū*. She assembled about 350 poems in a "poetic tale" mode, interspersing many with notes on the circumstances of composition. Teika accepted two. Combined with those taken in later imperial anthologies, twenty-four of her poems have the stamp of imperial approval.

As with the writing of her time, her prose sometimes employs *mōrōtai* or *rōka*, "obfuscation," and often does not refer to people by name. In contrast, her poems are notable for their simplicity and immediacy. Nakamura wrote that Ukyō no Daibu's poems evoked for him "tunes on a violin flowing out of a window on a dark night." In that, she reminded him not only of Kaga no Chiyo and Ema Saikō, poets included in this anthology, but also of Yu Xuanji (844?–871?), the Chinese poet who was executed for killing her maid out of jealousy; of Louise Labé (1526?–1566) and Marceline Desbordes-Valmore (1786–1859); and of Emily Dickinson.

I spent years not paying much attention to others' love affairs that I saw and heard about, thinking I wouldn't be like all those people. Among the many men I mixed with like the women I met morning and evening, there certainly were some who spoke to me in special ways. But, having seen and heard about what happened to other people, I would not respond, determined that such a thing was out of the question. But you can't escape predetermined fate. With one vexing thing unexpectedly added,[124] I was in such a chaotic state that I was back with my family. One day I was looking far into the west, at the treetops sunk in the color of the evening sun when the sky suddenly darkened and a shower came.

As the treetops reflecting the evening sun are bathed in a shower, my heart also darkens in no time

One autumn evening, a cricket that used to cry near the Empress's seat wasn't heard, then began to be heard elsewhere:

Abandoning the place under her pillow he's used to, bored, but still longing for autumn, O cricket

Made as though to urge you to brood and lament: the view of the unreliable autumn evening sky

Someone distancing himself isn't necessarily painful. But when he is within your view, he can upset you or break your heart, troubling you in a number of ways, as he did.[125] And so the year turned, and before you knew it, there was the enviable spectacle of spring. As a bush-warbler came to visit:

When troubled, I don't even know the heart of spring, what is it that the bush-warbler has come to tell?

For this and that he doesn't leave my heart, I think of him, I think I won't, and think more of him

When the person who used to preoccupy my heart[126] was still a courtier, he once accompanied his Minister father[127] to Sumiyoshi Shrine[128] to pay respects. Upon

---

124. The assumption is that Taira no Sukemori came into her life when she was enamored of Takanobu's courtship.

125. Evidently, Sukemori often came to visit the Empress, who was his aunt.

126. Sukemori.

127. Taira no Shigemori (1138–1179), Minister of the Center. Kiyomori's first son, he is described in the epic of the Minamoto-Taira war, *The Tale of the Heike,* as a counterweight to his father, who was arrogant, domineering, and insufferable.

128. Also Suminoe Shrine. It enshrines deities of navigation, ports, and poetry.

his return, he made a miniature of the beach on a dais with various seashells strewn on it and a forget-grass added on top and sent it to me, along with the following poem tied to it:

Because there is no use in being resentful,[129] I went to visit the grass known to grow on Suminoe Bay

In reply, because it was autumn, I wrote this poem on thin paper that was red on top and blue on bottom:

The Suminoe grass being nothing but your heart, I can only be resentful of my useless self

One morning after the snow had deeply accumulated, I was home, looking out at the wild garden, thinking of the poem "anyone who comes today,"[130] dressed as I was in a light-willow robe and red-plum thin silk. Suddenly he opened the door and stepped in, in a "withered-field" hunting garb, dark-red robe, and purple undergarment, so unlike my appearance, looking so elegant! I've never been able to forget this image of him, and the way it stays so close to my heart after all these years and months have accumulated is hard to understand:

Though years and months have accumulated, I still long for that moment, for that snowy morning

Because his heart was not what I thought it was, I was wondering if it would be best to go back to the days when I wasn't known by him and I didn't know him:

This evening his image rises more vividly than usual even as I wonder if I should end it now

No sooner do I decide, Well, then, I give up, than the weakness of my heart again intensifies

Brooding on the same thing on a moonlit night, I was looking up at the end of the room, when clouds cleared away even as I watched:

As I watch, a cloud clears away from the moon yet someone does not leave my heart and therefore

---

129. "Resentful" because she doesn't pay attention to him. Sukemori is being playful. *Urami*: "resentful" and "looking at a bay"; *kai*: "of use" and "seashells."

130. A poem of Taira no Kanemori in the *Shūishū* (no. 251): "In the mountain village the snow has fallen, accumulated, leaving no path; I'll look with pity on anyone who comes today."

During a period when he did not come to visit for a very long time, one night I was awake until very late, thinking of this and that. I must have shed tears despite myself. The next morning I noticed the light-indigo pillow was strangely discolored:

The scent he'd transferred washed away by the tears I shed, the color for a memento is no more

In the beginning I could not believe it was something that happened to everyone, and things would readily embarrass me. Fearing only what would happen if the ladies I saw morning and evening, not to mention the men, knew about it, I wrote things like:

Don't scatter them! If you did, how painful it would be: these suffering words on Mount Suffering

I'd been determined not to wander into the path of love yet have been pulled into a fateful vow

I won't live many years, I decide, and with that, single-mindedly, I console myself yet I'm still sad

Long ago, in a most unexpected place, someone I heard was more amorous than others[131] kept talking to a sophisticated nun until late into the night. At one point he must have become aware that I was close by. As it happened to be the tenth of Deutzia Month, he sent me the following poem through an intermediary, with the words, "The light of the moon is so blurred you must not be able to see what's happening":

With waves rolling onto the shore with rising thoughts, why should I be wetting my sleeves so?[132]

I replied:

Rising thoughts perhaps but with the waves going nowhere you have no cause to wet your sleeves

The sleeves of a woman[133] scooping salt, your heart, offshore wave, struck them, shattered, so I thought

---

131. Fujiwara no Takanobu.

132. This poem and the next depend on a string of associative words and puns. I take liberty with them in translating them.

133. *Ama* in the original means "nun," "fisherman," also, "fisherman's daughter," "prostitute"; here a woman who makes salt by burning seaweed.

He replied:

Rising only for you, rolling, my heart, the wave, doesn't stop for a second at a woman's beach hut

> Starting with such a lighthearted touch, we kept exchanging poems as though we were serious about it. But, determined as I was not to allow what usually happens in such a situation to happen to me, I was adamant about not going any further. Still, as soon as he learned about the unexpected thing,[134] he wrote me a poem hinting at it:

How envious! Which wind's pity has allowed the smoke of burning seaweed to flow toward him?

> In reply:

The smoke about to fade does not flow anywhere in the bay wind, staying simply adrift, lost

> He again referred to the same thing:

Ignoring me, the one you should love deeply, with whom have you allowed your heart to merge?

> In reply:

You flirt who makes love to anyone indiscriminately, even if I had feelings for you, I wouldn't show it

> Thus, nothing happened the way I wanted it to, and I was pondering on what chagrined me no matter how I looked at it:[135]

Having passed the Meeting Slope[136] I'm chagrined: How in the world had I begun the first step?

> He would send an oxcart for me and I would go to visit him. But just about the time I heard that a formal wife was finally to be set for him, I happened to see an ink stone near the pillow I had become used to. I pulled it close and wrote on the pillow:

---

134. Her liaison with Sukemori.
135. Indicates she ended up making love to Takanobu, after all.
136. Ōsaka (Ausaka): a barrier or checkpoint between Yamashiro (Kyoto) and Ōmi (Shiga). Because of what the name means, it symbolizes love-making in love poems.

His thought may move to another's scent, but do not forget, pillow used to me night by night

Soon after I came home, he sent word that he'd found my writing:

Your scent has moved both to my heart and to my sleeve; why is this request only to the pillow?[137]

During the same period, we once heard a cuckoo while in bed at night. Later, when I was alone and lying awake, a cuckoo flew by with a call that was no different. The next morning, when he sent me a letter, I wrote by way of responding:

That daybreak we spoke sweet nothings to each other; the cuckoo I just heard was no different!

In reply, he said what struck me as quite unlikely: "I, too, was just thinking about it":

Recalling, lying awake in bed, pitying myself: the cuckoo must have gone to you to tell my thought

After a long silence, he sent an oxcart for me. I hesitated, wondering if it would not be best for me to stay where I was. But, feeble-minded as I was, I went. When he saw me get off the cart, he exclaimed, "So you were alive!" A thought occurred to me when I heard that:

His remark "You were alive" intensifies my pain when I have spent days feeling I was not

After I left the Court, I did not really count on the man even though he came to visit from time to time. Indeed, my feeling was like "the Musashi stirrups."[138] And as days went by and as only distasteful things kept occurring, I felt I was in another world. So, to see what would happen, I decided to move to a different place and

---

137. In the fourteenth imperial anthology, *Gyokuyōshū*, this poem, no. 1566, is attributed to Sukemori, and the preceding poem, attributed to "a woman who was my lover," appears in its headnote.

138. Alludes to Episode 13 in *Tales of Ise*. A man assigned to Musashi Province found a woman to love there and wrote to his lover in Kyoto, saying that it was embarrassing to tell her about his new lover and painful not to, writing "Musashi Stirrups" on the envelop. Then he fell silent. After a while, his Kyoto lover sent him a poem, which, in paraphrase, said: "I count on you like Musashi stirrups; your not writing to me [or not visiting me] pains me, but your writing to me [or visiting me] annoys me." The episode may have some lacunae or narrative inconsistencies.

took out old letters and such to put them in order. Among them was one from him, in which he had repeated, "No matter what world may come, my feeling for you will never slacken." I wrote the following poem alongside those words:

Though you had made me think it would flow for long, now I cease to write you to my sorrow[139]

Not only was there no one to whom I could entrust myself,[140] but, within my heart everything was sad regardless of the time of day, and I remained pensive. Slowly autumn came. The sound of the wind,[141] which affects you in the best of circumstances, made me incomparably more pensive. When I looked at the sky where the Two Stars meet,[142] my melancholy simply intensified:

Having been pensive through and through, still I looked at the sky as usual where the Two Stars meet

While I lived in Nishiyama,[143] perhaps on the pretext that he had little time for himself,[144] he did not come to call for a long time. I noticed withered flowers and was prompted to write:

I have not counted how many days he has not visited, but the flowers seem to want to let me know

These flowers were on the branch he brought with him when he came to see me about ten days earlier. He inserted it into the blinds as he left:

At once piteous and painful does it appear: the bond between us we can't escape from life to life

One moonlit night I could not help thinking of him:

---

139. According to Takanobu's anthology, they exchanged several missives-cum-poems referring to "Musashi stirrups" before giving up. It appears that Ukyō no Daibu moved to a spot too far removed from the center of Kyoto for Takanobu's casual visit.

140. After leaving the court.

141. A harbinger of autumn: Seventh, Eighth, and Ninth Months.

142. As Tanabata legend has it, on the seventh of Seventh Month, Princess Weaver (Vega) and Cowherd (Altair) are given a once-a-year occasion to cross the River of Heaven (the Milky Way), meet, and make love. The suggestion is that Ukyō no Daibu is thinking of Sukemori now that Takanobu is gone.

143. Probably the Nishiyama Zenpō temple, west of Kyoto, where Ukyō no Daibu's brother, the monk Son'en, lived.

144. If it is assumed that Ukyō no Daibu is describing events around the year 1180, when the Minamoto clan revolted, Sukemori could have been busy indeed. As a male member of a military clan, he was by birth a commanding officer.

When I watch it with an image of his face deep in my heart, the moon is so clear
it is unbearable

Without any particular thought I was making the bed, when a thought
seized me:

With the image of the one I wish to be with come evening, I keep brushing dust
off his pillow

My yearning heart must lie alongside him, only the melancholy of my body having no place to go

I always thought of the same thing over and over again, so every time I'd say
to myself, "Oh, no, why can't my heart forget him?" But it was to no avail:

I try not to think such and such a thing happened but even as I erase the thought
I can't erase it

Once, while both he and I were saying meaningless things to each other, I
made an inadvertent misstatement, and he complained. Even such a thing was
pitiful and sad when I thought about it afterward:

How he did not miss a fragment of a word and took offense—even such things I
cannot forget

As to the world's turmoil during Juei and Genryaku,[145] there is no word
whatsoever to describe it, be it dream, illusion, misery, or anything else. No
matter how I looked at it, I did not know what to think of it, and even now I
feel I should try not to remember it. As for the autumn when the people I knew
departed from the Capital, I could say this or think that, but neither heart nor
word would be able to cover it. When the departure actually happened, since
none of us had known exactly when it would happen, all of us—those who
were close enough for us to see, as well as those who were far from us so we
only heard about them—were lost as if living in an indescribable dream.

When the world was in turmoil and the talk was that the future was definitely
uncertain, he was Chief Chamberlain,[146] and not only did he have little time to be

---

145. Most of the Minamoto-Taira War, which began with Yoritomo's revolt in Eighth
Month 1180, took place during the two eras, Juei (1182–84) and Genryaku (1184–85). With
large Minamoto forces pressing on Kyoto, the Taira clan fled the capital for western regions
on the 25th of Seventh Month 1183, taking with them Emperor Antoku, then only five years
old, and his mother, Kenreimon'in. With Gotoba ascending the throne the next month, Japan
had two emperors until Antoku perished with the Taira clan in Third Month 1185.

146. He was in that position when Kyoto was under mounting military pressure, from
First Month to Seventh Month 1183.

with me, but those around us also said we weren't being right and proper about it.[147] In consequence, the secrecy of our meetings became greater than usual, and even when we managed to see each other, it was with a good deal of hesitation.

"Now that the world has been thrown into such a turmoil, I have no doubt I will soon be among the dead," he said. "When that happens, I wonder if you will confer on me a dewdrop worth of pity. Even if you feel nothing, make sure to be a light on my road to darkness; after all, we have been close to each other for months and years. Or even if my life lasts a while longer, I am prepared to think that I'm no longer what I was. This is because once you start to feel sorry for this, miss that, or think of this person, there's no end to it. I'm weak-minded and I'm not at all confident about myself, so I determinedly regard myself as someone who is determined to discard everything and not to write letters to my people from whichever cove I might be in. So please do not think I'm neglecting you. I have decided to change myself in every way from this moment on. Still, I tend to feel the way I used to, and that pains me."

What he said was perfectly understandable, and that would leave me all the more speechless. Tears came out but no words would. Finally at the start of the autumn, I heard about the dream of dreams,[148] and there is nothing to which to compare my feeling at the time. Of course, anyone with any feeling talked and thought about the misery of it all, but I felt I had no bosom friend even among those whom I saw every day. So I was unable to talk to anyone, merely continuing to think about it on and on. But it was not something I could contain within my heart for long, and I could only face the Buddha and live in tears. Even so, not only is our life set,[149] but also I was unable to readily change my appearance,[150] nor was it possible for me to simply run away. I just lived on, to my distress:

Having seen distressing things without precedence, without compare, I loathe myself for still being

As the autumn wore on with me in an indescribable state of mind, I did not at all feel alive. One night when the moon was bright, the appearance of the sky, the way clouds rose, and the sound of the wind were particularly sad as I watched them, and as I imagined how he must feel, traveling with no known destination, my heart suddenly darkened:

Where is he? What kind of thing is he thinking, as he wrings his sleeves under the moon tonight?

---

147. In maintaining his liaison with Ukyō no Daibu when he had a formal wife.
148. The most unlikely event, to wit, the ruling Taira clan's fleeing the capital and, with that, Sukemori leaving her.
149. That is, she had no freedom to take her own life.
150. That is, take Buddhist vows.

At daybreak, at sunset, no matter what I saw or heard, I could not stop thinking about him even for a moment. In whichever way, I wanted to tell him what I was thinking, at least once, but that was not to be, to my grief. I heard by word of mouth how they tried to hold themselves[151] in this place or that, but there was no means of conveying my word:

Only of things I wish to say to him there are many, but unable to do so I shall perish in the end

Terrifying warriors[152] went down west in countless numbers. No matter what I heard, I was fearful of what I'd hear. Sad and distressed, I'd cry myself to sleep. In one dream, he appeared in a court cloak, just as I used to see him. He was standing in a place where winds blew noisily, looking around pensively. Disturbed, I awoke, and I had no way of describing how I felt. I thought that must be exactly the way he was, right at that moment:

Adrift amid the wild turbulences of wave and wind, he must have no time for respite under any sky

Perhaps an aftermath of my heart too disturbed, my body was feverish for a while, and I felt ill, too. I wished I could cease to be:

Before hearing the more distressing news in my distress, I wish I could place myself outside this world

I heard that Shigehira, Third Rank, Middle Captain of the Inner Palace Guards, having found himself in a distressing state, was in the Capital for a while.[153] Among those I was close to in the past, he was someone I saw morning and evening. He would say amusing things to us and go out of his way to help us people even with trivial things, winning our gratitude. I was distressed to wonder what retribution had brought this on. Someone who saw him said, "His face hasn't changed, and that made it even more difficult to look at him." The remark distressed and saddened me no end:

In the past when I spent morning and evening seeing him, I never imagined this would come to pass

---

151. The main Taira forces regrouped in several places as they were driven farther west along the coasts of the Inland Sea until they were destroyed in Dannoura.

152. Soldiers on the Minamoto side. Many were from today's Kantō region, which was regarded as barbarous and uncouth.

153. Shigehira (1157?–1185), Kiyomori's fifth son, was captured during the battle of Ichinonati on the seventh of Second Month 1184, and brought to Kyoto on the fourteenth. He was held there until the tenth of Third Month before he was sent off to Kamakura.

. . . Just about the time I heard about what had happened to his brothers,[154] I had a letter from him that wasn't cursory, and because I had a sure way of delivering a letter to him, I wrote, emphasizing "I shouldn't tell you anything like this":

My heart tangled like salt seaweeds in various ways, I barely feel able to gather them together

To think we are still in the same world is so sad, in the world where I am yet am not though I am

Speaking of his brothers:

Thinking of your thoughts, my thoughts shatter, and these added to my own thoughts, I'm very sad

In his reply to these, he said he was extremely happy to hear from me, adding: "Now that my life is likely to end today or tomorrow, I truly feel I've put closure to my thought on it. This is the only time I can say these heartfelt things":

Closure put to thoughts, I give up thinking yet keep going back, with so many things to think about

Now I decide: in everything I surely will not show any love, any compassion, or pay attention to them

Speaking of those who preceded him in death:

Even while we are when we are not though we are, having seen such distressing things is so sad

In the spring of another year, I finally heard that he was truly outside this world. I have no way of describing the time I heard about it. Though it was something I had thought about well before it all, I was simply bewildered. My tears would not stop, but since I had to control myself because of onlookers, though I didn't care what people thought, I said I was ill, and, covering myself with a counterpane, I spent days crying my heart out. No matter how I tried to

---

154. Sukemori's younger brother, Kiyotsune, feeling "like a fish caught in a net" between the Genji forces in Kyoto and a revolt in Kyushu, where the Taira clan had taken refuge, drowned himself in Tenth Month 1183; his older brother, Koremori, finding his position untenable in the schism among the important members of the Taira clan, did the same, in Third Month 1184.

forget things, his image lay alongside my body, and I felt as though I heard his words distinctly. Thus tortured, I had no means of detailing my sorrow. Even when we hear that someone has lived his preordained life before turning into transience, we say and think it's a sad thing. However hard I tried, I could not think of any precedence for this:

All in all, the world is transient and that is sad: someone who had no dream like this must have said that

After some time passed, someone wrote, "About your recent tragedy, I can only guess how you must feel," and I felt it was no more than a routine word of sympathy:

Be it grief or be it tragedy, I wish, I wish it were something the world says it is as a routine matter

As indeed is customary when you live on in this world, as nights passed and so did days, myself in distress, sanity nonetheless began to return, and as I went on thinking of various things, my grief, I felt, intensified. I was not the only one with whom he made a vow, which proved so transient, so miserable. Come to think of it, including those I knew and those I did not, many with connection to his family must have had this dream. For the moment, though, I felt my situation was without precedent. In the past, as now, there were only peaceful partings; at no time was there such a distressing one, I naturally thought. In any event, it was difficult to forget what I used to think about him. Come now, I'm going to forget it, I'd tell myself, but I could not, and that was sad:

Despite this parting without precedent, his image, lingering, lies alongside my body, to my distress

Come now, let us not lament these useless matters: would that I had the heart able to forget things

Though I decide to forget, I again go back; it would be sad indeed should I lose all traces of him

It must have been around the first of Twelfth Month. As night came, rain or snow, I couldn't tell, scattered, clouds moving turbulently. It wasn't all cloudy, and stars appeared and disappeared. When it was very late, around three in the morning, I thought, I pulled aside the silk coverlet under which I lay, and looked up at the sky. It was especially clear, and pale blue, and the stars, unusually bright and large, were out all over the place. They were mesmerizing, resembling as they did gold leaves scattered on paper dyed with daylilies. I felt as though I saw them for the first time that night. Before then, I'd been used to seeing the stars filling the sky, making it as bright as a moonlit night, but perhaps because of the occasion, I felt it was different, and that made me meditate:

Having been used to looking at the moon, I know tonight the profound feelings of the starry night[155]

When I went to Hiyoshi Shrine, the snow fell darkly, and it piled up terribly on the front board of my palanquin. After the vigil, on my way back to my inn at dawn, I lifted the blind, and the snow blew in sideways onto my sleeves and chest. I brushed off the snow on my sleeves, but it soon froze in spots. It was fascinating, but I had no one to show it to, to my sorrow:

What should I say my prayers for, when there is no way for the ice on my sleeves to melt away?

The surface of the sea[156] was dark green or black, fearsomely wild. The other shore, which was not far away and was in view, merged with the edge of the sky. A boat, which seemed to disappear into the cloudpath as it rowed, making a beautiful wake, looked, to my eyes, unfamiliar with the rough waves and wind. On the shore without tree or grass, the wind was unbearably strong. If I heard now, unexpectedly, that the one who entered the waves is in a place like this, I would stay here, however distressing living may be, I thought:

Were this the sea where I can meet the one I long for, I would step in to blend with the rough waves

A little past the twentieth of More Growth, because it was the day when the person who was fleeting turned into foam on the water, I performed Buddhist services, my heart focused on him as always, thinking only of him. But it was unbearably sad to think, "After I cease to be, who will think of him as much as this? No one will remember even the fact that I thought of him this much," and I couldn't help sobbing. This thought was even sadder than that of myself ceasing to be:

What can I do? Leaving aside the world after me, I wish someone would visit today, by then the past

---

155. The moon was viewed as an embodiment of the Buddha or enlightenment. Because of that perhaps, it—but not the stars—was an important topic for classical poets. Except as a topic for Tanabata, the Star Festival, during which Weaver Princess and Cowherd meet in the Milky Way, the stars were virtually ignored. This poem, along with its headnote, is an exception, prompting the great lexicographer Shinmura Izuru to single out Ukyō no Daibu as "the exalter of the starry night."
156. She visited Lake Biwa.

Kunai-kyō
(Died 1205?)

Kunai-kyō—literally, Minister of the Imperial Household—was a lady-in-waiting in the court of Retired Emperor Gotoba. Barely fifteen years old when Gotoba announced a 1,500-round poetry contest and asked her to join the ranks of contestants, she was no doubt exceptionally talented. For the contest, thirty of the best poets of the day were selected and asked to submit a hundred poems each. Despite her short poetic career, which spanned a mere five years, forty-three of her poems were included in imperial anthologies, beginning with the fifteen in the *Shin-Kokinshū*, for which the grand contest was held. Perhaps that intimidating honor weighed on her; she died young, most likely before she reached twenty. (For how she composed her poems, see the Introduction, p. xxxiii.)

Translated below is a passage from the *Masu-Kagami* (*Additional Mirror*), a court history that covers the period from the birth of Emperor Gotoba, in 1180, to the return from exile of Emperor Godaigo, in 1333, as well as a selection of her poems in the *Shin-Kokinshū*. The poem quoted in the passage was paired with one by the far senior Jakuren (1139–1202) and won, the judge of the session, Fujiwara no Tadayoshi (1164–1224), saying, "It is excellent both in form and content." Her father, Minamoto no Moromitsu (born 1131?), was one of the ten judges.

It is said that when the ruler himself is accomplished in the Way, the lesser mortals conduct themselves well. Probably because of this, during Gotoba's reign, there were many, both men and women, who were known to be excellent poets. Among them, the lady known as Kunai-kyō, being a descendant of the person known as Minister of the Left Minamoto no Toshifusa, himself a descendant of Emperor Murakami, was from what in earlier times was an exalted family; but she herself was a child of one who continued to be a lowly official and died without rising above fourth rank. Someone as young as she singing, as she did, of such unfathomably deep feelings in poetry is rare indeed. At the time of the 1,500-Round Poetry Contest, Retired Emperor Gotoba said to her, "The participants this time are all recognized people in this ancient Way of Poetry. You, Kunai-kyō, may still not be mature enough perhaps, but I thought it all right to ask you to join us. I hope you will do your very best to make good poetry and make me shine." These words made her blush crimson, and the way she sat with tears in her eyes touched even those endlessly more devoted to poetry. Now, the hundred poems she wrote were all excellent, each unique in its own way. Among them was:

> Light and dark: the green of the field's young herbs distinct in patches of
>   the fading snow

Imagining the green of grass, in varying shades of light and dark, as the snow that fell last year fades quickly here, slowly there—such a mind would be hardly possible for someone not mature. If she had lived to a ripe old age, she would have, we are certain, moved "the unseen gods and spirits." That she should have died so young is what we regret sorely, painfully.

From the Shin-Kokinshū

Suddenly darkening, the snow falling harder in the village, its footsteps though unseen the spring is come

On Blossoms[157] on the Lake:

Luring the blossoms, Hira Mountain winds have blown until a rowing boat has revealed its wake

On Blossoms on the Barrier Path:

On Meeting Slope a storm, blowing treetop blossoms, has turned the barrier cedar grove into haze[158]

On the Essence of Mountain Living[159] at the End of Spring:

Shining on the brushwood door the sun has left no trace, spring darkening with clouds at the rim of hills

As a Poem on Autumn:

Although there is nothing in particular to brood about, of the autumn evenings I ask my heart

On the Autumn Moon on the Seashore:

Sensitive Ojima fisherman's sleeves! They are not wet, are they, so the moon may lodge in them?[160]

---

157. Cherry blossoms are assumed.
158. Haze (*kasumi*), a spring phenomenon in poetry, is not possible in a storm, but the blossoms blown from the cherry trees among the cedars around Ōsaka Barrier have turned the entire grove into haziness.
159. "Mountain living" (*sanka*), as a set topic, refers to the life of an ascetic removed from the capital or the life of a rustic idealized like that of the noble savage.
160. Ojima, in Matsushima, is a pillow word for Matsu Province. As Matsuo Bashō,

The Moon after Rain:

Isn't she waiting for the moon in the village at the end of the clouds as the fierce rains recede?

On the Moon above the Chrysanthemums on the Woven Fence:

Waiting for frost the chrysanthemums on the woven fence take on the color of the moon at the rim of hills

On Mount Tatsuta the storm must have weakened at the peak: even the water uncrossed has torn brocade[161]

---

who actually went to see it nearly five hundred years later, says in *A Narrow Road to the Interior:* "The Ojima shore, connected to the mainland, is an isle jutting out into the sea." The poem alludes to a tanka on love by Minamoto no Shigeyuki in the *Go-Shūishū* (no. 827): "In Matsushima, the fishermen working the Ojima shore had sleeves that were indeed as wet as these." The poet's sleeves are wet with tears for unrequited love. Kunai-kyō twists the conceit that fishermen are uncouth and uses a metaphor for love, "wet sleeves," to describe an imagined reflection of the autumn moon. This is representative of the surreal poeticism of the *Shin-Kokinshū.*

161. Alludes to an anonymous poem on autumn in the *Kokinshū* (no. 283): "In the Tatsuta River maples flow chaotically! If I cross it the brocade will break in the middle." The conceit of course is that blown maple leaves have carpeted the surface of the river as with a brocade.

The Nun Abutsu (1222?–1283)

Abutsu served Emperor Gotakakura's daughter Ankamon'in and during that time was called Shijō or Ankamon'in Shijō. She was invited by Dainagon no Suke, a lady-in-waiting for Retired Emperor Gosaga, to copy *The Tale of Genji*. Dainagon no Suke was a daughter of the leading poet of the day, Fujiwara no Tameie (1198–1275), and Shijō ended up working as his secretary. Then she became his wife and bore him three sons. Tameie was sole editor of the tenth imperial anthology, *Zoku-Gosen*. His grandfather, Shunzei, edited the seventh, *Senzai*, and his father, Teika, the ninth, *Shin-Chokusen*.

Abutsu—Shijō's name after she took her Buddhist vows—has left us three important works: *Utatane* (*Brief Sleep*), a recollection of a failed love affair with a nobleman when she was in her teens, *Yoru no Tsuru* (*The Night Crane*), a treatise on poetics that she is believed to have written for her son, Tamesuke, and the *Izayoi Nikki* (*Diary of a Sixteenth-Night Moon*), an account of her 1279 journey to Kamakura for a lawsuit and her subsequent residence there. She brought the suit as a result of a dispute over the title to a manor in Harima Province. Tameie had initially given it to his first son (by another woman), Tameuji, then taken it back to give to Tamesuke, one of his sons by Abutsu. Abutsu died before the suit was resolved. Translated here are excerpts from *Yoru no Tsuru* and *Izayoi Nikki*.

The Night Crane: A Treatise on Poetics[162]

Read the Old Books

Since ancient times those who attained the Way of Poetry have left various writings for posterity, and these, of which there are many, are appreciated by various houses specializing in poetry and studied by individual poets. So it is silly of me to try to write down yet another set of words, and I do not know where to begin. But when it comes to pillow words such as *akane-sasu* ["madder-shining," modifying *hi*, "sun"], *hisakata no* ["of boundless light," modifying *tsuki*, "moon"], *ashibiki no* ["foot-wearying," modifying *yama*, "mountain"], *tamaboko no* ["spear-adorned," modifying *michi*, "road"], and *mubatama no* ["of the leopard-seed," modifying *yume*, "dream"], most treatises on poetry seem to say the same thing. I simply urge you to take a close look at those old writings.

Understanding the Heart of the Topic

In his treatise, *Shogaku Shō* [Guide for the Beginner], Fujiwara no Kiyosuke [1104–1177] says, as I recall, "In composing a poem, you must first thoroughly understand the heart of the topic."

---

162. In this translation, names, dates, and certain other pieces of information have been added in square brackets in lieu of footnotes.

Also, he says that it is very unseemly to incorporate all the words of the topic in the upper hemistich [i.e., 5-7-5-syllable unit] and, having nothing left to say in the lower hemistich [i.e., 7-7-syllable unit], just go on to say something meaningless. He says that when given the topic "deutzia flowers at a mountain hut" [*yamaga no u no hana*], someone composed, "The deutzia flowers blooming over a fence in a mountain village" [*Yamazato no kakiho ni sakeru u no hana wa*], but, perhaps because he did not know what to say in the rest of the poem, ended it by saying, "make you feel as though the side-wall were painted" [*wakikabe nureru kokochi koso sure*], which was funny. Still, I think that, depending on the situation, there are times when it is not a bad thing to incorporate all the words of the topic in the upper hemistich.

Nonetheless, with topics on love in which two ideas are combined, skilled poets used to make compositions, I think, that do not directly reveal but merely suggest the intent of the topic. On *aite awazaru koi*, "a love affair in which you go to see your lover but end up not seeing her," a poem by the Middle Councilor of Kyōgoku Lord Fujiwara no Teika reads, as I recall:

Iro kawaru Mino no Nakayama aki koete mata tōzakaru Ausaka no Seki

Past coloring Nakayama of Mino in autumn I again grow far from the Meeting-Slope Barrier

I think he made many such poems. I might have done for the lower hemistich something like *aute awazaru koi zo kurushiki*, "a tryst in which you are supposed to meet but don't is painful."

How to Compose a Tanka

In composing a tanka, I don't even have to say this, but you shouldn't think that you must begin with the first five syllables and then go on down.[163] That is not the case. Tameie constantly told me that the old model in composing a tanka was to work out the lower hemistich of 7-7 syllables, then think about the second phrase of seven syllables, then carefully determine the first five syllables in such a way as to make it fit into the beginning and the end. I think this was a warning that if you begin with the upper hemistich and go on down, your poem can end up becoming weak toward the end.

---

163. Japanese is written vertically.

On Allusion and Honkadori

It is especially in honkadori, borrowing phrases from another poem, that the distinction between skilled and unskilled hands becomes clear. These matters are also detailed in what Lord Teika wrote.[164] Indeed, a poem can sound particularly nice when it deals with a subject very unlike that of the poem to which it alludes, even when neither the borrowed phrases nor their positions are different. A poem by the natural poet[165] Lord Shunzei's Daughter, which I think is included in the *Zoku-Gosen*:

Sakeba chiru hana no ukiyo to omou nimo nao utomarenu *yamazakura kana*

They bloom but scatter, how depressing of blossoms *I think, but still cannot dislike* mountain cherries

A poem in *The Tale of Genji*:

Sode nururu tsuyu no yukari to omou nimo nao utomarenu *Yamato nadeshiko*

Related to the dew that wets your sleeves *I think, but still cannot dislike* the Yamato pink[166]

There is no difference in the borrowed phrases, but being a skilled person's work, Lord Shunzei's Daughter's poem is impeccable and sounds very nice. However, this is something you will find it hard to emulate.

The Matter of Diction

Tameie told me that you shouldn't delight in using words of the past in your ill-digested poems simply because ancient people used them in the *Man'yōshū* and the Three Anthologies. . . .[167]

At the same time, it is quite unseemly to use distinctive phrases of the poets in the periods more recent than the *Senzai* and *Shin-Kokin*, vying to seize them as if everyone else spotted them at the same time. It would not be good for the reputation

---

164. For example, *Eiga Taigai* (*An Outline for Composing Tanka*), translated in *From the Country of Eight Islands* (Doubleday, 1981; Columbia University, 1986), 202–4.

165. In those days a contrast was made between *uta-yomi*, a natural poet, and *uta-tsukuri*, a poet who toils at verse compositions.

166. In this poem, which appears in the "Momiji no ga" chapter of *The Tale of Genji*, Fujitsubo, the Imperial Consort and Genji's stepmother, indirectly tells him that her child—"the Yamato pink"—is in truth his, not her husband's.

167. The first three imperial anthologies: the *Kokin, Gosen,* and *Shūi.*

of the poets who originally used those phrases, either, so you must do your best to refrain from doing so, Tameie said.

In a poem of a contemporary lady-in-waiting occurs the phrase *tsuyu no tama-zusa* [epistle in dew]. Lord Shunzei was the first to use it in *iku aki kakitsu tsuyu no tamazusa*, "how many autumns have I written epistles in dew," and he wanted to set it aside for a while, I was told. You can say, of course, that the phrase is old now. It is in any case very, very indecorous to take a similar phrase from a poem so new that it will simply stare you in the face.

In composing a poem, you must make certain to calm your heart and weave words elegantly together, Tameie said. That is, if you say whatever comes to your head, simply imitate others, or only line up lightheaded words, and think you have understood it all, you will lose your equable mind, will not be able to use particles and auxiliary verbs properly, and will fail to balance the beginning and the end. Aren't there many such poems these days?

The Mutable and the Immutable

Also, as eras move from one to another, the *sugata*, configurations of poems, change. When you compare poems of ancient times with those of today, they are like fire and water, they say. Still, even among the poems of people of the Middle Period[168] and more recent times, there must be many that are not necessarily inferior to those of the earlier times.

Similarly, those who are regarded as skilled love to use the sentiments and words of ancient poems, which are elegant, never become stale in any age, and are interesting and refined, suggesting that there is no difference between past and present.

Buddhism and Poetry

In Buddhist teachings neither sin nor virtue is predetermined for anyone. Something strikes you and you are religiously awakened. The only difficulty may be to meet the right holy person at the right time. Indeed, you may feel lost as to whom to turn to. But as guides to Buddhist Law, holy sutras still exist in this world. As for guides to poetry, the *Man'yō* and *Kokin* still exist. How cannot someone who becomes religiously awakened and proceeds to religious training attain Supreme Bodhi even though this is the degenerate age of Five Impurities? To be religiously or poetically minded will depend on the person.

In carrying Buddhist Law forward or in helping the Way of Poetry forward, I don't think it matters whether the person's status is insignificant or not.

---

168. From about 1000 to 1200.

The First Order of Things: Feelings

Those who compose poems must regard feelings as of foremost importance. They must know *mono no aware*[169] and keep their mind clear. They must notice, and keep their heart alert to, the scattering of flowers, the falling of leaves, dew and showers, and when the leaves change color. No matter what they are doing, they must remain mindful of possibilities for poetry.

Fiction in Poetry

In poems on the four seasons, creating fiction will not do. You must simply compose poems by putting things elegantly together just as you see them.

In poems on love, there are many things that are ingenious and fictitious, but these are all right. Be it *makura no shita ni umi wa aredo*, "though there is an ocean below my pillow,"[170] or *mune wa Fuji sode wa Kiyomi ga Seki*, "my chest must be Fuji, my sleeve the Kiyomi Barrier,"[171] it is meant to express the depth of feelings. In tolerating outlandish comparisons, poems on love differ from those on the four seasons. This is what Tameie told me.

Still, fiction in poems on the four seasons may also be tolerated depending on how it is done. Beginning with the poem of Abbot Henjō (815–890),

> *Asa-midori ito yorikakete shiratsuyu o tama nimo nukeru haru no yanagi ka*

> Light green: the spring willow is like woven threads stringing together white dew like beads

mistaking one thing for another, as in

> *Asaborake ariake no tsuki to miru made ni Yoshino no sato ni fureru shirayuki*[172]

> In the dawn glow the white snow fallen in Yoshino Village almost seems the daybreak moon

---

169. "Ah-ness of things," sensitivity. In *Genji Monogatari Tama no Oguchi*, the *kokugaku* or "national learning" scholar Motoori Norinaga (1730–1801) famously argued that *mono no aware* is the ability to perceive things as they are and "has little to do with—nay, often goes against—the good and evil propounded in Confucian and Buddhist books," and that it is the purpose of all *monogatari* but especially of *The Tale of Genji*.

170. The ocean having been created by the tears.

171. Fuji, at the time an active volcano, is a metaphor for a "burning" heart; Kiyomi, a famous seashore and therefore associated with waves, is a metaphor for the "turbulence" of the heart.

172. Poem of Sakanoue no Korenori (active in the early tenth century). This is included in the *Hyakunin Isshu*.

and saying that cherry blossoms "resemble clouds" may be false but acceptable. In other cases, too, the injunction that things that do not exist shouldn't be described should be considered carefully.

Avoid Subjective Expressions

Amateurish poets love to use the expressions *ureshikarikeri* [I am so happy] and *kanashikarikeri* [I am so sad]. Unless the matter has to do with something truly happy or truly sad, these expressions should not be used, Tameie told me.

Do Not Mimic Contemporary Poems

Study carefully the well-known poets in anthologies of the past and recent times, whose poems are noble and elegant. Occasion allowing, pay attention to the heart of each topic as well, with discrimination. And try to emulate the outstanding poets when you see them. Never dream of mimicking or favoring the poems of contemporary poets.

Impromptu Composition

A poem made impromptu, in response to something unexpected, without letting the moment go, can be better than anything else, as long as you manage to say what you want to say that instant and do so in shapely fashion. Koshikibu no Naishi [died 1205] stopping Middle Councilor Fujiwara no Sadayori and saying,

> Ōe-yama Ikuno no michi mo tōkereba mada fumi mo mizu Ama no Hashidate[173]

---

173. This poem comes with the following headnote in the *Kin'yōshū*. As we have seen elsewhere, Izumi Shikibu, Koshikibu's mother, was a renowned poet, especially praised for her skill in turning out quick responses.

While Izumi Shikibu was in Tango Province with her husband, Yasumasa, a poetry match was held in the Capital and Koshikibu no Naishi was selected as a participating poet. Middle Councilor Sadayori came to her room in the palace and said, "What have you done with your poem? Have you sent someone over to Tango [to have your mother compose a piece for you]? Has your messenger returned? You must feel anxious." When, after teasing her like this, he rose to his feet, she held him back and made this poem.

In her poem Koshikibu uses two puns: Ikuno is the name of a place toward Tango and also means "to go," and *fumi mo mizu* means both "yet to step on" and "yet to see a letter." Amanohashidate, "Heaven's Bridge," is a famous "poetic pillow" in Tango. The poem is included in the *Hyakunin Isshu*.

The road to Ikuno and Mount Ōe being far away, I have yet to step on
Heaven's Bridge

and the cleverness of Suō no Naishi (1036?–1109?) responding to Major Councilor
Fujiwara no Tadaie (1033–1091),

*Haru no yo no yume bakari naru tamakura ni kainaku tatamu na koso
oshikere*[174]

In a spring night's dream pillowing your arm I wouldn't want to hear rumor
vainly rise

—these are examples in which human spirit has simply revealed itself in the manner of an expert thoroughly familiar with the Way of Poetry, and in this, there is
no difference between past and present.

Even though I have become an old decrepit tree in a valley now, if there were
people with similarly elegant minds, there is no reason I shouldn't be able to respond
to them as adeptly, I think, and I feel envious of the people of those days.

Diary of a Sixteenth-Night Moon

Departure

. . . while there are many examples of people who have edited anthologies, isn't
it the rare house indeed that has had two editors, each honored with an imperial
command to submit a collection to the court twice? I am involved with their descen-
dants, entrusted, by what karma was it, with three sons and with hundreds of poetic
documents. Also, my husband had said to me, "Help the Way of Poetry," "Bring up
our children," and "Keep up a memorial service for me after my death"—and firmly
pledged the manor at Hosokawa to me to do so. But its stream was dammed for no

---

174. This poem is included in the *Senzaishū*, with the following heading:

In Second Month, one night when the moon was bright, a number of people were
spending the night telling stories at the residence of Nijō-in, when Naishi Suō, lying
down, said in a whisper, "I wish I had a pillow." Hearing this, Major Councilor Tadaie
put his arm from under the blind, saying, "Do use this for a pillow." Thereupon, she
made this poem.

Suō's tanka uses a pun: *kaina* of *kainaku tatamu*, "vainly rise," also means "arm." The
blind (*misu*), made of fine strips of bamboo, was there because ladies were not supposed to
be directly exposed to men's eyes. Nijō-in is Emperor Goreizei's consort, Princess Shōshi.
This poem is included in the *Hyakunin Isshu*.

reason, so that the situation for years and months remained precarious enough to preclude either the means for lighting the candle for the Law and commemorative services or the means of protecting the Way, helping the house and maintaining the lives of myself and my children, even though we have, for some reason, managed to survive to this day.

I think nothing of my own life and would readily discard it. But however unenlightened it may be, the thought of my children would not allow it,[175] and I feel anxious when I reflect on the Way. In the end I decided that a cloudless truth might be revealed if the matter were placed before the Mirror of Justice in the East.[176] So, forgetting all the hindrances and turning myself into a useless thing, I made up my mind to allow myself to be lured by a sixteenth-day moon and set out. . . .

Even when I'm not negligent, our garden and the hedges tend to turn wild, but now—so thinking, I couldn't help looking around. Also, I was unable to console those who loved me as they wet their sleeves. I was especially pained by the Gentleman-in-Waiting[177] and the Gentleman of the Fifth Rank,[178] who seemed to have utterly succumbed to grief, although I tried to soothe them in various ways. Then I happened to look in my bedroom and saw my husband's pillow left as it was in the past, which renewed my sadness. So I scribbled near it:

Even the dust on the old pillow I have kept, who will brush it off after I leave?

Settling Down in Kamakura

The place where I settled down to live in the East is called the Valley-of-Moonlight. It is at the foot of a mountain near a bay, and the winds are rough. It is by the side of a mountain temple, quiet and desolate, and the sound of waves and the winds soughing through the pines are ceaseless.

Letters from the Capital started to arrive just when I was beginning to worry about them. The person for whom I had entrusted a letter with the mountain monk I'd come across on Mount Utsu sent me a reply by some reliable means:

Your travel robe, the tears added on Mount Utsu, must shower even when there's no shower

---

175. The Buddhist notion that parents tend to be misled into unenlightened ways because of considerations for their children—a notion well expressed in Fujiwara no Kanesuke's poem in *Gosenshū*: "Though my parental mind may not be unenlightened, I'm often lost to the Way thinking of my children."
176. Kamakura, where the shogunate with its administrative and judicial organs was situated.
177. Abutsu's second son, Tamesuke.
178. Her third son, Tamemori.

> Unexpectedly you set out on the sixteenth night, leaving the moon behind as keepsake

Because I had left the Capital on the sixteenth of Godless Month, she must have thought of the day, without forgetting it; that's considerate and touching of her, I thought, and again mentioned the sixteenth in my response:

> I hope to see you again in the end, being a sixteenth-night moon unexpected in the sky

Former Commander of the Outer Palace Guards, Right Division, Tamenori's daughter[179] is a poet often included in imperial anthologies. She is known also as Ōmiya'in's[180] Gon-Chūnagon. Perhaps because we talked to each other mornings and evenings on account of our interest in poetry, she wrote inquiring about my worries on the road, and one letter had:

> Far away I think of you, wondering how drenched your travel robe must be in the showers

In reply:

> Think, yes: both dew and shower as one made my sleeves drip over the mountain path

Her brother, Tamekame, similarly wrote about his concern:

> Having left our home town in showers, your travel robe in snow will be lucidly cold

In reply:

> My travel robe lucid in bay winds, Godless Month showering, in the clouds falls the snow

The person known as Lady Mikushige of Shikikanmon'in[181] is Prime Minister Koga's daughter,[182] and she is also someone with many of her poems

---

179. Tamenori (1228–1279) is Abutsu's son-in-law. The "daughter" is Tameko (Ishi), who died around 1315. A total of 180 of her poems are included in imperial anthologies.

180. Emperor Gosaga's consort, who died in 1292. She was mother of Emperors Gofukakusa and Kameyama.

181. Shikikenmon'in is Emperor Gotakakura's daughter (1197–1251).

182. Prime Minister Koga is Minamoto no Michiteru (1187–1248). The "daughter," also known as Sanjō, is thought to have died sometime after 1283. Fifty-two of her poems are included in imperial anthologies.

included in two or three anthologies beginning with *Zoku-Gosen*, as well as in the private collections of various houses; so, she is illustrious. Now she serves Ankamon'in as a lady-in-waiting. When I decided to set out to the East, I went to the Kitashirakawa Palace to tell her that I would be leaving the next day, but she was not there. With only one evening left before my departure, I was busy and had to hurry out without explaining what was happening. This had bothered me, so I wrote to her. Jotting down how forlorn I felt as the year drew to a close while I was away from home and how the snow fell without interruption, I said:

> Almost faint I watch the sky suddenly darken, the cloudbank beginning to turn to snow

Immediately, she replied:

> I'd been anxious for a good opportunity, when today, on the twenty-second of Priests'-Run, I received a letter I'd been waiting for—such a rare thing and a delight! My first thought was to tell you everything in detail, but this evening, with His Majesty visiting us to avoid an unlucky direction, I am too distracted to say whatever comes to my mind. How this goes against my wishes! That day when you kindly came to see me because you were leaving on a journey the following day, some young people had invited me to see maple leaves at the Peak Palace, and only later I learned what had happened. Why, I wonder, did you not inquire where I was?

> One side of my sleeve would have been soaked had I not known the day your travel robe left

And her response to my "beginning to turn to snow" was:

> You watch the sky darken and snow: I know how pitiful you are under the cloudbank

So, this time I responded only to her "not known the day":

> Why such hearty regrets, pretending not to have known the day my travel robe left?

Having heard that there would be a post early in the morning, I stayed up all night long writing letters to the Capital. To my Elder Sister,[183] who is particularly

---

183. Identified in a later passage as Naka-no-in no Chūjō as well as Sammi Nyūdō, but nothing else is known about her.

close to me, both of us depending on each other, I kept writing various things about my young sons. As usual the waves and winds were fierce, so I jotted down a poem describing things as they were:

> All night unable to end the tears or letters, I stay up alone amid the waves on the shore

Also, I wrote a letter to my younger sister nun,[184] who similarly missed and longed for me in the Capital. I gathered some bits and pieces of shore products and wrapped them:

> Uselessly harvesting seaweed and making salt, I long for you, my hometown nun

In due time, these two sisters sent me replies, which greatly touched my heart. . . .

Tamesuke and Tamemori Send Their Poems

Gentleman-in-Waiting Tamesuke sent down to me fifty poems,[185] without making a clean copy, saying he had just made them. His poems have certainly improved. I marked eighteen of the fifty as good. That was not quite right, probably the result of my unenlightened prejudice. Among them was a poem:

> Our hearts aren't separated but your travel robe's the white clouds beyond many mountains

He must have made this poem thinking of me traveling. I was touched and wrote beside it a reply in small letters:

> Could my longing heart be the distant white clouds morning and evening moving to and fro?

On the same topic of travel was also this one:

> Thinking of you on a transient grass-pillow night by night my sleeves grow laden with dew

---

184. Mino, who also served Ankamon'in.
185. A set exercise divided into the four seasons, love, and miscellany. Travel pieces are included in the miscellany.

I added a reply to this one, too:

> Autumn deep I cry on a grass-pillow, myself the bell insect I waved off, left behind

At the end of these fifty poems, I added words of criticism. I wrote an outline of how poems ought to be composed and listed some of our ancestors' poems, ending them with:

> If he saw these how glad would he be? So wondering I cry with joy on his behalf[186]

The Gentleman-in-Waiting's younger brother, Tamemori, also sent me poems, thirty[187] in his case, saying, "Please mark these and point out all that are bad." He must be sixteen this year. They read like poems, and I thought they were elegant—come to think of it, surely another shameless manifestation of an unenlightened heart! In this set, too, the poems on travel seemed to have been composed with thoughts of me. I had sent these sons the diary I kept while coming down East. I guessed they had read it:

> Parting with us, you saw the smoke from Fuji; even then your helplessness must have increased

I wrote a reply to this one, too:

> Parting with you transiently I still think of you, the thought like the smoke of Fuji that I saw

Dedicatory Poem: "Praying for Victory in a Lawsuit"

The *Diary of a Sixteenth-Night Moon* ends with a chōka. The unidentified 1298 copyist rounds out his copying of this memoir with an explanation of a few passages of the poem. It may be trimmed and expanded as follows:

"No traces of hemp are left" refers to a homiletic tanka that Hōjō Yasutoki (1183–1242), regent to the Kamakura government, composed: "In this world no traces of hemp are left; only mugworts grow as they please." In this verse "hemp" is a metaphor for an honest, righteous person and "mugwort" a metaphor for an evil, scheming person. Fujiwara no Teika included the poem in the *Shin-Chokusen*.

"Mugworts remaining" refers to a tanka that Lord Shunzei's Daughter composed and sent to Yasutoki in lieu of a petition: "If you alone know the number of traceless

---

186. "He" refers to her deceased husband, Tameie.
187. Another exercise set.

hemp, decide on the number of mugworts remaining." She was having trouble with income from her manor, which was in Harima, on account of the abuses of its military estate steward (*jitō*). Yasutoki, touched by her allusion to his own poem, promptly resolved the issue without going through the usual judicial procedures. Abutsu wasn't that lucky.

Lord Shunzei's Daughter was actually his granddaughter adopted as a daughter. Thus she was Abutsu's aunt officially and her sister-in-law actually. Either way, this is why Abutsu says, "we draw water from one stream."

"The clear water" and so on refers to an anonymous allegorical poem in the *Kokinshū*: "The clear water in the ancient field may be tepid, but those who know its true intent draw from it." According to one interpretation, the poem "means" to say: My beauty has faded but those who know my true heart remain kind to me.

In this country of Yamato,
   of Shikishima,
      when heaven and earth
began to open up long ago,
the rock door unlocked, those fascinating
words of *kagura* were taken to be poetry.
With that as a venerable example,
even in the Holy Ages poetry wasn't discarded.
Because with the human heart as its seed
it encompasses myriad sentiments
even devils and deities yield to, they say.
Outside the Eight Islands, in the four seas
waves remain quiet, undisturbed,
winds blow through the sky so gently
they do not rattle the branches, rain falls
at specified times, and so, following
each Majesty's imperial command,
along the bayshore of Waka seaweed
has been collected into many clusters.[188]
Even among them illustrious names
lasted for three generations,[189] the last
to his son making a special bequest.
Although I have evidence of this,
is it as penalty for his sowing a seed
in the belly of a lowly broom tree
which, I realize, is in Shinano?

---

188. Imperial anthologies of Japanese poems (waka).
189. Shunzei, Teika, and Tameie.

"With this serve His Majesty, help yourself
make ends meet" was his mandate.
Bordering Suma and Akashi,
a valley stream on Mount Hosokawa—
our meager lives hung on it as on a pipe[190]
but the water carried by it dammed
at its upstream source, we were now
like fish forced onto the land,
resembled boats, the rudder-rope lost,
with no one to turn to, at our wits' end.
Worried about my children, a night crane,
crying, crying, I came out of the Capital.
But I'm negligible: in Kamakura
where matters of governance press,
the leaves of the petition I had sent
were caught in the twigs of plum flowers,
and four years have since passed.
Where they go is unknown, in mid-sky.
Left to the winds, in my hometown,
the eaves must be in ruins; how spiders
have changed them, I know they have.
Should the writings left by generations
fall into decay, the Way of the Reed Plain[191]
would also die. What could we do?
The thought is not for my personal
grief alone but for the world as well
for which it will be cruel precedent.
For the future, in various ways,
he[192] wrote, left his brush marks.
Should anyone insist all these
are false, he ought to ask, yes,
the Justice Woods[193] that rights things
by offering mulberry adornments.
In this degenerate age prone to chaos
"no traces of hemp are left," I hear.
If this counsel isn't forgotten,
there should be someone who corrects

---

190. Hosokawa means "narrow river."
191. That is, the Way of Poetry. Ashihara (Reed Plane) is another name for Japan. Some texts give Ashigara for Ashihara.
192. Tameie.
193. Tadasu no Mori, the stand of trees that surrounds Shimogamo Shrine, in Kyoto.

distortions, or so deciding,
not thinking of myself, I implore.
Speaking of those days, indeed,
the person who lamented "mugworts
remaining" was rewarded with pity.
Ours is within the same Harima domain,
we draw water from one stream.
"The clear water in the field" may stagnate,
but if you trust "the true intent"
and, without further hindrance, decide
in my favor, there is no doubt,
the morning sun over Crane's Hill,[194]
the light of eight thousand reigns added,
this bright world will
    prosper even more.

Envoi

May your reign last long I pray mornings and evenings: I have described it today
   in Yamato words

---

194. Tsurugaoka, another name for Kamakura government.

Eifukumon'in

(1271–1342)

Consort of Emperor Fushimi (1265–1317), Eifukumon'in—Fujiwara no Shōshi's retirement title—composed tanka under the guidance of Kyōgoku Fujiwara no Tamekane (1254–1332) and became a representative poet of the Kyōgoku School. Tamekane, who was troublemaker enough to be exiled twice, urged poets to merge with nature. As he put it in *Waka Shō* (*Notes on Waka*): "Be it the flower or the moon, be it the scene of a daybreak or of a sunset, when you face a phenomenon, turn yourself back into it to become it, reveal its truth, embody its appearance and, facing it, entrust the working of your heart deeply to your heart, and leave the words to your heart." At one point, in his advocacy of a return to the *Man'yōshū*, a collection, it was thought, of spontaneous utterances, he wrote tanka wildly departing from the norm, provoking fierce condemnation, even lawsuits. His influence eventually settled into what might be called "meditative realism."

Eifukumon'in first appeared as an important poet in the fourteenth imperial anthology, *Gyokuyōshū*, which Tamekane finished editing in 1312 after years of conflicts with his fellow poets. Just about the time those editorial fights got under way, Eifukumon'in began to take part in poetic sessions and later helped a number of poets, generating a good deal of material for the seventeenth imperial anthology, *Fūgashū*, which was compiled in 1346 under the supervision of Retired Emperor Hanazono (1297–1348).

One notable incident in Eifukumon'in's life as a poet is her spat with Fujiwara no Tameyo (1250–1338) over his revision, without her knowledge, let alone consent, of one of her poems in the fifteenth imperial anthology, *Shoku-Senzaishū*, which he completed in 1320. As recorded in Hanazono's diary, when she noticed the revision, Eifukumon'in repeatedly asked Tameyo to cut the poem out, but he rejected her pleas (the entry on the 18th of Twelfth Month, 1325). The belief that an anthologist has the right to revise the poems selected as he sees fit survives to this day, in the practice among the heads—or teachers—of tanka and haiku groups to rewrite their members' poems at will, often on the spot.

Some regard Eifukumon'in as the last glow in the female line of court tanka. Of the great many poems she must have written, just about four hundred have survived, two hundred of them as *Hyakuban On-jika Awase*, a set of a hundred pairs of her poems arranged in a poetry-match format. Whether its compilation was by herself or someone else is subject to debate. The selections from it below are random and not in pairs. Poems on love, of which Eifukumon'in wrote a substantial number, are gathered at the end.

From the One Hundred Self-Matches

Still lucid midnight, it grows snow-overcast; then the clearing moon turns again into haziness[195]

In trees' minds flowers must be close: yesterday, today, the world overcast as spring rain falls

Lingering awhile over the flowers the evening sun, without really setting, has lost its light

Although, far and near, the haze is deep in hue, the willows along the bank remain shallow-green

At the waterfall the white flowers swirling up to the rocks seem to flow away, then go back again

Near daybreak, the moon faint on the rim of hills, the voices of returning geese are barely heard

Clouds of the evening shower not left, the sky clear, behind the blind climbs the evening moon

Even the voices of shirring cicadas are cool as a breeze blends with rain in the mountain dusk

Night deepening, what are the moon and the insects? The light and the voices grow limpid as one

Through the trees the moon falls into the garden on and off, turbulent near the eaves midnight pine winds

Migrating far away, the geese's voices grow distant in the colors of the clouds along the rim of hills

Eightfold mists rising on the mountainside, far away, autumn geese fly down onto the paddy field

---

195. Kyōgoku poets often described changes occurring over a long period of time. Lucidity (*sayuru*) suggests the lingering winter. Haze (*kasumi*) is a spring phenomenon. The meteorological shifts described in this poem occur during one night.

Enfeebled, dead paulownia leaves have fallen in the garden, the sounds of the rain
blending in a gust

Perhaps because it's falling on tree leaves that died and dropped, the shower sounds
enfeebled

Opening the morning door I hear near the eaves the treetop crows, their snow-deep
voices

The rain blending in the falling snow imperceptibly makes a sound on my darkening eaves

From Other Sources

The wilting wind having quieted down on the hedges, the rain cascades into the
small bush clovers

The sky chaste, the moon rises to the rim of hills where a gathering of clouds stays,
then dissipates

The sounds of winds fiercely move from treetop to treetop, gathered clouds cold,
a crescent in the sky

On a dark night mountain pine winds make a commotion, but in the treetop sky
the stars are in peace

Daybreak hesitant, the window dark, the sound of the night rain; awakening often,
my heart wilts

Bush clovers scatter in the garden, autumn wind piercing, as evening sunlight
fades on the wall

Where are the voices of crickets? Above the grassless garden of white sand, moon
of autumn night

Poems on Love

Suspiciously my heart grows disturbed though I had determined not to become a
brooding self

Suspecting he has another vow for the remainder of night, I cannot possibly tell
him it is still late

After parting the night is still deep; alone in bed, your presence lingering, I listen to the birds

Because I was so happy with love yesterday evening, today it adds another to my list of pains

I can reason with myself not ceasing to love, but I cannot forgive him for the distress of forgetting

"This is the end," I say and grieve for my life, but it is of no use to him who wants to stay away

Though I face a letter, thinking, "With a single stroke," I cannot write out my brooding heart

Not knowing of my heart this evening, he must be in some place else, vainly, he whom I think of

Before waking from the lingering dream of it as it was, I wish I could meet him again just as I did

Shōshō no Naishi
(Died 1264?)

Known more fully as *Gofukakusa*-in Shōshō no Naishi (Retired Emperor *Gofukakusa's* Major General Maid-of-Honor), she was the youngest of the three daughters of the portrait painter and poet Fujiwara no Nobusane (1177–1265). The title "major general" derives from the fact that, following an ancient Chinese tradition, most court ladies were given nominal military ranks. Here we cite her as the best-represented woman poet in the *Tsukubashū*, the renga collection compiled in 1357 by Nijō Yoshimoto (1320–1388).

The essence of renga, "linked verse," lies in the linking of two verses, 5-7-7 and 7-7 syllables (either may precede the other), and the linking often depends on wit and wordplay. This explains why most of the verses cited in the *Tsukubashū* and other renga collections come with verses to which the linking is made. Since wordplay is often lost in translation and requires explication, only a few examples are cited below. In each pair, the second is by Shōshō no Naishi.

Shōshō no Naishi's sister, Ben no Naishi (died 1265?), was equally adept at poetry, and the two women attending renga sessions, the hems of their scarlet skirts showing outside the blinds, presented an elegant spectacle, Yoshimoto tells us. Shōshō no Naishi is represented by fifteen pieces in his anthology; Ben no Naishi with thirteen.

the sleeves of the haze that has begun rising are still thin[196]

the sky is peaceful as the spring day breaks[197]

* * *

it has become a trigger to induce tears[198]

in the May rains the sweet flags on the eaves dripping[199]

* * *

On the night of the fifteenth of Eighth Month in the first year of Hōji [1247], at a renga session in the Sentō Palace:

---

196. 5-7-5. *Kasumi*, "haze," hides things, so it is a metaphor for clothes and related items. *Tatsu*, "rise," also means "to cut [in dressmaking]."

197. 7-7. Identifies what the haze is hiding, "the sky," and when, "daybreak."

198. 7-7. *Tsuma*, "trigger," also means "edge," "tip." "It has turned into the edge that has induced these tears" is a mysterious statement.

199. 5-7-5. Sweet flags or irises were put up on the eaves or the edge of the roof as a magic to repel fire and other evils. Shōshō no Naishi explains what has triggered the tears.

in this mountain village I have no letter from anyone alas[200]

there's soughing and it's a wind over bulrushes[201]

* * *

burning through midnight fireflies as my guide[202]

single-minded thoughts are agitated[203]

* * *

hear it and your sleeve's even more wet[204]

I walked over and saw the painful scene and so[205]

---

200. 5-7-5. *Tayori*, "letter," also means "visit."

201. 7-7. A rustling in the grass can be someone coming to visit.

202. 5-7-5. The firefly is a metaphor for someone who is in love but doesn't say so.

203. 7-7. A relatively straightforward linking. *Misao ni*, "single-minded," also means "unperturbed," "casual," as well as the pole used on a boat, which, by poetic convention, is associated with fireflies. Minamoto no Toshiyori has a poem in the *Senzaishū* (no. 202): "Pity, fireflies burn unperturbed [on a pole] when I think you can't help crying out in this world"—cry out, that is, if you are in love.

204. 7-7. "It" is some sad story.

205. 5-7-5. A relatively straightforward linking. The contrast has to do with "hear" versus "see."

Rikei
(Died 1611)

At least three military accounts by women survive from around 1600: *Rikei-ni no Ki* (*The Nun Rikei's Account*), *Oan Monogatari* (*Oan's Story*), and *Okiku Monogatari* (*Okiku's Story*). The latter two deal with the fall of Osaka Castle, in 1615. Tanizaki Jun'ichirō (1886–1965) incorporated with relish Oan's description of one of women's specialized tasks in time of war—the preparation of enemy soldiers' heads for inspection—into his novella *Bushū-kō Hiwa* (*The Secret Story of Lord Musashi*). Rikei reports the last days of the warlord Takeda Katsuyori (1546–1582), and her narrative is the best of the three.

The eldest daughter of Katsunuma Nobutomo (dates unknown), who had rebelled against the Takeda clan and was destroyed, Rikei was living as a nun on Mount Kashiwao when Katsuyori, his formal wife, then eighteen years old, and about ninety of their followers—more than half of them women: concubines, relatives, and ladies-in-waiting—reached her place as stragglers and met a gruesome death, on the eleventh of Third Month 1582. Katsuyori, a brave man but a failure as an administrator, was so unpopular that no one built graves for him or those who remained loyal to him. Rikei pitied their fate and wrote her account simply so that "at least their names may remain."

Rikei was apparently familiar with some military tales. She starts with the genealogical origins of the Takeda clan, her references to historical figures are assured ,if conventional, and her depictions of the suicide and killings to preserve honor and avoid capture are realistic enough.

Translated below are a passage describing the death of Katsuyori's wife and a set of seven poems Rikei composed as prayer verses (*myōgōka*) when she secretly visited the site of the final moments of Katsuyori and his entourage. These verses, which are part of her narrative, form an acrostic, *na-mu-a-mi-ta-hu-tsu,* "Glory to Amitabha," as well as "May they rest in peace." The set comes with Rikei's own comments on the first of the seven. The translation of the comments includes a few additions that were hard to avoid.

As her last moments drew near, the Lady must have become unnerved. Wondering what kind of goose[206] she might be able to entrust her words with to convey to her hometown, Sagami, and how she came to be what she was, she made a poem:

> Returning goose, I beg you to carry these words, to drop them in my old capital in Sagami

---

206. The role of the goose as a carrier of epistles derives from the Chinese legend about the warrior-commander Su Wu (140–60 B.C.E.), who, in enemy hands, sent his messages to his emperor by tying them to the legs of geese (note 33, p. 60). His captivity lasted for nineteen years.

Also, considering how aggrieved her siblings[207] would be after whatever happened to her:

Crying aloud, bush-warblers on the branch will surely miss the color of flowers doomed to fall

So she said. Her ladies-in-waiting told her that they were ready to accompany her in death and said:

The flowers too slight to count in blooming but never overlooked in scattering at spring's end[208]

When told that the enemy had pressed close, she said, "Pass me Volume Five of the Lotus Sutra." With it she calmed herself. The recitation of the sutra done, Katsuyori summoned Tsuchiya and told him, "Second her in her death." Tsuchiya said, "I will, sir," and placed himself in front of her. Looking at her for the first time so directly, however, he did not know how to strike her with his sword. Appearing to be not yet twenty years old, and dressed in various robes, she was so beautiful that even Yang Kuei-fei, Princess Sotōri, and Kichijō the Heavenly Maiden of the past could not have been more sensuous. Tsuchiya stood there lost, when the Lady unsheathed her protective dagger, put it in her mouth, and fell forward on her face. Seeing this, Katsuyori hurried up and seconded her. He then clung to her corpse and was unable to say anything for a while. . . .

. . . Because everyone in the Province was an enemy, there was no one who would defy the enmity and build graves for them. But someone who happened to lodge near the place one night went there secretly and, overcome with compassion, made prayer verses:

Native bamboo grove: all the flowers having fallen, only bush-warblers cry in the world

Mute the moonlight that entered the clouds, my heart has since wandered in the dark world

A pity: not yet daybreak a floating cloud hangs; all of us together the sixteenth-day moon

207. Katsuyori's wife was a younger sister of the warlord Hōjō Ujiyasu (1515–1571). Ujiyasu's eldest son, Ujimasa (1538–1590), was a distinguished warlord but committed suicide when Toyotomi Hideyoshi (1536–1598) attacked his Odawara Castle and defeated him.

208. According to another account, Katsuyori's wife, who had refused to return to her family despite his urgings, cut her hair and left it to be sent to her family with her death poem: "This world in disorder like my black hair, my dewy string of beads fades in endless thoughts."

*Mi*nd clear at the bottom of the water; sad that there's some muddiness in the bamboo world

*Ta*rrying, no one comes to visit your graves; autumn wind deeply resentful over the paddies, the kudzu field

*Hu*shed but I'll come to visit, parting the mossy underpath by the traceless hillside paddies

*Tsu*ris all you say but how could you deplore it: looked at closely, this is the ocean of emptiness

    In the first of these prayer verses, *take no hayashi* [bamboo grove] refers to the father and son of the Takeda;[209] *hana* [flowers] means what it usually does; *chiru* [fall] means "to pass away"; *mina* [all] means the entire clan. By *nao take no* in the first five syllables, I mean I still miss *Ofuya-sama*[210] even though so many people died. In the lower hemistich, when I say *yo wa uguisu* [bush-warblers in the world] I mean to say *yo wa uki* [the world is melancholy]. I also suggest *mata take no yo* [there will be again the world of the Takeda clan]. In each of these verses, I have put in such meanings.

209. The clan name Takeda means "bamboo paddies."
210. Kyoko Selden suggests that the word may refer to the father-son warlords Takeda Harunobu (better known as Shingen, 1521–1573) and Katsuyori.

The Age of
Haikai and Kanshi

As the tanka stultified under the burden of court-designated rules, the game was born of splitting the verse form into two and competitively composing the two parts and linking them alternately to make a chain; thus the renga, "linked verse," came into being. The sequential form, too, became rule-bound. Fortunately, it branched into orthodox and unorthodox, and the unorthodox branch, called *haikai,* "humor," became very popular, often veering toward vulgarity. Its main, enduring feature, however, was the use of daily language, which necessarily sought topics in daily life. The hokku, today called haiku, was the opening verse of the sequence, which in time became independent. Kanshi (verse in Chinese) saw a revival from the eighteenth to nineteenth century, when education spread among the commoners as well as the samurai class.

Haikai Poets as Eccentrics

Today's view of the haiku, a "poem recording the essence of a moment keenly perceived, in which Nature is linked to human nature," as expressed in the Haiku Society of America's definition, is, if anything, a consequence of the effort of the haiku reformer Masaoka Shiki (1867–1902). It surely does not reflect the view that prevailed during the latter part of the Edo period. Before Shiki attempted to introduce "literary" elements in the Western sense, haikai for most people meant a manifestation of a state of mind or attitude expressed in one of the three words: *fūryū, fūga,* and *fūkyō.* They refer, in varying degrees of intensity, to a liking for things somewhat unworldly or transcendental or to the object of that inclination, such as poetry, with the strongest word, *fūkyō,* corresponding perhaps to "poetic dementia." An old phrase for composing a haiku, *ku o hineru,* "to twist or turn out a piece," typified the detached, amused attitude taken in this genre.

One good place for gaining an insight into this is the *Haika Kijin Dan (Episodes of Haikai Poets as Eccentrics),* compiled by Takeuchi Gengen'ichi (1742–1804) and published in 1816, and its sequel, which was compiled by his son, Seisei (dates unknown), and published in 1832. So here we look at some women haiku poets as Gengen'ichi and Seisei saw them. In the following translation, I have added dates in brackets. Most of the poets cited here appear later individually.

SUTE-JO [1633–1698] was a daughter of the Den family, in Kayahara, of Tamba Province. From a very early age she showed signs of fūryū. In the winter of her sixth year, she made:

Morning snow figure two figure two wooden clog marks[1]

Because of this, one year, she received a poem from someone exalted:

Too good to be left in a weedy field this drop of dew

---

1. The Chinese character for "two" looks more or less like two horizontal bars, and Sute-jo in this piece describes the marks that the two-piece support of each wooden clog has left on the freshly fallen snow. Along with the story that a six-year-old composed it, the attribution of the "figure two figure two" piece to Sute-jo may be legendary. Although the story was repeated over and over during the Edo period, one of the maeku-zuke sets in *Inu Tsukubashū (Dog's Tsukuba Collection),* compiled by Yamazaki Sōkan (dates uncertain), reads:

one two one two I see the characters

in snowfall they wear clogs with broken supports

Whatever the connection, a mind that associates the marks of wooden clogs with the Chinese character for two and effortlessly describes the association is a prime example of fūryū.

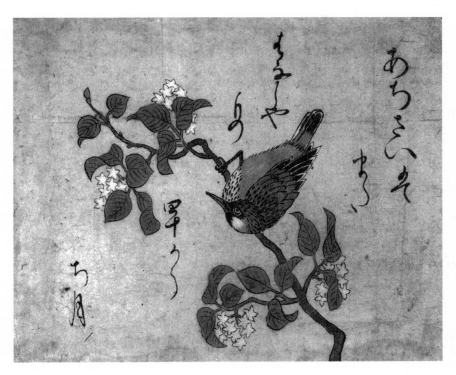

Chigetsu's painting of a titmouse perched upside down on hydrangea with a hokku which reads,
from right to left:

Achisai ha / mada / hana ja / mono / shijūkara

The hydrangea is still in bloom, yes, titmouse

❊

The nun CHIGETSU [1634?–1708?] hailed from Ōtsu, of Ōmi Province; she was
Otokuni's mother.[2] Both parent and child were partial to fūga. Both took Bashō as
a teacher. One year, when seeing Otokuni off to the East:

One would make a special trip to see the snow on Fuji[3]

---

2. Otokuni was actually Chigetsu's brother, whom she adopted. His dates are unknown,
but he has left a number of hokku, such as: "Even ark-shells must come out of the mud to
look at this autumn moon" and "The cat's paws don't get soiled this winter morning."

3. Because of his business, Otokuni traveled often and widely. The haikai implied that
he is lucky to be able to see Mount Fuji while on a business trip.

Mourning Ranran:[4]

> Crying out a rice sparrow spills a rice grain

> Bush-warbler! I rest my hands in the kitchen sink

> All the more you value your life cherry blossoms

Lamenting her decline in old age:

> My own figure looks pitiful in the withered field

Once, late in her life, Chigetsu took paper and a brush to Bashō and, holding the sleeves of her paper robe[5] together, requested that he write something on them for her to remember him by after his death. Bashō nodded in assent and wrote something on them, saying playfully, "Well, you are nearly sixty and ask me for something to remember me by after my death. How can I muster enough strength to do that?" It appears that she had sensed the nearness of her teacher's death. Before the end of the year she received the news of his death from Naniwa.

✳

SONOME [1664–1726] hailed from Matsuzaka, of Ise Province, favored waka by temperament, and had fūryū. In haikai she had Mitsu-jo for her teacher and attained its ultimate state.[6]

> Night storm! Lord Regent's hunted the cherry blossoms[7]

This is a variation of the piece on camellia Shinshi made about the same time, but we don't know who made which first.[8]

> Reaching out I pick flowers and blossoms as I go

---

4. Ranran was Matsukura Morinori (1667–1693), who studied with Bashō.

5. The "paper robe," *kamiko,* was originally worn by members of a religious sect but became, during Sonome's days, fashionable in the pleasure quarters. It's like Polynesian tapa.

6. Sugiki Mitsu-jo (1583–1647) was a renowned haikai poet of her day.

7. "Lord Regent," *Taikō-sama* in the original, refers to Toyotomi Hideyoshi (1536–1598), the warlord who unified Japan. He is famous for doing extravagant things. *Sakuragari,* "cherry hunting," is another expression for *hanami,* "cherry viewing."

8. Shinshi is a pen name of Takarai Kikaku (1661–1707), one of Bashō's top students. I was unable to find "the piece on camellia."

The child I carry piggyback licks my hair this heat

I exhaust all fancy ideas with my paper robe

All these manifest feminine sentiment and are admirable. When Ichū[9] left his hometown and went to Naniwa, she [Sonome] went with him and became his wife. Once, hearing that Bashō came by while on a pilgrimage, they requested his presence and regaled him. Bashō, struck by Sonome's deference and courtesy, made:

This white chrysanthemum doesn't have a speck of dust that hits the eye[10]

And Sonome followed it with a waki:[11]

water flows over fallen leaves in morning moon

After her husband's death, Sonome went down east and accompanied Bashō wherever he went.[12] After the venerable man died, she turned to Shinshi and studied with him. One year she set out on a journey, wandered about in Kyoto, and returned to Edo, where she settled in Fukagawa and earned her daily income as an eye doctor. According to her friend Kimpū's account,[13] she was by nature not conversant with quotidian matters and would cut a piece from the crimson-dyed silk of her sleeve to make thongs for her clogs or pick up the lid of a paper box for use as a water conduit. Such puzzling behavior is perhaps amusing in fūga terms. Later, she took Buddhist vows and shaved her head, but, strangely, she left about ten strands of hair in the middle of her pate. That she did probably because she was mindful of her Yuiitsu[14] past. The way she was, she surely achieved enlightenment in Zen principles, for in responding to Monk Unko, she wrote:

I have gratefully read what you said in your letter. "Not seeking the truth" and "Not seeking forgetfulness" are both foundations of the Great Way, as everyone knows, and I dare say there is nothing new about them. The way you act when you have reached one-mindedness and the root of all things, the willow is green, the flower is red, things are as they are, and you make hokku and write down

---

9. Her husband's name was Ichi'u. The poet named here is a far more famous one, Okanishi Ichū (1639–1711).

10. To commemorate her exchange with Bashō, Sonome called her own haikai collection *Kiku no Chiri* (*Speck of Dust on Chrysanthemum*). She published it around 1706.

11. See glossary.

12. Bashō died in 1694 and Ichi'u in 1703, so the description is in error.

13. Ikutama Kimpū (1667–1726). Kimpū wrote the afterword to *Tsuru no Tsue* (*Crane's Cane*), a haikai collection Sonome edited to celebrate her sixtieth year.

14. Yuiitsu is the name of the branch of Shinto established by Yoshida Kanetomo (1435–1511). Sonome's family followed it.

waka as you go along. If you say all this is rhetorical verbiage, all the sacred writings of Buddhism are also rhetorical verbiage. I hate anything that reeks of The Law. All I care for every day are prayers, hokku, and waka. It's good to go to paradise. Falling into hell is a blessing. . . .

❊

Shūshiki [1669–1725] was a resident of Edo, of Musashi Province. At first, while she was the mistress of the cookie shop Daimoku, in Terifuri-chō, her name was O-Aki. From an early age, she had indications of fūryū. One spring, when she was thirteen, she went to see cherry blossoms in Ueno. When she saw the cherry tree near the well behind the Kannon Hall, in Shimizu Temple:

The cherry by the well is risky for those drunk on sake[15]

The resident monk in those days was keenly interested in elegant things and collected every day the kanshi, waka, and haiku posted on the trunks of cherry trees, assessing and commenting on them. In the end he chose this hokku as the best from those years. No wonder the tree became famous as the Shūshiki Cherry for generations! When she became Shinshi's student:

Collecting clams women line up along rice seedlings[16]

She was so good at haikai she finally made it her profession.[17]

Blinds down, whose madam is on that cooling boat[18]

A warrior never learning from maples picks on a woman![19]

---

15. Getting drunk to make merry is part and parcel of *hanami,* cherry-blossom viewing.

16. *Shijimi,* here given as "clams," are tiny edible clams that grow in both fresh and brackish water; they also grow in rice paddies. Shinshi has a hokku: "A seedling lass plants toward her crying child." *Saotome,* here given as "seedling lass," is a woman young enough to be chosen to plant rice seedlings.

17. She became a *tenja,* a haikai judge.

18. *Suzumi-bune,* "cooling boat," is a boat for cooling off in summer. Well-to-do people used the Japanese equivalent of a houseboat. Women of higher social status were not supposed to expose their faces to the public, so when such people were aboard, the blinds were pulled down. The poet wonders what kind of elegant woman sits behind the blinds.

19. Alludes to the Nō play *Momijigari (Maple Hunting)* by Kanze Nobumitsu (1435–1516). The legendary warrior Taira no Koremochi, also known as General Yogo, is seduced, while hunting deer, by a noblewoman who is having an alfresco banquet to enjoy the autumn foliage. Wined and dined and made love to, he falls asleep, when the noblewoman, revealing herself to be a fire-breathing female demon, assaults him. But he successfully slaughters her with divine aid. Shūshiki was once invited to a samurai house for a banquet. One of the samurai guests got drunk and started to tease her. Thereupon she angrily made this hokku.

Living alone even a metal tripod for midnight tales

Her teacher indulged in licentious conduct all year round, with no set place to live, mostly staying in Shūshiki's house. For this reason, a while after his death, she used his haikai-judge stamp. Late in her life she is said to have passed it on to Kojū.

Once, a lord invited her to his villa. It was famous for its elaborate, beautiful garden, a glorious spectacle. Shūshiki decided it would be a heaven-sent occasion for her father to see it, so she brought him along in the guise of a servant, and he was able to enjoy the garden to his heart's content. A sudden fierce rain started. The lord called a palanquin for her to go home. Shūshiki, seeing her father having difficulty trudging alongside the palanquin, gave the bearers some errand to run and, while they were gone, changed places with her father—wrapping herself in his paper rain gear, putting on his bamboo-sheath hat, and tucking her hems up high—and went home, walking by the palanquin. We hear that no one noticed it. She is said to have expressed her filial piety in any way she pleased; this episode is a typical example. She died in the fourth month of the tenth year of Kyōho. Her death poem:

Even awakening from a dream seen, the iris color

❋

The one called the nun SHŌFŪ [1669–1758], in Ueno, of Iga Province, was a daughter of Ogawa Fūbaku and is said to have married into the Tomoda family, of the same fiefdom. She shed her hair after her husband's death and sought pleasure in haikai. She stands out in the Bashō School.[20] The following is known to be her distinguished piece:

Bright moon, hanging onto the porch pillar I turn round

She collected all her pieces in her lifetime and named the collection *Konohashū* [*Tree Leaves*]. It is regrettable that it is not widely known. When Bashō was still in his hometown and was known as Chūzaemon, she tended to his clothing needs, or so the story goes.[21] Later, she wrote him in Fukagawa, sending along a gift of what she called a Haikai Sleeve. She was eccentric enough to make something

---

20. Ueno, in Iga, is where Bashō was born and spent his formative years, hence the link between the two poets in this instance.

21. The link in such early years can hardly be substantiated, however; by the time Shōfū was born, Bashō was preparing to leave town. They did become acquainted much later, as Shōfū herself recorded. That happened when Bashō visited Ueno at the end of 1687 and stayed there until early the next year. It was either during that visit or another visit, after he completed his famous journey to the Interior, in 1689, that Bashō gave her the name Shōfū.

like that, to facilitate writing at a haikai desk;[22] it was a jacket, it is said, the right sleeve of which was shorter by just about an inch[23] (Tōyūshi has left a picture of it, but we'll omit it here). Her fūryū was incomparable.

※

CHIYO-JO [1703?–1775] was born in Mattō, of Kaga Province, and even when young, associated with members of the Shikō group.[24] After Shikō's death, she still could not find an appropriate teacher. Once, when Rogenbō, of Mino, came by on his pilgrimage, she visited him in his inn and became his student. She studied painting with Go Shunmei, of Echigo, and was good at it. Once asked to draw something and write a hokku complimenting it below, she drew a drooping morning glory above and below it wrote:

A morning glory thinks it perilous to bloom on the ground

This should show you how instantly, exquisitely, she could respond. When she went to bed for the first time with her husband:

If it's puckery I don't know but the first persimmon picked[25]

When she lost her child:

Dragonfly-catcher how far has he gone today?

Think of the deep feeling she shows in this piece. When Otsuyu, of Ise, wrote her his first letter, he scribbled the following in the margin of his letter:[26]

This nonflowering self must be a quiet willow

When she wrote him, she scribbled the following in the margin of her letter:

This nonflowering self must be a crazy willow

---

22. The "haikai desk" is *bundai*, an indispensable prop for any haikai session. Among the more memorable observations ascribed to Bashō is the one concerning this desk, recorded in *Sanzōshi* (*Three Booklets*): *Bundai hiki-oroseba sunawachi hogo nari*, "The moment you take [your haikai composition] down from the desk, it becomes waste paper"—that is, in haikai the process is what counts, not the result.

23. See Shōfū's section later in chapter.

24. Kagami Shikō (1665–1731), an influential haikai master.

25. This includes a pun: *hatsu chigiri* means both "the first pick" and "first love-making." It is entirely possible that her husband's name had *kaki,* "persimmon," in it, as in Kakiemon.

26. Nakagawa Otsuyu (1675–1739) was another influential haikai master.

Both left their provinces about the same time and each arrived back to his or her hut about the same time. When Chiyo read Otsuyu's letter and thought about his hokku, she saw the two pieces happened to come out of the same idea but decided, with admiration, that the choice of "quiet" was far superior to that of "crazy." She had the readiness to defer to others like that. Later she became a nun and called herself Soen. Evidently, she decided the only thing left for her to do was to study the Buddha's intent. On "The Threefold Worlds are all in the mind":[27]

Even a hundred gourds come out of a single vine

Even though haikai flourished in her day, few attained her exquisite state of mind.

＊

The NISHIJIMAS lived somewhere near Asakusa, Edo, and both husband and wife had a taste for haikai.[28] One night, when it snowed heavily, Nishijima prepared to go to someone's haikai gathering taking a boy clerk with him. His wife, seeing him off at the door, admonished:

If my child I wouldn't let him go with you in the night snow

Admiring this, Nishijima is said to have gone by himself.

＊

GYOKURAN [1727–1784] was always poor, but she served her husband well, remaining chaste.[29] They often wore each other's clothes, not disliking it a bit. Once, when he managed to buy some wine and tidbits and brought them home to enjoy with his wife, she played the koto, it is said, stark naked.[30]

---

27. This refers to the Buddhist proposition that all phenomena are the creations of the mind. The "threefold worlds" are the worlds of desire, form, and formlessness—that is, all phenomena.

28. Neither Nishijima nor his wife has been identified, but in *Itsuo Mukashi,* a collection of hokku compiled by Enomoto Kikaku (who has appeared in these excerpts as Shinshi), the hokku cited is attributed to Nozawa Ukō.

29. Gyokuran was a painter who preferred tanka to haikai but is added here to show what fūryū meant in those days. This episode appears in the section on her husband, the painter Ike Taiga (1723–1776), who wrote haikai.

30. This is reminiscent of William Blake and his wife, Catherine Boucher, romping naked in their garden. The two artist couples weren't far apart in time, either.

Den Sute-jo
(1633–1698)

Born to a wealthy family, Den Sute-jo married her stepbrother, Suenari, at eighteen and had five sons and one daughter. She, along with her husband, studied poetry with the famous scholar-poet Kitamura Kigin (1624–1705). After her husband's death she became a nun, as was often done; in her early fifties she became a disciple of the Zen master Bankei (1619–1690) and lived in a hut built next to his temple. The name Sute-jo means "abandoned woman," with *jo*, "woman," serving as what may be called a gender suffix. Contrarian names like Sute, "abandon," were common. Her name, after taking tonsure, was Myōyū, "delicate blending," and her Zen name, Teikan, "correct quietude." Her hokku use puns routinely. The following selection is made mainly to show her use of puns. Though today she is chiefly known as a haikai poet, she was good at tanka as well and left an acrostic sequence of forty-eight pieces, the first letters of which form the *i-ro-ha* syllabary.

Sute-jo's hokku celebrating the occasion of her taking tonsure. The top three Chinese characters say *Teihatsu o gasu*, "Celebrating my tonsure."

Negaeri no kokoro / yūran / mazu nademu

Turning in my bed I first caress my heart the valley orchid

Now let's pick but don't let young herbs out of your basket[31]

Looking at the water mirror the river willow draws her eyebrows[32]

The butterfly: distinct and not distinct from a flower[33]

Come autumn the paulownia tree will display a single leaf[34]

Day-darkener: when, even if left alone, the day will darken[35]

The moon in the sky looks comfortable beyond the blind[36]

---

31. *Iza tsuman wakana morasuna kago no uchi* in which *wakana,* "young herbs," also means "my name," and *na morasuna* means both "don't let your herbs out" and "don't tell your name." The hokku alludes to the song attributed to Emperor Yūryaku (418–479) and placed at the start of the *Man'yōshū:* "With a basket, a lovely basket, / with a trowel, a lovely trowel, / you pick herbs on this hill, child, / I ask you about your house, tell me. / This sky-filling land of Yamato, / I am the one who rules it all, / seated, I govern it all. / I will tell you / my house and my name." In ancient folklore, divulging one's name meant consent to marriage.

32. Alludes to Li Po's poem describing a woman's beautiful eyebrows as "willowy eyebrows."

33. *Chōchō wa hana ni wa narenu aida kana.* The pun may be orthographic: *wa narenu,* "can't become [a flower]," may also be *hanarenu,* "can't be separated from [a flower]."

34. *Kuru aki no kirigi wa misuru hitoha kana. Kirigi (wa),* "paulownia tree," also means "at the moment it's cut." The poetic belief had it that a single, heavy paulownia leaf falling signaled the arrival of autumn.

35. *Higurashi ya suttee oite mo kururu hi o. Higurashi,* "day-darkener," is a species of cicada so named because it shrills toward the evening.

36. *Tsuki ya sora ni iyoge ni miyuru sudare-goshi. Iyoge,* "look comfortable," includes the place name Iyo, which was famous for producing fine blinds.

Kawai Chigetsu
(1634?–1708?)

Born in Yamashiro (today's Kyoto), Kawai Chigetsu served in the Imperial Court for a while. The Kawai family into which she married was in the business of wholesaling and relaying horses. After her husband's death, in 1686, Chigetsu became a nun and adopted his younger brother Otokuni as her son, and the two of them joined the Bashō School. They were well-to-do enough to serve as patrons of haikai.

Sleeping alone through the night a male mosquito's lonely voice

In the spacious garden peonies bloom luxuriantly

Pointing his finger and stretching a child views the moon

　　Loving my grandchild:

I'll make a straw house for you for your rain frog[37]

Mountain azaleas, you look like the sea in the setting sun[38]

Since morning I wonder what I've done: spring evening

Every morning a wren pays me a quick, quick visit

Myself saying this but I become a child at flying fireflies

A cricket cries inside the scarecrow's sleeve

As though loneliness were his own: autumn dove

Spring awaited: blended in ice is dust and dirt

In an irrigation pond frogs are born as it warms

---

37. During wheat-harvesting time children used to make cages of wheat straw for green frogs' "funerals."

38. The original, *Yamatsutsuji umi ni miyo to ya yūhikage*, is rhetorically compressed and says, in paraphrase: "Are you saying that I should look at you, mountain azaleas, as the sea in the evening sun?" This hokku is regarded as one of Chigetsu's masterpieces.

Chigetsu's hokku on a fan, which reads, from right to left:
Yamatsutsuji / umi ni / miyo to ya / yūhikage.
Mountain azaleas, you look like the sea in the evening sun

Mesmerized by morning glories I take a nap

Calling out a rice sparrow spills a rice grain

>Among the hokku by various poets for the headnote: "Displaying Bashō's Self-Portrait in Otokuni's House on the 21st day":[39]

I start to speak to the figure in the portrait so cold

My own figure appears pitiful in the withered field

Removing its eyeballs the cicada has come out of his shell

If there were two we might fight over the moon tonight

Not knowing I've grown old: blossoms in full bloom

This autumn night when I think of it I'm ancient

---

39. Buddhist rite held on the twenty-first day after death.

Recalling my innocent days long ago:

Cooling off with mother's breasts, in father's lap

Visiting the abode of an old nun named Chigetsu:[40]

Stories of Major General the nun in the Shiga snow[41]

—Bashō

Grass broom's all there is for the elder's house snow[42]

Farewell Gift for Senna:[43]

Having heard "travels," even my heart now a flower field

HAIBUN

On Releasing a Sparrow

The willow's lower branches tapping my window, the fragrance of plum blossoms alluring by the eaves, and the sun sparkling, I recited "Unexpectedly you've come to visit,"[44] while dusting the sliding doors though not with "the jeweled

---

40. This is quoted from Bashō's writing. Toward the end of 1889, while staying in Zeze, Ōtsu, Bashō visited Chigetsu in the village of Ōgi to the north, in the area called Shiga. On that occasion, Chigetsu apparently told him that "the Major General of 'His Own Voice'" lived in retirement in Ōgi a long time ago. The person so referred to is the daughter of Fujiwara no Nobusane, who is especially famous for her poem *Ono ga ne ni tsuraki wakare wa ari to da ni omoi mo shirade tori ya nakuran,* "Not thinking, not knowing, that there will be a painful parting with his own voice the bird sings" (no. 794, *Shin-Chokusenshū*). About Nobusane's Daughter, see Shōshō no Naishi, p. 135.

41. Bashō puns on the place name Shiga, creating the sense of "telling stories." A typical salutatory piece in which the poet compliments his hostess, here in association with a famous poet of the past, this hokku was used to open a partial renga sequence, Chigetsu following with a self-deprecating piece, "over there the sand, here the tree-searer."

42. Chigetsu composed this apparently in response to Bashō's hokku when she remembered it much later.

43. Mikami Senna (1651–1723). Resident monk of Hompuku Temple of the Shin (True) Sect, in Katada, Ōmi. One of his hokku: "For baby grebes a willow sets up a separate house."

44. Partial quote from a tanka by Taira no Kanemori (died 990), no. 15, *Shūishū: Waga yado no ume no tachie ya mietsuran omoi no hoka ni kimi ga mimaseru,* "You must have seen the tall branch of the plum tree of my house: unexpectedly you've come to visit." The poem is based on the conceit that the visitor comes to see the plum blossoms, not the owner of the tree.

broom today on the first day of the Rat,"[45] when outside the door of the main room I heard some noise, and looked: there lay a baby sparrow with her wing damaged, chased perhaps by a falcon or a hawk. "What a lovely creature! This is something I'd have sought myself." I petted her and waited on her in whatever way I could think of. But nothing seemed to work, until I sought and acquired a grass called bastard gentian.[46] Then things turned around. As days passed, she grew close to me and missed me, much more so I felt than my grandchild. Just hearing my footsteps she would turn toward me and open her beak to wait for food. "I may be a horrible-looking old woman but I wouldn't cut your tongue off,"[47] I said. I also told the children not to do anything naughty to her. I even remembered how Lady Murasaki played as a child.[48]

Thus the spring passed, the summer peaked, and mid-autumn came. One day, deciding I'd never do it unless I did it now, I opened the door of her cage and let her go. But she came back the next day and again the next, staying close to her empty cage, acting as if she missed it, so I gave her some food:

Come around the equinox, my crutchless sparrow friend

45. A phrase in a poem Ōtomo no Yakamochi (718–785) made in a New Year's court ceremony held on the third of First Month 758: *Hatsuharu no hatsune no kyō no tamahahaki te ni toru kara ni yuragu tama no o*, "In early spring, on the first day of the Rat, today, the moment I hold the jeweled broom the string of beads wavers and tinkles." This New Year's rite, which followed a Chinese custom, entailed display of a ceremonial plow to symbolize the emperor's engagement in grain cultivation and a ceremonial broom to symbolize the empress's engagement in sericulture. A "string of beads" is a metaphor for life. The broom mentioned in the poem remains intact in the Shōsōin, in Nara. The poem originally is recorded as no. 4493 in the *Man'yōshū*; it also appears as an anonymous poem, no. 708, in the *Shin-Kokinshū*.
46. Medicinal herb used for rheumatism, neuralgia, and arthritis, St. John's Wort.
47. A folktale. A mean old woman cuts the tongue off her husband's pet sparrow when the bird licks her laundry starch. The old man visits his wounded friend and is shown two caskets to choose from as a gift. He takes the smaller one. Back home he opens it, and it is full of treasures. The jealous wife visits the sparrow and hauls back the larger casket. When she opens it, vipers and centipedes crawl out of it. Apparently a universal story, it first appears in recorded form in Japan as Tale 48 in *Uji Shūi Monogatari*, compiled in the early thirteenth century.
48. In the "Wakamurasaki" chapter of *The Tale of Genji*, the Shining Prince happens upon a lovely young girl at a temple he is visiting. When she complains that a servant girl let go a baby sparrow she was keeping in a basket, she is told that it is sinful to keep a living thing in captivity. She later becomes Lady Murasaki, Genji's wife.

Shiba Sonome
(1664–1726)

Born to a Shinto priest in Ise, Shiba Sonome moved to Osaka with her physician husband, Ichi'u (later, Isen), in 1692. Two years later the couple invited Bashō to their residence and had a renga session in which the haikai master composed the hokku and Sonome the waki (see p. 147). In honor of Bashō's hokku, she titled her book of haikai *Kiku no Chiri* (*Speck of Dust on Chrysanthemum*). While in Osaka, she thrived as a *tenja*, a haikai judge; some of the comments she left as judge suggest that she disliked "clever" pieces and pieces with "worldly" pretenses. After her husband's death, she moved to Edo, in 1705, and further studied haikai with Takarai Kikaku. In 1723 she compiled a haikai book, *Tsuru no Tsue* (*Crane's Cane*), to commemorate her sixtieth year. She was also adept at waka and dedicated 1,030 pieces to Ise Shrine in each of the years 1722 and 1724. Once she donated thirty-six cherry trees to the Tomigaoka Hachiman Shrine.

In a spring field a mindful person wears no makeup

 At the Miyakawa ferry the night was still deep:

The coloration only a little bit at spring daybreak

 A field at dawn:

Even before they bloom, lost in the others: violets

The robin's call falls and tumbles on the rock

 Leaving the inn while the morning is still dark:

To the sleepyheads don't show yourself, morning cherry

Clothes changed[49] you deliberately go to hold a neighbor's child

Show me where the gossamers fall, Sea of Grebes[50]

Insects' voices as night deepens sink into the stone

The cold of a cloud afloat drifting, the winter moon

---

49. *Koromogae*, here given as "clothes changed," refers to the custom of changing clothes on the first of Fourth Month, for the summer, and on the first of Tenth Month, for the winter.

50. Nio no Umi, another name of Lake Biwa.

Folded between tissues, and wilting, a violet

At Sonome's residence:

Deep inside the partition blind and elegant: north plum[51]

—Bashō

In reply:

Winter shower: your cypress hat will stay till flowering[52]

In autumn winds waves rough-roughing the plovers cry

I put my towel on my hat to dry in this heat

Bird messengers busily wheel over a winter boat

Coolness my back hair doesn't reach my collar

Coolness I put my forehead on the green tatami[53]

Already wine's splashed on my lap clothes changed

Amidst the tree-searer[54] spills a cow's noon voice

Living alone:

Leaves swoosh and a dog jumps, barks at the storm

The clouds white recently all day a stag calls

Tree leaves tear and shatter to bits so cold

Each wave rolling in collapses the plovers on the beach

---

51. *Nōren*, here given as "partition blind," is a hanging room partition made of simply designed cloths. *Kita no ume*, "north plum," echoes the expression *kita no kata*, "the lady in the north," an elegant reference to the mistress of the house because her room was usually in a quarter facing north. Bashō probably saw plum blossoms arranged in a vase in Sonome's room. This hokku is typical in its complimentary nature.

52. *Hana made*, "till flowering," is shorthand for "until cherries bloom in spring."

53. The tatami, which is the normal flooring for the traditional Japanese house, mainly consists of two parts: the body made from straw and the surface covering made from rushes. The surface covering becomes worn out easily so is changed from time to time. When it is new, it has the sweet smell of a fresh plant.

54. "Tree-searer" is a literal translation of *kogarashi*, a bone-chilling winter wind.

Ogawa Shōfū
(1669–1758)

Much of what we know about Shōfū comes from the preface to the anthology of her poems *Konohashū (Collection of Tree Leaves)*, which someone named Hakuzetsuba (White-Tongue Horse) the Old Man wrote at the request of Tōshū and Mijin, who compiled the book in 1758. Since Hakuzetsuba's preface is also typical of the genre, it is translated here. The anthology has poems neatly arranged by season and ends with a thirty-six-piece renga whose hokku was written by Bashō.

Preface to Konohashū

The Zen nun Chishū[55] is Tomoda Ryōbon's wife and Ogawa Fūbaku's daughter.[56] Carrying forward her father's wishes, she was wise in every way and even in the Way of Fūga bested most others. Along with her father and husband she studied under the venerable Bashō. She was especially close to him and was given the name Shōfū (Pine Wind). One year, in Western Kyoto, she became deeply involved with a woman of entertainment called Nokaze (Field Wind). Once, she took off her silk gown and exchanged it with Nokaze's, playfully remarking, "The wind has the habit of visiting the pine,"[57] and changed her name to Shōfū (Treetop Wind). She told other friends, "I'm sure my teacher will forgive me because the pines also have treetops."

Indeed, when Bashō returned to his hometown, he would sometimes stay in her place and, getting up or lying down, depend on her as though she were a cane. He preferred the length of the right sleeve of his brown jacket short, laughingly calling it a "haikai sleeve," or so this collection tells us. Now even the one he depended on

Faded away: the memory of the hands that sewed him lined clothes[58]

A deutzia-flower robe for her formal travel wear, in age she was not far behind Lord Shunzei.[59] Thinking of the lamentations of the person dedicated to this Way

---

55. The Zen name Shōfū acquired when she took Buddhist tonsure after her husband's death.

56. Tomoda Ryōbon (1666–1730) was a ranking samurai of the Iga fiefdom. Ogawa Fūbaku (died 1700) was a samurai of the Tōdō fiefdom.

57. The original is the lower hemistich of a tanka on love by Kunai-kyō, no. 1199 in the *Shin-Kokinshū*. The poem relies on three puns, so that it says, in paraphrase: "You've heard, haven't you, that even in the wind high in the sky the pine has the habit of making a sound—that the wind customarily visits the pine tree—but you are so absentminded you've forgotten to come to see me." About Kunai-kyō, see pp. 113–115.

58. This hokku is written as if it continued the statement made in the last part of the preceding paragraph. *Awase*, "lined clothes," indicates early summer. Shōfū died in Fourth Month, the first month of that season by lunar calendar.

59. Fujiwara no Shunzei, the greatest arbiter of poetry of his day. Famous for the banquet Retired Emperor Gotoba held for him to celebrate his ninetieth year.

of Poetry who was laden with memories of Bashō, her friends Tōshū and Mijin blended in a single volume the booklet called *Konoha*, in which our nun had carefully written down her pieces, things Bashō had written to her, hokku found on what appeared to be waste paper, and the pieces her grandson Kitan had remembered. They then asked me for a preface. I myself met and knew Bashō. As to the Way of Poetry, I heard and read Shinshi[60] and Tohō,[61] but, inadequate though I am as a follower of great men, declining the request would have been too ostentatious. Also, because of my friendship with Shōfū, I couldn't have remained silent. So I have penned this short piece in a simple attempt to copycat like a jay.

Time is Early Month of the 8th Year of Hōreki [1758]

Saigyō-an 76th Year of Age
Hakuzetsuba the Old Man

Staring the frog looks as if it's about to bring a lawsuit

Popping out the frog seems to have something to say

Fields and mountains feel ready for makeup in spring rain

Bush-warbler: your first call could have been a bit closer

[The preceding hokku was composed in response to what] Bashō said, "You have the first call all the time. You may go beyond the reasons for your first impression."

Not showing even the blue of the big sky: cherry blossoms

Far as the eye can see the cherry blossoms have lidded the sky

The skylark kicks down a clutch of cloud by five feet

Bashō always taught us: "As for the pine, learn from the pine; as for the bamboo, learn from the bamboo.[62] In fūga, I'd say what's devoid of falsity is

---

60. Takarai Kikaku, one of Bashō's earliest students, known for his "resplendent" hokku.
61. Hattori Tohō (1657–1730). He collected Bashō's observations in *Sanzōshi* (Three Booklets) and collected his hokku and other writings.
62. The pine/bamboo quote is among the most important dicta Bashō has left. As Tohō goes on to explain in what appear to be Bashō's words in *Sanzōshi*, "This means to separate yourself from your personal intent. If you interpret this 'learn' in your own way, you end up not learning anything. To learn is to get into the thing and, the moment it reveals its subtlety and you feel it, for it to turn itself into a poem. Even if you manage to express the thing revealingly, if it isn't a feeling that naturally comes out of the thing, the thing and your self become two separate things, and the feeling cannot attain truthfulness. It will be an artificial intent formed by your personal intent."

truthfulness." He greatly praised this hokku for its intent, which is something I haven't forgotten for a single moment.

In front of my hut I made a vegetable patch the size of two tatami and, watering it in the mornings, I've been looking forward to what it will bring:

A butterfly sucks the mouth of the flower I treasure the most

Spring passed, with no robes up to dry but cicadas' voices[63]

This rainy night no other sounds but clapper rails

Every year people delight me or I become aggrieved for my friends. I sleep, rise from bed, get my breakfast, eat my lunch simply to fill my stomach. Strike me or beat me, and I, a nun, remain not dead. I don't want to die, either.

Rain or shine my age grows long like a melon tendril

Under the snowy sky naked the winter melon grows fat

In praise of Bashō's portrait:

Both the haikai sleeve and plantain withered in the field[64]

As to what I call "the haikai sleeve" here, during the days when Bashō stayed with us, I would sew summer and winter wear for him. He preferred the right sleeve that was shorter by an inch. He used to say, with a laugh, "This is better for someone who uses a brush. You might call it a haikai sleeve."

RENGA

First Day of Frost Month in the 2nd Year of Genroku [1689],[65] at Ryōbon's House: Haikai[66] Kasen[67]

---

63. Alludes to Empress Jitō's tanka on p. 23.
64. "Plantain" is what the name Bashō means. He chose the plant for his *nom de plume* for the propensity of its large leaves to tear easily. That this somewhat bleak description is given in praise of the deceased master is also haikai.
65. That year, after carrying out his "journey to the Interior," Bashō went back to his hometown, in Iga, toward the end of the ninth month, and engaged in a number of haikai activities before leaving for Nara, toward the end of Frost Month.
66. See the glossary of terms.
67. Here the first six are translated.

Come, children, let's run about in the hailstones[68]

—Bashō

on this tray a cold camellia, narcissus[69]

—Ryōbon

after the feather duster's wind ceases, rolling up the scroll[70]

—Shōfū

squat-wrestling begins on moon's straw mattress[71]

—San'en

stags' voices: his borrowed straw coat provokes pity[72]

—Tohō

rustling, acorns fall on the mountain peak[73]

—Hanzan[74]

---

68. This is a typical hokku in a renga sequence: composed by the best in the group or the guest of honor and salutatory or complimentary to the host in character. Shōfū and Ryōbon had a number of children, so Bashō addresses them. The opening piece must also indicate the season of composition—here the hailstones indicate winter.

69. The second piece, called *waki*, is normally composed by the host of the gathering. It completes the statement made in the hokku by returning the compliment—sometimes, as here, in a self-deprecating manner. Ryōbon says the only thing with which he can welcome his honored guest is a tray of a camellia flower and narcissus. Ryōbon's piece alludes to a tanka in the *Fubokushō*, the large compendia of 17,380 verses compiled around 1310 by Fujiwara no Nagakiyo (dates unknown). The tanka may be translated: "If the service tray with anises placed on it has no rim, the beads [anise seeds] will not stay like hailstones."

70. The third piece, called *daisan*, must shift the focus from the preceding exchange. It usually employs a gerund, as it does here. Shōfū takes her husband's piece to mean a description of a tea ceremony. The feather duster here is one used for tea utensils. The scroll is one displayed in the alcove while tea is served. Nonseasonal.

71. *Izumai*, "squat wrestling," is a form of wrestling fought while sitting on a mattress. The scene moves from indoors to outdoors. The reference to the moon normally occurs in the fifth link in a thirty-six-piece renga. Here it is "brought up" by one link. The moon, unmodified, indicates autumn.

72. Among the people gathered to watch the squat wrestling is a poor hunter in a disheveled straw coat. The season is autumn.

73. The scene with the poor hunter is moved from some farmer's garden to the mountain. The season remains autumn.

74. Yamagishi Hanzan (1654–1726). Bashō's older sister's son.

Nozawa Ukō-ni
(Died 1722?)

Nozawa Ukō-ni's hokku began to appear in anthologies under her early name, Tome. It was in *Sarumino* (*Monkey's Raincoat*, 1691), though, that she made her name: thirteen pieces were taken in what is often described as the best of the Bashō School's anthologies. Her husband, the physician Nozawa Bonchō (died 1714), who for a while was among Bashō's most brilliant associates, edited it with Mukai Kyorai (1651–1704). Ukō took Buddhist vows in 1691, hence the conventional suffix *ni,* "nun."

When her husband decided to take Jirō to a night tea ceremony:

If my child I wouldn't let him go with you in the night snow

The light of stars was deceived: night winter shower

I blow on his chilblained hands: snowball-making

Amid the evening bell reverberating a cuckoo call

Child lost: his mother's heart the pampas grass field

Spring having let up sparrows chirp under the eaves

My body feeble, being prone to illness, I decided just combing my hair had become too much trouble and changed my appearance this spring:[75]

Both hairpins and comb things of the past: fallen camellias[76]

I invited someone along to pick young herbs:

In the spring field which grass gave me this rash?

---

75. That is, took tonsure. Why she did so while married is subject to speculation. By some accounts, she was in normal health.

76. Referring to this and the next hokku in his letter to her dated the 27th of First Month 1691, Bashō wrote: "Your two hokku truly impressed me. I see you haven't neglected [haikai since I left for Edo], and I am very happy. Of the two, the one about grass/rash makes me worry how your delicate hands and feet must be blistered; it's so vivid it conjures up an image. From the headnote to the camellia piece in Sarumino, people happily wonder what kind of beauty you are, what model of chastity you must be. I tell them, 'She is neither a beauty nor a model of chastity. She is simply a nun with a sensitive heart.' I hope you will work hard to make your heart even more sensitive."

I'd like to show someone greedy a cicada shell

> In the middle of Clothes Doubled, the nun Ukō wrote me a long letter, which had a hokku:[77]

My intent is clearly stated in cherry blossoms

---

77. This appears in *Minomushi-an Shū* (*Bagworm Hut Collection*) by Hattori Tohō.

Kaga no Chiyo-ni
(1703?–1775)

Chiyo has been compared with Bashō in fame, both while alive and after death. But, unlike Bashō, Chiyo has left us few verifiable facts about her life. As the scholar-poet Bessho Makiko put it: "Some say her husband died shortly after marriage, some that she remained unmarried; some say she had one child, some that she didn't; also, some say she was poor, some that she was well-to-do." In any case, Kagami Shikō, the greatest haikai proselytizer of the day, was the first to mention her importance. In a letter he wrote to a friend in 1716, he said: "In a place called Mattō, three li south of Kanazawa, there is a beautiful woman called Chiyo, in her seventeenth year since birth, a daughter of a tatami-framer. Toward the end of last year she happened to start hokku; a mysterious master from the start, she is now the talk of the three provinces of Echizen, Etchū, and Echigo."

Among the facts known: Chiyo took tonsure when she was fifty; her fame was great enough for someone to compile two anthologies of her work while she was alive, in 1764 and 1771; and in 1764, when a Korean embassy visited Edo, Maeda Shigemichi, the daimyo of her domain, Kaga (today's Ishikawa), asked her to add a selection of her hokku to his gifts to the embassy.

The following selection is made from the first anthology, which is arranged seasonally.

Spring

Seven grasses:[78] some grasses are exchanged with friends[79]

Dawdling on the road is part of young herb picking

If herb picking were work I wouldn't mind the coming of the dark

Seven grasses: there's too much of some, too little of some

The bush-warbler restates his song, again restates his song

The bush-warbler sings himself hoarse but the snow on Fuji[80]

---

78. The seven herbs that are collected in the field, minced, and made part of a gruel in the first seven days of First Month. There are some variations on the seven, but in an early listing they are *seri* (parsley), *nazuna* (shepherd's purse), *gogyō* (cudweed), *hakobera* (chickweed), *hotoke-no-za* (dead nettle), *suzuna* (Chinese rape), and *suzushiro* (radish). The custom harks back to the court ceremony of eating such a gruel on the first day of the Rat in the New Year.

79. Because you collect too much of some, too little of others.

80. The bush-warbler, a harbinger of spring, may warble on and on to say the spring is here, but the snow capping Mount Fuji remains.

Chiyo-ni's picture of plum branches. The hokku reads, from the right:
Saki naosu /ume no kokoro ya /toshi no / uchi
My heart like the plum reblooming before year's end

The green willow is quiet no matter where you plant it

Be it tied, be it untied, the willow in the wind

The butterfly moves her wings dreaming of what?[81]

A butterfly blows herself down with her own wind

The daybreak turns into cherry blossoms then the
    morning sun

In the blurred night I only ascertained plum blossoms[82]

I start to talk and take a second look in the blurred moon

Are they hard of hearing? I wonder: the pheasants call

From time to time the cloud loses track of the skylark

Summer

Deutzia flowers hold forth their light on the cloudy day

The sound of water returns to the water, then clapper rails[83]

---

81. Alludes to Chuang-tzu's dream in which he finds himself to be a butterfly fluttering about joyfully. Upon awakening, he can't tell whether he is Chuang-tzu in a butterfly's dream or a butterfly in Chuang-tzu's dream.

82. *Oboroyo*, "blurred night," assumes the presence of the moon. It means the same as *oborozuki*, "blurred moon." The blurring of the moon caused by the cirrostratus is regarded as poetically suggestive. Because of their strong scent, plum blossoms often became the reason for outings during the night.

83. The clapper rail's voice is a "clattering *kek-kek-kek-kek*," as Roger Peterson puts it. When clapper rails call to one another, all other sounds recede into nothing.

Chiyo-ni's self-portrait. The
writing reads mostly from left
to right, with the leftmost
four Chinese characters being a
Buddhist phrase: *Shinnyo jissō*,
"Truth is as things are."

> *Shimizu ni wa / ura mo /
> omote mo / keri / nakari*

> Clear water has neither front
> nor back

Only in the river the darkness flows: fireflies

The rice-planting song on the road though there's tomorrow too

In the morning the sky doesn't show the day's heat

Into the woods, and the woods are hot in their own way

Floating weed though a butterfly presses it down

Floating weed: does the cobweb moor it to the bank?

Waterweed flowers: what's that bird playing unwet?

Making the pine wind their own: cicada voices

Coolness: a heron's neck stretched all the way

I even forget my rouged lips at the clear water

Going along I again meet myself in the clear water

Autumn

Morning glories[84] when there are still lamps lit

The well bucket taken by morning glories, water sought[85]

Lightning:[86] on what does it leave its marks, going on?

---

84. By the lunar calendar autumn includes Sixth, Seventh, and Eighth months. As a result, the morning glory, the flowering plant of the summer in today's perception, falls in that season.

85. Chiyo's most famous hokku, which Daisetz Suzuki, in *Zen and Japanese Culture*, thinks is as important as Bashō's pond/frog hokku. However, Kōda Rohan (1867–1947), a great haikai commentator who wasn't averse to the notion of *zoku*—vulgar, common, quotidian—termed this hokku "fraudulent." More recently, Kawashima Tsuyu has said that "it reeks of *richiteki fūga*"—rationalized poetic air—"and can't be given high marks." From a translator's viewpoint, the word *morau*, here given as "sought," makes this piece untransferable into English. It is an active verb that means something between "to be given" and "to receive." The versions of Stephen D. Carter in *Traditional Japanese Poetry* and Patricia Donegan and Yoshie Ishibashi in *Chiyo-ni: Woman Haiku Master* are as unsatisfactory as that of Daisetz Suzuki in *Zen and Japanese Culture*; they use "beg" or "ask for."

86. Lightning became an indicator of autumn because of the belief that it helped rice to ripen.

The lightning must wet its skirt on the water

Seeing him off I can't take my eyes off the flower field[87]

Over the flowing water a dragonfly chases its own shadow

Paying no mind to insects chirping the night rain falls

I walk and walk yet the bright moon stays in someone's sky

Keeping the bright moon in my eyes I take a long walk

In the moonlit night a cricket comes out on a stone to chirp

Boats for the bright moon equally good, there or here

First geese fly past me leaving only their voices

Sewing clothes I drop my needle at a quail's call

Embarrassing the flowers and leaves, these long gourds

The color of water having turned red a stag calls

As if to pull together the evening dusk a stag calls

Winter

First shower:[88] a wind has passed through it without getting wet

When I became a nun:

No need to care for my hair my hands in the foot-warmer

Spilling, the plovers are picked up again by the wind

Each time the wind blows the plovers renew themselves

The first snow enough to unhinge the color of the crow

The first snow enough for a child to carry it about

---

87. *Hanano*, a field of wildflowers, is an indicator of autumn.
88. *Hatsushigure*: a light, almost airy shower that is a harbinger of the winter.

Arii Shokyū
(1714–1781)

Arii Shokyū, a village headsman's daughter, studied haikai with the samurai-turned-poet Fufū (1702–1762) in her late twenties, eloped with him, and went on to outshine her husband as a poet. Her most important work is *Akikaze no Ki* (*Record of an Autumn Wind*), an account of her journey inspired by Bashō's to the north, which he described in his celebrated "travel diary," *Oku no Hosomichi* (*A Narrow Road to the Interior*). She undertook her journey in 1771, remarkably, when she was fifty-seven. Bashō was forty-five when he took his. Though her route was different from Bashō's—she started out of Kyoto, Bashō from Edo—the two poets are thought to have covered about the same distance, of 1,000 miles, mostly on foot. Close to her destination, Matsushima, she fell ill. But she recovered and completed her journey.

What follows are excerpts from *Record of an Autumn Wind*. Asterisks indicate omitted passages.

When I first read an account called *A Narrow Road to the Interior,* I did not feel the urge right away but with time began longing for the route taken. Every year, each time spring came around, I thought of setting out with the haze. Yet old nun that I was, I was unsure of the great distance to be traversed, or else about barrier guards' permits, and as a result spent years and months to no avail. This spring, though, perhaps because some guardian deity of the road pitied me, Monk Shigen invited me along and I ended up going far beyond Ōsaka Barrier.[89] Not to mention the sky over the Capital, the grass hut I'd grown used to as my abode made me wonder "when again"[90] and I almost left dewdrops of difficult parting.

Yellow rose: though I don't say it's difficult parting[91]

---

89. *Uta-makura:* A checkpoint on the borders of Yamashiro (today's Kyoto) and Ōmi (Shiga) originally set up in 646; it was regarded as a place where you really left the Capital behind.

90. In 1167, Saigyō (1118–1189) visited Kamo Shrine before going on a pilgrimage to Shikoku. Forty-nine at the time, he felt that he might not have another chance to see his beloved shrine and composed a tanka: "Awestruck my tears fall on *shide* adornments as I wonder when again, deeply moved."

91. The original hokku, *Yamabuki ya nagori wa kuchi ni iwanedomo,* relies on a botanical pun. The shrub *yamabuki* (*Kerria japonica*) puts on yellow flowers, and yellow is sometimes called "the color of *kuchinashi*"—*kuchinashi,* cape jasmine or gardenia (*Gardenis florida*), being a shrub that also puts on yellow flowers. *Kuchinashi* literally means "mouthless," which here leads Shokyū to say *kuchi ni iwanedo.*

At Ishiyama Temple[92] we borrowed Monk Nange's[93] living quarters. When we went there to take our leave, a great many friends of ours had come from the Capital to see us off. They insisted they'd stay with us as long as our shadows remained on the lake, but we dissuaded them one way or another until the sound of waves as they turned back ceased.

*

That night we stayed in the monks' quarters at the foot of the mountain; we left near daybreak before we were able to say adequate words of thanks. The day broke and it was the first of Deutzia Month.

The wadding off we look destitute in our travel clothes

*

On the fifth, we walked on, looking at Mount Ibuki on the left. The storm affected me, and though it was Deutzia Month, it was cold. It must be at a time like this that deutzia flowers blooming on a hedge are mistaken for something else.[94]

We went farther and reached a place that they said was where the building for Fuwa Barrier[95] used to be. Now there were not even "dilapidated wooden eaves,"[96] only a patch of stone pavement remaining. Far above it, we saw straw houses here and there.

The eaves tilt toward deutzia flowers at Fuwa Barrier

In the middle of a field there was a lone tree called the Lookout Pine. It was the marker, we were told, of the robber something or other of long ago. Although it was a name linked to terrible crimes, that it was something ancient made it appear elegant.

We crossed the large rivers called Okoshi and Sunomata.

---

92. A famous temple located at the southern end of Lake Biwa, it enshrines the most admired statue of Kwannon, the feminine manifestation of Bodhisattva Avalokitesvara, and houses a room where Murasaki Shikibu is reputed to have written *The Tale of Genji*. The view from there in autumn is counted among the Eight Spectacles of Ōmi. Ishiyama, today's Ōtsu City, is an uta-makura.

93. The second half of *Record of an Autumn Wind* is an anthology of hokku Shokyū collected in relation to her journey. Nange's hokku: "Not the snow but evening haze buries the lake."

94. As, for example, snow.

95. One of the Three Famous Barriers: uta-makura. An ancient stronghold (*fuwa* means "indestructible"), it was abolished as early as 789.

96. Fujiwara no Yoshitsune (1169–1206) has a tanka: "The uninhabited Fuwa barrier-house, its wooden eaves dilapidated, retains only autumn winds."

*

We visited the Chiyokura.[97] For generations the heads of this house had carried forward poetic sentiments. Long ago the venerable Bashō once rested his walking stick here and left a casket that was part of his traveling accoutrements.[98] We took a look. It wasn't an ordinary kind of casket but more like a letter box, I thought. Unlike Urashima's jeweled letter box,[99] when opened, it had many old letters and things and made me think of the past.

*

On the fifteenth we left his place. The road immediately became steeper than the mountain path yesterday. Trees grew so thick in the depths of the mountains that we could not even see the sky. As we made our way between boulders that rose terrifyingly above us, worms called leeches dropped from treetops and bit into our feet to suck our blood. The annoyance was indescribable. When we were struggling like that, clouds gathered darkly and it started to pour. I felt I couldn't go another step, but there was no inn we could stay at. All I could do was cling to our guide's sleeve and push on, both rain and tears falling, until we came to Kanzawa, where we lodged.

*

We passed the Kiku River [on the eighteenth] and arrived at the Ōi River.[100] The water had risen because of the recent rain and ferrying had been suspended, resuming just today, we were told, to our relief. So we asked to be ferried. They put us on an oddly made board, and many people together carried it down into the river. Waves splashed over their shoulders. It was dangerous and terrifying, and I didn't feel I was alive. I kept my eyes closed, mumbling prayers, until the crossing was over. As if awakened from a dream, I turned to look. The place we had left behind was in the distance, and the people crossing looked like tiny water birds adrift in the waves. All extraordinary and novel:

Coolness turns to heat after depths shallows

---

97. A sake brewer. At the time, the master of the house was Chōra (1723–1776). His hokku: "Night by night the moon grows thinner with a stag's calls."

98. Chōra's father, Chōha (1677–1741), was given Bashō's casket as a gift by one of Bashō's friends.

99. The fisherman in the Urashima legend marries the Sea God's daughter, spends three happy years, and returns to his village with a box she gives him as a gift. He finds his village completely changed. Lost and confused, he opens the box, though the princess had told him never to do so. A puff of smoke comes out of it and turns him into an old man.

100. The Tokugawa government infamously maintained a ban on the construction of bridges over major rivers for purposes of defense. At such places "river-crossing men" (*kawagoshi ninsoku*) were stationed to carry travelers and their luggage, either on their shoulders or on carrying boards. The Ōi River was regarded as the most difficult spot to cross along Japan's main artery at the time, the Tōkaidō Road.

*

Over the Narrow Road of Ivy of the past young leaves luxuriated, and we could hardly tell it was there. We went farther to visit Saioku Temple, where Monk Sōchō[101] used to live. In the depths of a summer mountain the incense smoke from the Buddhist altar drifted fragrantly over the leaves of the trees and grass outside. In a pond made by damming a valley stream, the Moon-Spitting Peak cast its cool shadow.

His grave was under some conifers, and the scent of the flowers of its moss evoked the past. Some of the late-blooming cherry blossoms remained. I was reluctant to leave.

For the water shelf I pick summer flowers of a past spring[102]

We went as far as the station called Ejiri and stayed at an inn.

*

On the twentieth, as we passed Kiyomi Barrier,[103] I saw waves rolling over the rocks and couldn't help marveling how apt was the description in an old writing that they looked as if dressed in white silk robes. The view was so fine that I never tired of looking at it.

We came out on Tago Bay.[104] The sea was calm, and Mount Fuji, which we hadn't seen clearly till then, was in full view, the air clear, without a speck of cloud, way up to its peak. With most things, the real thing tends to be inferior to a pictorial depiction, but with Mount Fuji I was amazed to wonder how anyone could reproduce it in a painting. Each time we walked on somewhat and looked, the clouds that had formed over parts of the mountain shifted in various ways. The spectacle was so fascinating and incomparable I regretted that I had to leave it behind.

At the Fuji River:

Coolness since where Fuji first came into view

Staying at an inn in Hara, I got up and went outside to see Fuji during the night as well.

---

101. The renga master Saiokuken Sōchō (1448–1532).

102. *Akadana*, here given as "water shelf," is a shelf by a Buddhist altar or a grave where the water or flowers to be offered are placed. As the haiku scholar Fukumoto Ichirō has explained to me, *gebana*, here given as "summer flowers" but referring to the late-blooming cherry blossoms mentioned in the preceding passage, are the flowers offered during the *Geango*, a period of ascetic training that begins on the 16th of Fourth Month and ends on the 15th of Seventh Month during which the training monk confines himself in a single room and does not go out.

103. Uta-makura. It is said to have been located where the gate of Kiyomi Temple is.

104. Uta-makura. Famous for the tanka in the *Hyakunin Isshu* of Yamabe no Akahito: "On Tago Bay I go out and look: on the white-cloth Fuji peak the snow is falling."

On the twenty-second, in the castle town of Odawara, we inquired about a person named Bakuyu but were told he'd passed away during the previous winter. I felt there was nothing one could do with the fleeting way of the world. His son, along with his wife, graciously asked us to stay, so we did, overnight, and composed commemorative verse.

On the twenty-third we reached Ōiso, where we visited the Hut of the Snipe-Rising Marsh.[105] But the master wasn't home. Disappointed, I wrote down the following:

No snipe's call fills me with regrets: Fall of Wheat

But, as we were leaving, someone was sent to us to say the master was back home, and we turned back. We offered prayers to the statue of Priest Saigyō and visited the grave of the old gentleman Chōsui. The wind through the pines and the sound of waves striking the beach were sad for no reason, stirring sorrow even in me, an uncultivated soul.

On the twenty-fifth we paid our respects to the Fujiwara Training Ground and Enoshima, where, the sun setting, we slept with the beach for pillow.

On the twenty-sixth, to enter Kamakura we were walking along Shichiri Beach, then Yui Beach, when we saw that waves rolling in from the offing were as black as if ink had been poured into them. When we asked why, we were told that it was schools of bonito coming inshore.

Through the white waves snakily black: first bonito

*

We paid our respects to Tsurugaoka Hachiman Shrine and made a round of the five main temples, offering prayers at each. We lodged in a house in Under-the-Snow. Mine wasn't like the usual travel sleep; as I thought of the past at Valley-of-Moonlight,[106] the sound of the bell at Gokuraku Temple left a particularly strong impression.

Above deutzia flowers the bell sounds lucid Under-the-Snow

*

---

105. Saigyō wrote a tanka: "Even to me, an uncultivated soul, sadness is felt when snipes fly up from a marsh in the autumn evening." In reference to the poem, Ōyodo Michikaze (1639–1707) built a hut and gave it this name, turning it into a haikai-training place.
106. See p. 123 of the nun Abutsu's account.

On the first day of Seedling Month, at the behest of the old gentleman Ryōta,[107] we roamed the Sumida River by boat. I recollected the ancient tale of the Middle Captain[108] and couldn't help marveling how far we'd come.[109] We offered prayers at the grave of Umewaka-maru:[110]

Time streamers rise the Plum Temple affects us more[111]

   *

On the fifth we were invited to the Bashō Hut that Ryōta had rebuilt in Fukagawa:

Re-thatched the present becomes the past irises[112]

   *

Past the places called Gyōtoku and Kamagaya, the road opened onto a large plain. With no trees to stop under, we walked for about two li and came upon a village called Shirai, where there was a house selling water. Across from the house were leafy growths of trees on Mount Tsukuba, which looked invitingly cool. Back on the field, grasses grew taller than humans. A number of wild horses lived there. Horses would be startled by us humans and run; we would be startled by horses and try to escape. Wondering what sort of strange thing might be lurking there, I was fearful.

By the time we reached Kioroshi, the sun had set. From there we took a boat, but after rowing out about four li, we turned back because of an unfavorable wind. From

---

107. Ōshima Ryōta (1718–1787). His hokku in the anthology—"In May rains one night I secretly await the moon," which uses the usual pun on matsu, "pine" and "wait"—moved a Chinese stationed in Nagasaki named Cheng Jiannan to translate it into a five-character, four-line kanshi: "Summer long my grass hut is quiet; / every evening I sleep listening to the rain. / Before I know it, the moon's up, shining, / casting the shadow of the pine in the garden." Ryōta was very proud to learn this and promptly made a hokku: "In China a single unseen friend: first haze."

108. Ariwara no Narihira (825–880), the presumed author and protagonist of Tales of Ise.

109. In Tales of Ise, when Narihira reaches the Sumida River in his journey away from Kyoto and sees miyakodori, "Capital birds," he makes a tanka: "If your name is right, let me now ask, Capital birds: Is the person I love all right or not?" The miyakodori is the oystercatcher.

110. A legendary boy who was kidnapped and died of illness by the Sumida River. The Nō play Sumidagawa (The Sumida River) and other stories derive from the legend. The temple name Mokubo is based on an ideographic pun on part of his name, Ume, "plum."

111. On the Boys' Festival, on the fifth of Fifth Month, koi-nobori, "carp streamers," are hoisted into the sky.

112. This hokku was used to start a celebratory hyakuin, a 100-unit renga sequence. This shows the honor and respect accorded to her by her haikai friends.

the stern came a continuous rumbling as if an oxcart were being pulled out, and I could not even doze. Although it was a short night, I felt as if I'd lived a thousand years. As day began to break, I took a look and found that it wasn't anything like a cart but the boatman snoring. A person next to him shook him awake and said, "Put the boat out now."

The boatman said, "You're all so noisy. It's best to leave the boat up to the wind." He yawned, stretched his legs, and raised his arms. It seemed his height was greater than the length of the boat.

I looked upon the river, and its expanse was larger than two Yodo Rivers[113] put together. On the right, bulrushes, reeds, and rushes luxuriated; on the left was a scattering of houses. I asked the name of the river, and the boatman replied, "It's called the Toné River, ma'am, but also called the Bandō Tarō." He had a booming voice.

The reedbird's voice too fits the Bandō Tarō

On the twenty-second the wind still had not turned, and the boat didn't go that far, only reaching the bay of Katori around midnight. I had a sleepless night in the moonlight slanting in through the roof matting, got up as clouds began to appear in the east, and paid my respects to the deity.

We lodged in a place named Nojiri. Ours was a dilapidated house, but compared with a fragile small boat, it provided a comfortable place to sleep. On the twenty-third we reached Chōshi. As the tide rose up the river, it formed a stream, creating a spectacle you don't see in normal inlets.

In the rising tide in Chōshi seaweed runs swiftly

We visited the boat owner and were entertained as if we were old friends, which made me forget the discomfort of boat travel and the heat of the roads.

On the twenty-fifth we left Chōshi and lodged in Omigawa.

*

On the fourth [of Waterless Month] we crossed the border into Ōshū[114] and arrived at a castle town called Tanakura. For more than thirty days straight the sun had kept shining, the heat becoming more and more intense and painful. I hardly noted what was happening along the road, not paying attention to things to see. We sought an inn in early evening. What appeared to be its proprietor was an old woman. There were two other women, one around twenty, the other fourteen or fifteen.

---

113. The Yodo is the largest river in Kansai.

114. The borders of today's Fukushima and Ibaraki. The area north of there was generally called Ōshū, "The Interior Province."

Our room had a verandah, and sweet-rush placed in a mortar-shaped container emitted fragrance. In a thicket a narrow stream was visible, which gave a cool touch to the scene. When the evening moon set, fireflies flitted to and fro exquisitely. With a pleasant breeze coming in the open sliding doors, I was sitting there, looking out, when out of nowhere a man with a long sword on his hip suddenly crawled out of the garden and came to the other end of the verandah.

"What's this! Has a white wave[115] risen from that stream?"

I was terrified, and couldn't move. Then I sensed a woman quietly open a door on this side and slip out. She approached the man along the verandah.

"You keep saying that like a small boat pushing through reeds, you face too many obstacles to cross over here, but I fear some other beach offers you shelter," the woman said, sobbing resentfully. The man didn't speak for a while.

"Don't blame me so," he said. "The mosquito bites I got some nights back became terribly infected and painful and I didn't feel well enough to come here."

"The damned cat dropped the fish from the basket! Get the light!" the old woman growled in the kitchen.

The young woman stiffened and went inside, saying as if to herself, "I couldn't stand the heat. I had to get out the back door."

The man hastily disappeared into the night. So affairs of the heart are the same even at the eastern end of the land, I thought to myself, feeling gentle pity for the two.

*

On the twelfth we prostrated ourselves before the guardian deity of the road in Kasashima. We went to look at Middle Captain Sanekata's grave[116] farther behind the shrine. It was in a patch of pampas grass, a moss-draped marker. Winds from the peak and voices of cicadas naturally stirred pity in me. Preparing to leave, I imagined what it must have been like to leave one's remains in a desolate mountain like this, when travel always makes you melancholy and you long to be back in the Capital. As I thought of the ancient past, I couldn't help shedding tears. I tied some grass blades together as a farewell gift before moving on.

We went out to Iwanuma and saw the Two-Trunk Pine of Takekuma, of which it has been said "three trees."[117]

---

115. A robber, in reference to Chinese history.

116. Because of his ill-tempered behavior at the court, Middle Captain of the Inner Palace Guards Fujiwara no Sanetaka (died 998) was ordered by Emperor Ichijō (980–1011) to go to Mutsu, the outermost province, as governor, so that he might "see some poetic places." Though he was actually in his governor's post for three years before his death, legend has it that he fell off his horse and died on his way to his post because he didn't bother to dismount when he passed by a shrine for the guardian deity of the road mentioned in the preceding sentence.

117. Alludes to a tanka by Tachibana no Suemichi (died 1060): "The Takekuma Pine has two trunks; should a City person ask, 'How is it?' I'd reply, 'I've seen it.'" The poem relies on a pun: miki, "I've seen it," also means "three trunks" or "three trees."

Winds fragrant: which pine loves as husband and wife?[118]

We went to see a physician named Kyūsui and arrived in Sendai close to sunset. Now that the place riveting my heart[119] was almost within view, I was incomparably happy. Master Furukuni,[120] with whom I'd promised to meet, had arrived some time back, so we visited him at his inn, where we took off our hats and talked about recent poetic things. He had parted with us near Narumi, in Owari Province, and gone on ahead.

Around midnight I began to feel ill. Still, I talked poetry with anyone who came to visit. Though I could give only a string of brief responses to their kind words, it helped distract me from the pain of the illness. As days passed, though, the illness worsened, and just sitting up or getting up became painful. Even without that sort of thing, I was too old to be certain of myself. How sad it was to think I had plodded on to come to a remote place three hundred li away, yet could not go further! That I should have fallen ill when Matsushima was just one day away! Has the guardian deity of the road abandoned me, I wondered with some bitterness. Awake or dreaming, I kept thinking, "Who's waiting for Matsushima,"[121] unable to forget for a second, depressed that I might fade like dew on the grass by the road.

*

The Spirit Festival[122] time came. Even in the Capital it's a melancholy time. Ill on a journey, I sadly recalled the Scribe Tetsu's[123] verse saying, "Suppose I were dead, a spirit, I'd go back to my hometown."[124] For some reason I gazed toward the sky in the west.

---

118. The original: *Kaze kaoru matsu ya izure o sōfuren. Sōfuren* is the title of a Gagaku piece. Originally it meant, in Chinese, "The prime minister's lotus," but through a Japanized pronunciation it was taken to mean "Love between husband and wife." To paraphrase, this hokku seems to say, "The Two-Pine is playing 'Sōfuren' in the fragrant winds. I wonder which of the two trunks is the wife?"
119. Matsushima, the area in and around Matsushima Bay, Miyagi, which has about 260 pine-covered islets.
120. Better known as Ōtomo Ōemaru (1722–1805). He ran a successful business of postal runners (*hikyaku*) in Osaka, serving the three cities of Osaka, Kyoto, and Edo. Through his wealth, generosity, and wide range of associations, he became influential. His freewheeling style is representative of nonprofessional, nonsectarian haikai categorized as *yūhai.* Example: "Heaven and earth relaxing their hearts Deutzia Month comes." His travel diary, *Agata no Mitsuki Yotsuki (Three Months Four Months in Outlying Regions)*, describes his 180-day travels covering more or less the same provinces that Shokyū visited in hers. He undertook the six-month journey when he was eighty years old.
121. Alludes to Bashō's hokku: "Mornings and evenings who's waiting for Matsushima unable to forget?"
122. *Tama-matsuri, Urabon.* Usually held on the twentieth of Seventh Month.
123. The monk-poet Shōtetsu (1381–1459). Called Tetsu Shoki because he was a scribe at Tōfuku Temple.
124. "Well, well, suppose I were dead, a spirit, I'd go back to my hometown this evening."

For whom are you telling the future, tall lantern

From the twentieth onward, I continued to feel better, so decided to leave for the Narrow Road to the Interior.[125] My physician also gave me permission. On the twenty-fifth, I was helped into a palanquin made of woven bamboo and went over to Matsushima. Crossing the bridge built over the sea and arriving on the shore of Ojima, I realized that the view indeed included a thousand isles, far more than my eyes could take in. I was glad that I had lived long enough in this transient world, and for one day forgot the worries of all those years and months and the anxieties of the travels over such a great distance.

In time we put up at a thatched hut nearby. Even during the moonless evening I couldn't just sit idly. I pushed the window open and took in a sweeping view. Fishermen's bonfires were now visible, now not, in the spaces between distant isles, uncertain as to where to go. The moon for which I waited without falling asleep was clear when it appeared, casting shadows of pines growing on the isles on the surface of the sea, adding a poetic touch.

In Matsushima a thousand isles differ in the light of the moon

—Shigen

Sails too are counted in the mist among a thousand pine isles

As soon as the day broke, we paid our respects to Zuigan Temple[126] and from there climbed up to the Kannon of Wealth. The view below from the garden was another matter altogether.

Islands upon islands: beyond the pines migrating birds

On our way to Shiogama by boat, we felt, for about three li, as though we were in a painting; it was all exquisite.

Dew scattering on Hedge Island the waves bloom

We lodged on Chiga Bay. Now there were no fishermen making salt any longer; there were playgirls, instead. Late at night their singing voices touched me gently.

---

125. According to Bashō's companion, Kawai Sora (1649–1710), the "road" was within the premises of a peasant's house and along a paddy ridge.

126. Also called Matsushima-dera. Founded in 838 by Great Teacher Jikaku (794–864), also known as Ennin, of the Tendai Sect. The Kamakura regent Hōjō Tokiyori (1227–1263) converted it to the Rinzai Sect. It is the family temple of the Date, the hereditary ruler of the Sendai domain.

To wet our sleeves? Voices of insects living in seaweed

*

By the first of Eighth Month I felt normal getting up and lying down. Perhaps as a result, the voices of geese telling of the cold of night stirred strong yearnings for the Capital. On the fifth of Leaf Month, we parted with Master Furukuni and walked out of his inn. The reluctance to part we felt was more intense than that we'd felt leaving the Capital.

We crossed the Reputation River.[127] Taking the route we'd come, we said farewell to those who'd been kind to us. A gentleman named Kaisha,[128] in Koori, said he'd been waiting for us and entertained us, so we stayed in his house overnight. The bush clover blooming in his garden recalled the evening we'd waded into the plain.

Tell me how to sleep: we'd lodge in bush clover

We wanted to go to the Pine Grove of Kudzu but, told that the road would be bad because of yesterday's rain, ended up not going. We lodged for three days with Don-mei,[129] in Fukushima, who consoled us by asking us to stay. Uncertain days passed.

On the twelfth we came out at Shirakawa Barrier.[130] Both hills and fields were all colored; treetops, reflected in the river, made it look as though dyed Chinese-crimson, and I was reminded of the poem "Though I saw the Capital still in green leaves, fallen crimson leaves carpet [Shirakawa Barrier]."[131]

Frazzled since when, my hat: an autumn wind

There is a deity between Shirakawa and Shirasaka called Border Deity. It is said to represent the border between Michinoku and Shimotsuke. The spot where the Holy Man Saigyō made the poem saying, "clear water flowed,"[132] is by the water flowing between paddies. There are many willows along the stream.

---

127. *Natori-gawa*: uta-makura. Mibu no Tadamine (active around 900) has a tanka on love in *Kokinshū* (no. 628): "In Michinoku there's a Reputation River, they say, but it's painful to gain reputation where there's none."

128. His hokku: "'Do I smell?' says a willow falling upon my face."

129. His hokku: "Cuckoo, I've fallen asleep with the brush tip in my mouth." The suggestion is that the cuckoo, whose call is supposed to inspire a poem, didn't show up for so long that the poet fell asleep with his brush ready.

130. Uta-makura: one of the most important barriers or checkpoints in the north during the Heian Period. It was in today's Shirakawa City, Fukushima.

131. A tanka of the warrior-poet Minamoto no Yorimasa (1104–1180) included in the *Senzaishū* (no. 365): *Miyako ni wa mada aoba nite mishika domo momiji chirishiku Shi-rakawa no Seki.*

132. Saigyō has a tanka: "In willow shade on the roadside where clear water flowed, I stopped, saying, 'Just for a while'" (*Shin-Kokinshū*, poem 262).

Lured by the water being drained willows scatter

We lodged in a place called Ashino, near the willows.

*

We climbed Mount Nikkō and lodged in the monks' quarters called Ōshō'in. You could almost touch the clear moon close to the rim of the mountain. The multitude of flowers in the garden and the leaves on the mountains appeared to be vying in color, making me realize how things are at their affecting best during the night.

Waiting in the evening the light fills the latticed room

*

Down the mountain, in a place called Hoshina, I was attracted to a house that, though decrepit, had many cockscombs blooming close to its eaves, and sought lodging there. Just as it had appeared, once inside, we saw no tatami laid out but only a scattering of coarse mats on a floor of latticed bamboo. I was wondering how we could sleep in a place like that, when a woman who appeared to be the mistress of the house accompanied us to a room further inside where two tatami were laid.

"This is our Buddhist altar room," she said. "Recently I lost my most beloved child, who had just turned three, and today is the seventh day. I assume you're priests going to pay your respects to Zenkō Temple.[133] Please hold a memorial service for my dead child's salvation." We thought it was some karma to hear such a pitiful story, and prayed for the child, turning our rosaries over and over.

*

Now we arrived at Zenkō Temple. By then I easily might have died and gone "from darkness to a dark path."[134] But I'd managed to stay alive, by the Buddha's grace. I had no words to express my gratitude. We made a round of deep, dark places way below the Main Hall, praying. It was called the Six-Path Round, I was told. Faith deepening, I forgot all the troublesome affairs of the world.

---

133. Famous Buddhist temple of the city of Nagano. "Established in 670 . . . it is dedicated to Amida, Kwannon and Daiseishi, whose statues according to legend were miraculously carried there from Korea in the 7th century. The town of Nagano is often called Zenkōji, on account of this temple," according to E. Papinot in his *Historical and Geographical Dictionary of Japan*, originally published in 1910. Hoshina is only a few miles away from the temple.
134. Alludes to Izumi Shikibu's poem on p. 73.

That night we confined ourselves to the Main Hall, offering prayers all night. About the hour of the Tiger, sutra chanting started. About the time eastern clouds gathered, the doors to the sanctuary opened. With the lanterns reflecting on the brocaded curtains, the holy lights shone so brightly I almost thought the twenty-five bodhisattvas were descending to welcome me to Nirvana. That night for once I was able to forget the Capital as I single-mindedly prayed for my afterlife.

My mind clearing limpid with the moon moving west

Being so old, I could not possibly hope to come here again; so, finding it hard to leave the place, we stayed in the Main Hall for two nights.

*

I fell off my horse at a place called Nakakubo.

A bagworm, I fell off yes but on wildflowers

*

On the fourth [of Ninth Month] we left the inn during the night and rested in Moriyama. When I saw "all the underleaves [that had] turned color,"[135] I recalled how we'd gotten wet from the drips off young leaves. Everything I saw or heard soothed me, making me feel that any sufferings from illness, the fatigue on the road, and all the other things that had happened to me had been a dream.

Past Seventh Hour, we arrived at Ishiyama and untied our *zuta* bags in the living quarters of Seson'in. Perhaps because all the virtuous men had prayed for me morning and evening, I was paying my respects here for the second time without mishap, the shabby old self that I was, I thought, all because of the blessings of the Buddha's Great Compassion and Great Sorrow. We talked, teary or laughing, until evening; then we climbed up to the Main Hall and recited a sutra in thanks that all our wishes had been fulfilled.[136]

Then we went to the Moon-Viewing Hut. The sky was clear with an evening moon. Wondering if the wind was in tune with the Rhythm, we stayed there for sometime.

Soughing soughing bulrush sound in the Biwa sea

---

135. Ki no Tsurayuki (892?–945?) has a poem "Both white dew and showers having leaked through, all the underleaves have turned color."

136. Monk Nange made a celebratory hokku: "Straw coats and hats untied we celebrate with leafed rice-cakes."

Taniguchi Den-jo
(Died 1779)

Den-jo was a well-known haikai judge, along with her husband, Rōsen (1699–1782), and their adopted son, Keikō. In 1789, Keikō compiled an anthology of his adoptive parents' writings, *Haikai Umiyama* (*Haikai: Sea and Mountain*), which includes fifty-five haibun by Den-jo—the largest haibun collection by a woman known so far. Translated below is a small selection. It ends with the afterword Den-jo wrote to *Tamamo Shū*, an anthology of 117 women's hokku compiled in 1774 by Yosa Buson (1716–1783). I am grateful to the poet Bessho Makiko for introducing me to Den-jo's writings.

The Pillow

In spring when the haze spreads and induces sleepiness, your lower arm is too high for a pillow if you raise it and too low if you lay it down. A pillow made of a bundle of silk tied together is likely to appear soiled in your dream. Such were the uncomfortable thoughts I was having, when Master Lotus gave me a beautifully lacquered pillow made of wood[137] as a New Year's gift. I pulled it close to me as a well-devised companion:

> The moment I fall asleep I bake some millet cakes

The Happiness of Being Childless[138]

In our society we treat children as treasures. I won't talk about the earlier days because that might simply bore you. In more recent times, though, except for those who are from an old family blessed with genealogical distinction from generation to generation, those who, with luck, have managed to save a great deal of money, and those who are able to provide themselves with the three necessities of life—clothing, food, and housing—it should be happiest to be childless.

When you think of it, if poor people didn't have children, you'd have a shortage of women and men you could employ as servants, so you can't really be one-sided about this. If there weren't people who turn their children into money, there'd also be a shortage of bushes where young bachelors can dump their *klesa*.[139]

In any case, I haven't been blessed with much luck since my youth, spending years

---

137. Because of their elaborate hairdos, commoners in those days, both male and female, often used wooden pillows.

138. As Bessho points out, during the Edo period a man could divorce his wife if she failed to produce a child within three years of marriage.

139. Buddhist term for "moral depravity; in particular the 'three fires' of hatred, lust and illusion which must be eliminated on the Path" (Christmas Humphreys, *A Popular Dictionary of Buddhism* [Citadel Press, 1963]).

and months barely afloat or else sunk, thinking that my only good luck in my lifetime has been not having a child. If someone says to me, "Well, then, you don't know what fine feelings are,"[140] I'll simply cover my ears with my hands and watch these flowers:

Kerria rose: in the continuing good weather my flowery heart[141]

The One Lost in the Darkness

There's something that troubles my mind, and I ponder the matter unable to keep my eyes shut throughout the night. In this world, because of the various ways we are, our thoughts may move from the darkness on account of children to the darkness of the passage of love, but we are lost in the darkness all the same.[142] I have no children and because I'm clumsy I haven't known the heart of being in love. When it comes to learning, I'm even more in the dark because I'm short of talent. Be that as it may, in this melancholy world you can't escape the darkness. When I think of my past and future, for no reason I become sad and the tears trickle down to my pillow. The rain falls hard. This, too, is the darkness of Seedling Month.

Mosquito net hanging, apart a lamp: that too is darkness

Sometime in the evening not just one but two insects that looked like butterflies got in the lamp's fire and died. Perhaps they, too, were lost in the passage of love. Not knowing what else to do, "May you play with dew on the same lotus in the afterworld," I prayed and, removing them, placed them elsewhere.

A Fire Close By

A fire is said to occur when a thriving city becomes ill. From winter to the three spring months things were in turmoil and few people saw the coloring of fields and mountains. Meanwhile, this year government edicts being particularly stern,

---

140. Alludes to Section 142 of *Tsurezuregusa (Essays in Idleness)*, by Yoshida Kenkō (1283–1351?), which begins: "Even someone who looks heartless sometimes says something nice. A rough warrior who looked terrifying asked a man who happened by, 'Do you have children?' The man replied, 'No, I don't have any,' and the warrior said, 'Well, then, you must not know what fine feelings are. Your heart must not know compassion, and that terrifies me. Only by having children do you learn what fine feelings are.'"

141. *Yamabuki*, "Kerria rose" (*Kerria japonica*), is a flowering bush. Because of the poem of Prince Kaneakira (914–987) included in the *Go-Shūishū* (no. 1154), *Nanae yae hana wa sakedomo yamabuki no mi no hitotsu dani naki zo ayashiki*, "Sevenfold, eightfold, the Kerria rose blooms but mysteriously does not bear a single fruit," the plant is automatically associated with "not bearing a single fruit."

142. See Izumi's tanka "From darkness to a dark path," on p. 73.

it was all quiet as we watched cherry flowers as carpeting snow, then eyed deutzia flowers as beautiful snow. "So you've managed to hear the cuckoo; I envy you," so said close friends among us to one another.

It must have been in the early afternoon on the ninth day of the month.[143] The Fire Boy rose and stepped out. Because the wind was a southerly and fierce, an abundance of what looked like blacksmith's sparks came flying toward where I live. The racket made in trying to fend them off was so terrifying that I can hardly describe it. I wrapped what little I have in a cloth, ready to run out. But Keikō's daughter, who is two years old, lay in bed, utterly untroubled, occasionally yawping, a pitiful sight. My Pekingese danced around our feet, getting in our way, as we ran hither and thither. Near the eaves the female and male sparrows kept coming and going to bring food for the chicks they were raising in the honey locust. If the burning reached them, they'd go up in a puff of smoke along with the tree, I thought. All these things presented a picture of the confusion that is our world. Someone looking at me must have thought the same thing.

The wind changed to a westerly, so this time we had a narrow escape. But the wind kept blowing on and on, never allowing peace of mind.

In rain clouds the cuckoo must long for the sky

Ink-Stone Box

Among the three kinds of beneficial friend,[144] the one who gives me things is Tairi near Tomigaoka. Previously, he'd given me something that made me happy, but this time not only was it a furnishing I'd thought about and wanted to have for some time, but also its lacquering was done in the old style, with summer insects flitting elegantly over irises. Placed near the window where I commune with friends of the world I have yet to see, they make me of think of the balls that glow during the night.[145] Truly, to my eyes, they are like an interval of sunshine during the May rains. To express my gratitude though I can only convey one hundredth of what I feel:

Study hard, do you say? This ink-stone box of fireflies[146]

---

143. Deutzia Month or Fourth Month.

144. Alludes to Section 117 of *Tsurezuregusa*: "There are three kinds of good friend: (1) a friend who gives you things; (2) a physician; (3) a friend who is wise."

145. Floating phosphorescent balls were believed to be human souls; so were fireflies, as in Izumi's tanka, "Brooding," p. 77.

146. Alludes to the Chinese legend about Che Yin: "His family was often too poor to buy oil for lamps, and so in the summer months he would fill a gauze bag with several dozen fireflies and use it to light his books, thus continuing his studies far into the night" (Burton Watson, trans., *Meng Ch'iu: Famous Episodes from Chinese History and Legend* [Kodansha International, 1979], 120). The Japanese lyrics for *Auld Lang Syne* incorporate this story and the story about Sun Kang, who used snow for the same purpose.

The Pekinese I Raised

The Pekingese I raised with my own hands had glossy hair like black velvet. Built like a work of art, she never left the hem of my kimono as I walked about doing things. If I went out, she would lay her ears back, droop her tail, and look pensive. If I came home late at night and rapped on the door of my hut, she would run to welcome me before everyone else, overjoyed. I have no child but came to understand the sentiment "Longing for you, your infant child waits at the gate." In summers she would sleep inside my mosquito net; in winters, under my coverlet. Thus we were never really separated. And ten years quickly passed.

Today she suddenly fell ill. She seemed to die, but revived, three times. Then her soul was gone somewhere. Hoping she might come back to me once again, I wrapped her in silk tonight, so I might take her to a funeral in the field early in the morning:

To my eyes, too, the night and the morrow: the fall of dew

Chiyo and Utagawa: Two Women

Chiyo, of Kaga,[147] decided in her youth to follow fūga rather than the Wifely Way. Now she has become a nun named Soen, I hear, and is no longer unfamiliar with her afterlife. I admire that. Meanwhile, Utagawa,[148] of Mikuni,[149] being a river bamboo, plays with fūryū on her own bay, waiting to become the boat, the white elephant,[150] even while helping people of this melancholy world soothe their klesa. Shall I praise the former's void or shall I praise the latter's substance?

Shine, illuminate, moons of Kaga and Echizen, for two nights

Someone who acquired and mounted a decorative sheet with the two poets' hokku asked me to write something in praise of them. That is what I have done.

---

147. Kaga no Chiyo-ni. See pp. 166–170.

148. Utagawa, "Song River," is the *nom de guerre* of a prostitute famed for her haikai. Her personal name was Gin; her family name is unknown. When she became a nun, she assumed the name Myōshun. She was born in 1717 and died in 1776. Here are three of her hokku, courtesy of Bessho Makiko: *Okusoko no shirenu samusa ya umi no oto*, "Depthlessly, bottomlessly cold: the sound of the sea"; *Hitosuji wa yanagi ni omoshi takatsuburi*, "For one strand the snail's too heavy for the willow"; *Mushiboshi ya koishiki fumi no tamoto yori*, "Summer airing: a loved one's letter out of a sleeve." Members of the gay quarters figured as haikai as well as tanka poets throughout the Edo period. An unusual collection in this regard is *Momohagaki*, compiled in 1826 to commemorate the 100th anniversary of the death of the Yoshiwara prostitute Tamagiku, who died at age twenty-five, as a result of excessive drinking.

149. Of Echizen (today's Fukui), famed for its porcelain.

150. On which the Bodhisattva Samantabhadra, the All-Compassionate One of Perfect Activity, rides.

In Praise of Tobacco

There are a great variety of things people in this world have fun with, but many are beyond our reach. Among such things, though, tobacco is the one pleasure both the poorest men and the poorest women can enjoy as they please. In spring, you regard the smoke as a gossamer-like haze; in summer, it may rise and turn itself into a cloud peak. In autumn, it's equal to a torn fragment of cloud; in winter, it's smoke rising from a charcoal kiln away from a fire tub. Thus, there's nothing amiss about it in each of the four seasons.

Or, when your friend prepares to leave, you can take out what's called "holding-him-by-the-sleeve tobacco" to keep his affection a while longer. Truly, though I'm not in a cove where fishermen live, the smoke grass moves the tides in and out.[151]

Now, I have a friend who had cut herself off from this for years, but who, in place of something else, came back to this poetic intermediary. I was so happy that she did:

Get this: chrysanthemums, cherry, and new tobacco

Joking with Shishimin[152]

About the time the winds coming over bush clover began to chill me, I was padding clothes with cotton, working with litter all around me, when Shishimin, who happened by, put me down with a laugh, saying, "Leave things like that to someone else. You aren't good at it, you know." So I said to him playfully, "Don't you think it, sir? When General Big Cold and Adjutant General Little Cold[153] wearing ice swords attack you with armies of hailstones and cold showers from front and rear, their white banners of snow flapping in the cold wind, how do you propose to defend yourself if you don't have a single layer of plated armor?"

"Pad them"—so the crickets tell us urgently

Just a Wall Between Us

The old man Chikkan, though a good friend of mine in flower and moon for a long time, seldom had a leisurely talk with me because he lived beyond a river, beyond a

---

151. "Though I'm not," etc., forms a tanka in the original. The reference is to salt making on the beach, which entailed the burning of seaweeds.

152. "Lion Asleep." Another nom de plume of Den-jo's adopted son, Keikō. Keikō means "Chicken Mouth," and it is a direct reference to the ancient Chinese proverb "You may become a chicken's mouth but not a bull's arse."

153. *Daikan*, "big cold," refers to the middle of Twelfth Month, and *shōkan*, "little cold," to the early part of the same month.

bank. At some point this year, though, he sought out housing just one wall beyond me and started living there. I was so happy that I joked about Mino and Ōmi:

From a single pot we eat, friend, night's clams[154]

The Anxieties of Seeking a House

The house where we lived until last year used to worry us; its eaves leaning, it might have collapsed any moment in the wind and rain. The owner of the house to which we then moved is a rich man. He was having a splendid structure built in the village of Negishi, with all the artistry of carpenters lavished on it, everything polished, constructed in such a way that he might enjoy every view of the flowers, the fireflies, the moon, and the snow. It was while readying himself to move into it that he said to us, "Come live in my old house. I wouldn't feel comfortable allowing someone whose whereabouts are unknown to me to lodge in it." We were more than happy to accept the offer. We hastily put things together and transferred ourselves there. It was mid–Leaf Moon. Long ago a woman sold her house,[155] but I merely wanted a place to fend off the rain and dew:

A house bought, at Ise's back I view the moon[156]

I made this to show I'm different.

I thought we could live there as endlessly as an endless ivy. But shame on me: Its owner told us that because the village of Negishi was too far from his physician and thus inconvenient, he'd have to come back here at the start of autumn this year. There was nothing we could do about it; the place was his own. Not having a piece of land large enough to allow a gimlet to be planted, we could only be embarrassed about ourselves. We tried to find another place we could move to but couldn't find

154. Alludes to the hokku placed at the end of Bashō's account of his journey to the Interior: "A clam separates lid from flesh as autumn departs." For the complex pun of Bashō's hokku, see H. Sato, tr., *Bashō's Narrow Road: Spring & Autumn Passages* (Stone Bridge Press, 1996), 153–55.

155. Alludes to a tanka of Ise in the *Kokinshū* (no. 990), which comes with a heading: "Having sold my house, I made this poem": *Asuka-gawa fuchi ni mo aranu waga yado mo se ni kawari yuku mono nizo arikeru*, which relies on two punning words: *fuchi*, "depth" and "stipend," and *se ni*, "to shallows" and "money." One sense of the poem: "Though not like the Asuka River where depths turn into shallows, my house turns into money."

156. The punning word here is *uraya*, "back," which also means "bay hut," in reference to the place name of Ise.

one quickly. We aren't like the Great Hermit, who said he could move to any place he wanted to by loading whatever he had in his hut on just two carts;[157] nor are we like a snail, a creature who casually walks about, carrying himself and his house; nor, because we have things that follow us, are we, I said to myself, like a hermit crab, who's casual about his lodgings. With sweat on our faces:

What to do: the residents change like dew on the grass[158]

Afterword to Tamamo Shū[159]

Our Under-the-Sun is a nation of waka, and you can't really count, they say, the number of women poetic saints who have moved Heaven and Earth and touched Demons and Deities.[160] There are also numberless people who, picking up the outer leaves of their thirty-one syllables and arranging the five-seven-five, do not limit themselves to the flowers only when they are in full bloom or to the moon only when it is cloudless,[161] but let their hearts walk to the fields and mountains near and far for the flowers, the snow, and the cuckoo, playing freely as they please. The person who has assembled the pieces of these people for printing to create a precedent for those who come after us is, happily, someone who aids us. He then asked me to add a few silly words of my own. I declined, but he wouldn't allow it. So I ended up preparing ink on the ink-stone and taking up my worn-out brush.

Eastern Capital
Den-jo

---

157. In his famous account of his hermitage, *Hōjōki*, Kamo no Chōmei (1153–1216) describes his hut as *hōjō* (ten feet by ten feet) and seven feet high, which can be readily taken apart, adding that he needs only two carts to carry all he has, his hut included.

158. Alludes to the hokku Bashō put at the start of his account of his journey to the Interior: *Kusa no to mo sumikawaru yo zo hina no ie*, "In my grass hut the residents change: now a dolls' house."

159. Chiyo-ni wrote the preface.

160. Alludes to the preface to the *Kokinshū*, partly quoted, p. 43.

161. Alludes to Section 137 of *Tsurezuregusa*: "How could the flower be seen only in full bloom, the moon only when it's cloudless?"

Tagami Kikusha
(1753–1826)

This poet was born to a samurai-physician in Nagato (today's Yamaguchi) and named Michi; she was married at age fifteen. When she was twenty-three, her husband died. A year later she received her haikai name, Kikusha (Chrysanthemum Hut), from a local haikai master. At twenty-eight, she set out on the first of her many long journeys, taking Buddhist tonsure at the outset of that trip. During that first trip she studied tea, calligraphy, and the koto (the seven-string variety) and in her forties learned to write kanshi. Like Chinese literati, her aim was to master the four arts of koto, go, calligraphy, and painting, though she chose tea in place of go. A born writer who was happy to try any mode of expression, Kikusha, unlike most other haikai poets, was at ease composing tanka as well. In one of her early trips she retraced backward the entire route Bashō took in his famed journey to the Interior. She eventually traversed on foot a total of 8,000 kilometers, or 5,000 miles. Kikusha's complete works of over 1,000 pages were assembled and edited by Ueno Sachiko and published in 2000. What follows is a sampler of her many and varied writings, mostly taken from *Taorigiku (Hand-Picked Chrysanthemums)*, which Kikusha assembled to mark her sixtieth year.

I was separated from my husband when young and because I had no child to inherit the house, I adopted a son of someone I knew and left the household affairs to him. Now that I had plenty of time to kill in this floating world, I thought of paying my respects to shrines and temples as I went along to meet people famed under heaven, and on the very day I thought of that, I set out on a journey all alone:

The moon for hat I hope to play under the traveling sky

Prepared to leave Kyoto to set out on a journey, I enjoyed the spring brocade of the Capital and, passing over the mountain to Shiga and about to enter the Ōmi Route, the spring colors of the lake waters[162] captured my eyes in many ways.

The end of the lake visible in a flower blizzard

I climbed [Mount Obasute][163] and was looking at the moon well into the night, but long before I had enough of it, suddenly the sky flashed and tor-

---

162. Lake Biwa.
163. Literally, "aunt (or old woman) abandonment." Famous for an episode in *Tales of Yamato* describing a young man forced to abandon his old aunt to save food, it is also known for an exquisite view of the moon. Kikusha climbed the mountain on the 11th of Sixth Month 1782.

Kikusha's painting of an orchid. The hokku reads, from right to left:

Asakaranu / ka ya oku tsuyu no / asa na yū na.
Never shallow: dew laden with scent mornings and evenings

rents of rain began to fall. The thunder and lightning were ferocious. It was an extraordinary turn of events high on a mountain surrounded by deep valleys. The hills nearby began to crumble. Fearful that I might lose my life any minute, I crawled in between the rocks I came upon and, shrinking my body, I intently prayed. Gradually, the day broke. There happened to be a man named Dengorō. He and his wife were gentle-hearted and kind. The previous evening, while engaged in farm work, he had seen me go up the mountain all alone, but for some reason things changed suddenly and there were fierce winds and rain all night. Concerned about me and unable to sleep, he decided to come to look for me. Happy to find me, he comforted me and took me to his home for further care. I was able to extend my life at the time solely because of the couple's kindness.

An old woman abandoned in a village such kindness O cuckoo

From Nakakomatsu to a place called Koide I went by horse. When we reached a wide wild plain, my pack-horse man, who looked down and out and forlorn, said, "This is an ancient battlefield where Lord Yoshiie[164] once encamped.

---

164. Minamoto no Yoshiie (1041–1108), a warrior-commander famous for his exploits in subjugating the northern tribes.

That's why it's called the Camp Field. Please make a hokku for me, ma'am."
He then pulled out a sheet of paper tucked in his wretched straw-rope belt and
inserted it into the saddlebow. I was deeply touched that he, though looking
uncultivated, wasn't what he appeared to be:[165]

Rice up to dry, such a peaceful world the Camp Field

Another year, after paying my respects to Ōbakusan,[166] which is in the village
of Uji:

Coming out of the mountain gate it's Japan a tea-picking song

Lord Tō, former Minister of the Right, gave my seven-string koto the name
Flowing Water and a tanka to go with it. I was overwhelmed with gratitude.
Around the twentieth of the same Ninth Month, he held a wind and string
gathering, inviting me to it to listen to the music. The moon was shining
brightly over his garden.

TANKA

Had I expected to see it today: autumn night's moon above the peak shrouded with
white clouds?

In Nagasaki, on the fifth [of Fifth Month 1797], I watched the boat race:[167]

KANSHI

I'd heard in this land there are Chinese influences.
On the fifth I watched dragon boats dominate the strait.

---

165. A pack-horse man asking for a poem recalls a similar episode in Bashō's account
Narrow Road to the Interior. Asama-naru, "uncultivated," is a word she also applies to her
own appearance when she is refused lodging some days later.

166. Manpuku Temple. It was founded by the Ming Zen Master Yinyuan (1592–1673)—
Ingen, in Japanese—in 1665. In architecture, language, and most other things, the temple
remained heavily Chinese. The temple was also known as Ōbakusan in reference to the
mountain where Yinyuan's Zen sect was headquartered.

167. Nagasaki, where many Chinese traders lived, had customs showing Chinese influence.
The festive boat race is one of them. Elongated boats, each manned by twenty to thirty-five youths
and carrying a large drum or a gong in the middle, race with one another. The race is said to have
started in China to express sympathy for the patriot-poet Quyuan (343–277 B.C.E.), who, in grief
and disappointment, committed suicide by throwing himself into the river.

Kikusha's painting of (perhaps) bamboo. The hokku reads, from right to left:
Soyoge soyoge / tsuki wa oboroyo / kimi ga aki
Sough, sough: the moon on a blurry night, autumn in Your Reign

Racing, crossing, they came fighting, manly, exciting.
No need to talk about Quyuan's grief a thousand years ago.

HOKKU[168]

After race boats cross the sea returns to normalcy

The following year [1802] as well, I stayed in the Muneoka family's Shōuen [Plantain-Rain-Garden]. Cared for by the couple's sincere kindness, I went on to stay another year, exchanging many poems.

---

168. Coupling a kanshi and a hokku (and sometimes a tanka) was sometimes done.

KANSHI

Upon Leaving

Traveling to the sky's end I'm always free.
Floating clouds, flowing water, thoughts never cease.
East, west, south, north, no footprints of mine,
day or night a tumbleweed left to the wind.

HOKKU

Like a kite, its string cut, I'm blown on by a cloud

RENGA

The third year of Bunsei [1820]:

A tea-cookie hailing from Seiryū [Green Willow] Village in Kambe [Deity's Door], Province of Ise,[169] even its name, "Nanking Okoshi,"[170] being extremely rare, I thought of presenting it to the lord[171] as a New Year's gift. On my way up to his residence as I brought it along:

Divine wind: Ise *okoshi* arrived from the Willow[172]

—*Kikusha*

fragrant in the green spring the color of tea[173]

—*The lord*

the *manzai* with all felicitations getting laughed at[174]

—*The lord*

---

169. Where the Grand Shrine of Ise is located. Ise Shrine is the residence of Amateraru Ōmikami, the Sun Goddess. Ise Bay is famous for the *kamikaze*, "divine wind," and *kamikaze* is a pillow word that modifies Ise.
170. A rice-based cookie with sesame, beans, nuts, peanuts, seaweed, and oil mixed in it. The word *okoshi* also means "coming from" or "arrival from," as well as "generate (a wind)"—the pun Kikusha uses in the hokku that follows.
171. Mōri Motoyoshi (1785–1843), the eleventh lord-president of the Nagato fief. He took interest in a wide variety of arts and was Kikusha's close friend.
172. The willow is the seasonal word for spring; paying respects to Ise Grand Shrine is also associated with spring.
173. Motoyoshi congratulates Kikusha and himself by noting that the cookie she has brought as a gift is good for tea. *Niou*, "fragrant," also means "clear," "beautiful."
174. The *manzai* is a New Year's performer who in semiformal attire delivers felicitations on the arrival of the New Year, perhaps with some amusing asides. In this instance, however, the performer was too focused on the felicitations part to remember to be entertaining.

saying, "You're a lovely child," I hold him by the hand[175]

—Kikusha

to whom shall I lament my secret thought?[176]

—Kikusha

treated to dinner, untimely, something I can't eat[177]

—The lord

adding to the feeling the pine conspicuous the moon this evening

—The lord

through the long night cranes exchange their feather robes[178]

—Kikusha

Eight Pieces for the Front[179]

---

175. A scene in the crowd who has gathered to watch the *manzai*. Following three links that deal with spring or the New Year, Motoyoshi shifts to a nonseasonal description.

176. The apparent innocence described in the preceding piece is taken to mean something totally different. The child may be the result of a secret love affair. If that interpretation is right, it is a "love" link—*koi*, "love," being one of the two important topics in a renga sequence. The other is the moon.

177. The "secret thought" turns out to be about something other than a love affair: A guest invited to a sumptuous dinner finds himself being served something he can't eat, because of allergy or some other personal reason, but he can't be so rude as to tell that to the hostess.

178. In classical poetry the cranes are often depicted as nestling in pine trees. Whether this is contrary to nature I have yet to find out.

179. From the way the sheet of paper for renga is folded and the way its "folds" are named, this description suggests that Kikusha and Motoyoshi meant to work out a sequence of one hundred pieces. But, from what was customary in Kikusha's days, the duo probably did not intend to go beyond the opening section of eight.

Ema Saikō
(1787–1861)

Saikō, who distinguished herself as a kanshi poet, must be counted, in one modern scholar's estimation, among the three greatest women poets Japan has produced—the other two being Princess Shikishi and Yosano Akiko. Contemporary assessments of her achievements were no less great.

A daughter of a well-to-do practitioner of Chinese medicine, Saikō was encouraged to paint and write from an early age. When she was twenty-six, she met an ambitious scholar of Chinese studies, Rai San'yō (1780–1832), who promptly fell in love with her—a sentiment Saikō reciprocated. Though San'yō's wish to marry her was not fulfilled, he became her teacher in kanshi, and their affection for each other endured, sustained by correspondence and occasional meetings. San'yō lived in Kyoto, married; Saikō lived in Ōgaki, in Gifu, unmarried.

Saikō recorded her daily life in her kanshi. The selection that follows is arranged chronologically.

Viewing Cherry Blossoms

In Second Month of the 11th Year of Bunka [1814] I Followed San'yō Sensei and Tōan Sensei to View Cherry Blossoms on Arashiyama[180]

Breeze, and good weather settles in, gentle sun harmonious.
Small groups, lightly dressed, pass by us one after another.
No regret that it's three days too early to view the blossoms.
With all branches in full bloom, many will be drunks.

Green, Round Shadow

In Mid-Fall, of the 11th Year of Bunka [1814], I Went to Myōkō Temple. On My Way Home I Lost My Umbrella, so for Fun, I Made This Poem

Your green, green, round shadow was never away.
A while ago I welcomed you from Kyoto, home.
Your lid shielded my updo, always my companion,
handle in my hand's custody, you followed me everywhere:

---

180. Several months after becoming Rai San'yō's student, Saikō visited him in Kyoto. She was twenty-seven. Carousing under cherry blossoms is part of the flower-viewing tradition.

on clear days when I went for mushrooms on autumn hills,
in a breeze, at a spring temple, where I was flower-drunk.
So, why one morning did you abandon me and leave?
Fearful of the sun, I hunger for you as for the morning meal.

Living Quietly in Early Winter

This isolated village, I'm content, is far from urban dust.
My tiny tiny quarter is full of more than I can enjoy.
A slender pipe diverts water from the spring to wash my inkstone.
I change the window paper so I may read books better.
The leaves fallen from the *feng*[181] I call a maid to sweep away.
The frozen roots in the herb garden I hire an old man to plow.
Days are short, but to me, a woman of leisure, they feel long,
as I recite poems, learn to paint, rather than make myself pretty.

A Woman's Room in Spring

Near the window, swallows, in pairs, chatter away;
beyond it, pendulous, pliant, a willow with its branches new.
Leisurely, with scissors in hand, sitting all day,
I've made light clothes, but feel too lazy to try them on.
The days are finally longer, I see, and evenings short;
incense in the duck-shaped censer dead, ashes still warm.
Afraid only that the spring light will soon fade,
I glance at blossoms fluttering down beyond the blinds.

Bamboo in the Snow

> I Studied Painting Bamboo with Ink for Twenty Years but Was Unable
> to Paint Bamboo in the Snow, Until One Day the Snow Pressed Down the
> Bamboo; I Moved My Brush Fast and Also Made a Poem[182]

Before my window the snow presses down beautiful bamboo.
I playfully take up a purple brush, my hands both cold.

---

181. A species of the witch-hazel family originally from Southern China and Taiwan.
Its resin was used as medicine.
182. This happened in 1821.

The first time in twenty years this difficult
   moment:
Heaven has opened a copybook for me
   to see.

Sleepless on a Moonlit
   Night

The autumn night, limpid, often startles
   me out of dreams.
Among the trees a crow caws, twice,
   three times.
The clepsydra, rather slow, adds to my
   collar's cold.
The sputtering lamp darkens, making the
   window light.
A couplet, in this idleness, I manage to
   get.
All feelings are spawned while on the
   pillow.
Tossing, turning, sleepless, thinking of
   an old friend,
I happen to see the moon clear, close to
   the roof.

Growing an Orchid

I brought a humble orchid into my
   room
and have since, for years, been intent on
   nurturing it.
A light shower, and I've taken it outside,
delighting in the sprouting purple buds.
Mornings I watched it, evenings I caressed it,
examining the flower buds a number of
   times.
I've taken up the brush to paint its piteous figure,
composed poems to praise its lasting grace.
From the care needed to raise an orchid,
I've learned how people bring up children.

Saikō's painting inscribed with the poem,
Bamboo in the Snow

Parting with My Dear Friend Tōjō on a Boat[183]

Vales and hills, I haven't exhausted this clean fun,
yet the return-pole is set and I can't stay.
I hate the Nagara River this streak of water,
swishing, urging the passengers to send the boat down.

I've managed to dress to go home, my heart pained;
frost assailing my robe, the day breaks.
The mist's about to dissipate, the hills to brighten;
the light boat, with a pole, starts down the river.

The light boat runs swiftly, melancholy on board;
a thousand hills pass by before I bat my eyes.
What can I do with the rapids busily sending us down?
I part with you and I again part with these pretty hills.

Forbidding My Sister Sake

My good sister has a sick habit,
mostly generated by sake.
What to do is to wet one's lips with it,
but she's grown to be like her sis.
When moonlight's on our green blind
or plum lends its scent to our window,
my heart yearns to simply get drunk with her;
my mouth doesn't dare ask her to have a drink.

Winter Night

Father opens European, Dutch books;
Child reads Tang, Song verse.
Sharing this single lamp,
each traces his own source.
Father reads on and never rests,

---

183. In Tenth Month of 1826, Saikō, fulfilling an earlier promise, visited Murase Shikin (1791–1853), whose penname was Tōjō, in his village, Kōzuchi, Mino (northeast of Ōgaki), and stayed with him for three days, with Tōjō giving her a tour of the place and hosting a gathering of poets. A sequence of three poems.

child, tired, thinks of chestnuts, yams.
I'm ashamed I am, in spirit, so far from father,
who, eighty years of age, has no mist in his eyes.

Painting

To do a painting and argue if it looks like life,
that's an approach a child might take.
Who is it that said this so very well?
Old gentleman Dongpo[184] no less.
I take his word and make it law.
Suppose I drop ink on paper,
the square foot turns into the Xiaoxiang,[185]
and a hundred shapes rise from the brush tip.
Paint well what you have in mind,
there's no need to fear praise or criticism.
Call it hemp or call it rush,
the designation's wholly up to the viewer.

My Soul So Familiar with the Flower[186]

My soul so familiar with the flower,
I can divine the blooming time.
One bright day I made preparations fast,
wanting to seek the fragrance far away.
The morning sun rose, I started out,
and before evening sun inclined, found lodging.
The brush and inkstone, and a packet for verse,
I have an old servant to shoulder them.
Now I'm ready to meet Kyoto flowers
to make their clean bliss mine awhile.

---

184. Su Dongpo (1037–1101), better known by the older romanization of his name, Su Tung-p'o, was a Chinese painter-poet regarded as having started the literati tradition of painting bamboo. Saikō took his words to heart.
185. An area in China famous for its "eight views."
186. In the spring of 1830 Saikō went to see San'yō in Kyoto for the seventh time. The year was intercalary, with Third Month repeated, and she was able to prolong her stay by that much. This poem describes her leaving home for Kyoto.

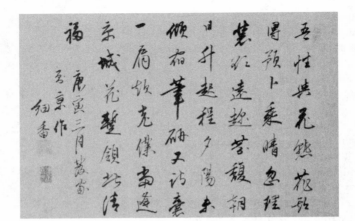

The poem, *My Soul So Familiar,* in Saikō's own calligraphy.

By the Rainy Window
I Spoke with Saikō about Parting

by Rai San'yō[187]

In this detached room with a low lamp, stay awhile for fun;
until the new mud on the way back dries, you better wait.
On the other bank the peak and range have fewer clouds;
in the next house strings and songs at night have peaked.
This spring being intercalary, you, my guest, still stay,
but night-long rain has pitilessly left few flowers intact.
Mino for which you are about to leave isn't far away,
but having grown old I expect it to be hard to meet often.

Parting Melancholy

San'yō Sensei, along with Three Young Men, Nakajima, Isagawa, and Shion-
oya, Came to Karasaki to See Me Off; I Wrote the Following and Presented
it to Him, as Well as to the Three Men.

We've walked together for several *li,*
regretting our destination isn't farther away.

---

187. When the time came for Saikō to go back home, San'yō gave her a farewell party
in his house, on the west bank of the Kamo River, and wrote a poem for her.

Your reciprocal thought being intense,
parting melancholy continues to grow.
Disturbed green, the trees in the wind;
remaining reds, the blossoms after rain.
Out of this mountain, soon to part our sleeves,
my heart is broken in the evening sun aslant.

Under the Pine Tree at Karasaki
I Said Farewell to San'yō Sensei

I stand on the shore; you are in the boat.
Boat and shore, facing, are tied by parting sorrow.
Gradually you fade into the lake haze, grow small,
and I blame the wind filling your sail.
Under the pine I linger, unable to leave,
but the expanse of blue waves is empty, vast.
I've parted with you seven times in twenty years,
but no parting difficult as this to explain to myself.

Mother's Death

> In Tenth Month, in the 2nd Year of Tempō [1831], Mother Died, and I Stay
> Home. Because She Was My Stepmother the Mourning Period Was Shorter.
> Still, Though I've Already Taken off my Mourning Robe, I Cannot Bear the
> Pain. So I've Written This Poem to Express My Sorrow.

Bearing me and rearing me,
which was a greater favor?
No love in your arms for the first three years,[188]
but for forty long years I watched your face.
Just like a sweet gourd vine entwining a crooked tree,
I did not think of a different mother who bore me.
One morning, eternal farewell, dark and light apart,
the blue sky spread calmly through my tears of blood.
Your voice and form still in my ears and eyes,
asleep, my soul is often easily startled.
A wind in the inner room desolately stirs the blinds,
and I wonder if you called me from above my pillow.

---

188. Saikō's own mother died before she reached the age of three.

Again

I inspected your clothes chests, donated them to the monk.
Still your scent remains and I cannot resist the tears.
A breeze to the drape for your soul leaves the incense cold.
Half the night a freezing rain, before the altar, the lamp.

In his old age losing his spouse,[189] I think of his grief,
the only thing left to soothe himself now, a female child.
Tears over the sorrow of your death keep rolling down,
but feigning cheerfulness I wipe them secretly while tending him.

Reading The Tale of Genji

Who is this who took up a red-lacquered brush to depict life,
and has for a thousand years intoxicated the reader's heart?
The analyzer of all these subtle things proves to be a woman, yes,
naturally different in love of elegance from a man.
In spring rain, cutting wicks, evaluating a hundred flowers—
his yearning for incense, pity for jewels, began with this.
Across the Milky Way, in evening, magpies span a bridge;
letter sent at daybreak by the blue bird, the messenger.
Moonflower by an ordinary fence, the night, the loss;
Cicada Shell, her dress, the light, half a husk.
Summer insects, burning, throw themselves into a flame;
spring butterflies madly dance on the wing enamored of a flower.
A cat with no manners flips aside a pale-blue blind,
but the lunar resident remains obscure in the palatial depths.
After many clouds are befriended, rains caressed, he is torn,
quietly shedding tears into cold ash, in feeble candlelight.
These fifty-four books and millions of words
are in the end all about that one sentiment: love.
In love there are joys, pleasures, there are sorrows, hurts;
above all, love is to be noted when it is requited.
Do not blame her[190] that things become excessive through the tale:
she simply wanted to explain all that she knew of love.
With a lamp lit by my small window, night quiet and still,
I, too, remain intent on puzzling things out in depth.

---

189. Reference to Saikō's father, Ransai.
190. The author, Murasaki Shikibu.

Of Myself

A dream, so swift, now someone a half century old;
private thoughts, endless, darkly pain my heart.
The moon wanes, the moon waxes, from full to new;
flowers fall, flowers open, in autumn, again in spring.
Paintings I once did seem to be by a different hand;
books I once read feel new as I read them again.
I only hope to remain more or less trouble-free,
now with my parent in his room, old and ill.

Watching the Flood[191]

The water, rising in Shinano and Echizen,
branches out, enters Mino, and flows.
Persistent rains soon create waves,
violently swelling from summer to fall.
The Kiso River grows most urgent,
muddy swirls spreading, insouciant.
The estuaries are a land of carried soil,
yearly accumulations forming hills.
New paddies, however, exist in Owari,
something that worries us in Mino.
Ah, Mount Stars still has the rock to which boats were moored.[192]
How do we know mulberry fields won't become a sea?[193]

Occasional

A rivulet and tall trees surround my brushwood gate,
settled long here, east of the castle, in a fertile land.
Nothing to do in the old age heaven has offered me,
with all sorts of growths having taken root.
The yeast that intoxicates me, this taste in a cup,
I paint bamboo: reeds or hemp? these brush stains.
Don't know: in a previous life I must have been a nun;
I love this quiet simplicity away from dust and noise.

---

191. In Eighth Month of the third Year of Kaei [1850].
192. Reference to a local star festival and the legend that boats used to be moored to a rock on a hill during the floods.
193. "A mulberry field turns into a sea" is an old Chinese phrase meaning a dramatic change that can occur in this world.

Occasional

In the west and east friends seldom grow remote in
    heart.
Old and lazy, I let their letters pile up unanswered.
Once in a while, when I manage to respond to many,
I have a cup of spring brew and feel my mind expand.

Earthquake

> On the 4th and 5th of Eleventh Month in the
> First Year of Ansei [1854] the Ground Shook
> Terribly, and I Composed This to Document
> What Happened.

Roof tiles flew, houses wanted to collapse,
people, stampeding, trampled on each other.
On the cold night all slept outdoors,
no time even to repair makeshift shacks.
Some rode in palanquins with no bearers,
others lay in boats not being poled.
Sleep wanted, sleep was hard to come by,
painful moon at once horrifying and faint.
Daybreak, both small and big acute with hunger,
    cold,
the frost on the clothes covering them as white as
    snow.

Poem for a Painting

In the garden a wind rustles the bamboo.
I can't help feeling the clear, hot sky.
Afternoon nap by a cool window,
in peaceful sleep I hear a heavenly sound.

Saikō's painting inscribed with
Poem for a Painting

Untitled

To spend my leisure time I have a way,
which other people needn't know:
I've just painted three stems of bamboo
for which I've written a poem with a rhyme.

—*Saikō at Seventy-two*

Untitled[194]

My age: seventy-four,
feelings colder than ashes.
Not ill but growing thin,
I'll make a smaller padded robe.

Saikō's painting with the poem
"To spend my leisure time"

194. Saikō's last poem, written toward the end of 1860. She died nine months later.

Kamei Shōkin
(1798–1857)

When the kanshi poet Hirose Tansō (1782–1856) visited her father, Shōkin wrote a kanshi for him. Tansō was impressed and wrote a poem in response saying that she conveyed the poetic style idealized by Confucius so well it was embarrassing to think that Japan had extolled for a thousand years writers like Murasaki Shikibu and Sei Shōnagon, who were obscene—obscene in the sense of writing about amorous relations between women and men. Shōkin at the time was eleven.

Untitled[195]

Japan's number-one plum
will open for you tonight.
Want to know the flower's true intent?
Come, treading the moon, at midnight.

Evening View of a Spring River

Sun's glow shines on the river, sand birds white;
evening mist dissipates, a thousand mountains red.
Beautiful women from whose houses walk in spring,
sleeve to sleeve going home along the willow road.

Describing a Riverside Village

Golden rice cloudlike covers a thousand paddy ridges,
farmhouses are delighted with the bumper crop.
Old men and women drum the pots, crying out in joy,
the village boys on stilts kicking up dust.

---

195. Shōkin is said to have written this poem when one of her father's students slipped a love note to her.

Hara Saihin
(1798–1859)

Saihin, whose childhood name was Michi, studied Chinese classics and kanshi with her father, Kosho, who was promoted from a low position to president (*saishu*) of the school of Akizuki, a small fief in today's Fukuoka, and to fief treasurer (*nandoyaku*) because of his learning and reputation as a poet. In 1812 the lord-president of Akizuki suddenly stripped Kosho of his positions, forcing him to "retire." Saihin continued to study and teach with him and after his death, in 1827, spent most of her time trying to reestablish Hara as a house of learning and to raise money for publishing a collection of her father's poems.

Saihin traveled widely—carrying a sword on her hip—and lived for twenty years, from 1828 to 1848, in Edo, where she tried to establish herself as an independent Confucian scholar. Her kanshi is said to show strong influences of Li Po and other Tang poets and is characterized as "masculine."

Spring Rain

Pliant, pliant, restless clouds rise;
swirling, swirling, fine rain falls aslant.
Warm mist wanders over willow streams;
spring trees enclose several houses.
In the valley fountain voices echo;
on the pond embankment grass adds to its hue.
I do not know, before it clears up again,
how many branches will brew blossoms.

1817

Finding Myself on Mount Fuji in a Dream

(First in a two-poem set)

The mountain, so divine, named Incomparable;
blue sky, white sun, the snow rose steeply.
Zou's Vast Ocean lay small in my eyes;
Zhang's River originated below my feet.
Before me I saw stars return to where they lodge.
Looking down I heard the Immortal chant midair.
A poem made, I was about to surprise the Creator:
pillow and bed, wind cold, the mountain moon low.

A Quiet House in Early Summer

Green trees, layered shadows, a lodge with water and rocks;
the mugwort and sagebrush uncut bury the stone steps.
The swallow before the blind has flown into the setting sun;
the shoots in the bamboo grove have grown in the new rain.
While drinking I'd fallen asleep over a pot of sake
and was too lazy to put away the books unfinished on my bed.
To kill time, all day, sitting under a tall pine tree,
now I see a solitary cloud come out of a cave and spread.

In the Spring Rain
I Think of My Hometown

A lone guest upstairs, I think of many things,
while watching the smoky rain tangled like threads.
Spring on heaven and earth, warbler's calls trail;
home beyond clouds and hills, letters are slow.
A flute, plum blossoms fall in my melancholy,
Fragrant grass in a dream, I write it in verse.
Homesick, unsettled like willows in the wind,
all day swaying, I cannot hold myself down.

1821

Impressions of Nagasaki [196]

I'd long heard about Chinese verse and prose;
Chinese say, The river crossed, burn the boat.
But, for verse as spear, brush deployed, no one is my rival;
pigtailed, head shaven, awkward, they can hardly write.
Green-eyed aliens leave in the autumn moon before dawn;
red-robes' guns tear the clouds above the sea.
Though Nagasaki is minuscule, a bullet of a land,
its hills and streams are all beyond the ordinary.

1823

---

196. Saihin exchanged verse with some Chinese traders, "native" users of classical Chinese, and apparently bested them. This instantly became legend.

Leaving Hometown for Edo

Up early, greetings to my parents,
New Year I leave my hometown.
At the gate the willow I planted
is particularly hard to part with.
Offerings to our ancestors:
May Father and Mother prosper,
I the traveler be peaceful.
I drink cup after cup to ride a whale,
I drink cup after cup to ride a whale.
That done, I'm ready to travel.
Now I am twenty-eight,
ashamed to think how Liang left Nanyang.[197]

23rd of First Month, 1825

Seeing Hakusei off to Bizen[198]

Life is filled with separations.
Seldom can we gather our heads.
The autumn wind blows on falling leaves,
scattering them swiftly, bleakly.
Three children from the same root,
we are like duckweed, restless.
Last year all alone I was a guest in Kyoto,
at the clouds, with the sea, lamenting my wandering.
Parents were unhappy, thinking of me, their child,
tramping and trekking, fearing no highwaymen.
Grief and joy, not many days we've held hands,
but you brothers follow each other to Rocky Bear.
Of your pain, above all else, I shall never speak,
knowing how you feel as autumn turns to winter.
I, Hin[199], will stay by our parents' side, sharing their joy.
Come, relax and take care of your chronic illness.

Fall of 1826

---

197. Zhuge Liang (131–234) was a Chinese military strategist who, as legend has it, left farming in Nanyang at age twenty-seven to help a regional warlord defeat Emperor Wu's army.

198. Hearing about her father's illness, Saihin hurried back from Kyoto. But then her brother, Hakusei, had to leave for Iwakuma to nurse his own illness.

199. Abbreviated reference to herself.

Occasional

I recall: Father, now dead, after his resignation,
took his family to distant San'yō to roam.
Ten poems in *Fragments from Wanderings*
explore Hiroshima and Miyajima.
Afterward he never tired of roaming as he pleased,
leaving or staying just as a white cloud does;
in each place formed a society, himself its president,
prominent in the literary field, with no competitor.
He always said, "My friend of the past is Li Taipo.
A poem done, my brush can let the Five Mountains fly.
I only regret I did not live with you, in your days,
smash the Yellow Crane Tower of the Immortal,
get drunk, remain so for months on end
and when dead bury my bones in the wine dregs."
The tenth year of Bunsei, spring, New Year,
when at sixty-one, the zodiacal cycle turned,
my mentor, simply bored by the human world,
suddenly left in "duck shoes" into the distance.
As I recall the places he visited in his roaming,
winds stir the trees draped with melancholy rain.

1827

A View from a Boat

A light boat, unmoored on the beach with white gulls,
sets sail into the distance, toward invisibility.
A wind falls and the vapors are all the more white;
the tide flows, and blue above a giant turtle is a solitary peak.

1827

Responding to Kyōhei[200] Sensei in Verse

You as Father's friend, I'm solitary and am not.
With you I come to know all the men of letters.
In my heart I hold an ambition, though small,
have again wandered afar to this corner of heaven.
A migrant goose, flying, calling, lost in the marshland,

---

200. Rai Kyōhei (1756–1834) was a Confucian scholar and poet and an administrator in Hiroshima.

Brooding, dreaming about my family, I head for Edo.
Should I fulfill my plans while young,
some eccentrics might appear who follow me.

Fall of 1827

Fish Offered and Brought

Fish that are whiter than gems:
with some I made a bowl of soup.
Its flavor so light, incomparable,
my teeth feel gradually refreshed.

New Year, 1828

Responding to Takahashi Sōzan
Using the Same Rhymes[201]

Leaving this place, alone, again I turn east;
our souls will mingle across a thousand li in dreams.
My home at heaven's end, when can I return,
my steps like willow flowers, flying, left to the wind?
You are the only person I've found sympathetic of late;
I'd like to see you again, if possible, before you grow old.
Each time you find a startling phrase in verse exchanged,
please write to me about it in your letter.

Early summer of 1828

New Year's Day

The bell in the bell tower struck a hundred and eight times,
my dream of being home broken, the sky's already light.
Clear morning, myself in the mirror, I pity my illnesses,
several strands of gray hair sprouting to frame my melancholy.
Poetic sentiments long abandoned on account of medicine,
I've thought of going home vainly as if chasing the setting sun.
For ten years a solitary guest because of father's will;
how could I return home without making a name?

1837

---

201. A rock with the first four lines of this poem inscribed on it in her own hand stands
next to her grave.

Going to Mukōjima with Two Gentlemen:
Watanabe Tōri and Hirose Baitan

Each time I see someone from the west,
I'm thrilled, feelings unbound.
Especially with an old acquaintance,
it's as though facing a spring wind.
The long pain of being a guest
melts like ice and I feel at peace.
We set off to the Sumida River,
traipse amid myriad blossoms.
Mokubo Temple Umewaka's grave:
Mother and son, each pained, unable to meet.
Two men accompanied by a woman,
we forget male or female, feel the same.
The view in no place is my possession.
We all laugh: We've turned into hermit crabs.
For myself I'm troubled by no gainful pursuit,
traveling quietly to the west or to the east.
Just let me ask the Creator about this:
Is anything under heaven not a wanderer?

Third Month, 1837

Nabuto Island

Sky and sea a single azure in a hazy expanse,
the space for the phoenix, boundless, leads nowhere.
People tell me: Bowheads come here chasing sardines,
prompting the fishermen to shout and run about crazily.

1848

Calling for Sake

As for sake you need only a sip,
drinking-money doesn't have to be much.
When my poesy runs dry, though,
I call for a cup and make verse, drunk.

1848

Thoughts at the Year's End, Using
Lu Fang's Rhyme Scheme[202]

Wanting to comb my unkempt head,
I sit alone before a clear mirror.
Each strand unable to block old age,
so many worries for sixty years.
My thoughts like steaming stones,
when will the time for dead ashes come?
Going against Brother Haku's request,
I vainly grieve the passage of days and months.
Perverse, pushing for impossibilities,
late in life I grow even more insane.
A child of an honest government official,
how can I forget: The poorer the more resolute?

1856

While Roaming in Amakusa[203]

Near where Japan's land ends,
I climb a height and explore the distance.
Within my sight nothing blocks the view,
the setting sun between sky and sea.
Afar I think of the State of the Sages,
a sunflower tilting toward the evening sun.
Once Manchu Qing disturbed China,
culture no longer followed the old.
Added to this was British violence,
cruelties poisoning all the young.
For defense there were no more men,
in fierce chastity only Liù's daughter.
Shaven-headed, pigtailed sojourners
fear the dogs like tigers and wolves.
Once you learn how to read and write,
you lament, unable to forget the outrages.
Come now, all this has happened overseas;
I won't vainly tax myself with these sorrows.

1856–1857

---

202. Lu Fang (1125–1210), also known as Lu Yu, is regarded as the greatest poet of the Southern Song dynasty.
203. In 1842 when the British fleet annihilated China's Eight Flag Troops in Zhapu, Liu's daughter chose to die rather than subject herself to rape by British soldiers. Her virtuous deed was extolled in a series of poems.

On Mount Aso

On the 22nd [of Ninth Month 1857] I Was Up Early and Climbed Mount Aso;
I Use Shuryō's Rhyme Scheme[204]

Mount Aso rises, builds up high into heaven,
cloud ladders, stone bridges, break, link up again.
Wind forms under my armpits, clouds around my feet,
and make me want to follow an immortal walking midair.
I look around and the peaks are like children, cousins;
ahead of me rises forlornly the top of Kujū.
White clouds in heaven fly, inexhaustible,
smoke everlasting since the Bun'ei era.
Clouds and smoke rise and fade day and night,
lamenting the human world perhaps, ever changing.
Having come afar to this famous mountain,
I'd like to state my impressions in one verse.
A fountain always rises to reflect the five colors
unlike the dead ashes never burning again.
We ply our canes, roam, step on charred stones,
the mountain spirit not angry at our dust marks.
Day short, sun dipping west, we're far from home;
like skewed fish humans go on down below.
I beg you, look: In Miyaji, last night's rain,
already frozen among mountains, is white as snow.
On this trip, without depending on Mr. Murai's sons,
my old legs wouldn't have gotten me this wondrous scenery.
Here's a stone where naturally you can rub ink:
I'll wield a brush awhile to write of this mountaineering.

---

204. Kataoka Shuryō (1715–1768) was a Confucian scholar and poet of the Kumamoto
fiefdom. A large stone at the top of the mountain has an indented flat top that makes it look
like a naturally made ink-stone.

Takahashi Gyokushō
(1802–1868)

When Gyokushō published a collection of one hundred kanshi in 1849, Ōtsuki Bankei (1801–1878) wrote a preface and said: "The house in which Gyokushō was born is located east of Sendai Castle, in the most prosperous part of the fiefdom, where rich merchants' houses stand roof to roof. Gyokushō studied literature hard and also pursued calligraphy, in which she established her own school. Not long afterward she struck out for Edo and started teaching Chinese prose and poetry and became widely known. Hearing about this, the wife of the lord-president of the Sendai fiefdom invited Gyokushō to her official mansion, had her lecture on Chinese classics, and presented her with a crested kimono. This was a great honor."

In the Rain in Early Spring

With no sake, no flowers, time passes vacantly.
Spring cold, coarse and prickly, brings gooseflesh.
New mud and drizzle, too lazy to sally forth,
alone by the window I go over yesterday's go game.

Suburban Walk on an Autumn Day

The wind penetrates my collar, making me feel light;
the setting sun will exhaust its light before long.
On a wild bank insects chirp, clear, pleasant to the ear.
Where autumn grass is deep, I walk, and I walk.

Untitled [205]

Lively, fish and shrimp fill the boat with noise.
Back home I take up the lamp; it's already twilight.
In a blur I marinate our catch and resume our feast.
We still have half the fragrant sake left in the keg.

---

205. One day Gyokushō went boat-fishing downstream of the Sumida River.

Red Plum

Warmth has entered its sensuality, making it outstand;
corals, clusters of gems, adorn its many branches.
Evaluation's of no use, all prattling wasted.
Just call it a beautiful woman, tipsy, and that will do.

Autumn Morning

My neighbor, sleep-greedy, hushed, makes no sound.
A leisurely person, I'm up early, like the cawing crow.
Before my gate there's already someone with his wares,
an oxherd who's come to sell several kinds of flower.

Year End

A few leaves left on the calendar and I'm alarmed.
In everything I feel lost, the world presses ahead.
The little girl doesn't know I'm up against the wall,
saying merely, "How many days before the New Year?"

Paper Curtain

On the four sides walls set up to block frost and wind,
the lamp lit lightening the air, I feel my mind melt.
On a pillow I wake from dreams, the day yet to break,
and wonder if I'm in the midst of white clouds.

Yanagawa Kōran
(1804–1879)

When she was six or seven, Kōran, whose childhood name was Kimi, began studying Chinese classics and verse composition with a monk who was her grandfather's younger brother. In her teens she became a student of her second cousin, Yanagawa Seigan, (1789–1858), fell in love with him, and at age sixteen married him. Although their families, in Mino, were both well-to-do, they were sometimes very poor, because Seigan was determined to make a living as a writer.

Soon after their marriage Seigan left her to travel, telling her to study part of the *San-ti-shi* (*Verse in Three Styles*), an anthology of mid- to late Tang poetry. But in the two years he was absent, she studied and memorized the whole book, which consists of 494 poems. Shortly after Seigan's return both set out to travel to Kyūshū and did not return to Mino for four years. They then left to live mainly in Kyoto or Edo when not traveling.

In the 1840s Seigan became a leading figure in the movement to "revere the emperor and expel the foreigners," as foreign pressures to open isolationist Japan mounted. In 1858, days before a mass arrest of such political activists began, he died of cholera, but Kōran was thrown in jail. Though a great many were executed, she was eventually acquitted.

Late in her life she founded a private school and taught with some of Seigan's students. She also excelled in painting and playing the koto.

Traveling at Year's End, I Speak My Mind

At an inn window to whom to tell my inner thoughts?
Again I see in the east wind the Big Dipper turn.
The oriole, welcoming spring, is truly beautiful,
white plum blossoms, like snow, already seductive.
Darkening and pathless is the way to serve my in-laws;
bright and shining is my heart longing for the sages.
Cold and destitute, how can I know the beauty of braids,
sewing with a needle, washing clothes, from year to year?

1822

Thinking of My Hometown:
Two Poems

1
Going west for a thousand li, then going farther west,
the clouds and mountains recall people far away.
And here in the water outside the Karukaya Barrier
I seem to hear the voice of Papa calling to his child.

2
As the blossoms scatter, the green grows even newer;
each time the seasons change tears wet my handkerchief.
Distant, I know cherries, bamboo shoots are now served,
a joyous gathering of sisters minus one.

                                                                            1824

Leisurely Composition on a Summer Day

Bored, I tossed needle and thread, couldn't take them up again;
beads of sweat through my robe when I woke from a nap.
Sand scorched, gold melting, the noon grew even hotter;
I pitied the garden flowers drying up and dying.
The evening came and slowly cool breezes rose,
a slice, an early crescent, slim as an eyebrow.
Jasmine blossoms open, their fragrance filled my hand;
I held a stem near my hair and snowflakes fell.

                                                                            1824

Raising Bamboo[206]

A suggestion of spring thunder and they snake about,
raising their heads, in no time a swarm of them.
Dew washes their golden tubes, making them gleam;
wind blows on their brocade sheaths, making them fall.
Who said for months he did not think of meat?
How could we do without you a single morning?
The greediest must stop wielding their tongues:
I need to see them erect, sweeping the highest clouds.

---

206. Po Chu-i has a poem, "Eating Bamboo," which includes the line "Every day I added
them to dinner and for long had no thought of meat."

On Returning Home

(Two from a three-poem set)

1

Drizzling, mountain rain green,
sandals and cane hurry themselves.
Climbing, climbing, I reach a height
and at cloud bottom first see my home.
I imagine my sisters, old and young,
in advance bringing out a pot and cup.
Last night the lamp must have spat out wicks,
the magpies chattering themselves hoarse.

2

Going, going, the village road smooth,
froggy frogs raucous in the spring paddies.
An old farmer raises his eyebrows,
looks at me, and comes to greet me.
Welcoming my return he talks and talks
and his warmth touches my heart.
Clouds remain but it finally lets up,
the evening sun on my brushwood gate.
I enter and before we exchange words
the whole family bursts into tears.
The surprise over, joy is born:
we talk and smile, laugh noisily.

1826

Thoughts on Traveling

(Two poems)

1

A duckweed for years on end against my wish,
again with bedding wrapped I leave my brushwood gate.
A little better than a parasite using someone's fire,
why dislike the road dust soiling my travel robes?
Wayside chrysanthemums, hostless, are skinny,
but water's edge white herons, fish caught, are fat.
When will the society of glory and shame come to an end?
Is it superior to life in the hills, machinations severed?

2

Light flows with travelers, busily, busily;
autumn deepens while I journey, brood miserably.
Falling on my hat coldly a rain of yellow leaves,
the afternoon air scents my robe with winds over rice.
Chinese classics no less than my lifetime work,
I tend to neglect sewing clothes, work requiring days.
I can't compare with the wife who lifted the dinner tray,
but on these journeys I luckily serve Hong of Five Sighs.[207]

1829

Making a Poem at Night While Ill

From year's end to early spring my illness has subsided
but the doctor nonetheless allows no verse composition.
Back turned to the fading lamp I neglect scissors and measure;
on a pillow, pensive, I dream of my brothers, old and young.
The devils' chief, lazy, must have left my life alone;
the snail's horns broken, I'm exempt from vying for my name.
Enfeebled, fearing most the ferocity of the threat of wind,
I turn away from the poet's window, the snowy moon bright.

A Great Famine

In the Fall of the 7th Year of Tempō [1836] I Write Down My Impressions of
the Great Famine. Student Momiyama Happens to Present Us with Freshly
Harvested Rice. So I Refer to It in the Fourth Line.

Even in normal times I see dust on my rice steamer;
now with persisting rains famines recur everywhere.
For a long time our whole family has eaten only gruel.
A blessing then, a sack, we happily taste new rice.
People must have neglected their productive work,
for how could heaven choose to murder humanity?
The blue sea turned into paddies wouldn't provide enough,
unstoppable heaven and earth filled with refugees.

---

207. As the *History of the Later Han* tells it, Liang Hong married Meng Guang, who,
though known for being not particularly beautiful, had expressed the desire to marry him
because of his reputation as a wise man. She served him reverentially, hence "the wife who
lifted the dinner tray [to her eye-level]." Hong left an elegy that used the word "sigh" five
times. Kōran proudly regarded herself as Seigan's Meng Guang.

Occasional

We sell writings for a living in lieu of sericulture,
our rags the laughingstock of the vulgar often enough.
In talent and eloquence I've never aspired to be a Daoyun[208]
but recluse, I luckily manage to live with Tongming.[209]
A floating cloud, the world is but an illusion;
quiet water, my heart could be absolutely clear.
Because heaven wants to push a bud toward the Way,
it first makes me suffer cold and starvation.

1837

Winter Daybreak

Struck once, a bell startles me out of a bad dream.
No living things are exempt from life's struggles.
Look, over castle trees the moon slightly inclines
and cold crows, starved sparrows, cry out like that.

On the Way from Katsuyama to Yawata

Fearful of the heat, in fresh sandals, I leave before dawn.
The whole world is hushed, only roosters calling.
The gleaming stars my faint guide, their light fading,
the vault now turns scarlet, bringing in the early day.
Along my path the cool soppy dew finally disappears;
before me, in the village, as I walk on, heat haze rises.
Below a cliff shops are placed, two or three of them.
Good, I'll rest in layered mist, in mountain-water cleanliness.

1841

---

208. Daoyun is a woman of great literary talent mentioned in the *History of the Jin*.
    209. Tongming was the childhood name of Tao Hongjing (456–536), a man of erudition who preferred to be a recluse but was often consulted by Emperor Wu, of Liang. Kōran compares Seigan to Tao Hongjing.

Traveling Late into the Evening

Who says, "Since ancient days traveling has been hard"?
Wandering, at each place a smile melts my tired face.
Evening geese pasted in the sky link up, again break;
cold clouds pregnant with snow build up, again separate.
A thin moon is ready to sink, its light a delicate glimmer;
a feeble fountain, though almost dried up, keeps purring.
Not worried that in the year's last month I still travel,
I look at withered woods and hills in night's light.

3rd of Twelfth Month, 1846

Occasional

In my forties, so many worries, my decline palpable,
the house has no swaddling clothes or lovely infant in them.
Out of nowhere comes a yellow butterfly, notices how I feel,
and adorns a scarlet branch of pomegranate.

1848

Song of Buying a Koto[210]

The fifth year of Kaei, summer, Fourth Month,
a merchant came, carrying a koto, and boasted:
"An instrument like this is rare in this world,
its lacquer's so old the crazes are fine as hair."
I'd longed for a koto for a number of years
but hadn't thought to see a beauty so suddenly.
Its aged air, solemnly wafting up, struck me:
delight to the eyes, joy to the heart, block to the mouth.
I'd heard that plum blossoms are prized as crazes;
indeed, rarest flowers dotted the snake belly.
I thought it was at least five hundred years old
yet it hadn't the slightest scratch, front or back.
Engraved below its head were the letters "Old Dragon,"
the seal saying, "Laughing freely in fine scenery."

---

210. The koto described here is now part of the museum holdings of the Board of Education of Ōgaki City, Aichi.

Equipped with both name and substance, impeccable,
it was like a prince being disciplined, attractive.

Dragon, Dragon, I can't fathom how you transform yourself,
hiding, visible, leaping, flying in perfect time.
I do not know how many generations you've lived through,
but you acquit yourself like a virtuous dragon.

Scholars in most cases have no extra funds,
still less a poor woman who's hard pressed.
How could I afford the price of a bunch of cities?
Hairpins removed, skirts sold, I barely managed.

The wise by tradition never respect possessions,
giving full care and attention to a koto alone.
A koto cordons off the wayward, the dishonest,[211]
this is why you can't leave it for a second.
Don't you see the harmony of music relies on the Six Tones?
Get it right on wind and string and the house is in order.
The Five Positions well met, the core can't be afar;
yin-yang helping each other, the medium won't be lost.
From kings, dukes, down to officials, commoners,
who can afford not to play the koto, small or large?
Oh, when music attains harmony, subtlety enters the divine;
else no skills would be needed between heaven and earth.

I Bought a Koto and Played a Piece on it

I stand in my upstairs room and the rainy season lets up;
mountains and streams expand, bringing my heart peace.
Floating clouds and willow flowers vanish without a trace;
like water naturally flowing east, the koto has an ancient voice.

---

211. *Qin,* the Chinese word for koto, is similar to *jin,* the word meaning "forbid," "proscribe," and the two characters also look alike, hence the saying "*Qin* is the same as *jin*." In Japanese, the two characters are pronounced the same.

Jailed[212]

The whole land overturned, angry waves raged.
How could a mere widow clear such slander?
My heart transparent as ice, I trust in my future.
I've never sought to pull strings through bribery.

23rd of Twelfth Month, 1958

In Jail

Who would subject a lone phoenix to a dirty net?
Captured in flight, dance forbidden, she's trapped.
But glory and decline, adulation and insult, are the norm.
Who would second-guess the ineffable deity of heaven?

29th of First Month, 1854

Out of Jail

Anxiety and hardship now approached a full ten days;[213]
the heart, put to a hundred tests, revealed its divinity.
I'd known luck, the very best, would come if I waited,
that three uninvited guests would come with help.[214]

16th of Second Month, 1859

---

212. Because of her association with the antigovernment movement, Kōran was arrested, interrogated, and jailed.

213. "Ten days" is *rhetorical*; her imprisonment actually lasted nearly five months where foul conditions often made a two-month imprisonment fatal.

214. Alludes to the *I-Ching*.

Furukawa Kasame
(1808–1830)

Not much is known about Furukawa Kasame except that when she died, her grieving husband, Yokokawa Bankyū, put together a collection of her hokku, along with a number of hokku and other writings her friends composed in memoriam, and published it under the title of *Hagi Darani* (*Bush Clover Dahrani*). According to Josetsu, one of the two people who contributed prefaces, Kasame composed hokku "while she mended clothes, with crickets shrilling, faced a lamp in the night's cold, rose with the bamboo stirring by the window, and worked as bush clovers wavered in the garden. . . . In early Waterless Month she said she didn't feel well, took to her bed . . . and just around the Souls' Festival . . . became as voiceless as a cicada shell." Her childhood name was Matsu. She had three children.

Spring

What I hear are all birth-cries in early spring

Bagworms, too, have become spring: plum flowers

Seaweed's fragrance: the old monk is fond of eating

Always in haste the swallows never forget their house

How peaceful: the Mount Fuji you see from the bridge

While you yawn the skylark has gotten in the grass

Rain or wind the cherry flowers worry us

Summer

Peonies bloom and no more grasses around them

I re-look, still mistake my house in young leaves

In the dark bedroom I release wrapped fireflies startled

Luxuriating branches much heavier with cicadas' voices

Her child fell asleep but still her hand moves the fan

Her child asleep she slips out to cool off awhile

Autumn

Lightning: I return again to see my child's sleeping face

Casting his net he's covered the lightning

Loneliness can be fun, too, with insects' voices

In autumn wind clinging to a leaf a cicada shell

Darkening the evening sky snipes rise

Pasania nuts: the sexton's fond of children

Autumn cold: numberless stars cover the boat

The pillow at this inn's dirty: the night's cold

Winter

At a tree-searer I'm awakened from a kabuki dream

The first snow's gone the moment you praise it

The cold night: the sound of a needle by a lamp

> By a lantern I wait for my husband's return, thinking how cold it must be in the streets:

Under the winter moon my heart walks here and there

Sakuma Tachieko
(1814–1861)

Tachieko, née Hiroe Kan, was born to a soy sauce brewer in Akamagaseki, at the southern tip of mainland Honshū. Her family was literary and artistic, and their associations included the kanshi poets Rai San'yō (1780–1832) and Hara Saihin (1798–1859). She studied painting and calligraphy with notable teachers and became skilled enough as a painter to be listed in the catalogue *Nanga Painters: Past and Present,* published in 1855.

Tachieko's first marriage failed. During her second marriage, she met Sakuma Tane (1803–1892), a tanka poet. It was love at first sight for both. But Tane was a low-ranking samurai in retirement, with scarcely any income, and their life together was a perpetual struggle. Tane often traveled to sell his writings, while Tachieko taught sewing and the reading of Chinese classics.

Some years after her death, Tane collected Tachieko's writings in a two-part book called *Kurehatori (Twill).* Book I contains 156 tanka on spring, 74 on summer, 119 on autumn, and 66 on winter; Book II, 91 tanka on love and miscellaneous writings. I thank the feminist scholar Shiba Keiko for making me a photocopy of the handwritten *Kurehatori,* and the scholar Kyoko Selden for transcribing Book II on the computer for me.

The following selection is made from the tanka on love, except for the last, which is from the miscellaneous writings.

My heart burning with an unknown thought the rain falls knowingly and wets my sleeves

My heart robbed by someone I saw and began to love I'm in deep thought despite myself

The sea may turn into hills, mountains into a river, but the vow I vowed can't be changed

Waiting so long for someone not coming I resent the moonlight shining into my bedroom door

So happy I forget what I meant to say: the night we meet we spend in dreams till break of day

In love in love I'm overjoyed to see you yet apart from this why is my heart so agitated?

The happiness of meeting now a dream the reality is this pain at morning's parting path

You and I both in love with the Each-Other River: how deep, how shallow, come, let's compare

Resentful of birds' calls we talked well past midnight: now a memory to me sleeping alone in bed

Forgetting I confuse this morning with yesterday this long spring day in thoughts of love

The months and days without meeting so painful one night's thoughts are a thousand nights'

I, thinking of you, am like the snow uninterruptedly, timelessly falling to accumulate, accumulate

Quickly changing, your heart's unreliable, comparable to sky where showers pass

I'd think nothing of my life in dying for you; what's painful all the same is just longing for you

> For months we exchanged letters; then we met and made a deep vow to each other. He came to visit for the first time and after staying awhile left.

In love in love we meet, the night, so happy; all the more painful today, this parting path

> When I made a print of the shape of my body for him and sent it to him, I wrote the following on it:

May you long for me from this shape till we meet: I tried to transfer my deep heart playfully[215]

Looking at the Moon

This year, we've had a great deal of rain since spring, and we didn't have four sunny days out of ten. Especially during the rainy season, it was unreasonable, the way it rained so hard. Even after Waterless Month arrived, the rain persisted, and it didn't let up. As it kept on falling, we, staying inside, even felt like doubling our clothes, far from saying anything like "Can't stand the heat." We all frowned,

---

215. The original plays with the word *kata*, "shape," and *katami*, which means "look at the shape" and "memento," "keepsake."

complaining bitterly, "What if this . . . ?" Finally, though, on the twelfth day, the wind shifted, and the rain clouds disappeared somewhere. The sky was refreshing, and the landscape for the first time was summer's.

In any event, for us who mingle in society at large, things can go wrong, and unwanted things can happen often enough. This time, for a certain reason, we had to move about eleven li north from here to live in a cove named Yadama. My dear husband, having a number of things to worry about, had to wander from place to place, spending most days on the road. We, at home, could only wonder how he was, when he might be coming back, never feeling at peace, hoping to hear from him like a cuckoo's single call. And the summer wore on in vain.

It was at such a time that, though it was at the height of heat on a hot day, he had to go to a village about five li from here. I was unable to stop him, and he was cheerful when he left, making me feel all the more inadequate and miserable. He hadn't been feeling well, especially since Seedling Month, when his stomachache worsened. But he pushed ahead, ignoring it. The heat continued day after day, so that grass and tree seemed to wilt.

One such evening I was with my young ones, wondering aloud how he was, what he might be doing, to console ourselves. The sky was unusually clear, with not a single cloud. The light of Leaf Month rose, brightening the whole world, so that, facing it, I almost felt embarrassed. My two children and I were on the verandah. I pulled up a pillow and lamented, "From where do you think your father is looking at this? It must be on an occasion like this that someone said, 'All the ministers of Kamakura are in tears.'"

> Induced by the light of the moon all so clear I feel mysteriously sorrowed
>   by things

I whispered this, when there was the noise of someone pushing and opening the latticed door. Wondering who it could be, I looked, and it was one of the young men who come to this house mornings and evenings. He was like a family member, and I talked to him while lying down. In a while my children fell asleep. I put them in a mosquito net. I made the young man read a Chinese classic. Again there was the sound of someone coming. "Well, now, his aunt and his mother together rose up to the moon!"

Soon the other youth finished reading and came out, so the three of us talked about nothing particular, until it got awfully late. The two men rose and left. I went out with them and locked the door to the gate. Preparing to go to the bedroom, I looked up. The moon in midair was still clear.

> Strangely, as it grows late, I'm moved to wish the moon will remain clear
>   in the sky

In what kind of hut is my husband lodging tonight? How is he looking at
the moon?

And I had another thought:

The days are so hot as to tear apart the soul: may you come home soon,
without incident

Interludes

A Brief Survey of Senryū by Women

The 5-7-5-syllable senryū, like the hokku, derives from the longer verse form of renga. But unlike the hokku, which normally deals with natural or seasonal phenomena, the senryū is expected to deal with matters of human and social nature, often in a playful, satirical, or knowing manner. The hokku—called haiku today—carries a seasonal reference; the senryū doesn't have to.

The distinction between the two genres of verse has been tenuous at best from early on, however, and in recent years the blurring of the differences has become such that Ōnishi Yasuyo has said, "If someone asks me how senryū differ from haiku, I tell the inquirer that the only distinction that can be made is by author's name"—that is, if the author is known to write haiku, the pieces he or she writes are haiku; if the author is known to write senryū, the pieces she or he writes are senryū. Ōnishi herself is sometimes listed as a senryū poet, sometimes as a haiku poet.

Modern senryū, which dates from about the time of the haiku reform efforts of Masaoka Shiki (1867–1902), has taken such divergent perspectives as idealism ("the theory," as an English dictionary puts it, "that the objects of external perception, in itself or as perceived, consist of ideas"), proletarianism, social realism, and individualism ("the tendency," as a haiku dictionary puts it, "to sink deeply into one's own individuality").

One senryū observer has noted that if the period of 250 years since the senryū was established as a genre were to be divided into five ages, this would be the fifth, and women writers have dominated it. In the early part of the twentieth century, women senryū writers were, the pioneering Inoue Nobuko said, "fewer than the stars at daybreak."

What follows is a brief survey of senryū by women. Most of the selection is made from Taira Sōsei's anthology with commentary, *Ryōran Josei Senryū* (Midori Shobō, 1997).

Sakai Sobaijo (Died 1952)

A mother of seven children, Sakai Sobaijo was one of the first women to take up senryū in the Meiji era. Her husband was Sakai Kuraki (1869–1945), a leader in the Meiji senryū revival among whose senryū is "Kuraki has become a fool called a teacher," which is a twist on an anonymous senryū, "He's not such a fool as to be called a teacher."

At every command he gives the second lieutenant jumps up

In a sudden shower a woman covers her obi first

Unable to compose a single piece on plum flowers she comes home

She says "sheeee!" to a burglar thinking he's a rat

Receiving the evening sun a fishing boat is left in the dark

Itō Masajo (Born 1882)

"A woman experiences frustrations," Itō Masajo said, "as an old woman, a little girl, a bride, a second wife, and a widow. She must capture such weaknesses" in her senryū. She was prolific and once turned China's classical novel *The Water Margin* into a sequence of 285 senryū. But she had disappeared from the senryū world by 1920.

Cupid often runs out of arrows and is lost

Deep deeper into the night O O atop the waves[1]

Shimoyama Kyōko (Active in the Early 1900s)

Welcomed by the Tokyo senryū world as a "genius" in 1904, she helped found a senryū association in Osaka in 1909. Later, she apparently faded away.

The powder peeled off from her face the summer Fuji

Sewing the myopic person ends up sewing her nose

Out of a wildly hairy shawl a human head

In thin rain atop a guillotine a crow caws

She snaps her white fan open and a head rolls

----

1. A *bareku*, a piece whose real meaning lies elsewhere—in short, an erotic piece.

Inoue Nobuko (1869–1958)

Married to Inoue Kenkabō (1870–1934), the first "giant" in modern senryū, Nobuko established in 1929 an association of women senryū writers—the first of its kind. A nurse during the Russo-Japanese War, she protected and promoted the proletarian, antiwar senryū writer Tsuru Akira (1909–1938) at the risk of government persecution. In 1937, when he was jailed, she was also arrested.

The moment it blooms with full force it's cut

A beautiful day turns into a beautiful night

My heart is like a ceaselessly rolling stone

I protect my heart's light from being blown out

How weighty is the one approaching his last moments

The derangement of my soft fingers touches a flower

I open it I close it but my hand's still empty

From a whole array of colors I find white

The evening primroses stack up the light of the moon

No matter how I sit I only see myself the way I am

One leaves then two and I'm alone with the dead[2]

Kataoka Hiroko (1890–1975)

Admired by her fellow senryū writers as "the Venus of Okayama" (Okayama being the prefecture where she was born and spent her life), Kataoka Hiroko was praised by Inoue Nobuko for the "wide range of poetic sensibilities and for the lack of sentimentality" she showed in her work. The last two in the following selection have to do with her husband, a fellow senryū writer, on his deathbed.

---

2. In memory of her husband, Kenkabō. In a 5-5-7-syllable format, this poem was originally printed in three lines.

Days continue with my heart like a wasps' nest

For sharing joy this mosquito net is too small

Leaving brightness on the water the twilight falls

Oh well then I'll just turn into a snake's heart

Making not the slightest move my nerves sharpen

I firmly held it and it was a fragile hand

In a hospital ward just the two of us the night the rain

Mikasa Shizuko (1882–1932)

Regarded as representative of the Shinkō (Newly Rising) senryū movement.

Today too darkens bringing closer the day we'll meet

The heart wanting to be loved presses on my loneliness

As if collapsed into crying the woman guffaws

In secrecy I touch something I shouldn't be touching

I've preserved the redness of my lips today as well

Yoshida Shigeko (Active around 1930)

Yoshida Shigeko was married to the adopted son of the famous patriot Yoshida Shōin (1830–1859) and was a devout Buddhist.

Deprived of all their possessions a winter stand of trees

Holding loneliness in her arms she's left behind

Even my hair refuses to be easily combed this morning

Keeping quiet she is inside all sorts of partitions

Having totally naked our hearts hold each other

Taking one off taking two off like a human being

The moment we hold each other our masks are gone

Ōishi Tsuruko (Born 1907)

Ōishi Tsuruko was a daughter of Inoue Nobuko and Kenkabō.

Walking side by side the warmth on the side where you are

I love senryū suffer senryū and it makes me live

I break the wall I break history[3]

Miura Ikuyo (Born 1912)

Miura Ikuyo uses punctuation, including dashes, and spaces. She also ignores syllabic count often enough that some call her pieces "one-line poems" rather than senryū.

Distant whistle—a hag lives alone under the River of Heaven

We date on a flaming day a skink for a pet a snake for a pet

The moonlit night I hung my slough on your treetop

I plant a cactus in my eyes and give up

Dangling from a liar's throat an emergency exit

I knocked my head and sand spilled from my eyes

---

3. In 5-7 syllables.

Kondō Toshiko (Born 1915)

When Kondō Toshiko was fourteen, her mother was murdered by a passerby. It was after that incident, she said, that she was drawn to senryū.

The loneliness of knowing today too I read books

The corpse of silence shutting up the past

You walk you run and you're still on the earth

Worm infested the flower can't help but bloom

My life a single drop of love between heaven and earth

Usui Kanojo (Born 1925)

Arriving at senryū at age twenty-five, Usui Kanojo has served as a permanent judge at the Tokyo Senryū Association since 1988. She often ignores syllabic count and employs punctuation.

I'll trust this man for now I take off my *tabi*

My will—toward the sun my hands are red

His lies were his only truth eternal sleep

The nails, feeling the autumn white[4]

Great desert—a human breaks his measure off

I keep hugging my self that's different from my age

---

4. In Chinese tradition, autumn is called "White Emperor."

Kuwano Akiko (Born 1925)

From 1973 to 1980 Kuwano Akiko was the senryū judge for the Hokkaidō edition of the daily *Yomiuri*. In 1988 she won the Senryū Ze Prize.

The snow's falling the snow's falling these two breasts

Lightly lightly a butterfly lies dead on the canvas of snow

My skull squeaks right in the midst of ecstasy

Hayashi Fujio (1926–1959)

Her husband killed in war, Fujio was active in senryū for only about three years before she died of a stomach ulcer, but she has greatly influenced those who have come after her.

Seeking despair secret fire O burn

I close my eyes I drop into sex the bottomless swamp

I submit to a single male the male's arrogance

These breasts not to give to a child I a woman

Delighting in its voluminousness my black tangled hair[5]

With the tip of my tongue I roll the delightful evil

Once a month to face the beast I want fire

The whole thing the whole of it slips in I slip in

The bed's screams on night's swing I ride

---

5. Yosano Akiko: "Black hair a thousand strands of hair tangled hair thoughts so tangled thoughts tangled!" See p. 267.

Saigō Kanojo (Born 1928)

Saigō Kanojo started writing senryū in 1953 and has remained active since. She once headed a group to study the genre.

The light falling on her aslant she's an ordinary woman

He leaves and I put away the lonesome sound

Tokizane Shinko (Born 1929)

Compared to Yosano Akiko in tanka, Shinko has been the most influential senryū writer for the last few decades, her liberating boldness attracting many admirers.

So I hate him to the very end I dress to kill

Love achieved at 4 o'clock the 4 o'clock train leaves

Savage love's what I want I say smokestack

Completely beaten oh I'm a chicken stripped naked

Since I became again a wife who laughs often winter

Kill your wife and come visit me wavering wavering

Morinaka Emiko (Born 1930)

In 1981 Morinaka Emiko became a senryū judge for the national broadcasting corporation, NHK; she now works as an instructor at the NHK Academy of Distance Learning.

The pale moon whose are these tiny breasts?

On a promise not to bear a child we meet snow ceaseless

I think of the day my bones will collapse rustling

The bell insect[6] dies the bell insect's food remains

I like humans I'm being drunk with humans

I've never eaten breakfast with a man

Kodama Yoshiko (Born 1934)

Kodama Yoshiko learned about senryū in 1952 while in a sanatorium. Since 1988 she has been independent, not associating with any group.

I'm in the shadow of countless prostitutes

Conflict at the base of this silvery night

Mayumi Akiko (Born 1934)

In 1983 Mayumi Akiko won the Fukushima Prefecture Senryū Prize.

Though hugging each other my back suddenly feels cold

Let me eat you you eat me to become nothingness

Though lying close to each other two separate snails

Kino Yukiko (Born 1936)

Kino Yukiko took up senryū at twenty-nine. In 1982 she founded the Bangasa Kikyō Senryū Association and became executive director of the All Japan Senryū Association in 1991.

In too much sorrow I sleep with my mask on

---

6. *Suzumushi (Homoeogryllus japonicus)*: a variety of cricket. Prized for its quiet, limpid sound and called the king of singing insects.

Matsuda Kyōmi (Born 1942)

Arriving at senryū at thirty-seven, Matsuda Kyōmi has won a variety of prizes, among them NHK's Kyūshū Contest Special Prize.

Suppressing yawns suppressing myself I remain wife

Combing my hair in love I scatter and spill sparks

Having my lover unbutton me early summer

Every time I weep I rise to my feet like a man

Seino Chisato (Born 1948)

In 1986 Seino Chisato created "senryū performances" to stress the "physicality" and "eroticism" of senryū and staged one-woman shows in Himeji, Okayama, Tokyo, and Kyoto.

The night I meet my younger brother I'm a Klimt woman

I bought at a kiosk and brought home as the sound of waves

Running down the giraffe's neck the orgasm

Seeking love just as a Javanese lizard calls

Hasegawa Hiroko (Born 1948)

Hasegawa Hiroko started by submitting senryū to daily newspapers in 1968. A resident of Matsue, she won the second Education Minister's Prize for National Culture.

I like the wind born when I turn the page

The sun sets now in the shape of a breast

I gargle my mouth I gargle but the man remains

Love is when the peach quietly goes on ripening

Lover when the tide is full let's meet again

I put in the blender your long sentence

Ōnishi Yasuyo (Born 1949)

Ōnishi Yasuyo is at the forefront of "New Wave" senryū writers. She teaches at Kansai Gakuin University while running a restaurant.

I'm being rocked by the train rocking with shame

A single fish crosses the Ice Age

My bones and cherries are in full bloom

Having also learned to be ill I take off my flower robe

Lifelong I count dandelions count clouds

When vermilion peonies start to collapse I hug fire

In Clothes Doubled my reproductive organ dies beautifully

The metaphysical elephant drinks water from time to time

Akimoto Miyuki (Born 1957)

Born in Hirosaki, Aomori, Akimoto Miyuki became a member of a local senryū group in 1990. Two years later she won the Meyanagi Prize.

The dog's balls have a line I'd like to rape

I take a deep breath and become pregnant with fireworks

A crayon breaks and a contrail is left behind

Killing the sound of waves I'm cutting scallions

Stepping on my shadow I arrive at the winter sea

What is this loneliness the mud on a yam

A Brief Survey of Haiku by Women

From the seventeenth century onward, the hokku was a more or less independent verse form, but Masaoka Shiki made its independence final by declaring the sequential verse form of renga—of which the hokku was the opening part—to be "non-literature." Shiki also helped replace the term *hokku* with *haiku*.

After Shiki's death, in 1902, those who studied haiku with him split into two camps: "traditional" and "nontraditional." The former group was famously (and dictatorially) represented by Takahama Kyoshi (1874–1959) and his magazine, *Hototogisu* (*Cuckoo*; Shiki, which is a pen name, also means cuckoo); the latter less famously by Nakatsuka Ippekirō (1887–1946) and his magazine, *Kaikō* (*Crab Apple*). Kyoshi held *kachōfūgetsu*, "flower-bird-wind-moon," to be the true subject matter of haiku and stuck, usually, to the *yūkiteikei* format, 5-7-5 syllables with a seasonal reference. Ippekirō, in contrast, did not require seasonal references and, more important, advocated *jiyūritsu*, "free rhythm."

The traditional and nontraditional groupings are, however, simplistic and do not begin to suggest the whole range of approaches and expressions attempted even within the traditional camp, as may be discerned from the following selection of haiku written by women in the twentieth century. The selection owes much to *Joryū Haiku Shūsei* (*Collection of Women's Haiku*), compiled by Uda Kiyoko and Kuroda Momoko (Tachikaze Shobō, 1999). The large anthology contains twelve thousand haiku by eighty-one haiku poets. Some haiku poets with more substantial selections appear individually elsewhere.

Abe Midorijo (1886–1980)

A member of *Hototogisu*, Abe Midorijo became a leading poet in the group. In 1932 she started her own magazine, *Komakusa* (*Horse Grass*), which survives to this day.

Autumn wind a horse loaded with stones doesn't move

A dog sharply looks at a dog in a distant withered field

Just like ripples the geese grow far away

Mists spouted and the number of fireflies has increased

Haikai heavier than life I await a butterfly

Hasegawa Kanajo (1887–1969)

A member of *Hototogisu*, Hasegawa Kanajo became a leader of women's haiku under Kyoshi. For her achievements as a pioneering woman haiku poet she was decorated.

At the rain clouds again mountain azaleas flare up

A morning wind a cat walks around the mosquito net

Spring clouds not moving a boat advances

The spot where the dog sits is bald on the spring lawn

Takeshita Shizunojo (1887–1951)

A member of *Hototogisu*, Takeshita Shizunojo formed the Students Haiku Association while working as a librarian.

Short night my child with not enough milk obstinate

Short night shall I toss away my child crying for milk[1]

In the act of breastfeeding alone my spring passes away

Long night the woman falls asleep like a silkworm

Hydrangeas friends who lose their husbands increase[2]

---

1. The last part of this haiku consists of five Chinese characters, which form a sentence in classical Chinese and which are then given a reading in colloquial Japanese. You might call it a bilingual joke.
2. Japan's war in China was worsening.

Sugita Hisajo (1890–1946)

A member of *Hototogisu*, Sugita Hisajo started a haiku magazine for women, *Hanagoromo* (*Flower Robe*), in 1932; it lasted for five issues. Kyoshi initially showcased her but later "excommunicated" her. She had nervous breakdowns and died in a mental clinic.

The flower robe shed strings cling to me colorfully[3]

A moonflower about to open with its folds deep

Mending socks I became not Nora but a schoolteacher's wife

The mountain cuckoo creates echoes as it pleases[4]

Spring night suppressing sleepiness I comb my hair

Hair rolled up I remain immersed in long night's bath

The Genkai[5] with its roaring darkness wild geese shout

I hate Kyoshi I hate Kanajo my unlined sash[6]

Hashimoto Takako (1899–1963)

Famously inspired by Kyoshi to write haiku at a party she and her wealthy husband threw, Takako was not strictly a *Hototogisu* person. Her initial guide was Sugita Hisajo. She wrote a number of haiku about her husband, who died in 1932.

Up close to his face near death I say the moon's shining

In the moonlight I sleep with one who's alive dying

Snow fierce how I went out of breath when hugged

---

3. *Hanagoromo*, "flower robe," is a flowery kimono worn for viewing cherry blossoms. The original, *Hanagoromo nugu ya matsuwaru himo iroiro*, plays with the word *iroiro*, which, though here given as "colorfully," means "various" (strings).
4. Kyoshi selected this for the Landscape Academy Prize.
5. The strait between Korea and Kyūshū, reputed for its rough sea.
6. Hisajo had a fallout with both Kyoshi and Kanajo.

Snow fierce I die not knowing any hand but my husband's

Toward a man strangling a chicken the snow sweeps

Perambulator sidewise against summer's roaring waves

In the spring lake I wet my fingers and mourn for her

Myriad greens there on my forehead the iron bar[7]

A wasp struggles in order to live or to die?

Snowy day my bathed body I caress each finger each toe

Snow fierce how many the things I leave unwritten[8]

Mitsuhashi Takajo (1899–1972)

Takajo first studied haiku with an editor of *Hototogisu* but was later drawn to *Bara* (*Rose*), a magazine founded in 1952 by the radical modernist Tomizawa Kakio (1902–1962).

Autumn wind fainter than the water the fins of fish

A woman stands alone ready to cross the Galaxy

Even the day heaven and earth are quiet ants hurry

Hard to die can't stand living this late summer light

With nothing to hold on to I hold on to a cold wind

Holding a fireball in my heart I deteriorate

Under dead leaves an earthworm turned into a nail

There's a single ant the ants are everywhere

A thousand insects shrill one shrilling derangedly

---

7. Visiting the mental clinic where Sugita Hisajo died in a jail-like room.
8. Found in her bed after her death.

Shimizu Keiko (Born 1911)

Shimizu Keiko initially studied haiku with her brother-in-law Akimoto Fujio (1901–1977), an advocate of proletarian haiku; she later joined Nagata Kōi (1900–1997), an ardent student of Zen. She regards the haiku as "a short poem with seventeen syllables"—the sort of conception that is possible only in the milieu where the view prevails that haiku is different from *shi*, a blanket term for non-tanka, non-haiku poems.

The snow accumulating a single ax lies quiet

The overcoat being black the snow starts anon

The tree-searer's rapids night's no-man's slope

With a caged badger I share a cake 'cause he's old

Waking from a nap I drink water and lose appetite

I open my palm and the snow falls swiftly

In my mouth a limb of a thrush resounds

Even a wasp • a man • death is beautiful in the distance

If you die you're forgotten that's good the summer moon

Katsura Nobuko (1914–2004)

Katsura Nobuko started by submitting haiku to *Kikan* (*Flagship*), a magazine Hino Sōjō (1901–1956) started in 1935, advocating liberalism. She has received a number of awards, among them the Order of the Sacred Treasure.

The moon's so pure I end up hating my spouse

My soft body I let it into the moonlight

Under a spring light to my consternation my solitude

In mid-heaven geese utter the voices of living things

Window snow with my female body I let the hot water overflow

With silk I wrap my body the autumn having arrived

At the end of the day the sun shines on a black swallowtail

In North Country a moth dances out onto a Nō stage

Amid cherry blossoms a bell makes a sound totally dark

Kitahara Shimako (Born 1917)

Shimako has been associated with several magazines, among them *Kanrai* (*Winter Thunder*), edited by the traditionalist Katō Shūson (1905–1993).

On a snowy field his thick throat stretching a rooster calls

I wrap scallions in a newspaper where I read about Picasso

A plowing bull terrifies beaten he turns up his eyes

I count the stars I count the bones and I fall asleep

A butterfly flits and I think of the butterfly having parted with her

Suzuki Shizuko (Born 1919)

Suzuki Shizuko started writing haiku during the war and collected them in *Shunrai* (*Spring Thunder*) in 1946. But it was with her second book of haiku, *Yubiwa* (*Ring*), in 1956, that she distinguished herself. The book contained pieces that candidly described the sexual and other turmoil in the years immediately following Japan's defeat, in 1945. After publishing it, she faded out of the haiku scene.

In autumn rain someone pointed to a mole on my nape

In the hot bath my breasts are dear this autumn night

Putting up with the dryness of my lips the night is long

Opening winter pear I'm surprised at my flirty self

In my body your blood flows I can stand sitting right

Immersed in sensuality immersed in it the ripe pomegranate

I like glasses roses rains stations fingers spring thunder

Already I have two affairs running an avalanche

Lovemaking a quiet rain stays and surrounds us

My naked body on my thighs run blood vessels blue

Sexual desire wild clouds quickly change their shapes

This moonlit night I keep thinking of something not right

This flowery night an alien soldier and I finger-mate

Being a prossie may be good eating ripe persimmons

In the sleet the amount of money someone's given

Cosmos and things blowing gently I can't die

To a brothel this road leads in the moonshine

The summer citrus's sour now the hell with virginity

Tsuda Kiyoko (Born 1920)

Tsuda Kiyoko studied haiku with Hashimoto Takako, beginning in 1923, then with Yamaguchi Seishi (1901–1994), one of Kyoshi's "four leading students."

From the spring sea easily a gull flies up

A swimming girl her hair also follows the flow

$\alpha \beta \chi$ the crows in a greenfield

Truly when I die I will not give you a phone call[9]

No direction no time no distance the desert day breaks

A desert tree I DO NOT KNOW the Japanese

The spring river the blind water's indigo thick

Terada Kyōko (1922–1976)

When seventeen Terada Kyōko developed a lung disease that remained chronic for the rest of her life. She received the Modern Haiku Society Prize. She also wrote scripts for the radio.

Winter full moon in the midst of my own scent I sleep

I look down but can't avoid the butterfly's light

A dragonfly touches it a wind touches it my father's large earlobe

On a snowy night my hairpin has the smell of the sea

The snow melting mannequins utterly naked on a truck

Kumagai Aiko (Born 1923)

A student of Katō Shūson, Kumagai Aiko won the Modern Haiku Society Prize.

On Constitution Day I'm with weeds on a mountain

My crotch of Original Sin is hot collecting plums

A urinal remains standing after a fire

This is a wrinkled town "Don't throw away kittens"

---

9. Because of the use of the katakana syllabary, this piece gives the impression of a telegram.

With fire clams open the Old Testament

Ants • lizards have no voice their love fierce

I look down my torso gone molten the day the war ends

The flesh called tongue twists around white peach flesh

An eel cries like a woman who's burst out sobbing

Thirteenth moon the corpse's vagina's like fire

Yagi Mikajo (Born 1924)

An ophthalmologist, Yagi Mikajo started writing haiku as a medical student. She studied haiku with Hirahata Seitō (1905–1997), in the first half of the 1930s a leader of the Shinkō movement, which attempted to "modernize" haiku—an anti-Kyoshi movement. Mikajo founded her own magazine, *Hana* (*Flower*), in 1964.

The birth cry between my thighs stretches into budding-tree darkness

Bikini in the distance my two children are both in the rebellious phase

A soprano and the lightning-shaped sense of pain

Full-blooming forest's genitals' branchial respiration

Father's death

Each and every strand of his silver hair glistens death

A toad crawls out onto a sleepless map in red and black

Transparent in the sea light a running bull's history of plundering

The deep-sea fish falls apart the moment it moves

I seek Kama Sutra on a seashell mound on a deserted isle

Yamada Mizue (Born 1926)

Yamada Mizue studied haiku with Ishida Hakyō (1913–1969), who pursued "the meaning of life" through haiku. She won the Kadokawa Haiku Prize and the Haiku Poets Society Prize.

The straw hat soft to my hands the summer ends

Never saw again on the coffin the winter wasp

On a hot day a nap resembles death a little

Withered rushes the distant ones first in the evening glow

I pick a snail as it faintly puts up resistance

Trying to escape its own fire a firefly flies

On a frosty night one, two books on how to die

Miyoshi Junko (1926–1985)

Miyoshi Junko's haiku first saw print in *Gumpō* (*Swarm of Bees*), a magazine started by the policeman haiku poet Enomoto Fuyuichirō (1907–1937). She was the first recipient of the Corona Prize, in 1964. She was ill for some years before her death.

Slight cold the night's faucet shut still leaks

At once a stranger the one I parted with under flaming heaven

The night we met can't take the snow scent off my black hair

Sinking my washed hair I make the water abundant

A shrike's sharp call put my life out of whack

Ikeda Sumiko (Born 1936)

Ikeda Sumiko studied haiku with Mitsuhashi Toshio (1920–2001), a member of the Shinkō Haiku movement. She won the Modern Haiku Society Prize. Her haiku are sometimes hypersyllabic and do not scan.

In Waterless Month the drips from my aimless oars

Having bloomed I wrote and both breasts and moonflowers ended up blooming

I'll give you a blue rose it's up to you to despair

In a housewife's summer my fingers stuck to the ice

In their usual positions my husband the tea canister the gecko

Diving grebes popping grebes do their numbers jibe?

I love living the beginning of winter resembling spring

When it's cold I wear more clothes when I miss him I meet him

By habit I've come home under the spring stars

Before I knew I was born a human   and *you*?

When you stop growing you're an adult the spring evening

Under the ceiling between my thighs the warm amniotic fluid

In this country I was born and give birth moss maples

Every time I wake up my bed I see is older

If it's cold I wear more clothes if I miss him I meet him

In haiku history sale bans • arrests • earthworms that chirp[10]

---

10. The old haiku tradition held that *mimizu*, "earthworm," chirped or cried.

Ōki Amari (Born 1941)

Ōki Amari studied Western painting at Musashino Art University and haiku with Kadokawa Gen'yoshi (1917–1975).

With father ill it is as though the sky had thin ice

Origami cranes strung together burnt in the witheredness

Lying on its back the baby shark was breathing

There's no peacefulness of dying in the winter sea

Naruto Nana (Born 1943)

Born in Seoul, Naruto Nana studied haiku with Nagata Kōi. A winner of the Modern Haiku Society Prize, she teaches literature at Kyōritsu Women's University.

Saw peonies and then saw gorillas and came home

In spring darkness I've become pregnant with a piece of jade

It's *negative* then it's *positive* the summer sea

Evening cherry blossoms at times appear like dorsal fins

Just about ten cicada shells smell of the snow

Going over the sea that one swallowtail is today's betrayal

At six at dusk the daddy longleg's legs all fallen

On my soul a cat's footprints blue Waterless Month

The moon rises on a plate a single decomposed pair

Metaphysics two snakes begin to rust

Out of loneliness I give birth to snakes dragonflies

Side by side with the life called dog I sun myself

Takazawa Akiko (Born 1951)

Takazawa Akiko studied Russian at the Tokyo University of Foreign Studies and haiku with Suzuki Murio (1919-2004), who started out as a sympathizer of the Shinkō Haiku movement and later wrote nonseasonal, increasingly abstract haiku.

Right after an ecstasy snow falls on my hands and feet

My folds cold a wave-surging orgasm

5 • 4 • 3 • 2 • 1 • 0 the naked tree

At autumn evening I was asked where are you going?

In Tokyo a thousand full moons • manholes

Matsumoto Kyōko (Born 1958)

After graduating from the Buddhist University, Matsumoto Kyōko studied haiku with Itami Mikihiko (born 1920), an important member of the Shinkō Haiku movement who strongly advocated the use of interlinear breaks (*wakachigaki*). See the Itami Kimiko section, pp. 352–353. Her first book of haiku, *Remon no Machi de* (*In the Town of Lemon*), in 1987, was welcomed as youthful haiku of a new generation.

Deep-sea fish   after being with you I'm all alone

Cranes' courtship dance   such is weightlessness

I was hugged in my dress   I heard a shooting star

Just *kill me* for a woman only a blue sky

Nakayama Mickey (Born 1947)

Nakayama Mickey started writing haiku as a member of a haiku group when she was forty-three and went on to win five prizes in the next seven years, including the Haiku Poem prize, in 1997.

We the progeny of Atlantis the sardine clouds

Silvery pampas grass   is this really your last trip

An evening sun that can't set fluttering a harmonica

Come March intending to be playful clouds form

Toward a full moon I pedal my bicycle which is blue

I burn letters because it's such a beautiful sky

Cell memory thrown into turmoil   marine blue

Where's Heaven? Where is it? Falling leaves fly

Closest to Hesperus lies your train stop

Flowing toward my hometown spring's Milky Way

Symptoms of deterioration so vivid my sunshine

His back in the distance drenched in the moonlight

Water's dream   ice's memory   emerald

Beginning to run where the cats turn into peacocks

The Modern Age

Shimazaki Tōson (1872–1943), whose first book of poems, *Wakana Shū* (*Collection of Young Herbs*), in 1897, marked the arrival of new poetry in Japan, recollected in 1904, when his first four books of poems were issued in a single volume, the excitement he and his fellow poets felt in creating a "new style" of poetry in their own language.

> At long last, the time for new poetry has come.
> It is like a beautiful dawn. Some shout like ancient prophets, some call out like poets of the West, all as though intoxicated with a bright light, a new voice, and imagination.
> Youthful imagination, awakened from a long sleep, adorns the language of our folk. . . .
> Many in the throng of new singers are just simple youths. Their art is childish, imperfect, and yet also without falsity, without embellishment. . . .
> It is said that poetry is "emotion recollected in tranquillity." Indeed, my songs are confessions of fearful struggles.
> Grief and suffering remain in my songs. When you think of it, it is good to speak out. It's good to speak out without hesitation. . . .

Tōson's poetry, in fact, immediately, profoundly, affected the young men and women of the day, among them Yosano Akiko, the first poet to appear in this section. In particular, the cry of O-Kume, one of "the six virgins" given voice in a group of six poems, is thought to be the direct antecedent of Akiko's more assertive tanka such as, "Spring's short how can life last forever I said made his hands grope my strong breasts." Midway through a nine-stanza monologue O-Kume implores: "How can't you tell that my love for you, / having touched your manly hand, / would not cease, oh, unless I transferred / my lipstick to you, to your mouth?"

Here it may be apt to note that Japan's ending its isolationist policy in the mid-nineteenth century worked wonders in literature. The first known Japanese anthology to be translated into a foreign language was the *Hyakunin Isshu*. F.V. Dickins, a physician attached to the British Navy, rendered it into English and published it in London, in 1866; it is a marvel of freedom in approach to translation. The first systematic attempt to introduce Western poetry in Japanese translation was made in 1882, and its three compiler-translators were a sociologist, a botanist, and a philosopher—none a scholar of literature or a poet. The first comprehensive anthology of verse composed by Japanese was one of kanshi. A Chinese scholar compiled it at the request of a Japanese journalist, and it started publication in China, in 1883. And the journalist, Kishida Ginkō, had earlier collaborated with the American missionary-physician James Curtis Hepburn on the first Japanese-English dictionary, which was published in London, in 1867. The romanization Hepburn devised is used to this day.

Yosano Akiko
(1878–1942)

Born to a well-known confectioner in Sakai, Akiko (née Hō Shō) won national notoriety and admiration with her first book of tanka, *Midaregami* (*Hair in Disorder*), published in August 1901. At times mesmerizingly narcissistic, the collection of 399 pieces spelled out a young woman's sexual thoughts and acts. "Not even touching the blood-tide in my soft flesh aren't you lonely you who teach the Way?"—so she said in an often quoted piece. But the man who "taught the Way," Yosano Tekkan (1873–1935)—the founder and publisher of the romantic poetry magazine *Myōjō* (*Venus*)—was living with one of his former students, who was pregnant. The literary critic Takayama Chogyū (1871–1902) thundered, accusing Akiko of "licentious sentiments and shallow philosophy," and Sasaki Nobutsuna (1872–1963), a poet and a scholar of classical Japanese poetry, judged that *Midaregami* was "pernicious to the human heart and poisonous to social education."

But *Midaregami* had a liberating effect on young men and women at the time, and its hold remains powerful today. The tanka poet Mizuhara Shion (born 1959), for one, has called *Midaregami* "an epoch-making work that sought beauty by reaching a woman's deep [psychological] strata," concluding that it is "a collection of nightmares that reveal themselves at least once to the dullest and most banal of women."

Akiko married Tekkan in the fall of 1901 and went on to have six sons—the sixth one died shortly after birth—and six daughters by him, while remaining superhumanly active in a range of literary endeavors and women's education. In poetry alone, she wrote fifty thousand tanka and seven hundred shi. Among her other works that are still widely read today is her translation into modern Japanese of *The Tale of Genji*.

From *Midaregami (Hair in Disorder)*

Cochineal Purple

Hair five feet untangled soft in the water the maiden's heart I'll keep secret won't let it out

The girl twenty flowing through the comb the black hair's haughty the spring how beautiful

Dark red whom shall I tell about it the blood wavers thoughts of spring life in its prime

Toward Kiyomizu passing Gion cherry moonlight night everyone I see tonight is beautiful

Clouds blue Summer Princess who's come her morning hair beautiful it flows in the water

Yosano Akiko at the time
Midaregami was published

Akiko in later years

Night's Deity come morning rides a sheep home I'll capture and hide it under my
pillow

Not even touching the blood-tide in my soft flesh aren't you lonely you who teach
the Way?

He not allowed to go the darkening spring evening laid on a small koto my tangled
tangled hair

Arm for pillow a strand of hair snapped I heard it as a small koto in spring night's
dream

Hot bathing at a spring's bottom a small lily flower its twentieth summer I see as
beautiful

Disturbed heart hesitant heart persists, for the god stepping on lilies I can't cover
my breasts

On her scarlet rose her layered lips do not allow a song without a soulful scent to
ride

Now here when I turn to reflect my love was like a blind man unafraid of the
dark

My tangled hair made back into Kyō Shimada the morning he's still in bed I shake
him awake

My painted parasol thrown onto the other shore grass I cross the brook spring
water warm

Cuckoo it's one li to Saga three li to Kyoto in Kiyotaki of water the day breaks
so fast

Pressing my breasts I softly kick the mystery curtain here the flower's vermilion
is intense

Somehow I felt you waited for me have come out into a flower field this evening
moon

Hot bathed and out of the spring what touches my skin is the silk of the harsh
human world

My light dress its two-foot sleeve sliding down it a firefly flows away into night
wind blue

Leaning on an evening door you sing a song: "I left my melancholy home I'll
never return"

I see it as my spring figure twenty years old a light-colored peony vermilion at
its base

Just to see I touched it with my young lips how cold was the dew on the lotus
white

Spring rain dripping on a swallow's wings I'll receive it to smooth my morning-
slept hair

White Lily[1]

You brood I brood our hearts now inseparable are you White Bush Clover am I
White Lily

The three of us are siblings down and out in this world I first blurt out at an inn
in West Kyoto

One room away I heard you breathe from time to time the night I dreamed I held
White Plum

---

1. Tekkan at the time had at least three lovers: Hayashi Takino, with whom he had just
had a son; Akiko; and Yamakawa Tomiko. Each woman had a nickname: Takino was called
White Peony; Akiko, White Bush Clover; and Tomiko, White Lily. The pen name Tekkan
means "branch of a plum tree."

Not saying not asking just giving a nod we parted the day was the sixth the two
and the one

Things can be cruel in Kyoto I start to write and look down at the Kamo River's
white

Twenty-Year-Old Wife

You leave I'm Mount Wu spring's one-night wife do not think about this till the
next world

Our hearts' clear water overflowed turned muddy you are a sinful child I'm a sinful child

I miss the hot spring scent the plum scent the darkness I leaned on an inn door
waiting for you

Twentieth year my life has so little happiness may the dream I see now be
peaceful

Black hair a thousand strands of hair tangled hair thoughts so tangled thoughts
tangled!

Spring Thoughts

Spring's short how can life last forever I said made his hands grope my strong
breasts

The vow fulfilled the evening rain flowers black my five-foot voluminous hair is
light

So I may punish a man of many sins I'm made with clear skin and long black
hair

You're ill I'll turn my thin arm around your nape so I may kiss your fever-dry
mouth

A Selection of Non-Tanka Poems

In September 1904, when Akiko published the poem that follows, "May It Not Come to Pass That You Die," she was attacked by would-be patriots, among them the scholar of Japanese literature Ōmachi Keigetsu, who called her "a traitor, a rebel, a criminal who ought to be subjected to national punishment." Japan had gone to war with Russia, and Luxu (Port Arthur), where Akiko's brother was sent, had become the largest battleground. In an effort to scale the Russian fortress, General Nogi Maresuke, commanding the Third Army, repeated frontal assaults, creating immense casualties. For the four-month-long assault and defense of the fortress, Japan and Russia would end up deploying a total of 145,000 soldiers, of whom 78,000 became casualties, 18,000 killed. It unnerved the Japanese high command and drove soldiers' relatives to despair.

May It Not Come to Pass That You Die

*Anguished over my younger brother, who is in
the army laying siege to Luxu.*

Ah, my younger brother, I weep for you,
May it not come to pass that you die,
Because you are the one born last
Parents' love is greater that much,
But did they make you hold a blade,
Tell you to kill human beings,
So you might kill humans and die,
Have they brought you up till twenty-four?

Being the master of a proud old house
Of merchants in the town of Sakai
Destined to inherit your parent's name,
May it not come to pass that you die,
The Castle of Luxu may be destroyed,
Or may not, how can that matter,
It's no concern of yours, no such
Requirement exists in a merchant's house.

May it not come to pass that you die,
His Majesty the Emperor would not
Himself go out to fight, would He,
To make each shed the other's blood,
To order you to die in a beastly way,

To tell you that a man's honor is to die,
His Majesty's heart being deep,
How would he think of all this?

Ah, my younger brother, in battle
May it not come to pass that you die,
In the autumn that passed Father died,
Our dear Mother, surviving him,
In the midst of her grief and pain,
Her son summoned, is left to keep house,
In His Majesty's reign, in peace, they say,
Mother's gray hair can only increase.

Prostrate by the blinds she weeps,
Your wife, so new, innocently young,
Have you forgotten her, think of her,
After less than ten months separated,
Try to think of a young woman's heart,
If not you, the only one in the world for her,
Ah, whom else could she count on,
May it not come to pass that you die.

When I Hold a Hand-Drum

When I hold a hand-drum, the voice
Of my older sister, young, comes afloat,
An outer robe on her, flowery,
Older sister's face, beautiful,
Amid cherry blossoms, with blinds,
In a high house overlooking the Uji River,
Sister and I stayed one spring night,
Which dazzled me, how can I forget,
Yes I know, you, having been born
From a different womb, till fourteen
Didn't know Father's love firsthand,
Even during the five years you were home,
Though you were home you weren't at ease,
Then your first love that didn't show,
Hid in your heart a burning thought,
Married to someone you didn't like,
Careful to suppress your weeping,
You the fragile one smiled a smile,

Saying something in a fleeting way,
Ah a dream, wasn't it, such a short life,
You passed away at twenty-eight.
When I think of you, once again
I can only weep for your fate.

Man's Chest

A sword a master forged,
Shorter than a foot,
I think of its sharpness.
At times I want urgently
To get a triangular-tipped scalpel
From someone in a foreign land.
The instant the gleaming blade
Touches the chest of the man I hate
Blood drips down my sleeve,
Splatters on my fingers, scarlet,
Thinking of it I smile to myself,
Even my body trembles pleasantly.
At that moment I'll forgive
The unspeakable heart of the man I hate.
Having said this, on his chest
I want to stab, come night,
I place my brow, feel peace,
Entertain dreams, yes, that's me.
And the man, as if he'd missed me,
Hugs me tight against his chest
And falls asleep, I've yet to forget.
Should he say if as a joke
I won't give you my chest today,
I can imagine how lonely I'd become.

The Day the Mountain Moves[2]

The day the mountain moves has come,
So I say, but no one believes me.

---

2. Written for the founding issue of the magazine *Seitō* (*Bluestocking*), which the feminist
Hiratsuka Raichō started in September 1911. Raichō appears next.

The mountain has just been asleep awhile.
Once in the past
It was all afire, burned, and moved.
But no one needs to believe that.
People, simply believe this:
All the women who've been asleep, now awake, are on the move.

The Woman

"Don't forget a whip,"
Spake Zarathustra.
"A woman is a cow, is a sheep."
I'd add to it and say,
"Let her loose in the field."

Autumn

Autumn is a thin wine cup, isn't it,
Like the one that touches the basin and sinks tinkling an insect cries.
Autumn is Younger Sister's parasol, isn't it,
Its delicate handle made of jade,
The bright, yellow sun shining on it.

Or else, autumn is a twenty-three-year-old in modern style.
Dressed in bluish gray indigo and svelte,
Against a light-brown ground, with many golden threads, and square,
    her China-woven sash dazzling,
In a corner of a park she passes the shadow of a tall maple,
Her eyes a little downcast, she intently looks at a display of snow-white
    chrysanthemums.

She then turns and catches my eye.
"My, so good to see you," she hurries to me.
"How come you've become so skinny," says she
As my older sister might who was separated when ten years old,
What a gentle, gentle autumn this!

In Praise of May

May is a fancy month, a flower month,
The month of buds, the month of scents, the month of colors,
The month of poplars, *marrons, plantanes,*
Azaleas, tree peonies, wisteria, redbud,
Lilacs, tulips, poppies,
The month women's clothes turn
Light and thin, the month of love,
The festival month Kyoto residents
In twirled crowns, arrows on their backs,
Compete in horse races,
The month girls in the City of Paris
Choose for the Flower Festival
A beautiful, noble queen;
If I may speak of myself,
It's the month I crossed Siberia, crossed Germany,
Longing for my love,
And arrived in that distant Paris,[3]
The month to celebrate our fourth son,
Auguste,[4] born last year,
With irises, swords, and streamers,
The breezy month, the month of
The blue moon, of platinum-colored clouds,
When the bright sky and the hemp palm
Outside the window of my small study
Remind me of a Malay island,
The month of honeybees, the month of butterflies,
The month of birth when ants turn into moths[5]
And canaries hatch their eggs,
The sensual month, the month of flesh
That somehow incites you,
The month of *Vous voulez* wine, of perfumes,
Of dances, of music, and of songs,
The month of the sun when
Myriad things inside me
Hold one another tight, become entangled,
Moan, kiss, and sweat, the month

---

3. Akiko traveled to Europe via Siberia in 1912.
4. During that period, it was fashionable in certain circles to give European names to children. The Japanese name of Akiko's fourth son, born in 1913, was Iku.
5. Akiko got an entomological fact wrong here.

Of the blue sea, of the forest, of the park, of the fountains,
Of the garden, of the terrace, of the gazebo,
So here comes May
To toss at us a giddiness
Sweet as the lemonade you suck with a straw
From a thin, skinny glass.

Auguste's Single Strike

My lovely two-year-old Auguste,
I write this down for you:
Today, for the first time,
you struck your mother on the cheek.
It was the power of your life
that wanted to win—
the genuine power for conquest
took on the form of anger
and a spastic fit
and flashed like lightning.
You must have been conscious of nothing,
must have forgotten it at once.
But your mother was shocked,
was also deeply happy.
You can, some day, as a man,
be on your own defiantly,
you can be on your own purely, resolutely,
also can love man and nature decisively
(The core of conquest is love),
also you can conquer suspicion, pain, death,
jealousy, cowardice, derision,
oppression, crooked learning, conventions,
filthy wealth, and social ranks.
Yes, that genuine strike,
that's the totality of your life.
Such were the premonitions I felt that made me happy
under the pain of the sharp blow
you struck with your palm
as a lion cub might.
At the same time I felt the same power
lurking in myself
and even the cheek you didn't strike
became hot like the cheek you did.

You must have been conscious of nothing,
must have forgotten it at once.
But when you've become an adult,
take this out and read it,
when you think, when you work,
when you love someone, when you fight.
My lovely two-year-old Auguste,
I write this down for you:
Today, for the first time,
you struck your mother on the cheek.
My still more lovely Auguste,
you, in my womb,
walked through Europe, sightseeing.
As you grow up,
your wisdom will remember
the memories of those travels with your mother.
What Michelangelo and Rodin did,
what Napoleon and Pasteur did,
yes, it was that genuine strike,
that ferocious, blissful strike.

The First Labor Pains

I am ill today,
physiologically ill.
Wordless, eyes open,
I lie in bed before birth.

Why is it—although
I've almost died a number of times,
though I'm used to the pains, the blood, the cries,
I'm trembling with anxieties and fear I can't control.

A young doctor tried to soothe me,
describing the happiness of giving birth.
I know such things better than he.
What's the use of that now?

Knowledge is not reality,
experience belongs to the past.
Everyone, please be quiet.
Please do not step out of the bystander's position.

I'm all alone,
all alone in heaven and earth;
biting my lips quietly,
I'll wait for my own strength I cannot resist.

Giving birth, in fact,
is the creation of a single reality
that explodes from inside me,
with no room for good or bad.

Now, the first labor pains. . . .
The sun immediately pales,
the world coldly quiets down.
And I am all alone. . . .

Scarlet Plum

Oh, a branch of
Scarlet plum blossoms
Atop a florist's loads,
Are they perhaps the blossoms
A mother and a daughter who are *pauvre*
In a dark corner of a tenement,
In the wintry light
Of patched sliding paper doors,
Faces down, few words spoken,
Crafted by hands, employing
Meager cloths, glue, scissors, a branch,
And fingers that turned pale?
Piteous blossoms,
Blossoms stringing together
Tears, artifice, and red balls of unglossed silk,
I like you so much I feel sad.
Why,
I am in you,
You are in me.
You and I are
Exposed to severe cold and north wind,
Fearfully, timidly, smiling,
Awaiting March.

Hiratsuka Raichō
(1886–1971)

She was born the third daughter of a government official and named Haru. A top student throughout her school years, she enjoyed an unusual degree of independence and liberty. While attending Japan Women's College, a nonsectarian institution established in 1901 by Naruse Jinzō, an educator who studied theology in the United States, she started her religious and philosophical search and in the end found her spiritual home in Zen. In 1908 she attempted a double suicide with her teacher of English.

In 1911 she founded a magazine for women's writings, naming it *Seitō* (*Bluestockings*), and took up the pen name Raichō. The title of the manifesto she wrote for the first issue, "In the Beginning, Woman Was the Sun," went on to become the most frequently quoted slogan for the women's movement in Japan, although the article itself, as she later admitted, was a little too spiritualistic. (The first half of the manifesto is translated here.) *Seitō* quickly turned to women's issues and was attacked as the mouthpiece for the New Woman. When that happened, Hiratsuka penned a piece to assert, in a mainstream magazine, "I Am a New Woman." *Seitō* was banned twice before it was discontinued, in 1915, because of poor sales. Her first collection of essays was also banned, in 1914. One of her models in women's issues was the Swedish social educator Ellen Key (1849–1926).

In 1920 Hiratsuka founded the Society for New Women and in 1930 the Consumer Union. After Japan's defeat in the war, she became active in the peace movement. In 1953 she founded the Federation of Japanese Women's Associations. One of her mottoes was "To live is to act. Not just to breathe."

In the Beginning, Woman Was the Sun

—On the Occasion of Starting *Seitō*—
First Issue of *Seitō*, vol. 1, no. 1, September 1911

In the beginning, woman was in fact the sun. She was the true person.

Now, woman is the moon. She is the moon with a pale face like someone sickly, who lives by relying on someone else and shines by someone else's light.

Here *Seitō* has raised its birth cry.

Seitō, which became possible only by the modern Japanese woman's brain and hand, has raised its birth cry.

Things women do today merely invite the laughter of ridicule.

I know very well what hides under the laughter of ridicule.

And I'm not in the least afraid.

But, what to do with the painful sight of the shame and opprobrium that women themselves have renewed, again, upon themselves?

Are women worth vomit so much?

No, no, the true person—

We've done everything today's women can. And the child we've given birth to, giving it all our heart, is this, *Seitō*. Even if it is a retarded baby, a deformed baby, or a premature baby, we can't do anything about it; we must be content with it for now.

Have we given all our heart to it? No, who, who could be content with it?

I have renewed, again, greater discontent upon the women themselves.

Are women so powerless?

No, no, the true person—

But even I do not overlook the fact that *Seitō,* born of the thriving sun of midsummer, has enough fierce passion to kill extreme heat with heat.

Passion! Passion! We simply depend upon it.

Passion is the power to pray. It is willpower. It is the Zen power to meditate. It is Shinto power. In other words, it is the power to concentrate spiritually.

The only gate that leads to mystery is called spiritual concentration.

Just now, I said mystery. But it isn't the kind of artificial mystery that tends to be drawn on so-called reality or, apart from reality, by sleight of hand, by a mere cleverness, or else by nerve. It isn't a dream. I must make it clear that it is a mystery that is reality itself, which we can only see at the lowest depths of our subjectivity, in the interior of deep human meditation.

I think I will seek genius at the very center of spiritual concentration.

Genius is mystery itself. It is the true person.

Genius is neither male nor female.

Male and female, such sexual discrimination belongs, in stages of spiritual concentration, to the self in the middle or lower stratum, to the self incarnate that must die, must perish; it cannot occur in the self in the highest stratum, the true self that is immortal.

I once did not know there were women in this world. I did not know there were men.

Many men and women were reflected well in my mind. I never saw them as men or as women.

Nevertheless, many a reckless action that overflowed from excessive spiritual power could not in the end be controlled, and plunged me into an almost unsalvageable exhaustion.

The deterioration of personality! In fact, this for the first time showed me socalled woman. And at the same time so-called man.

Thus I learned the word *death* in this world.

Death! Fear of death! One who once under heaven and earth played on the shore of life and death, but then, O, one whose legs tottered in the face of death, one who was to perish, so-called woman.

One who once lived in the uniform realm, one who then in the mongrel realm could hardly breathe with her chest, one who was impure, so-called woman.

And, I came dangerously close to falling in step with the throng of spineless fatalists who do not know that one's destiny is something one shapes for oneself—O, just thinking of this, cold sweat breaks out on my flesh.

I wept, bitterly wept, that the strings of the harp I'd played day and night had loosened, that they had lost verve.

When I knew that personality had formed in my self, I was abandoned by genius. Like a heavenly maiden robbed of her heaven-flying feather robe, like a mermaid pulled up on the land.

I lamented, painfully lamented, that I had lost my bliss, my final hope.

For all this, I was also, and always, the master who controlled anxiety, loss, exhaustion, derangement, destruction, and all else.

I have followed my own path without rest, with the right I acquired for having always been my own master, content that I am an autonomous, free person who controls herself, never regretting my own self trapping me into self-destruction, no matter what incident happened, one after another.

O, darkness, and absolute light, of my hometown.

The sun that illuminates with brilliance and heat that overflows out of itself and nurtures all things is a genius. It is the true person.

In the beginning, woman was in fact the sun. She was the true person.

Now woman is the moon. She is the moon with a pale face like someone sickly, who lives by relying on someone else and shines by someone else's light.

We must now recover our sun that was hidden away.

"Reveal my hidden sun, my latent genius!" This is our incessant call to our interior, our irrepressible, inerasable thirst, our final, whole, personality, and the only instinct in which all mongrel, partial instincts are unified.

This call, this thirst, this final instinct turns into passionate spiritual concentration.

And where it culminates, that's where the exalted throne of genius shines forth.

Fukao Sumako
(1888–1974)

After losing her father at age four, Sumako, whose original name was Ogino Shigeno, was adopted by one family after another well into her twenties. Fukao Hironosuke, a railroad engineer and poet whom she married at twenty-four, died when she was thirty-two. With Yosano Akiko's encouragement she started writing poems. From 1925 to 1928 she lived in Paris, befriended Colette, and became Colette's devoted translator. In 1930 she became a special correspondent for the daily *Mainichi Shimbun,* which enabled her to stay in Paris once again, this time for a year and a half. During that time she took Dr. Toulouse's course on sexology at the University of Paris; she turned what she learned into her book on that subject, published four years later.

In 1939 she went to Europe for the third time, to represent Japan for the Japanese-German Friendship Society. In 1957 she lived in Paris again and while there represented Japan at the fourth gathering of the World's Democratic Women, held in Vienna the following year. She kept publishing poems, essays, stories, and translations throughout her long life.

"Pity the man. . . ."

Pity the man,
born with an innate loneliness,
unable to part with its dark shadow,
working morning to night
at a government office he disliked,
with no time to make the poems he wanted to make,
afraid of touching the inheritance from his ancestors
and not even buying the piano he wanted to buy,
just keeping his mouth shut, just sighing,
only going as far as using a Meisen futon,
and dying at thirty-five,
ah, pity the man!
Nonetheless, I who, left by him,
have to think of these things,
am even more to be pitied.
Ah, pity the man!
Ah, pity me!

The Room

It was like a
one-eyed monster.
It was like a cave
where lives were entombed.
A single small window
greedily sucked in
the faint evening light.
From there the world
looked like a ghostly human soul,
blue, small, trembling.

It was full of sighs, sneers,
groans, sobs, footfalls of things,
in an amorphous way.
The smells of aphrodisiacs, smells of furs,
smells of ecstasy, smells of sadness,
smells of flames, smells of blood,
drifted faintly as if not there.

It was like a place where you lived in death.
It was like a place where you were dead while alive.

It was a room.
It was a mysterious room,
that my soul, passing by,
happened to see, once.

How to Write a Poem

First, push the door of the cage open
and free the songbird used to singing.
Spring rituals begin then.

My Residence After Japan's Defeat

Spring 1947

On the torn shōji
soiled swans flap, flap.
The mirror is covered with cracks,

the rose in the vase thoroughly beaten.

Outside the window
everyone's soiled as soiled can be.

The earth, out of oil, is rickety-rackety.
Isn't there a room for rent on some star?

Like a greedy crow I
bite into enormous sufferings. . . .

Public Bath

Let's at least regard it as the Jordan River.

Miss Fuji Who's All Alone and Beautiful

> From the lakeside of Léman
> I looked up at Mont Blanc
> With Rousseau, in ecstasy;
> I looked back at the city of Léman
> With Rousseau, in ecstasy.

Humph, you say Miss Fuji?
Nothing exciting, I say.
In the winter mirror that's coldhearted and clear,
a *new look* in classical white,
come on, who are you copycatting?
From the roofs of the *barracks* of Tokyo,
You're just the proverbial crane in a garbage dump.
Some pale-faced poet may twist it
and call you a swan in a swamp.
I'd love to strip you of that white.
First, I hate the pose you strike.
I'd smash it up and ditch it in the brothel ditch.
Ahhhhh, the holy land Tokyo of the brothel ditch and *barracks*.
In this cold
it swarms with flies, lice, and bipedal beasts.
Listen, Miss Fuji,
I look at you from here

and you are certainly an aristocratic lady.
Humph, Miss Fuji who's alone and beautiful, they say.
Foreigners say, don't they?—
Fujiyama, sakura, geesha girls.
So you put on haughty airs.
The Rockies are the world's treasure trove, they say.
Olympus is the world's culture, they say.
And what on earth do you say you are?
Don't be shy, put your hand out.
A lot more than that.
You see that?
Politicians or artists,
they are all sticking their hands out.
Like fishing poles.
Anyway, I can't stand graceful pretenses.
Miss Fuji of catty tameness,
Miss Fuji of self-complacence,
do you know anything like shamelessness?
Know something called the flower of evil?
Scribbled on your white shoulders
are 31 syllables and 17 syllables—
a pretty poetic pose, I'd say.
Humph, I'm the holy Mary Magdalene,
Miss Fuji Miss Noble One,
how about a shot of rotgut?
Tastes real neat, I tell you,
though I do have scotch, gin, and Old Parr.
Now souped, eyes barely seeing, shoes torn, drunken ship,
reeling to right, reeling to left—
after all, this life is zigzaggy and bizarre.
I'm soiled, dirty.
Listen, Miss Fuji who's all alone and beautiful,
So you are still there.
What! Face to face with the dandy Diet?
Stop that, I say.
All it has inside it are quacks.
You're too good-natured for words.
Look, how utterly clear the winter mirror!
I'd like to spit at it.
Come now, let's go on pilgrimage to Damascus on a ship, shoes torn—
methane gas, acetylene, yakitori, ammonia,
pickpockets, thieves, guntoters, cutpurses, murderers, burglars,
the homeless, the dead in the gutter, orphans, streetwalkers, bosses—

Just a minute, watch out!
A dagger flashes.
Who is it hanging out there?
A what?—
You're over sixty but still have to sell your womanhood?
You have to powder your face garishly?
My goodness.
You say it's warmer under a tree than in jail?
You say you can see the Great Dipper out of your garbage can?
What, do you want to sing?
Good, go right ahead and sing.
The rage now boogie-woogie, "Rose of the South,"
Anything will do.
Look, here's a black baby
dumped.
He's so cute.
A discard accompanied by milk, I see.
Shall I take him in and bring him up?
How about Mr. Mendel?
He'd say he'll turn yellow in three generations.
What would you say,
Mr. Lycenko?
Come, Miss Mink of ¥50,000,
you put on a lot of airs but that coat doesn't look right on you.
Listen to me now, Miss Housewife of ten-yen cuts,
no matter how you look for them,
you won't see anything cheaper than ¥10.
Ahhhh, the holy land Tokyo bustles so,
a truly attractive city of the world!
Germs flourish
in the germy delta that is Tokyo.
Come, Miss Fuji the aristocratic lady,
Miss Fuji who's all alone and beautiful,
Here everyone's soiled, dirty,
I myself am soiled as soiled can be.
Now, I see, the night's curtain is about to come down.
Mr. Lanky Sperm,
Miss Big-headed Fungus Mushroom Ovum,
soon it'll be time for lovers.
When evening darkness presses upon you . . . I see.
Then the winter mirror turns into sooty glass,
right? Miss Fuji who's all alone and beautiful,
your figure, well,

what's all the fuss,
will be just the roof of a *barrack* a little larger than usual.
See this dry wind that just blows and blows!
Ahhhh, I want to pee.

Spring

In a green-bamboo basket
duck eggs.

I heat bath water
with cherry petals.

Okamoto Kanoko
(1889–1939)

Born to a well-to-do landowner in Kanagawa, Kanoko started publishing her poems
at age sixteen and joined the *Myōjō* group the following year. When she was twenty-
one, she eloped, which led to her first nervous breakdown. The next year, she married
Okamoto Ippei, who went on to become a famous cartoonist; she also joined the feminist
group *Seitō,* which published her first book of tanka, in 1912. The marriage between
Kanoko and Ippei was full of strains—Ippei actively seeking sex outside their home
and Kanoko openly carrying on love affairs, though they did so by mutual consent.
All this led to her conversion to Buddhism and pursuit of Buddhist studies. Although
she did not publish her prose work until 1936, three years before her death, she was
prolific in that branch of writing. The first full-scale collected works, 1974 to 1978,
required an astonishing total of eighteen volumes. She published about six thousand
tanka during her lifetime.

From *Ai no Nayami (Sufferings of Love)*, 1918

Sufferings of Love

You being away from me makes me lonely you being pretty by my side too torments me

Deeply I again miss you keeping quiet my washed hair scattered over my back
this noonday

The nail I bit unthinkingly has a light mark of lipstick left on it how sad how
lonesome

Reflecting how terribly lonesome I am now I cannot see myself consoled by your
"youthfulness"

When he thinks so much of me why does it sprout in me? *Jealousy* it must be
jealousy it must be

Painful to be uselessly *jealous:* Permit me to be in love with him God beautifully
gently

Perhaps because you are in love without a suggestion of *jealousy* innocently you
are beautiful

Feebly feebly a mosquito whirs around a room where the two of us *sobbing* keep
silent

Even before the tears have dried a smile has risen to his cheeks suddenly
beautifully

Healthily I think of you: a *scattering* of white flags blooming toward summer
daybreak

Out of the station the two of us what soaks our eyes green first is the young bamboo
on the hilltop

Off the train hearing its whistle along a distant field path we walk into a sparse
stand of trees

When I turn to look at you lagging behind the high-noon sun's dazzling on your
new hat

On the roadside grass *dust* is somewhat white the two of us walk silent under the
noon sun

The *parasol's* handle I grip is sweaty how many miles away from the city have
we come?

The one who knows both my sorrow and my joy not by my side the high noon is
so quiet

Not knowing when I'll be healed of this illness I spread a new sheet again on my
bed

Early Autumn

Dreaming of your hometown's soft mountain range I feel at peace night after
night

Place your cold black front hair *vividly vividly* first against my cheek I'm sober-
ing up

How brittle the married woman's affair her gold hairpin sliding tangles her side-
locks

Both my child and my garden's small grass asleep lovely will you forgive me for
my love?

From *Yokushin (Bathing Body)*, 1925

   Still Life

Cold still in spring the morning's bright in my room I look at the apples' glow this way that way

Vermilion apples' glow glow culminates I can't do anything so lovely on a Goguryeo plate

Stripped naked I hold up one I hold up a single vermilion apple in the morning bathtub

Left on a medicine shelf the vermilion apple so lovable I pick it up again and immerse myself

Except for my palm on which the vermilion apple rides I've immersed myself in the bath

My body immersed in the bath gradually warming up I can hardly bear up a single apple

Immersed in the bath and taking a close look I find the apple's *core* slightly crooked

How dense the morning bath's steam I look and the shelf-apple's vermilion seems remote

On my palm warm from bath immersion I place the vermilion apple oh how lovely it is!

The *apple* I brought I caress quietly in my palms and that done immerse myself and take a bite

My teeth take a bite and the apple's vermilion rind tears smudging faintly its soft-snow flesh

One bite another, and at the *apple's* sourness I tremble faintly in the morning bathtub

The Great Quake[6]

—meeting the disaster in Kamakura

Before I can tell whether I'm alive or dead the voices of people calling for help strike my ears

Where's the person screaming? I go to the right and it isn't to the right it can't be to the left

I rise to my feet and look about for a while: within my view nothing but standing trees

Beams of every house laid on the ground, now unhindered the wind blows through treetops

Pulling myself up from the bottom of muddy sand where I was lost I first see a faint white sky

His wounded arm bent a man accepts meager food with his other hand and walks away

The collapsing itself is sad enough: flames licking the houses what kind of act is this?

Corpses equally burnt, among them a mother holding a child: I step up close stare at them

My eyes used to the ghastliness the corpse of a mother holding her child makes me weep

Unable to keep standing looking at the corpse of a mother holding her child I simply kneel to pray

---

6. The Great Kantō Earthquake, which struck on September 1, 1923, claimed 3,400,000 casualties, of which 105,069 were killed or missing. The epicenter of the quake was in Sagami Bay, so the damage in the cities surrounding the bay, such as Kamakura, was great. As Kanoko suggests, a great part of the damage was caused by the ensuing fire, which raged for three days in Tokyo. Of those who perished, 58,000 did so in that city; the number compares with the more than 80,000 killed during the U.S. air raid of Tokyo in the early hours of March 10, 1945.

That second the great quake tore the ground apart I was thrown away with pieces
of mud

I rise to my feet and look: my house or the houses the others lived in no longer
exist

Not knowing the ground could be torn in a second in so ghastly a way I had lived
in such peace

Astonishment followed by astonishment sorrow followed by sorrow I can't tell
between the two

Long inured to astonishment, flames rising up near my body, I stand dazed, staring at them

People and houses utterly shattered: on Mount Kamakura the green of pines just
intense

Those Crushed to Death and Those Burnt to Death Lie Together:

Trampling on the corpses near and far all night long packs of wild dogs never stop
howling

From the east the sun has risen the morning after heaven and earth were turned
upside down

Among humans parents were shattered children burnt; only birds call playing
joyfully

Amid heaven and earth turned upside down the morning glories on the fence grow
more intense

Takeuchi Rie
(1901–1958)

Born in Takamatsu, Rie began taking part in leftist activities in her late teens; the consequent police harassment continued until after the Second World War. She published poems and short prose pieces while working in offices and factories and, beginning in 1937, while running a bookstore. In 1934 her twelve-year marriage was dissolved, leaving her with five children. On May 25, 1945, during the incendiary bombings of Tokyo, her second daughter, Yoshimi, suffered severe burns. From her thirties onward Rie had to cope with bouts of rheumatism or arthritis.

The Cart

(Late May 1945)

The light of a sooty lantern
goes ahead, the color of apricot, wavering.

Within the circle of
its dull light
the cart follows the path, rickety-rackety.

Lying in the futon on the cart
my seventeen-year-old daughter horribly burned from an air raid the other night.
Myself, leg injured,
I crouch next to her.

The possessions piled at the end of the cart
are the scanty bedding and cooking utensils
we've managed to get hold of.

In this narrow land,
things and lives
burned up one after another,
we tend to be bound up by the fury
that we can't even become monkeys.

Still
what a pitch-dark
night.
From the shelter for air-raid victims in Ichigaya
to the temporary residence in Nando-chō

Takeuchi Rie

it isn't such a long distance,
but my son holding the shafts
my son pushing the cart from behind
my daughter holding up the lantern
all are exhausted, panting,
and to my daughter who has burns
these vibrations must make
the road feel a hundred miles long.

Worse,
the town that burned and collapsed stinks,
the remnants of buildings
piling up black in the darkness of night.
At the bottom of it all
still flickering, smoldering,
are the pale flames on human bones.

Is this
what once was Tokyo?
The skin of what once was our fatherland,
its greed plastered into its mask

The light of the sooty lantern
continues to waver on,
wavering.

And we
still can't say we are victims
for at any moment too frightening
we might be smashed into bits,
mother and children,
fragile lives gathered together,
the cart following the path, rickety-rackety.
Weaving through the sheer darkness
from one crease to another,
the apricot-colored, solitary light.

Bathing

(Late August 1945, at the place to which we were evacuated)

Lilies are carelessly blooming.
Pinks, cosmos, globe amaranths are also
luxuriously abloom in this farmer's garden
where I set up an old laundry tub
and bathe my daughter
who has burns on face and hands.

Until the other day
small aircraft continued to whine
in the Ibaraki sky, which is now refreshingly clear,
with only the clouds drifting toward Hitachi,
leaving soft brush marks.

Into the hot water
filling the darkened tub to the brim
I help my daughter with her useless arms,
and my fingertips tremble.

As I pour warm water on her
from shoulder to back,
from back to hips,
the smooth skin of a seventeen-year-old girl,
with soap bubbles on it, emits a fragrance,
and her wet down gleams, sparse.

And yet
her hands rolled up in bandages,
hands made to look like tree stumps,
uncertainly afloat in midair,
sitting in the tub, disheartened,
my daughter so disfigured.

Loess-like medicine
pasted thick
on the skin burnt black,
her face whose form has collapsed,
cocking her face that can't be called a face,
apparently listening to some sound,
my daughter so disfigured.

Methodically scrubbing her,
I think of
one thing,
just one thing
that, like a wind sweeping through the field,
keeps ringing in my heart.

Even so,
you, flowers in the garden,
being not in the least arrogant.

Avoiding the others' eyes,
I caress my daughter's body,
I wash and cleanse her—this, rolling down my cheek,
is not a tear.

It is sweat.
It is a drop of sweat wrung out of
the skin of a mother who has shrunk, innocent.

Crawling

One doctor said
it was arthritis.

Another said
rheumatism.

Many a syringe needle was stabbed
into the veins of my withered arms.

And my legs
ceased
to move.

From room to room
I crawled
slowly.

After sasanqua flowers scattered many times,
one morning, when pussy willows spread ash-silver,
unexpectedly I stood on my legs,
just like that.

To give it a try,
I walked and walked.
And behold,
the burnt-out town of vending booths
was frozen in a large crystal basin,
and ahead of it,
on the slope densely covered with ferns
new people
were rolling down.

Having seen them,
my legs lost their gravity once again.

I crawled again
slowly.

On the terribly bumpy road
I crawled about,
injuring my fingertips.
Something like the body odor of a reptile
suffocated me.

A Single Excess

I was staring at
the several bees swarming
over a single rose, when a smattering of sand
fell on my cheeks.

That instant
I also saw a smattering of sand fall
from the round small eyeballs
of a hen intently scratching the ground
at the fence.

Kaneko Misuzu
(1903–1930)

Born in a port town in Yamaguchi, Misuzu proved to be a natural in the new, thriving genre of children's songs. She began publishing in magazines in 1923 and saw fifty-six pieces in print in the next five years. The unstinting praise she won from the poet and songwriter Saijō Yaso (1892–1970) was a special encouragement to her. But her marriage was an utter failure. On top of his licentious conduct, her husband forbade her writing and corresponding. She gave birth to a girl, and a separation followed. She became ill. Threatened by her husband that he would take her daughter away after their divorce, she killed herself.

In her brief life she wrote a total of 512 songs. After her death 24 more pieces saw print, but apparently none of her songs were set to music in her lifetime. During the late 1990s she was "discovered" and became popular. The movie *Misuzu*, made in 2002, is based on her life.

Fish

I'm sorry for the fish in the sea.

The rice is grown by farmers.
The cows are raised in the meadow.
The carp are fed in the pond.

In contrast, fish in the sea
have nobody to care for them.
They haven't even played pranks
but are eaten like this by me.

I'm truly sorry for the fish.

Early Autumn

Here's a cool evening breeze.

If I were in the country, I'd now
be taking a black bull home,
the sea's evening glow far away.

It's the time a thousand crows fly home,
cawing in the aquamarine sky.

Have they picked eggplants in the field?
Is it about time for the rice to bloom?

Lonesome, lonesome is this city,
with nothing but houses, dust, and sky.

Funeral Day

Each time I saw someone's funeral
adorned with flowers and flags,
I wished I had a funeral, too,
until just the other day.
But the one today was no good.
A great many people were there, yes,
but no one would talk to me.
The aunt who'd come from the Big City
kept silent, tears in her eyes.
No one scolded me, no,
but somehow I was scared.
I made myself small in the store
until like a rising cloud a long
procession left the house.
It left me more lonesome still.
The one today was truly no good.

Transferred Boy

The boy who's come from elsewhere
is a lovely boy;
how can I become
a friend of his?

During the noon recess
I look out;
he's leaning on
a cherry tree.

The boy who's come from elsewhere
speaks like elsewhere;
what words shall I use
to speak to him?

On our way home
I happen to look;
he's already got
a friend.

Country

I just really want to see

small oranges ripening gold
on an orange tree,

or figs, still babies,
clinging to a fig tree,

and ears of wheat blowing in the wind,
and a skylark singing.

I just really want to go,
though it must be in spring that skylarks sing;
when, and what flowers,
does an orange tree bloom?

In the country
I only see in pictures,
there must be many
many things that pictures
do not show.

The Blue Sky

The vacant sky,
the blue sky,
like the sea
on a waveless day.

I'd like to leap
into the midst of it
and swim away,
far away.

The streak of white foam
I then make
will turn into a cloud
just as is.

The Grave of a Goldfish

Dark, lonely, in the soil,
what is the goldfish staring at?
The flowers of weeds in a summer pond,
the phantom of the swaying light.

Quiet, quiet, in the soil,
what is the goldfish listening to?
The footfalls of a night shower,
soughing over the fallen leaves.

Cold, cold, in the soil,
what is the goldfish thinking of?
Her friends of long, long ago
who were with her in the vendor's pail.

The Elephant

I want to ride a giant elephant,
I want to go to the Indian Nation.

If it's too far away,
I at least want to grow small,
so I can ride a toy elephant.

The rape field, the wheat field,
what deep forests they would be!

The beast there I drive out
would be a mole bigger than an elephant!

Come evening I'd stay in a skylark's inn,
seven days and seven nights in a forest.

When I come out of the deep forest,
dragging a mountain of game,

how beautiful the avenue will be
lined with milk vetch,
the sky I'll look up at from there!

Good-bye

Mother, mother, wait for me,
I'm very busy now.

I'd like to say good-bye to all,
to the horse in his stable, to the chickens
and itsy-bitsy chicks in their chicken coop.

If I could see yesterday's woodcutter,
I'd like to go to the mountain for a while, too.

Mother, mother, wait for me,
I have some things I'd forgotten.

I'll look at roadside dayflowers,
smartweed flowers, the faces of this and that
flowers I won't see when I go back to town,
so I'll remember them well.

Mother, mother, wait for me.

School

Some children came by boat,
some came over a pass.

At back a mountain, cicadas droning,
in front a bank with reedy winds.

Beyond the paddies you saw the sea,
full sails, reefed sails going by.

The snow would fade from red tiles,
the peach would bloom in the blue sky;

by the time new pupils arrived,
grebes and frogs would be calling.

A black bundle on my back,
I too picked red strawberries.

O, school with those red tiles,
your roof reflecting in the water,

like that reflection in the water,
you now exist only in my mind.

The Fallen Leaves

The back entrance was full of fallen leaves.
Shall I sweep them away, secretly,
before anyone knows about it?

When I thought I'd do it on my own,
I was happy about myself.

When I gave a single sweep,
a music band came by in front.

I thought I'd do the rest later and ran,
and followed the band to the bend.

And when I came back I saw
someone had swept the leaves clean
and had thrown them all away.

Hayashi Fumiko
(1903–1951)

As is clear from the title *Hōrōki* (*Diary of Drifting*), her 1930 book that suddenly turned her into a best-selling author, Fumiko, daughter of itinerant vendors, spent a wretched life until her writings began to sell. She worked at whatever job she could get and moved from one man to another. The income from the book (and the resulting status) enabled her to travel to China and Manchuria, then to Europe. For the rest of her life, she remained prolific and traveled often. During the war she was a member of the Pen Squad, a group of writers assembled to promote Japanese military causes.

Fumiko, who sprinkled *Hōrōki* (and other prose writings) with poems in the manner of "poetic tales," published some of them in *Aoi Uma o mita* (*I Saw a Pale Horse*), in 1929, a year before her autobiographical account came out. Among her early literary associates were anarchists and dadaists. That, and the so-called Taishō Democracy, during which "countless isms" (Fumiko's phrase) flourished, accounts for the seemingly throwaway, at times sexually explicit, phrasings in her early poems. Her style becomes muted with her second book of poems, *Omokage* (*Vestiges*), in 1933.

Tired Heart

That night—
on a table in a café
a face like a basket of flowers cried.
Who cares
if a crow caws on a tree.

Night is pain—
my face
held up with both hands,
tired of green powder,
was dragging the needle of twelve o'clock.

Sobering Up

My dear world!
I'm drunk now.

The walls of my apartment are blue like crackers
and my purse has 30 sen[7] in it.

---

7. Before this monetary unit was discontinued, the sen was to the yen what the cent is to the dollar.

Since it's raining I'm going to get wooden clogs.
Getting me drunk, he said,
I won't say anything, please simply love me,
so I'm loving him without saying anything and yet
I'm sad. . . .
Tomorrow night I'll go to a marriage *arrangement* agency
and find a man—

My rent is ¥35, you see.
O I think I'm going mad.
I work hard for a month
but my husband's as *insidious* as a sea cucumber.

Like smoking a cigarette I'd like to try a kiss.
I don't need any lover.

Just for a month
I'd like to eat white rice.
My mother is rheumatic
and I'm nearsighted,
but drinking is bad for the brain—
I used to send 50 sen each time,
but now she's separated from the man,
and I feel dizzy.
50 sen and 35 yen!
I wish it could drop from heaven—

Kiss

The night I first knew kissing,
cherries in their *glorious splendor*

The moon was red—

At the man's lips that seemed to slurp blood
above all
above all
the moon went on pirouetting.

Quiet Heart

Late at night
in the distance a cock is crowing.
Tomorrow I'll buy rice with this:
on the orange crate, my desk,
I've written a fragrant tale for children.
If it becomes money
my fantasies will fade away in the white electricity late at night.

Tired, I counted with my fingers:
I haven't eaten rice for two days,
I'm very cold,
and, listen, my stomach is clanging
like a bell.

I'll put a pot on the hibachi,
place a bundle of noodles in it and eat.
Outside the wind seems cold
but it's a wonderful moonlit night.

Looking at the steam rising like white threads,
I am as happy as a baby, I tell you.
The children's story written,
the noodles now beginning to cook. . . .

The withered narcissus I had a week ago
incites an absurdly sad mental state
but thinking of tomorrow, I firmly hold back my tears
and stare at my white hands.

Once I had someone who wrote me love letters, come to think of it. . . .

A Dream I Had When I Lost a Job

The night so dark it could almost burn
the moon ducked under a tunnel,
offshore a white sail was sliding clip-clop.
There, I, fired by a soap factory,
kept my hands coarsened by soda to caramel brown
immersed in perfume, crying.

I don't know how far I'd walked,
but I saw a fire in the darkness.
Conveniently I got hungry.
It was a Chinese restaurant.
Loaded with freshly roasted pork,
one plate 8 sen.

The Chinese chef with gleaming eyes
made me hot.
Without moving, our arms touched each other,
when the Chinese chef let a snake coil around his, *hee, hee. . .*
I brushed his long hair up,
he was my lovely lover.
His magic snake jumped off!
The blue foam turned into solid soap.
My lover and I rolled in the field and, our small fingers linked, kissed,
but he said, I can never make a living with a lover,
and tried to smash through my small chest.
Red sparks turned into solid soap.
I wanted to stuff my face with Chinese food
and started to run blindly.
Bam! My chastity was blown away.

The Heart

This is an old, travel-worn trunk.
A mirror, a soiled puff,
a silly music box,
an old card,
a blank diary,
an old book without a preface.

This is a windowless room.
A pale rose,
a still life of a fish,
a bundle of love letters,
a nail-clipping implement,
and a mynah bird who can't sing.

Melon[8]

I used *every means I knew* to raise
enough to buy a honeydew
and took it to him.

Thereupon he wrote, with a straight face,
a note to someone else's wife:
"On my desk is a melon, ma'am;
it would be nice to eat it with you."

On my way home from him
I bought a pear melon for 5 sen,
stripped myself naked,
ate it by myself, joyfully.

---

8. The honeydew and some other exotic melons, usually regarded as gift items, are notoriously expensive in Japan and have provided Americans visiting Japan with an endless source of wonderment and mirth. It's amusing to see that the situation was the same in Fumiko's day.

Matsuda Tokiko
(1905–2004)

Born a miner's daughter in Akita, Tokiko went to Tokyo in 1926 and became an active member of the labor movement and the Union of Proletarian Writers. She won her first literary prize for a short story in 1928 and later won other prizes. As a member of the Japan Democratic Writers Association, she maintained her proletarian sentiments to the end of her life.

Breasts

Born proletariat,
born with malnutrition
born with father in jail
but, my child,
in your voice crying with hunger
I discern new strength.
Your destiny and your food
now boiling with a vengeful will,
these bone-dry breasts.

1928

To My Father

Teeth bared, you barked at me.
A maul held high, you chased me.
Your teeth were bluish yellow with gunk and frustration.
Your eyes blazed, burned a feeble and useless me.
Only with that memory I grew up, Father.
My appreciation of you as father surreptitiously revives in my blood flow today,
    today
I'm remembering you, Father, weeping.
In a winter mining town of blizzard and humiliation,
exploited by those bastards, I raised pigs.
Hating you, Father, trudging in the thigh-deep snow,
you were the one I hated the most, I thought, it wouldn't do just to stab you to
    death!
My hatred awakening, my body frazzled,
spring came late to the mine,
the flame, the sun, crackling the silver-white mountain range.

A young man, a young man's words, his powerful arms!
I just wanted to shove you aside, to get away from your eye.

Father,
you had thousands of days of humiliation, even your daughter adding to them,
that's my regret, my hatred of those bastards you faced all alone.
Now, what am I to weep over?
Over you, in my attempt to awaken you, to get through the pains of my struggle.

Father, dear,
exasperated with daily living, simply believing in victory,
you weren't afraid of whittling your life away.
Your teeth,
your arm, maul swung up,
that, that is what I inherit.

1932

Untitled

Another siren. . . .
Where can we run?
Into a closet? Into a shelter?
If further inside the shelter is a graveyard, so is its entrance, so is the path to it

Bark, bark, air-defense wardens, cops, don't bark at us.
Does anyone linger, not wanting to save his life?

Here they come.
Earth quakes,
shelter quakes
"It's aaaal right."
"It's aaaal right."
"No, don't cry."
"Come, take my breast."
"Come. . . ."

Mrs. Landlord,
let's not cry.
You shouldn't cover your baby with your body like that.
He won't be able to breathe. . .

They're dropping 'em. . .
This earth quakes,
they're dropping 'em. . .
Where's that?
Whose turn is it to die? They're dropping 'em. . .
This earth quakes.

Steady.
I curse 'em . . . curse 'em . . . curse 'em . . . curse 'em. . .
I'm still alive,
I'm still alive.
This anger,
this anger
Still they're dropping 'em,
dropping 'em,
dropping 'em,
dropping 'em. . .

1944

Resident Registration

No question, I, too, am Japanese.
Address: N Ward, Tokyo, Japanese Nation.
Eyes: brown.
Hair: turning gray.
Teeth: rotten.
Inside my ribs a nest of tuberculosis. Except it's congealing.
Stomach: generally greedy.
Bottoms of my feet: callused.
Livelihood: abundance of tax-free well water, which I mainly praise,
and the clarity of the same tax-free water, which I celebrate every morning.

Parents: in graves.
Spouse: in hospital.
Children: growing fast, but mysteriously, they spend days sighing, gnashing
    teeth.
Happened to be born in the Japanese Nation, this is my 16,900th day.
Experience: all in all, nothing but humiliation and self-contempt.
Bitter tastes have shrunk my tongue.
The days I spent, praying to the Chrysanthemum Crest pasted garishly on the high
    peak of Fuji, above the clouds, far in the distance, I was a degraded hungry
    ghost,

until at last
I was covered with the fires of domestic and foreign devils, but didn't die.
Yes, sir,
my two feet remain sucked in the squishy soil of this nation.
Yes, sir, I, too, am like a clump of this soil.
Am also like a grass or tree, or like a beast,
am also like night dew, or like a wind.
But even if you plant rice or wheat seeds in my arms or legs, nothing will grow
    there.
This is my registration.

1948

Nagase Kiyoko
(1906–1995)

Born in Okayama, Nagase was first inspired to write poems by Ueda Bin's translations of European poems, published in 1905 under the title *Kaichō-on (Sound of Tides)*. Married at eighteen, she published her first book of poems, *Grendel no Haha (Grendel's Mother)*, in 1930. The title poem is based on *Beowulf,* which she read in English in high school. At forty she took up farming. In 1963 she began work for the World Federation. In 1982 she became president of the Society of Okayama Poets. In 1987, at age eighty-one, she published *Akegata ni kuru Hito yo (You Who Come at Daybreak)*, which won a prize. The last two poems of this selection are taken from it.

Winter

I've gotten beautiful stripes.
In the glittering wind and light,
in a terraced field surrounded by mountains—
stripes of brilliant emerald green and kite-brown.
Cultivating and sowing I've made them.
The bamboo thicket swaying in the wind is also mine.
Because only I am aware of its beauty.
Those mountains to the east are also mine.
As if enjoying various hats,
there, blurred in the morning haze,
they have light-pink tops
where deities sleep like butterflies
before flying away.
Dressed as a peasant woman, wrists and collar tight,
I climb up the slope
and the slippery blue mountains
link up toward the distance just at the height of my shoulders,
as if they could readily become my scarf any time.
The mountain for the setting sun is Mount Shinden.
These days the sun sets right behind it,
rays of light shining out like the Buddha's halos,
from both its right and left shoulders.
Then the clouds turn into golden streams
and pour into me.

The grasses have blown their seeds away,
the leaves left hugging the ground, colored.
Winter having arrived, I begin to see the beauty of each leaf.
Mountains and rivers made part of my body,
I spend the winter like that.

Lighting a Lamp at Night

Just as the silkworm makes her cocoon,
so I make my own night;
weave the night and make a room.
Under a deep violet starry sky,
lighting a lamp for me alone,
I make a small oval world.

The day exists for everyone.
During that time I work, forgetting everything.
At night everyone recedes into the distance.
All visible things become invisible
and for my willful self,
gently, thoughtfully, disappear into the dark.

Within the lonely world for me alone
I gleam as moss and fireflies do.
Hoping to live a good life,
deepening my longing for things beautiful,
I knit several quiet lines
with fingers soiled during the day.

That which filters through my daytime self filled with painful heat
and turns it into a transparent drop,
a drop of night world:
a small lonely world where I light my lamp,
an oval world that exists for memory and prayer,
a quiet path between today and tomorrow that I take alone.

Deceive Me, Please, with Gentle Words

Deceive me, please, with gentle words.
Delight me, please, with a warm voice.
I'm inexperienced, but accept, please,
my thoughts for you, and praise them.
Ah, that you need me more than anyone else—
deceive me, please, with a grateful smile.

When you do,
will I think highly of myself and grow arrogant?
No, no,
I'll simply capture your deceit like a pliant vine
and lean on it to rise to my feet.
I'll become far, far more gentle,
far, far more beautiful,
a woman whose heart works wonders.

Ah, I grew up in too much of a wasteland.
My starved heart wants only one thing:
The delight of thinking
that you're delighted by me.
Understand this
if as scantily as dawn dew or breeze,
and my eyes will come alive, youthful.
Happy and brimming with tears,
I'll be deceived, deceived, and be rich.
Ah, lead me, please, with gentle clapping
as you might do a blindfolded tag player.

Prayer

Give me simple joy.
Let me discard bitter reflections of wisdom.
Give me glittering joy of flesh.
Give me the joy of grass and tree blown in the wind.
Let me discard the roaming of one night.
Toward a blue dawn, let me wash my bleeding soles
in a quiet purling stream.
Let me be endlessly beautiful.
Let me and the one who is hurt because of me
live together.

When he is about to strike me,
let me be even more accepting.
Sorrowed by his regrets,
I always stay under his whip.
Absolve my heart of its long forbearance and pain.
Revive me with very simple joy.
Ah, I choose burdens too often.

A Woman Sings

Having few friends,
you watch only me.
And you scold me,
scold me as a thoughtless woman.
No   no
No   no
still not enough proof of love,
it's disgusting that you don't always look happy,
it's disgusting that you can't predict today's weather for me.
You say only impossibilities I can't help.

I'd like to begin learning magic.
I'd like to stop your criticisms with a single glance.
I'd like to put your mind to sleep with a single finger.
I'd like to go out on a broom every night.
Letting my hair stream like smoke,
I'd like to jump over a mountain ridge.
Laughing at your scolding,
I'd like to fly into the glistening moonlight.

Being simple,
you don't think of my deadening sufferings.
Nonetheless you will nonchalantly go to Heaven.
And I, having wished for magic, fall to Hell.
Ah, and that makes a distance of ten billion years that can't be leapt across.

Combing

Have you come to comb me,
to turn my hair long and pliant?

When you're gentle, you are always in midair.
I turn toward you, smile,
and throw thoughts and words that flutter like doves.
Yet the moment I meet the actual you
I'm defeated, shattered.
My smiles wilt, I turn pale.
Always, always,
you test me like that.
No longer able to tell which is the real you,
I feel lost, I doubt.
Is this all right with you?

Like a tall wild chamomile
swaying in a breeze toward dawn,
I grew up free in an untamed land.
On my own,
I would rely upon my mind.
Yet your combing
shakes me, hurts me;
it leaves wounds on my skin, on my heart,
as a sled does on the snow.

And yet I always remember
how shallow my love is,
that I don't understand your meaning, you having grown up willfully.
I'm sure I need more and more of
uninterrupted waking, uninterrupted pain.
You really have come to comb me, haven't you,
to turn my hair long and pliant.
Ah, ah, because, I'm sure,
my hair is too tangled, too twisted.

My Aged She-Devil

My aged she-devil who lives in the cavern,
coughs on a cold frosty morning,
now visible, now invisible, between sun and moss.

My Grendel's mother—
threatening the king's castle with howls,
smashing his arrogant feast,
she took back her son's arm

that was mounted high on a beam.
She grabbed like straw bundles the necks of
warriors who put up a fight, and chortled—
One who dashes over the fields alone,
one who lets her hair flow like rain clouds,
lilies fall,
thistles are splattered with blood—

In the light toward dawn,
all alone, shining alone, sublime,
in her mind there's no king,
outside herself there isn't a single law.
She eats wild beasts, wears their hides;
her heart is darkly torn, body lacerated,
her teeth are as white as the waves rolling in from the North Sea when she
   guffaws.

For a long time an aged she-devil has lived in my cavern.
Oh, could it be her?
No urbanity, no gaiety,
the only thing I sharpen: tusks of egotism.
My copper-hued hair now withered,
only my eyes are red, about to be buried in wrinkles.
I still think of the freedom of my youthful days,
my legs stand like those birch trees upon the hill
but now I have no way of leaping across a valley.

Under the starry sky, I barely avoid frost in my cavern
and warm the dreams of the good old days.

Waking, my aged she-devil
coughs,
stirs to cook broth,
now visible, now invisible, beyond the moss.

Fujita Fumie
(1908–1933)

Born in Kagoshima, Fujita Fumie studied at a normal school and worked as a schoolteacher for a year. She edited and published two magazines in 1930 and died a month after publishing her first book of poems, *Yoru no Koe* (*Night's Voice*), in 1933. She apparently attracted attention with both her unusual poems and her exceptional beauty; she seems to have sent her photographs to a number of correspondents. Her poems suggest she had tuberculosis, but her death was so sudden that it was rumored to be suicide.

Night's Voice

> —*Ah, Seigneur! donnez-moi la force et le courage*
> *De contempler mon coeur et mon corps sans dégoût!*
> "Un voyage à Cythère"
> —Charles Baudelaire

Night's voice, why have you come so far?
Listening to you coughing,
I become unbearably lonely.
But I fawn on you, *mon ville natale.*
Because when I'm with you,
I feel a little richer.

Woman with a Black Shawl

Along a golden seashore
I always walk with you, black shawl.
Tangled hair falling over your brow,
two eyes feverishly opened,
O
with what kind of feeling do you look at me?
Your noble, beautiful limbs
always cover my ferocious bosom,
O you are gentle,
you are gentle as a giant tree.

Hungry   and angry,
I wander on, spasmodic,
past the rear gate of youth astride sadness.
I pity you as you are linked to me.

Departing Summer

My surroundings have grown utterly gaunt.
O now my eyes can only see your pretty feet, lord.
Your fiery brow,
your thick, sharply closed lips,
I can still remember clearly:
your fragrant hair and wheat-hued taut skin,
your suffocating hot kisses,
your violent, stormy caresses,
lord, don't you also remember them?
The star-sprinkled festive night sky the double-bed,
the grass chamber by a dark, moist waterway,
ah but the ceaseless, persistent lovemaking
had tired me out.
Yet as I listen to your footfalls as you leave without a word,
my body, look, begins to tremble like a calf.
Distant tyrant, have you finally set out on a journey
this year as well, unaccompanied by a good woman, stone for your pillow?

In Illness

> La chair est triste, hélas! et j'ai lu tous les livres.
> —Stéphane Mallarmé

Finally defeated in battle like an evening sun
I lie fallen.
Every day I make many a white sailboat
flow over the hot sea.
It's like making my children flow
or like making your children flow;
it's unbearably fearful.
I've never resented as much as I do today
the distance that sternly sits in this world.

In Illness

Even while the moon opens like a flower
the weeping of people
carries the sky like soot and smoke.
Why does only loneliness go on growing fat?
Everything lays its corpse like a white coral
on light's wasteland.

Trusting

I trust the thread
and sleep with my life hanging from it.
Quiet music envelops me like misty rain
and, holding my cold hand, walks on.
O, "You may drive out Nature with a pitchfork,
yet she still will hurry back," Horace said.

Festival of Solitude After Carnal Excesses

Why do you not deign to
raise your voice?
Your brow like a feverish patient.
Your eyes like ripe fruit.
O
vain weight casts its shadow on your cheeks.

About Myself

I've never had eyes with no clear outlook at any time,
a shadow of a sorrowful length,
and fiery cheeks.
Only when I'm disturbed by an aurora-like chill
I become beautiful.

Sick Body

Blue cells aflame roses are in bloom.
At the root sobbing, sobbing.
Something like magnesium.
The warm, very warm
bloody odor of the flesh.
At times avalanching in the barracks-like body
hollow coughs occur among my chilly ribs.

A crippled demon who, resembling a tree-shearer, drags its pitiful black shadow.
I knock on the hard crust of the earth and sleep in a cold jail.
Where shall I tie up my white bosom?

Evening.
Piercing my ravaged eyes a smoke of laughter faintly rises.
Shattered into a thousand pieces and fallen, something lies at my feet.
Pity, something like a column of fire glances off my eyes and flutters down.
I know nothing. Know nothing.
Why doesn't that tree have a single leaf?
Why are withered creepers entwining the fence?
Why are your distant eyes so obvious?
Something fierce tries to drive my sick body
like an enraged lion.
Ah yet I always conspire with a familiar death,
gripping in my snow-like hand a permanently unyielding purity.
Sad!
Kicking away the man-woman bond the Yalu River goes on opening up!

Fujiki Kiyoko
(Dates Uncertain)

Fujiki started publishing haiku in 1933, became a prominent figure in the Shinkō Haiku movement, and disappeared in 1940, when the movement's leaders were arrested for advocating liberalism and "antitraditionalism." One feature of Shinkō Haiku poets was rejection of seasonal elements, but Fujiki often employed them. The haiku selected here were all published in the magazine *Kikan* (*Flagship*), which played a leading role in the Shinkō Haiku movement.

In an old bed a devil grabbed me by my black hair

Ears of wheat reveal the depths and shallows of the sea

Only a horsefly's voice annoying my ears I make unlined clothes

Pity the stokers at the ship's bottom summer has begun

Early autumn's good my veins transparent arteries pulse

Early autumn's good ocher-colored my limbs my body

An Oppressed Wife's Memo

Lonely spring a wife lives as if she were machinery

A white moon turns into gold above young leaves

May has come has come riding the blue of the tides

Rainy season desolate I find myself with peanut shells

The quiet sound of a falling mosquito resounds in my body

As a katydid I feel as if noonday were sinking

A girl's limbs are thin and wise air-conditioned

Oppressed by the sea in twilight I await a train

Through my temples a locomotive dashes dark

Knotweed growing thin falls into the typhoon zone

Insomnia

Covered by the sounds of insects lies a brain

In winter rains I'm listening to a nurse's tale

A Parting

The day my black hair's heavy and cold we part

The night I give up and sew the needle shines

A spring evening I ride a car with an ordinary man

A spring evening is wound down toward the apple skin

Trees budding officers and men quietly return[9]

The scent of a perfume so lively sudden loneliness

Summer deep I sleep the day with my own smell

Coming away from parting I drink hard cold water

Fingerprints of desolation everywhere clouds white

On the tatami of August a woman has grown fat

Katydids my perspective gradually narrows

In a monks' quarter I swallow down painful love

---

9. In one of a famous pair of photographs chronicling Japan's war in Asia, a regiment is shown leaving the barracks in neat formation; in the other, the same regiment is shown returning, its size much reduced, and many of its members carrying white wooden boxes in front of their chests containing the ashes of comrades killed in battle.

White noon no white letter comes knocking

I wouldn't want war and women to be separate

In deep autumn I go on traveling unenlightened

Boy going to war reticent the sukiyaki singeing cooks down

Killed in battle all his thirty-two teeth untouched

With dusk slow to fall gruel's cooking at my feet

Here's life the fruit juice amber-transparent

Under a clear sky healed I smell my own loneliness

Having gotten used to the depth of war I love a dog

Not being the widow of someone killed in battle loneliness

Friend's husband in a distant battlefield the sea glistens

I turn off the lights and enjoy the solitude of solitude

Having lived single-mindedly I've lost my goal

Satō Sachiko
(1911–1998)

Born in Miyagi to Christian parents, Sachiko began publishing poems and other writings soon after arriving in Tokyo, in 1929. Because of her involvement in the proletarian movement, she was jailed twice and had to remain underground for several years. She did not collect and publish her poems in book form until 1980.

The Road to the Sea

Let us go to the sea, children.
To the town bathhouse, it's 2,000 yards.
The road to the sea is 1,200 yards long.
Let us go to the sea, children.

*

Ducking under cornstalks, withered as they stand,
we walk across the ridges.
In the unkempt summer grass
lies a traction engine rusting red.
Around the scattered rails rusting red,
squeakers, rice-pounders, lord grasshoppers
flutter up from our feet as we walk,
exciting you to no end.

*

In the puddle, boom, boom,
bullfrogs play the contrabassoon.
Long-legged waterfowl forage.
At a clear wing beat, we look up.
Piping above us:
a flock of plovers with white breast feathers.

*

Taking valuable time from my meager work,
I walk along a grassy path with my children:
buds slightly opening from their edges,
hasty evening primroses, Chinese agrimony.
Picking them, we go, and mother's heart
leaves her household accounts book, grows wide as the sea.

The Doll

Excited by the one-eyed doll
bought at an autumn fair for farm implements,
my daughter doesn't stop prattling as we walk.

Mother, listen, mother,
What is the man there doing,
buying a doll?

He must have a small daughter like you, Hako,
at home, too.
She must be waiting for a souvenir.

I feel sorry for him.
He must have gone to war, too.
Is his leg growing back?

A while before, scared,
she was peeking from behind her mother.
She's five years old this year.

I stop, and she turns a puzzled look
up at her mother.
Remember, child, until you grow up,
what you've seen with your round eyes.

Anemophile

What kind of wind has brought her here,
to a seashore village where beach peas bloom?
A girl with flaxen hair.

Born of the foam on the waves?
Her eyes are aquamarine.
Covered with sand, today, too, alone,
she chases small crabs on the beach.

Please do not stare at me so,
with your chestnut-round eyes,
your astonishingly white skin
showing through your hook-torn hole.

You beckon her to come closer,
"You, bitch!" she spits, and runs away.
A girl, is she five perhaps?
May the sun take loving care of her!

A Child's Invitation to a Banquet

Come out, Mama, the evening glow's so pretty!
The infant's excited voice calls to mother in the kitchen.
    If you can stop using your knife,
    if you can leave your oven,
    go out, just for a while.

Reflecting the evening glow,
a flock of herons, gold-tinted paper pieces,
flies toward the setting sun
against waves of clouds with hems.

Come out, look at it.
To a pleasure at hand, to a joy at hand adults overlook,
to a banquet a child invites you.
    I'll let myself be invited to a banquet
    by children who've grown up without knowing the war,
    by children who don't think of air-raid hellfire when they look at the evening
    glow.

To make peaceful the sleep of children
who need not fear air-raid shelters,
whose dogs aren't shot by machine guns,
whose dolls and picture books aren't burned.

To ensure today's peace after the painful sacrifices
of children who can no longer raise their voices,
of children who retain atomic injuries
    six thousand mothers gather,
    scientists of the world gather.
    I can hear their voices from my kitchen window.

Come out, Mama!
    A child's voice is shouting.

Sagawa Chika
(1911–1936)

Born in Hokkaidō, Sagawa studied to be a teacher of English. Arriving in Tokyo at seventeen, she quickly came to know several poets and writers. She saw her first translation—of a short story by the Hungarian writer Ferenc Molnár—printed the following year and her first poem, "Konchū" ("Insects"), the next year. Her nonlineated, prose translation of James Joyce's *Chamber Music* was published in 1932. Though she translated mostly "conventional" writers, in her own poetry she came under the influence of surrealism, which had just been brought to Japan. In 1935 she was diagnosed with terminal stomach cancer and died in January the following year. *Collected Poems of Sagawa Chika* was published in July that year. Among those who wrote tributes to her were some of the more prominent poets of the day.

Insects

Insects multiplied with the speed of an electric current.
Licked all the inflammations of the earth's crust.

Turning its pulchritudinous costume inside out, the night of the metropolis slept
    like a woman.

I now dry my shell.
My scaly skin is as cold as metal.

Half of its face smeared with paint, this secret is known to no one.

The night brings to ecstasy the woman with a mole who freely rotates a stolen
    expression.

My Photo

The sudden arrival of the telephone surprised the villagers.
Well, now, do we have to move somewhere?
The village chief hurriedly took his blue jacket off.
After all, mother's account book for small expenses was correct.
Farewell, blue village! The summer like a river ran away again chasing those
    people.

At the deserted station a rooster in a red chapeau got off the train.

The Rusted Knife

A pale blue evening climbs the window.
A lamp hangs down from the sky like a woman's head.
A dense black air fills the room—a blanket spread.
The books, ink, and the rusted knife seem to deprive me of life little by little.

When everything was jeering,
the night already resided in my hand.

The Blue Horse

The horse ran down the mountain and became deranged. From that day she is
    blue food. The summer, having dyed the women's eyes and sleeves blue,
    cheerfully spins in the town plaza.
Because the guests on the terrace smoke cigarettes so much the tin-like sky is
    graffitiing the rings of ladies' hair.
I think I'll throw away sad memories like a handkerchief. If only I could forget
    love, regrets, and enamel shoes!
I didn't have to jump from the second floor.
The sea rises to the sky.

Clairvoyance of the Color Green

the clairvoyance of a single acacia leaf
May   there the angels discard their clothes   legs soiled with green
the smile that chases after me   the memory turns into a swan's throat and
glistens in front of her

now   where has the truth gone
the music of the birds solidified with night dew   the picture of trees printed
    on the sky's wall   a green wind quietly brushes them off
pleasure is calling from the other side of death   the other side of the earth
I see for example the sun grown heavy falling down toward the blue sky

run!   my heart
turn into a ball   and to her side
and through a teacup

—love one on top of the other   make us unhappy
the wrinkles of milk quaver   and my dream rises

Fragments

A unit of blue officers with military caps of cloud is lined up.
They cut down the head of the night from an endless hole.
The sky and the trees, one lying upon the other, seem to vie with each other.
The antenna runs across above them.
Are flower petals afloat in the space?
At noon, a pair of suns run up to the gladiators' stadium.
Soon summer emotions rusted red will also sever our love.

The Sea of Memories

Hair wild, a mad woman's drifting, chest bared.
Flocks of white words shatter on the faintly dark sea.
A torn accordion,
a white horse and a black horse foaming violently cross it, galloping above it.

White and Black

A white arrow runs. A night bird is shot and flies into my iris.
Constantly it interrupts my fig sleep.
Silence likes to stay in my room.
They were the shadow of a candlestick, the pot of plucked primula, and the chair
    of peach-blossom heartwood.[10]
I keep watching time and flame entangled glide around the window.
Oh, today, too, a man with a black face comes,
beats into a mess the flower garden of my heart, and flees.
Rain, who comes in boots,
do you trample upon the ground all night?

The May Ribbon

outside the window the air laughed loudly
by the shadow of its multicolored tongue
leaves turning into a flock blew
I couldn't think

---

10. "Peach-blossom heartwood" is a literal translation of the four Chinese characters given. A possible typo, but one never knows.

is anyone there
I stretched my hand into the darkness
and touched nothing   but the wind's long hair

Dream

The reality that collapses only in midday's naked light. All the treetops are bones.
Her back turned to the transparent window she can't explain. Only, her ring repeated
its reflection many times. Dazzling stained glass, vainly decorated time. Again
they'll make a detour of the house and choose a boisterous path. Sweaty dark leaf.
The wind on it is a cripple and can't move. Denying the phantom of the darkness,
I know. That people are mistrustful. Outside salty air is duping a soul.

White

on the lawn wavers like a flame
an amethyst button glistens
you slowly descend toward me
a mourning dove cocks its ear to his lost voice.
The net of the sunlight passing a treetop.
The green terrace and the dry pistil.
I remember to wind the timepiece.

The Green

from the morning *balcon*   surges wave-like toward me
overflows everything around me
on a mountain path I almost drown
unable to breathe I trip and catch myself many times
the town in my eyesight opens and closes like a dream turning
around them they begin to collapse toward me with a terrifying speed
someone has abandoned me

The Bride of the Sea

I wake at the sound of a wind that passes by, meandering through the dark sea of
   trees.
Beyond the cloudy sky
a cuckoo calls,
Go home today, go home today.
Where can I go back to?
For me to reach behind noon
the bush of gooseberries and giant knotweeds was too deep.
The apples in my fading memory
were in full bloom.

And so was the invisible scream.

Rush through the wet path in the windbreak,
and you come to a dune with sorrels and wild strawberries.
These glisten like gems and are tasty.
The sea, foamy,
must be spreading laces.
The short train is facing the metropolis.
Disliked by an evil god,
only time piles upon the tips of waves and is blinding.
From there I wait for someone's words
and listen to a song that pushes me up to reality.
And now I surmise people, like parasols,
are about to enter the banquet of trees covering the ground.

1. 2. 3. 4. 5.

Under one of the trees lining the road a girl has her green hand raised above her.
Surprised by her plant-like skin, I look and in time she takes off her silk gloves.

Ogawa Anna
(Born 1919)

"During the postwar poverty," Ogawa wrote, "I lost my father and three children one after another. I started writing poems while raising the two children I was endowed with after that." She was over fifty when she published her book of poems *Nyoshin Raihai (In Praise of the Female Body)*, in 1970. Born in Shizuoka, she became, in 1969, a leading participant in the antipollution campaign against the building of a large power plant in the estuary of the Fuji River. Her second book of poems, *Fujigawa Ugan Kasenshiki Chizu (Map of the Riverbed on the Right Bank of the Fuji River)*, in 1978, won the Shizuoka Poet prize. Ogawa Anna is the pen name of Ashikawa Terue.

On a Quiet Night a Storm Was Forecast

Before my children came to me,
what were these small, piteous things doing? I sometimes wonder.

"Before you were born from my tummy, Ryū-chan, you were a small seed, weren't
    you?"
The child must be fascinated by the same question.
He thinks he was, before birth, a small, hard seed, and yet he was in his mother's
    womb.

On a lonely, lonely, quiet night of a new autumn when a storm was forecast,
like a mammalian parent lying amid her children asleep,
unobtrusively warming their bodies,
I sniffed at my children's smell
and thought intently, intently, about God
who had brought us together.

In Praise of the Female Body

I had assumed I had nursed my mother in her sickly last years as best I could. But
once, when I, with a rag, was cleaning my house, which was quiet and hushed after
everybody was gone, the thought suddenly erupted out of nowhere and overflowed
that I, a child, in the end had always remained in my mother's palm. . .

When you purify a woman before sending her off,
the moment that induces the most sadness comes
when you clean that part of her.
Even with someone who had grown old and, at the very end,

like a wintry stand of trees, attained the state of quietude,
though you'd called her Grandma, when you find it to be unexpectedly beautiful,
like a snowy morning, pure, pacific,
how bitter and remorseful you feel, thinking back on your behavior
that wasn't up to the mark on most days.
Not all of those who were born from it
have ever thought kindly of the pain it had
when it gave birth to them.
Withdrawn, forgotten,
it had been protected by a single heart for many decades.
The sorrow of someone who can move neither her arms nor legs, suffering from
   a long illness,
comes from the pain of exposing it when it's soiled,
not having a hand to cover it in embarrassment.

Having given birth many, many times,
suffered, agonized, and lived,
it is now wilted. When you finish purifying it
and gently close it again for her,
do you think you receive something from a single human being, quietly, gravely,
to inherit it, to pass it on?

Father and I

Before he was yet to meet me,
what a lonely young man he must have been!
He was a clean young man who would swim straight toward the offing in the blue,
   deep-blue evening sea.

His shapely nude body heading overarm toward the offing
I think I clearly see.
The taste of the tide he splashed through in his loneliness
suddenly touches my tongue, my shoulders, I feel.

When he met me,
what a happy father he must have been!
He must have looked at me as if *he* had been born to this world.
And completely forgetting about the sea
he waded straight to the other world.

I know:
because he truly met me,

he took on the heavy load of sorrow and helplessness of this world.
Still, he never once regretted it.
From time to time he would remember himself before he met me,
the blue, transparent loneliness of that autumn sea.
Each time he would grip my hand even more tightly to live on,
holding it intently, until I shook my hand and twisted it free.

When he died,
he went away, carefully holding his own palm his child had shaken off,
deeply, deeply believing he'd been born to meet me.

The Woman's House

The house is the woman's.
It has an amazing number of cabinets and pockets where she hides a great variety
    of things.
Have you ever wondered: What if the woman dies first?
Yes, well, yes, the woman feels completely safe about them.
The cabinet there, the pocket there—they are like "nonbeing" that is "being," which
    has accumulated the years and months that appear transparent and are utterly
    nontransparent which the man left behind or the woman just arrived can't see,
    and that therefore have erased a vast amount of time.
They're schemed in such a way that you can't get hold of them even if you see
    through them or scoop them,
but only someone who has folded her heart in the house for many decades can
    take them out freely.

The man has no place in which to hide things,
and feels immediately lost even with a letter a woman gives him on a street.
Indeed, in the house, he's naked and is too busy uneasily looking for a place in
    which to place himself.
He sits on a floor cushion his woman has set up, receives tea from her,
and finally lays himself next to her, in the only space left for him.

The Palm

The palm of my left hand grows itchy.
Wants to caress something.
Wants to touch something.
Feels a terrible, itchy lust.
Tonight the palm of my left hand
has turned a light cherry color.

The Real Being of Ducks

If the world is like glass,
today its mirror surface is utterly dark blue.

The sandbank with withered reeds burning yellow,
flocks and flocks of ducks swim about,
Prussian blue, green-gold.
In the distance gulls dance a rondo,
inlaying paradise.

Suddenly, however, the ducks fly up,
fly up glitteringly
from the dark blue mirror surface,
betting on a moment's shattering.

In the deep void peering out of what has dropped away, the cave,
was the inner side of the world.

Map of the Riverbed on the Right Bank of the Fuji River

Clusters of Fuji City factories press on the east bank. From the stomach-shaped port hiding behind them coffee-colored substances are vomited to be discarded on the bank to the west. This mudflow of civilization is layered on the Map of the Riverbed on the Right Bank of the Fuji River.

The six bridges for the Tōmei Expressway, the National Highway No. 1, the Tōkaidō Railway, a pipeline for industrial water, the Shinkansen, and a bypass are all arteries of Japan, and from the point where another bridge can't possibly be built the virgin land designated as a "river site" finally begins. The sea is close by.

People must want to take flight from where a river ends. There is a hang-gliding place. You walk past it, and the fishermen who have lost their beach are doing the least they can do: to spread nets and dry shrimp on them.

Around you are beach peas, convolvuluses, melancholy you climb up and there white flowering thorns,[11] marsh, pampas grass, patch of miscanthus, tufts of reeds, rushes in the evening sun.

Because I come here from time to time I know human intervention is gradually affecting the original landscape of the estuary. The field of pampas grass eagles inhabited has been scythed, and the ancient mirror that was once hidden has turned into a hand mirror that reflects the sun. The delta tucked

---

11. Buson's hokku: *Ureitsutsu noboreba shiroki hana-ibara.*

away amid the rushes once had, like a woman's body, veins crawling and spreading all over it, but as it was sucked off by drainage canals, the woman walked away from the river.

The willful midriver shoals were taken away, and only a single spot is left for gulls to bloom. Ducks, led from one place to another, are now given a small swamp protected by an estuary sandbar. The autumn wind has lost its fangs or its razor-sharp sword to abruptly slash at us.

I walk over the short prairie where rushes and reeds have been mowed toward the estuary where the autumn sun fully falls and ducks live. Because the sea is close by, every time there is the groan of the sea I hear ripples lapping at the roots of miscanthus and see here and there ducks sleeping with their blue color hidden, ducks preening, also ducks afloat in the distance. I remove my binoculars and take one step forward, and they dance up, flapping, all over the virgin field.

At that moment, the ducks, hung in the midst of the horizon, the water, and the sky, splendidly demonstrate the structure of the height of their habitat. Surprised, I confirm: the river site map is not a plane.

When a heron pulls its thin leg out of the mud, what it's touching is the ground, a substance deeper than the water. It is the real mud that the heron's soles touch, not my hips sitting in the grass, not my hand pulling a tuft off a reed.

The wind continuously talks to the flowers of the reeds, and the flowers of rushes never cease to hang round the evening sun. The skin of the beach that is like a virgin's lips is where what is in the sky and what is in the ground leave a stamp attesting to their wedding. A skylark's song of songs always makes a vertical musical score. A flock of ducks is a net that links itself to sky and field.

And even on a map of a river site government officials spread before them, the evening sun leaves an ineradicable stamp.

Spring Evening

With my son who returned reticent after drowning the kittens whose eyes hadn't
    yet opened,
I tried to pick up various topics of conversation with the tips of my chopsticks,
but his face must have packed into it the long twilight of the estuary; with the time
    before darkness still lingering,
it sat there, a little pale, shaped like a stomach.
We had no choice but to remain silent, digesting.

Suddenly I thought I heard the midnight door groan open
as the young Shakyamuni[12] stepped out.
Indigo darkness was visible through the crack of the door.
I remembered I had run away into that darkness.
I had opened the door many times, had second thoughts, and come back.
You can send back the white horse in earnest
and leave permanently,
or you can ask the clothes back and wear them again.
You can also push open the many doors of your life to go out
and come to visit as a traveler.

While I was going through such thoughts,
the spring evening had completely darkened.
Then my son switched on the lamp on the table.

The Gleaming Silk Cocoon

Even if what is enveloping me when life quietly revives
is something like a silver-gray silk cocoon,
I should think it would be faintly lit from inside,
a body of dull light.
In the darkness
I'll be staring at this phantasmal light.
I may be one old woman,
but I am quietly burning,
a gleaming silk cocoon enveloping a pupa.

---

12. One of the names for the Buddha.

Ishigaki Rin
(Born 1920)

After finishing junior high school, Ishigaki found employment at the Industrial Bank of Japan and worked there until her mandatory retirement, in 1975. She has said of her poems:

> There are poems that are neither dadaist nor surrealist, poems not written with any particular [ideological] awareness such as that of the proletariat, but are labeled "poems of daily life" or "poems of working people"—poems, in short, that are closely linked to the kind of work the poet does, to the type of department she works in.
>
> This is so much so that I'm tempted to ask half-jokingly if even poetry has been unable to escape the trend toward specialization and fragmentation of modern times. If people have noticed what I've written at all, it is because I've stuck to the standpoint of a working person.

Ishigaki's first book of poems, published when she was thirty-nine, was titled *Watashi no mae ni aru Nabe to o-Kama to moeru Hi to* (*The Pan, the Pot, and the Burning Fire I Have in Front of Me*). She published three more books of poems before they were assembled in the complete works, published from 1987 to 1988.

Atomic Fairy Tale

The war began.

Two planes flew up from two countries
and simultaneously dropped atomic bombs on each other's countries.

The two countries were destroyed.

The only survivors in the whole world
were the crews of the two planes.

How they lived, sadly
and intimately—

That, perhaps,
may become a new myth.

(September 1949)

Greetings

to the photographs of Hiroshima

Look,
this face burnt shapeless,
a person who was in Hiroshima that moment,
on August 6, 1945,
one of the 250,000 burnt shapelessnesses.

That which is no longer in this world—
nonetheless,
friends,
let us once again look at our own faces
facing each other,
today's healthy faces,
morning's fresh faces,
not a stain of war-fire left on them.

I look for tomorrow's expressions in the faces
and I feel a chill:

When Earth owns hundreds of atomic bombs
and walks on the borderline between life and death—
why are you so peaceful,
so beautiful?

Listen, quietly:
isn't something coming closer?
What we have to see is before our eyes,
what we have to select
is in our hands.
8:15 a.m.
comes every morning.

On the morning of August 6, 1945,
all the 250,000 people who died in one second,
were, like you
and me at this moment,
peaceful, beautiful, off guard.

(August 1952)

Landscape

Wait, and he won't come,
if he won't come, who will wait—
I tell myself
but because he doesn't come, I wait.

You've receded too far to call by name,
you no longer show even your back—
you come from the horizon,
rushing in like the tide,

you rush in
but never make me wet,
stopping short at the tide-line far below,
exasperatingly undulating.

On the hillside
I turn dry like sand;
behind my eyelids dims
the seascape's daybreak and night.

That Night

A woman who's made her own living
and is pushing forty,
I feel as if the grave illness
that lays me low and doesn't allow me to get up is a lover.

No matter how I groan,
none of my friends is here to feel the pain for me;
on a bed in a corner of a third-class ward
my lonely heart, which poverty has made incapable of
turning even to relatives for love, begins to melt.

Tomorrow when they operate on my spine,
I'll say to my illness, gently:
Listen, I don't mind dying.

The sufferings of a sleepless night
can't be greater than
living after this.
Oh I'm tired,
really tired.

In the white arms
the sheets silently extend,
I play,   *It hurts, it hurts!*
this boisterous night,
a festival for me alone.

Miniature Clams

At midnight I woke up.
The miniature clams I'd bought in the evening
were alive in a corner of the kitchen
their mouths open.

"In the morning
I'll eat you,
every last one of you."

I laughed
a witch's laugh.
After that
I could only sleep through the night,
my mouth open slightly.

Island

I stand in a looking glass.
A dot,
a small island.
Separate from everyone.

I know
the island's history.
Its measurements.
Its waist, bust, hip.
Costumes for each seasonal occasion.
Warbling birds.
A hidden fountain.
Fragrance of flowers.

I live
on my island.
Cultivate it and build it up.
And yet
I can't know
everything about this island.
Can't settle on it forever, either.

In the looking glass I gaze:
myself—a far-off island.

Greeting with a Smile

I begin to take myself apart.
With the care of boning a cooked fish
for an infant child

with the strength of plowing the earth for sowing
in the direction of a cloud, thinning, flowing in the wind

with the timeliness of a green apple
welcoming its season for ripening

with the love for old tiny forms
unraveling my late mother's hand-knit sweater

With a smile I greet the person
who never tired of telling me what to do
after the moon became full

I begin to take myself apart.

Cliff

At the end of the war,
they flung themselves one by one
from the cliff of Saipan—those women.[13]

---

13. In the Battle of Saipan, from June 15 to July 9, 1944, the 71,000-man U.S. forces, accompanied by large-scale bombardment and bombing and strafing, annihilated the 31,000-man Japanese forces, leaving less than 1,000 alive to be taken prisoner. A great number of civilians, including women and children, who lived there as sugarcane growers and such, threw themselves to death off what was later called Suicide or Banzai Cliff.

Virtue, obligation, appearance,
and such.
Driven by fire, by men.

They plunged because they had to plunge.
The place they went to with no place to go to
(A cliff always makes a woman upside down)

But you know what?
Not one of them has reached the sea yet.
Fifteen years since then,
I wonder what's happened.
I mean, that
woman.

Festival of the Blind

A person has
two faces.

On the head, eyes, a nose, and such,
on the body,
another set of eyes, a nose, and such.
(This set, since some time in the past,
the person has been concealing.)

The two breasts are
unseeing eyes;
the blind one knows
that though unseen, something is there.

What is there
she tries to make sure, touching them.
One day
at the joy and sorrow of what she made sure
her eyes became moist,
she shed white tears endlessly.

A child who grows up with white tears.

The tiny dent in the middle of the belly
is the primeval nose,
which, in distant days,
from its mother's womb,
sucked up mysterious things.
From there blew in smells of flowers,
fragrances of tides,
the winds and the light.
The nose has those first memories
tucked deeply
in its soft folds.

Below the nose, a grass bush,
a woman or a man
has ferns growing round an old marsh,
beneath the ferns insects chirp,
many tongues flare.

The tongues know
of the good food about to be arranged
on the sea-like table:

fruits
rare in any country,
resplendent dinner
no cook knows how to make,
liquor of fire.

People the world over
throw away all their clothes
and go to the table.

The festival of the blind,
drums of the festival,
bonfires without heat, without color.

Iijima Haruko

(1921–2000)

Iijima started writing haiku after delivering her husband's pieces to his haiku group, Ashibi, in 1960, because he was laid up with tuberculosis. She published her first book of haiku in 1972 and her sixth in 1996. Her pieces "preserve the essence of traditional haiku and at the same time show an avant-garde orientation," according to one critic. Known as an able critic, Iijima is cited here to demonstrate the commonly accepted practice of *jikai*, "self-explications."

Izumi no soko ni ippon no saji natsu owaru

At the bottom of a spring a single spoon summer ends

1964

It was about five years after I started haiku. In those days I often traveled to the mountains. It was just about the time my brother-in-law built a small mountain house in Tadeshina. The highland scenery was something new to me, and our family went there often.

In those days I made a great number of haiku that used the highlands and mountains directly as their material, but not one piece among them deserves keeping. This one, however, may convey to some extent, I think, the feeling a highland resort in late summer. But I did not actually see a scene such as described here. The impetus for making this was that in my neighborhood in Tokyo I had seen a great many metal tops of coke and juice bottles stuck into the road before a tofu store that sold them. This is the last healthy piece, so to speak, in my haiku work, and in that sense I am fond of it.

Ichigatsu no tatami hikarite koi otorou

In January the tatami gleam and the carp deteriorate

1970

This has nothing to do with any concrete scene. It is perhaps a mental landscape that has accumulated in me during the period from my birth to adulthood. I grew up in a typical middle-class house in Kyoto, which means that I didn't live my daily life in an atmosphere as authentic as this. But if you are born and grow up in Kyoto, shrines, temples, and preserved places, mansions, and high-class restaurants—in other words, the kind of time and space embodied in the ambiance of "In January the tatami gleam and the carp decline"—are everywhere around you; you don't have to go out of your way to look for them.

Perhaps the attachment to and the rebellion against such a world is the starting point of my haiku.

Hotaru tobi utagai-bukaki oya no hashi

Fireflies flit a deeply suspicious parent's chopsticks

1970

There is a bus road from Kodama-chō on the Yataka Line that leads to Minano, in Chichibu. That the small stream that runs along it is a habitat for fireflies I learned from newspapers, and this is a haiku I made when I went to see it. I waited for long, long hours until the summer sun set. And then waited in the darkness. In time a single firefly emerged from the depths of the stream and I was narrowing my eyes to concentrate on it when, all of a sudden, the surrounding darkness was all fireflies. As an actual scene, the fireflies I saw then were fully sensual and exotic, and I, as a woman haiku writer, might have wanted to make a more sensuous haiku, but what remained with me was a poor man's piece like this. It appears that the feeling I had while I, seated on a small bridge and waiting for fireflies, was chatting for a while with an old woman who came to wash her tools used for spraying insecticide, ended up in this haiku after some twists and turns.

All this means perhaps that in our age we can no longer be as simpleminded as to link the firefly to female emotions or narcissism.

Hikitsuzuki mi no soba ni oku yuki-usagi

I continue to place next to me the snow-rabbit

1974

For a while during my grade school days we lived near the Nin'na temple, in Omuro, Kyoto. The area was still utterly suburban, and fields spread from our backyard to the forest of the Myōshin temple. One fragment of my memory from those days is a snow-rabbit. On a snowy day, on the porch, I made a snow-rabbit. Whether I made it by myself or there was someone else, what happened before or after, I have no recollection whatsoever. I don't remember the cold of my hands, either. The only thing that remains, in isolation, is the snow-rabbit on a lacquered tray placed on the porch. Come to think of it, I saw the real snow-rabbit only this once.

But this haiku did not begin with the snow-rabbit in my childhood memory. The word "snow-rabbit" opened the way. The word "snow-rabbit" is at once the real snow-rabbit that fades away on a tray even while you are looking at it and the white rabbit that leaps about in the snow eternally, freely. It may be that the real snow-rabbit's readiness to fade away, its fragility, ensures its eternal existence.

Ningyō no dekiagaru hi no fuyu no kawa

The day the doll completes itself the winter river

1976

I once saw a dance drama in which an old doll maker falls in love with the doll of a beautiful young woman he is making with great care. The place is Okinawa, and the doll is made from a screw pine. To avoid the old man's love, the doll returns to the original tree just before it is completed. The way it transformed itself into a screw pine with leaves swishing, disturbed, was realistic.

That was how I was inspired, but the doll in this haiku can be any doll. It can be an ordinary doll that an ordinary person makes. And the place can be anywhere as long as it's where you can see a winter river. A winter river, I think, helps expand time and space to some extent. This is a piece that some may say is too ordinary, but I think its relaxed tone is its one merit, if there is any, and it's a piece that I, as its writer, can't discard, though I can't explain why.

Waga basshi tatsu tōrei no Girisha no ichiba

My last child stands in winter splendor's Greek market

1977

A haiku that came into being at a meeting in which the topic given was *ichiba*, [market].This was when we had a haiku meeting at the Bashō Hut in Sekiguchi with young members of Taka [Hawk], with Abe Kan'ichi also invited.

I was at a loss with "market." It is a word on Mr. Abe's turf. Or else it would be a market where I go every day to buy vegetables and fish, but that might make the matter too quotidian. Out of desperation I started to wonder about bazaars in foreign countries—Persian markets, Arabian markets, Turkish markets, Greek markets. When I reached this last, I do not know why, but I remembered a scene where Princess Medea, played by the late Maria Callas, bathes her own child she is about to kill. Then without much ado this put itself into this form.

I wasn't confident that Greece has "winter splendor," but I was much relieved later when I saw, in a Greek movie called *The Record of a Traveling Performer*, a fine day after snow among the hills and a deep blue sea in winter. I have never been to Greece and I have only one child, a daughter.

Nakajō Fumiko
(1922–1954)

Born in Obihiro, Hokkaidō, Nakajō began publishing tanka when she was thirteen. In 1939 she moved to Tokyo to attend the Tokyo Academy of Home Economics and studied tanka with the noted scholar of classical Japanese literature Ikeda Kikan. Married in Sapporo, in 1942, she was divorced after giving birth to four children. In 1952, she had her left breast removed because of cancer, then her right the following year. In 1954, her cancer recurred. In April a sequence of fifty tanka by her was published in the monthly *Tanka Kenkyū,* and in May a sequence of fifty-one in *Tanka,* with Kawabata Yasunari's endorsement—a very unusual step. In July, her book of tanka, *Chibusa Sōshitsu* (*Losing My Breasts*), appeared. In August, she died.

In 1955, the actress-director Tanaka Kinuyo made a movie about Fumiko, *Chibusa yo Eien nare* (*Be My Breasts Forever*), with one of the top stars of the day, Tsukioka Yumeji, playing the poet. The love affair Fumiko had after losing her breasts added to the drama.

After pressing the stamp of divorce I stand with no self-confidence was I a terrible wife

Husband you've become a total stranger though my flesh retains the warmth of your palms

Though it may not be because I'm depressed I thirty am quick to notice male vanity

Translucent in the sun clouds flow spring is at hand I in the rumor: "She readily falls"

Although in a pale blue wind secretly he holds me I no longer have taut slender hips

I let an owl and tadpoles and flowers and love live together in me I being female

In the surgery the disinfectant smells strong the misery that's come over me is no mistake

Being operated on the anesthetic lures me into the past when my nude body was happy I see now

Coldly the scalpel takes my breast into the distance where the voice of attachment taunts me

As long as I burned I gave my breasts to my lover not knowing when the cancer germinated

Lips pressed on them my breasts were hot while the cancer tauntingly grew in secrecy

Since the moment I was carried out of the surgery I've been jealous of fresh pointed nipples

Out of dead flowers I'll weave a garland to hang on my chest the breast will not return to me

The shore where among white jellyfish my breast floats I'll look for it by sleeping again

Wasn't there in antiquity a woman illicit like me punished by having her breast sheared off

New cancer drugs far from perfection classroom marmots sleep hushed the night cold

Where my breast was sewn flat I think of the years and months it will crack and dry

Reflecting my breastless self like a fish like a bird the mirror shows me no mercy

Intently waiting for a kiss that drools with gleaming saliva this morning I'm an infant

Even the night white rabbits countlessly shine and leap virgin sleep doesn't come back to me

As though unable to suppress its fury the cancer emerges again in my breast I console

Having moved to a bed emptied by someone who died I switch off the lightbulb making shadows

May the breast cut off not turn dark hastening its burial the snow falls and falls

Having many scar streaks on my chest I must be truthful even when I'm being false

My white breasts seem to be buried there radiating phosphorescence the swirls of the night

To me the sleepless night comes with a toad, a black dog, someone drowned, and the like

Nomura Hatsuko
(Born 1923)

The Battle of Okinawa, from late March to late June 1945, claimed 110,000 soldiers and 120,000 civilians on the Japanese side, and 12,000 soldiers on the U.S. side. Nomura Hatsuko, born and raised in Okinawa, became an elementary school teacher upon graduation from normal school, in 1943. Almost all her pupils were killed in the three-month-long slaughter. Nomura based the following tanka mostly on the recollections of one survivor of the Himeyuri (Star Lily) Unit, Miyara Ruriko. The Himeyuri Unit, hastily assembled to work as nurses, was made up of 150 women students of a normal school and 50 female high school students. The group soon retreated with the disintegrating Japanese forces under fire to the southern tip of the island, where they tended wounded soldiers gathered in caves. Only a handful of them—nurses and soldiers—survived. Nomura's sister was one of the victims.

Nomura is engaged in a campaign to teach children the horrors of war.

With the bombardment at Minatogawa the U.S. assaults the island from land and sea and sky

(7 a.m., March 23, 1945)

At once the entire land of Okinawa becomes a fiery sea throwing its residents into an uproar

Reluctant to leave their schools and part with friends the young women head for the battlefield

(March 24, 1945)

Deranged a soldier steals, devours the riceball given to a soldier who's lost both his arms and legs

Every time the soldier whose jaw is shot through tries to speak maggots splutter out of it

Maggots thriving lice wiggling in the cave the stench of blood • feces • urine • pus suffocates

Carrying a cut-off arm or leg out of the cave to throw it away a young woman has goose bumps

No drugs just take maggots off wounds help them piss carry dead bodies the whole day exhausting

As a *barometer* to measure lack of oxygen in the cave they light a candle which
promptly dies

Driving civilians out of a safe cave they requisition food as well saying it's the
army order

(Move to Third Surgery Cave; Night, June 18)

A gas canister shot into it the cave turns into an inferno with screams of I can't
breathe

(June 19, at Third Surgery Cave)

Her nose covered with a towel wet with her urine she seems to have fallen asleep
as in a dream

White flowers blooming! she reaches out for them on the cave ladder, maggots
flourishing

On a friend's corpse framed with maggots maggots maggots lies an old woman's
white-haired head

Walking over corpses walking over them all flee in chaos civilians soldiers chaste
young women

Itami Kimiko
(Born 1925)

Itami began studying haiku with her future husband, Itami Mikihiko (born 1920), in 1946, then continued with Hino Sōjō (1901–1956). Kimiko and Mikihiko became members of the magazine *Seigen* (*Blue Darkness*), when Sōjō founded it, in 1949. After Sōjō's death, Mikihiko took over the magazine as publisher. The monthly continues to this day with Kimiko as editor.

An advocate of "rigorism, realism, and lyricism," Mikihiko has used interlinear spaces in his haiku—a practice known as *wakachigaki*—from the outset. In 1961 he explained that he used spaces to clarify the meaning (or images), express internal pauses and turns, strengthen the rhythm, and eliminate the discrepancies between meaning unit and syllabic unit when the haiku is written in one line, without spaces, without punctuation. In addition, he has argued that haiku using modern Japanese (as opposed to classical or pseudo-classical Japanese) require an average of nineteen, rather than seventeen, syllables.

Kimiko, who also employs spaces in her haiku, has published a dozen volumes of haiku, beginning with *Mekishiko-gai* (*Mexican Shells*) in 1965, and has won several prizes. She has also published several books of non-haiku poems.

To a daughter looking down at her math   the sea that was blue

Betting on an unknown future   the parasol opens

At land's end tails turned to the sea   fish dry

Bashful at grandfather in the Buddhist altar   suntanned sisters

Mother's lachrymose last years   cherry blossoms abundant

Given a Mexican shell[14]   by a boy with pirate's eyes

Taxidermist's noon   about time we saw a ship

The offing where sunfish live in view   for the boy dark tatami[15]

If I die   even then the wind will blow on the elm

---

14. "Mexican peacock abalone," which grows to twelve inches.
15. Kimiko's younger brother, who died at age four.

White too intense a color   for a girl in gym clothes

Warships' labyrinth   in the mirror are sailors' backs

The smoked fish shop begins to darken   earlier than the inlet

Twilight at a naval port   narcissus and iron smell

Russian lumber   cold and large   going through town

Loaded horizontally in a lift   iced fish

Alongside a stand of trees to be cut   the setting sun

The back of a sweetfish angler grows transparent   past noon

Can eternity ride on my palm?[16]   the garden of quince

For fear of death is it?   the luridly colored Buddha and roofs

Stone stairs to the sky   the whereabouts of Van Gogh's ear unknown

Peach-colored nuns' robes   drift   in a boiling bazaar[17]

Bruges twilight   a swan floats prayer-shape

Narcissi absorb all sounds   a monastery

Like a long diary   the snow falls   golden anniversary

I meet a fish in meditation at a Black Sea restaurant

Chasing land-mine-hit legs   the Angkor Wat wind

Between heaven and earth   tree frogs are born in foam

Light hubbubs of electric currents   a beauty salon

---

16. May allude to the folk belief in the Buddha's omnipotence. Whatever a human being does takes place within the confines of the Buddha's palm.
17. In Myanmar.

Shinkawa Kazue
(Born 1929)

In 1943, when she was a high school student, Shinkawa began studying poetry with the famous songwriter and scholar of French literature Saijō Yaso (1892–1970). In 1953 she saw her first book of poems in print. Since then she has published over thirty books. She has also worked as a judge in poetry contests, an editor, and an anthologist. In 1983, with Yoshihara Sachiko (1932–2002), she founded *La Mer*, a quarterly of women's poetry, which continued until 1993. In the fall of 1999 she received the Rekitei Prize for her lifetime work.

Don't Bundle Me

Don't bundle me
like gillyflowers
like white scallions.
Please do not bundle me. I am ears of rice,
the golden ears of rice that scorch the chest of the great earth
in the fall, as far as the eye can see.

Don't pin me down
like an insect in a specimen box
like a postcard arrived from the highlands.
Please do not pin me down. I am flapping my wings,
am the sound of invisible wings
ceaselessly touching, feeling the expanse of the sky.

Don't pour me
like milk diluted by dailiness
like lukewarm sake.
Please do not pour me. I am the sea,
the bitter tides the rimless water
that rises vastly at night.

Don't name me
daughter wife.
Please do not keep me sitting
in the seat set up in the ponderous name of mother. I am a wind,
a wind that knows the apple tree
and where the fountain is.

Shinkawa Kazue

Don't partition me off
with commas and periods into several sections.
And please do not fussily write me off
like a letter that comes with "Good-bye" at the end. I am a sentence with no end,
a line of poetry that, like a river,
continues to flow and expand.

The Birth

You came to fill a new space.
When the clouds toward daybreak acquired a rosy light
and the air made gentle ripples
you emerged abruptly
and turned a cute pistol
against your surprised mama.

Oh how can I embrace this
pulsing small lump of <life>
without trepidation, without fear?
My sin, my recklessness,
pitiful child.

Your mama completely forgot
to attach angelic wings
to your back.
My sin, my recklessness,
your mama was in such a hurry
that she completely forgot
to make your tiny palm
clasp a leaf of tricks. . . .

Having no coat, wearing no shoes,
how do you plan to cross
many a cold night?
You'll stumble many times,
each time hurting your toes, red blood oozing.

Life means
to make payments constantly,
to be chased constantly.
You will be scared, grow breathless,
and chew on a bitter blade of roadside grass,
thinking I wonder what?

But you sleep innocently.
As if to say this is your payment today,
you wet your diapers spectacularly, boldly,
and with marvelous cries
rip the night apart,
brazenly issuing a command
to the whole world.

The Door

Whenever a deadline approached
I would grow even more reticent
and making my workroom stagnant as the dark bottom of the sea
let my fish scales glow quietly by a rock all day.

At such a time
you would come down the hall with your infant steps,
stop in front of the stubbornly closed door,
and call your mother's name with a tireless passion:
Mama! Mama! Mama!

Watching silently from inside
the blue-green handle turn, click-click,
your mother's eyes would begin to see, with painful clarity,
a rabbit caught in clairvoyance,
your small figure on tiptoes holding on to it.
In the end I'd lose
and open the door wide.
You'd quickly run up to me,
brightly scattering the cries of a brave soldier
taking back a prisoner, how innocent of you!

You call the swivel chair covered with faded velvet Mama
and turn my world like a top.
You call a pen Mama
and tell me to draw
on the blank margins of my lined sheet
lots and lots of choo-choo trains.

One day
out of a very gentle feeling
I kept company with you from morning, all day.
You were in a terribly good mood
and were twice as good a boy as usual. Yet,
remembering I don't know what, suddenly you tossed off your toys,
ran to the study where I wasn't, that day,
and called out:
Mama! Mama! Mama!

Listening to your voice
I felt oddly lonely.
For you
what was wanted was always behind the door.
The person who'd open the door after your repeated calls
and pick you up had, for you, the reality of mother.
Listening to your voice
I gradually became unnerved.
In time I became inorganic

and standing close behind you
raised a pitiful cry:
Me! Me! Me!

When the two of us
violently pushed the door open
I definitely saw, I thought:
seated in the old swivel chair,
facing a lined sheet spread on the desk,
and drawing one picture after another
of the matchbox choo-choo train you liked, weeping,
a profile of the real me—

Sleepless Night

A needlefish that can't die at the bottom of a creel.
A heterogeneous fabric in a dyeing vat.
Hyacinth grown in the water, excessively white, thin roots.
A foundling of the wind which, having lost its direction, is bewildered, a small
    cloud.

Hot Late Summer

What to do with the rose in my garden,
this remaining rose?

I ended up looking at the abandoned garden.
My old mother, senile, asleep,
carelessly showed it
because of the unusually humid heat past noon
with no autumn wind to stir the blinds.
The withered gate that couldn't possibly have
anyone to wait for or to visit
was not so much obscene
as openly, casually, innocent.
Having hurried past the verandah outside her chamber,
I wipe the sweat that covers my skin.
The heat of this year, this crazy heat.

What to do with the rose in my garden,
this private rose?

Spring Cold

So it may light your way
when you visit me again tonight,
as I'm sure you will,
I leave the light by my pillow on and close my eyes.
The backs of my eyelids
are like lanterns with lit candles.

In that light
peach blossoms fall, fluttering, fluttering.
It must be because you are coming,
I won't call it crude behavior,
slightly tipsy,
hitting, hitting flowering branches.
Yet you are like a silhouette on the paper sliding door
no matter how much time passes,
only peach petals remaining pink.

Fluttering, fluttering,
have I cried a little?
The lanterns waver,
your silhouette smudges and fades,
and tonight's dream
has turned into nothing but chilly, cold petals.

The Remaining Summer

To see him off, I stand at the gate after the rain.
The ivory roof of his car
has scarlet smudges of crepe myrtle
that the hard rainfall awhile back struck down.
——Shall I wipe them off?
——No, not necessary. It would wet your hands.
By the time he returns on the superhighway to his office downtown,
the roof will be dry, and so will the flowers sticking to it,
leaving no trace, blown away by the wind,
that's what he's figured out in his head.
The brief conversation like a bird's bath,
the faint scent transferred,
will fade, will be forgotten,
by the time he pushes the elevator button,

the transience of it all like an exclamation.
He's someone who promises to come
but often doesn't,
so when he hurries away without even saying, "See you again,"
how can I, in the future, wait to see him again?
Telling myself not to wait anymore
I end up waiting again, morning and evening, which terrifies me.
Allowing the scattered red flowers, the last of this summer,
to smudge both heart and eyes, I remain standing,
thinking of the sadness of flowers
that peel off the roof of a speeding car
and are lost one after another.

My Bedcover

I love using my bedcover made in India
which has flowers and birds embroidered in variously colored threads
on simple, coarse cotton fabric.
At night when I need only to peck at a little bit of sleep
I don't have to unroll a sea of sensuous silk sheets under the lamp
so I lift the cover slightly at one edge
and let my body slide under it.
When I pull it, together with the bedding, up to my cheeks and close my eyes,
I reach a very peaceful state of mind.
It must be because I feel, gently placed on my chest,
the hands of an Indian lady that carefully moved a needle
using hand-woven woolen threads, each hand-dyed,
the hands of a woman who must have accepted silently, for many years,
so many sorrows.

Speaking of India,
a writer who said he'd been invited to and stayed in a vast mansion
of a certain poet of the Tagore family
once came to visit and said something like this:
    "Even among the servants
    the caste system holds absolute sway.
    You just ask for an ashtray
    and the message is passed down through lower classes.
    All that complicated stuff beats me."

If I rank myself à la that country,
I am neither of the *brāhmin* (priests) class nor a *ksatriya* (noble)

but at best a *vaisya* (commoner).
I do not know to which class the Indian lady who did the embroidery belongs,
but even if she is a *sudra* (slave)
or an even more miserable untouchable,
at least on this bed
we are equal.
The evidence is this:
The flowers touch my cheeks
and the birds, fluttering, fly down to the rim of my sleep
and try to look into my dream.
The three blue stitches laid out wave shape
must mean the sacred river, the Ganges.
Sometimes, as though for ablutions in the lake beyond the forest,
she and I become naked
and splash water at each other in sheer delight.

The Snowy Morning

The snow that hadn't fallen for a long time
even after winter came
must have begun falling at midnight:
Having turned the withered lawn and trees in the garden pure white
it keeps falling.

This thing so voluminous—
In what kind of bag had heaven stored it?
As if heaven had held it back
patiently
before opening it at last,
the snow continues to drop unstoppably,
drop continuously.

If heaven had held it back as best it could,
it must be sorrow,
not joy.
At heaven's sudden confession
the world has turned quiet, hushed.

How long do I have to hold back my sorrow
before letting my heart open
so it may become as beautiful as this,
as pure as this?

. . . so wondering
I stand, gazing out at the garden
beyond the glass door.

Odes to Fire, 2: "When the water called me. . . ."

When the water called me
my body spilled from the log bridge
and before I took another breath was held in the river's arms.
I flowed. The water sang.

—— Your red clothes, wet, open,
  are beautiful like a water flower.
  Let me give this flower to the water god
  as soon as possible.

But at that moment
with a voice stronger than water's someone called me.
I opened my eyes a little. It was the riverbed
and a fire was burning.

—— We can't offer this healthy girl
  as a sacrifice to the water.
  We'll just give her clothes to him.
  Come, burn like me.
  Totally naked, you enchant me.

Myself enchanted, I stared at the fire.
My body became hot and my life caught fire.
My girlhood of "shoulder fabric"[18]
flowed away, along with my clothes, in the hometown river;
I left a red flower, first sign of womanhood, abloom on a pebble
and began to walk.

Sometimes even now, far or near,
the water tries to lure me with his sweet song.
And each time I freely release my clothes to him
and become naked.
I make a fire and from near it
start out once more as if for the first time.

———————

18. *Kataage:* Children's kimono have extra fabric on the shoulders to enable their
enlargement as children grow.

Odes to Water, 11: Sagami Bay

"Take the intestine of the sardine.
It grows S-shaped, and when it grows longer,
 it coils around the first S-shape, like this, from both sides.
 Exactly the way we wind a hemp rope when we put it away. . . ."
A restaurant in Aburatsubo Marine Park.
Drawing a picture on a paper napkin on the table
and explaining
is the world-famous ichthyologist and director of the aquarium here, Dr. Suehiro
 Yasuo.
"When it comes to flat fish like the flounder,
 the way it coils is like this, swirl-shaped. . . ."
While listening to him, before I know it I turn into water
and, twisting, coiling, whirling,
pass through a fish's stomach.
This is because when led to the room for filtering seawater
I dipped my fingertip
in the water in the tank and licked it a bit.

"There are a great variety of fish, many,
 but if you captured a monster fish like Nessie,
 do you think you'd like to bring him to this aquarium?"
"What I think is, that was a kind of mirage
 that a rising air current at Loch Ness showed.
 Mirages are not confined to deserts, you see.
 Oceans and lakes show similar mirages at times.
 Rather, the coelacanth,
 this fish is not an insubstantial illusion,
 but it's proven it still lives off the east coast of Africa.
 You know, it was thought for a long time
 that this fish emerged in the sea 400 million years ago
 and became extinct several thousand years ago."
400 million years!
For a second the color of the Doctor's eyes was fabulously deep.
I stared at it as if touching the mystery of the sea.

That life came into being first in the sea
I'd read somewhere before.
Because of that or something, the amniotic water that protects the fetus
has, I am told, the same substance as seawater—that is, the brine.
Will the fact that I gave birth to a child
allow me to say I was once a sea?

After leaving the aquarium I took a taxi
and crossed over to Jōgashima now linked by a modern bridge.
I climbed the stone steps with swamp lilies blooming on both sides,
stood on the level ground where a lighthouse was, and gazed at the sea.

Even so, ocean,
what in the world are you?
Enveloping two-thirds of the earth
like an amnion, with this stupendous water—
You are, just as you are, supposed to be a big answer
but you always leave me in the form of a question.
You don't even show me a mirage as the Doctor mentioned,
remaining quiet, calm, shining in the evening sun, ocean, ocean.
You pretend to keep billions of doors open, but are closed, ocean, ocean.
What really are you,
when a faint taste of salt earlier
still lingers on my lips?

Katase Hiroko
(1929–2006)

Born in Fukuoka to parents who were both Presbyterians, Katase spent her adolescent years, from 1939 to 1946, in Beijing because her father, a physician, was assigned to teach at Beijing University. She majored in English at Tokyo Women's Christian University and wrote about Virginia Woolf in her graduation paper. From 1957 to 1988 she published six books of poems and won prizes for two of them. Among the poets she translated for book-length collections are Kathleen Raine, H.D., and Ted Hughes.

Daybreak

A car packed with howling small angels
draws toward me.
Fragments of a dream still glisten.
On a dark bed
my immature white breast is tormented.
A single night has torn yesterday and today apart.
The white wall and the window and the light
the world had changed.
Shaking your blind small face,
searching for a nipple,
you, terrifying joy!
Dawn swirls out of the window.
The voice that's leaving appears, disappears in a stand of trees
and the day is bright with a curse
because it has made sadness its own.

Time of Love

Blindfolded by large palms—
we disappear beyond the horizon,
in each other's arms, headlong;
baby carriage, coffin, and torch course through
our blood vessels.

Seeing nothing,
hearing nothing,
ducking under the orbits of blinding clouds and pale underground,
stars, thorns, and mud,
we wept for our selves that were ceasing to exist.

We saw things
that were incomparably beautiful,
that were superabundant,
but could not grasp any of them.

We heard words
that had never existed,
that were being whispered as if overflowing,
but could not memorize any of them.

In the midst of things flowing toward us endlessly
we, almost hurt, wanted to close our eyes,
but our eyes opened with forced ecstasy.

Receding, our giant backs darkening—
daybreak flying-fish, seaside chimney, shining stand of trees,
woman in evening glow washing a hoe with water, white town,
night's mountain and marsh, countless other things passing by—
we now wished
to be

seen by them,
memorized by them,
while touching the sky with our tentacles of despair.

Mother and Child

Cold rain falling in the window;
darkening, you and I
face each other:
prototype of dialogue
of such solitude.
Suddenly raised from my nipple,
your face
goes over my shoulders
and spreads beyond the window.

Birth

At night's base
the shark-like loneliness

of time and space
took a bite from my flesh.

Twilight:
trembling lump of flesh
bloodied beside me,
when I held in my arms
you who still held the void on your back,
what was distant suddenly came close
and crept into my blood.

The new possession awakened a new possibility,
loss:
if you are truly life,
to that extent you are death.

My death that stepped outside,
a horizon that leaps up and leaps down
while annihilating me from inside,
O, how painful it is
to possess an infinity,
to be caressed by the hands of infinity,
tiny fingers that grasp me
from sky, from sand, from inside a fire, from a collapsed wall!

Laughter,
you've come from the other side.
Surrounded by giant witnesses,
the sun, the mist, the waves point at you,
saying they won't forget you—
I escaped
that trap of cold sweat, that flesh-tearing pain,
that loss of blood,
that convulsive curtain of the night,
I passed through them all.
Even so, now
I cannot escape you,
you, who are so powerless,
you with your fragile twilight grip.

I was struck by what had emerged:
fingers, calves, nape, ears,
every dent, every furrow

that was being etched in the backlight,
how precisely life, in its unprepared way,
goes on revealing what's hidden!
Life lays down a trail
to the distance where joy becomes abstract,
the distance from which death returns.

No matter how many times I close my eyes,
the shadow that stands on my horizon doesn't disappear.
Like the shadow of a small tornado or lava,
what's there is what wasn't there yesterday.
Is today as accidental?
You, who never try to turn back
and question your raison d'être,
you limit yourself to the sky black,
you are the end, an existence.

Like a petrified small owl,
captured by an invisible, persistent eye,
facing a shadow coming nearer with huge wing beats,
you are surrounded by life
so vivid and abundant.

Lovemaking

In the darkness
the noble bridegroom's smile
is bloodied before I know it.

In the darkness and light both drowning,
the man's dark flesh
torments what it loves
with solitary power.

The cruel brilliance of the fire set to a ghetto
that burns up from the horizon of embrace.

The eyes rimmed with uneasy flames
stare at each other
as if staring into the darkness itself
as if it were something to be penetrated.

The man holds the woman tight
like a prayer before battle. . . .
in the flow of the night
where everything collapses soundlessly—
he covers with his body warmth, as with a shield,
her cold nude body as exposed
as Judgment Day:
this recovery of the throne in the course of time

———— ripening female body,
   you are a new border where I am prostrate,
   the dawn of a still unknown country or city,
     half asleep, half awake;
   there's the laughter of a child who's coming

O, green treetop that grows wet at dawn,
peach that fingers tear apart

The woman's limbs suffocate
in the river of melancholy and bitter pain of all males
that flows out of the giant Adam,
in the hot night's forest filled with
the restless Cain's footprints and panting.

They are the pillars of fire that burn
distantly in the sky of the dreams of the dead,
testimony to an invisible country

Suddenly, out of the woman's depths
the darkness of the strata deafened for thousands of years
gushes out;
in that deep shout of conception
the two no longer recognize each other's face or body.

A sense of death begins to fog the surroundings.
Now void mates with void,
the flesh no more than a light trembling
at the rim of a world that can't be seen.

Delivery

tom-tom   tom-tom
screeching wild birds   contracting ocean   dark brown
group figures shooting arrows at the sun   from virgin forests
to deserts   to water's edge dyed by Sirius
stirring night's luxuriant leaves   drums respond to one another
what old news is it   holding in a vat-coffin
a bronze mirror and sword adorned with the sea's variegated stones
and listening
tom-tom   tom-tom

paradise
a semblance of God that comes through a forest filled with light
in military uniform   eyes bloodshot
gun muzzle turned toward me
tom-tom   tom-tom
in body's depths grow waves winds
from among disturbed treetops rise drum sounds
woman wakes from pain
on cold birthing chair white-clad figures look down upon

gripped by night's heavy gills
gray flesh dripping with sweat being shattered
facing the sky above a town asleep
open exposed thighs
burning like a secret furnace   brimming with darkness a hole
dug out hollow
a wet black small head appears disappears
. . . .
woman lies on her back
like something that has reverted to original material
nameless   soft
beside a fountain of fragrant ripe wine—
has the birthing chair that's faded away
enveloped in bloody mist   emitting hard light
plunged into a shining orbit
floating up out of darkness bitter rock-like
breasts   white hair   meteoric face

time that wells up like endless donations

makes everything breathe
like a bridegroom of sadness
in the white night made by the burps
of those that go through the eye of a needle
their four limbs bent

Tada Chimako
(1930–2003)

Tada was inspired in her late teens by the poetry of Hagiwara Sakutarō and Nishiwaki Junzaburō to write poems. *Hanab*i (*Fireworks*) was published in 1956. It was followed by nine collections before the definitive edition of her complete poems appeared, in 1994. Her seventh, *Suien* (*Water Spray*), published in 1975, was a small collection of tanka. Tada occasionally attempted rhyme, one of the few modern Japanese poets to do so. Her eleventh book of poems, *Kawa no Hotori ni* (*By a River*), published in 1998, won the Hanatsubaki prize and her twelfth, *Nagai Kawa no aru Kuni* (*A Country with a Long River*), in 2000, the Yomiuri Bungaku prize. In November 2001 she was found to have cancer. While ill, she wrote haiku, which were collected in *Kaze no Katami* (*The Memento of a Wind*) after her death. Tada majored in English at college and is known as a distinguished translator of French writers such as Marguerite Yourcenar (*Mémoires d'Hadrien*), Claude Lévi-Strauss, Georges Charbonnier, Antonin Artaud, and Saint-John Perse.

After a Storm

Night having receded,
the sea was quiet, dozing,
with a wrecked ship
like a prayer book it had read to sleep lying on its chest.

I

Joyfully as a cabbage
I'm planted in the ground.
Carefully strip me
of the words I wear,
and you can prove my absence;
nonetheless, that I have a root, too.

Convergence

The rain washes away the remaining summer,
in the garden a soaked dripping autumn crouches.

My tongue, cold as a clam,
imprisons soft words
in its shell grown used to the tides.

Tada Chimako

I put a wet stone reflecting my eyes
on a thinly spread palm,

and my long gaze in the end returns to itself,
abandoning a memory
that lists and sinks like a wrecked ship in the distance.

Legend of the Snow

And finally the snow began to fall
after the rain, wind, and sand

Stopping the hands of all clocks
the snow slowly went on piling
on the steeples of evil intent
on the castle walls of foul distrust
on the ruts of the wheels that struggled with black mud

Enveloped in the snow cocoon
the town became a legend
became a white pumice gravestone
with countless holes bored in it by the souls, the noctilucae. . .

(however ill and emaciated, old people
all become beautiful before dying)

Where was reconciliation?
The human town forgot weight
and precariously trembling as a single flower
atop a thin stalk
kept opening one white petal after another
(like a deep gentle wound
that turned into a holy theater)

Where was prayer?
The snow that began to fall at last
after the wind, rain, and sand
laid a white day upon a white night
and never ceased.

Darkness

The pitch-dark night sky
is packed with roses.
Tens of thousands of roses stir.
I can sense this,
that the heavy night dew falling on my nape
is the sweat of the roses jostling one another.

The Mirror

*

The mirror that is always slightly taller than I am
laughs slightly after I do.
I blush red like a crab
and cut with scissors those parts of me protruding out of it.

*

I bring my lips close to the mirror and it clouds
and I vanish behind my own sigh
just as for example an aristocrat vanishes behind his crest,
just as a hoodlum vanishes behind his tattoo.

*

This mirror, a graveyard of smiles, traveler,
go to Lacedaemon and tell this:
that, heavily made up, a grave painted white,
only a wind blows through the mirror.

Orpheus

When I turn to look, someone dies.
Twilight of the snake in the valley,
footfalls on dead leaves cease
and I become solitary as a pebble.

Who were those who died?
By turning to look,
how many people have I killed?
I light a lamp of grapes resplendently,
I wear thick glasses,
but such questions are now too dark for me.

(In any case, when was it
that I passed through a long tunnel
to a border station with a grave marker
to welcome a faceless bride . . . ?)

Transparent water climbs up my back
and flows down, counting the number of vertebrae.
And ahead of me a forest of lusts burns out.
(Which god set it on fire?)
One shadow, extending its arms and charred black, and another tilt
and in the semidarkness the thickness of ashes increases.
The season to operate on the totally blinding cataract. . .

Having swallowed the bride
the lips of the earth no longer open.
My lips, too, do not move.
I will not play the crescent moon
again
to turn the night into morning,
oblivion into song.

By the emaciated river of Thrace
I grab a viper with a crushed head
and throw it as far as I can, behind memory.

Making Up

Facing the mirror I lightly make up
This is what I always do, a custom every night
What isn't a custom
Tonight I become a boy!

A dress shirt and a blazer for a fifteen-year-old boy
Slacks also for a fifteen-year-old boy
These mysteriously fit me right
And I become a boy just before his beard begins to grow

This gamble, it doesn't cost much
Isn't even as risky as a gamble
I may replace a jack with a queen
But it's all right: No one will notice it
(Its rusted hull repainted
Its prow loaded with eyes
The ship launches from orthodox time)

From now on I won't envy any man or woman
Won't need perfumes or two revolvers
If I want to, I can become
A concrete woman
An abstract boy

The night has deepened
Preparations done I'll go now
To someone who's neither husband nor lover
Farewell, strange boy in the mirror
Who's about to become a man, until the daybreak smelling of mother's milk

Yesterday's Snake

> *The Three Realms are illusion; they are merely the work of the mind.*
>
> Ten Stages: Avatamska Sutra

Yesterday, in a dream, I saw a beautiful snake.

In truth, it wasn't in a dream but surely in the garden that I saw the snake. In the farthest end of the garden where the rain fell quietly, at the base of a stone wall, in the only spot still left white.

But today it's clear, and the wet twilight snake won't appear again. That large snake striped white and gray, his body wrapped in perfect scales, who showed only alert coldheartedness. Putting up with my stare, he didn't even stir.

(Behind my back a valley stream was making a deep rushing sound)

I whistled once toward the darkening ground. That instant the snake put out his tongue—or, rather, put out his tongue and pulled it in with blinding speed.

A faintly vermilion, pointed tremolo. . .

Tongue pulled in, he started to advance slowly. Very slowly—and yet, the scales all over his body trembled dozens of times a second and, the scales trembling, his body smoothly slid forward. . .

Not at all changing his wavy form undulating at three places between head and tail, making the tip of his tail vanish while simultaneously raising his head forward, forward.

(Do people call that swift appearance-disappearance advance?)

The snake slid into the dense grass bush at the root of a pine, and I was left alone in the rain, umbrella in hand. Like a tall mushroom tilting gravely.

Yes, that must have been a dream after all. A long slim dream that, undulating, raised itself and vanished.

(The resplendent vibrato of white and gray of the scales all over his body!)

This garden itself isn't that garden of yesterday. It has dried up in every nook, it has no shade, and the sound of the valley stream has grown shallow.

I surely had my eyes open in the dark illusory rain.

And I myself surely was a mushroom, that instant, in a corner of the garden.

From the tanka collection *Suien (Water Spray)*

Moonlight

Black hair spreading in the water by the boulder sways once, a waterfall begins to roar

Autumn water flowing over my eyebrows in the shallows of a daybreak dream a
   scarlet crab lives

Evening glow shines on the root of my nail the moon doesn't become a half moon
   waning waxing

Heaping up an abundance of eyelids I can't sleep this fall a single rose remaining
   vermilion

I pluck I pluck petals off a chrysanthemum the floramancy done stamens vie with
   one another

Water Spray

By the water my soul is what's delusory bellflowers purple clouds the shadows
   pass

In the midst of travel the traveler doesn't pass his shadow turning in the midst of
   autumn grass

What passes is the season   the touring wandering stage   hides its shadow in
   the bottomless pit

Past a water village a grass village the road ends where the bones live here in a
   stone village

Water spray rising envelops a waterfall like a glimmer of light at the end of the
   night

Emerging in the darkness of ferns and still quiet the illusory waterfall as my
   travels end

Holing Up in a Kitchen

A purification rite
And cut
On the cooking board for sacrifices
Tubes rise one after another
For example tubular cuts of a fish ring-cuts of a carrot
Surrounding an absent corpse
Like *haniwa*[19]

---

19. Clay or earthen figures made to decorate mausoleums in ancient Japan.

The water remains cool in the Aquarius
Let the water catch fire and burn
On the distant shore where saliva rises
Teeth all lined up
Wait for the fading of reds and greens

The firing ceremony
The dissolution and transformation in a tightly sealed pot
The plants are no longer plants
The animals are no longer animals
All things will be reduced to ideas

The priest pacifies the furious bubbles
Reverentially holds a pestle of eternity
And deliberately stirs earth water fire wind

Fear of the Kitchen

No matter how peaceful a house may be, it has, by necessity, one room tainted by murderous omens. There, people wield murderous weapons in broad daylight and slaughter pitiable small animals. Those who are already corpses are skinned and cut into pieces—on the sacrificial platform called the cooking board.

The cooking board is purified by blood. You wash the blood off with water and detergent merely to return the sacrificial platform in a state of extraordinary exhilaration to the state of carte blanche and make it wait for another purification.

The cook is a priest who sanctifies the corpse to turn it into savoriness in the mouth. His clean white robe signifies his priestly status.

Even a dainty fruit knife acquires, doesn't it, the features of a nakedly murderous weapon when it stabs an apple's red cheek?

That white box that makes a manmade Arctic materialize in a corner of the warm kitchen. A refrigerator or a freezer. It is a space of a different character in the bright, heated kitchen and, like the murderous intent in a tiny corner of the brain of a smiling man, hermetically seals its fatally cold air, along with its darkness, and never lets it out.

The plucked birds and beasts stuffed into this white box—how they resemble the frozen corpses in the morgue!

A room equipped with a number of gas burners where you can freely cook and broil. If you feel like it, you can even turn the knob on and just leave the burner unlit. Your kitchen will soon turn into a perfect gas chamber.

And when you put a whole chicken or turkey on a broiling pan into the oven and close its door, don't you think of the steel door that seals in a cadaver at the crematorium? Even the meager oven in my house can readily broil your baby.

The fury of the water that's put on the fire and made to boil—well, that's hard enough, but how can we wash away its resentment as it's left in the kettle to slowly turn cold?

In the peaceful kitchen, stacked pure-white eggs keep a precarious balance, and a highly sharpened meat knife is suspended above the cook's head like a Damoclean sword.

Taoyuan, or Earthly Paradise[20]

Go through the tunnel and there's the cemetery hill.
Peaches are blooming.
Father and mother are warbling.
On the slope the westerly sun shines on
a solitary boy's playing all by himself
and an old grave keeper's dozing.

Visit this quiet hideaway village.
Bamboo shoots sprout near your feet,
and so do some new gravestones
during the hesitant second
when a peach petal leaves its branch
and dances down onto the grass.

Go through the tunnel and it's the world of peaches.
Ideographs are left to the stones.
Reflecting the boy's laughter in a glistening way,
the water of the Netherworld is purling.
Dyeing the grave keeper's white head red,
a distant past glows in the evening sun.

---

20. *Taoyuan (Where Peaches Luxuriate)* is an earthly paradise in Chinese legend. Once a fisherman, going upriver, found, beyond a peach orchard, another world where people who had escaped the horrors and deprivations of wars were living in peace and happiness.

Year's First Dream[21]

Listening to the year-end bell,[22]
I stuck a finger into the golden skin of an orange
when, as if pushing it back, an old man put his head out of the torn part.
—Come in awhile. It's warm inside.
(But how can I go in?)
The moment I peered into the hole, I was sucked into it head first,
and the next moment I was sitting in the orange.
The walls of the round room were covered by something fluffy and white
and, yes, it was "warm inside."
Placed before the old man was a go board.
He must have wanted someone to play the game with.
I chose the black stones, he casually beat me,
and gave me an orange from a tray.
When I stuck a finger into its fragrant skin,
another old man put his head out.
—Come in awhile.

How many round rooms,
how many oranges within oranges did I go in to play?
When I woke the first day of the year, my body was soaked
by a brilliant golden fragrance.

The Mysterious Female or Sheep Valley[23]

This is a valley where sheep well up,
clouds well up, sheep well up,
a fissure covered by white cotton
that smells of amniotic fluid.

---

21. Almost anything that happens or anything one does for the first time in the early part of the year is regarded as auspicious or otherwise treated with deference.

22. *Joya no kane:* At midnight on the year's last day Buddhist temples begin ringing bells. The bells are struck 108 times, each strike designed to dispel one of the 108 *kleśa,* or emotions or temptations that disturb the quiet of your mind and prevent you from achieving enlightenment.

23. Poet's note: "The quotations are taken from *Lao Zi* [*Lao Tzu*]. The story about Prime Minister Lord Li derives from *Xuan-shi-zhi.*" Translator's note: Prime Minister Li is Li De-yu (787–849), and *Xuan-shi-zhi* is a collection of mysterious stories compiled by Zhang Dou (dates unknown).

Lord Li the Prime Minister in his dream walked on a mountaintop
and saw a vast valley buried under sheep.
The shepherds said,
These are the sheep you, sire, will eat in your lifetime.

Some years later Lord Li was demoted.
By fortune telling, the monk told him:
You are expected to consume 10,000 sheep in your lifetime.
So far you have eaten 9,500.
There still are 500 left.

Thereupon 500 sheep were delivered as an offering.
The monk sighed and said,
Here we have all 10,000 sheep.
I must tell you your life is finished.

His soul visible through his lonely face,
Lord Li reached this valley he'd once seen in his dream,
pushing aside the clouds welling up, the sheep welling up.

This valley is "the Gate of the Mysterious Female."[24]
Because it goes down to Yin City it's named Yin Gate.
It has lips that move constantly,
which, being moist with netherworld water, are named Yin Lips.

And here there are teeth,
rugged teeth of rock
to masticate all the dead.

"The Valley Deity doesn't die."
"Empty and inexhaustible."[25]
Endlessly giving birth,
the Valley Deity nonetheless wails.

24. Section 6 of *Lao Zi:* "The Valley Deity doesn't die; it's called the Mysterious Female.
The Gate of the Mysterious Female is called the Root of Heaven and Earth." Both "the Valley
Deity" and "the Mysterious Female" are understood to be metaphors of the Tao (the Way).
25. Section 5 of *Lao Zi*. The reference is to bellows, another metaphor for the Tao.

Inanna Inside Us

From Chimako to Kazuko,[26] *late fall 2002*

The oldest goddess in the world[27]
in the oldest country in the world
(even so instead of being raised to heaven)
descended to the netherworld.
In passing through the first gate she took off her sash and veil,
at the second gate, her bracelets and rings,
as she descended, took off more
until with only her beautiful naked body clothing her
she descended to the bottom of the netherworld.
And like a dog she was hung from a nail, they say.

And so, my friend, I was secretly afraid:
My poor offering
to the oldest and the newest goddess of poetry
might herald some ominous signs. . .
But I also thought:
The goddess of poetry, like that old goddess,
like the woman diver of this country who rises from the bottom of the sea
(yes like "The Woman Diver" of the Nō play who took the jewel back
from the Dragon King and rose to the surface of the sea)[28]
kicking with those beautiful legs that ominous wave of emphysema,
kicking open Pluto's hard seat,
pushing aside "layer upon layer of waves,"
was bound to rise and step forth bathed in the light of rejuvenation. . .

Blessed be the small corals surrounding
your nude form like lambs.

---

26. Farewell to Shiraishi Kazuko, written a few months before her death. For Shiraishi, see pp. 388–397.

27. The Sumerian goddess Inanna is often described as "the oldest goddess."

28. A play about a female diver who retrieves a crystal ball from the Dragon King who stole it during its transference from the Chinese Court to the Japanese Court. A female diver, who has given birth to a boy by a nobleman visiting her village, offers to bring back the ball, which has a figure of the Buddha in it, for a promise that her child would be made a nobleman himself. At the Dragon Palace under the sea, she breaks into the stupa enshrining the ball, cuts her chest open to protect the ball from "the mouths of evil fish and crocodiles" that guard the palace, and is hauled back up into her boat. But she dies—of her self-inflicted wound and the lacerations she received from the attacking fish. The play, which combines folktales and Buddhist and other elements, is old and its writer is unknown.

Revealing them from the waves
you will toss them back.
And I, again tracing the path to the dark, dazzling secret rites
from the first gate to the second,
will try to grab you by the wrist, by the ankle,
so that I may grip firmly
what we have shared
in the crystal ball like a drop of blood. . .

Farewell-to-This-World Haiku[29]

Riding from one blade of grass to another the wind goes where

---

29. After she was diagnosed with cancer, Tada began writing haiku under the poet Takahashi Mutsuo's guidance. This is the last of the about 160 she wrote.

Ōba Minako
(Born 1930)

Since her debut novella, *Sambiki no Kani* (*Three Crabs*), in 1968, won two literary prizes, Gunzō and Akutagawa, Ōba has won most of the major literary prizes—Tanizaki, Noma, Kawabata (twice), and Yomiuri—for her stories and novels. She lived in Alaska for eleven years. She published just one book of poems, *Sabita Kotoba* (*Rusted Words*), in 1971. She is a member of the Japanese Academy of Arts.

Love That Doesn't Work Well

1954

Your words are like
wet origami sheets.

My words are like
congealed pine resin.

I tried to make a crane out of a red wet origami sheet;
the sheet tore and dyed my fingers red.

You are sneezing
with black pine resin stuck on the tip of your nose.

Parting

1953

In a battle that was eating into me inexorably
of ridicule, hatred, and pity,
when your eyelash, a blade,
slashed my lips,
I laughed, cackling.
The laughter, more than loud weeping,
was a coarse laceration.
The blood that spurted up immediately congealed into
a needle of grume riding a razor blade.

The Tachikawa Scene

1952

A friend of mine, who reads palms, once worked part-time as an interpreter-cum-salesgirl at a shop selling pearls to American soldiers in Tachikawa. (This was during the Korean War.)

Soldier with eyes as blue as marbles:
"I'm interested in a long necklace of pearls. I'm going to send it to my mother as a gift."
Salesgirl:
"Let me see your palms."
"How is it? What's my fortune like?"
"How old are you?"
"Eighteen."
"You may be killing someone; if not, you may be killed by someone."
"Is there any way I can change my fortune?"
"Let me see now. Stay still as much as you can. Don't do anything, try to be alone as much as you can, and think hard how all this has come about. Then, you may be able to end up neither killing nor getting killed."
"I'm going to Korea."
"Take a pearl from the necklace you're going to send your mother and keep it with you. I'm sure it will protect you."
The salesgirl took a pearl from the ones strung together before attaching a hook to them and wrapped it in paper.
"I'm going the day after tomorrow. Would you see a movie with me?"
"Yes, thank you. But tomorrow I have something else to do."
"Well then, would you write down your address for me?"

The salesgirl received love letters from the battlefield.
Three came, and that was the end of it.

The salesgirl was listening to the radio.
It was saying an American soldier assaulted and killed a Japanese girl.
The salesgirl was reading a newspaper.
It was reporting Korea was full of prostitutes. As in Japan.
It was also reporting there were part-time student jobs available sewing together the corpses returning from Korea.
Sitting in the pearl shop, the salesgirl was watching, through the window, again, women in long flouncing skirts hanging onto the arms of American soldiers.

Poison

1954

Oh, please,
do not tease me.
If I misunderstand you again,
I might actually use the poison
you gave me.
When that happens,
please do not blame me.
I wouldn't in the least mind of course
if you were to believe
I've been too kind
to you.

But, please
take precautions
so I don't have wrong ideas.
Let's stop having trysts
near the rainbow bridge in the evening haze.

Life[30]

1967

Women inspect catalogues and do shopping,
have dinner with someone amidst gossip.
They get depressed when someone's happy,
consoled when someone's a little unhappy,
but stop thinking when someone's too unhappy.

And men, too,
perhaps because of this Information Age,
become uneasy when alone,
comforted when with someone else.
And when there's nothing particular to talk about,
they feel relieved,
confirming that there's nothing particular to talk about.

Old people,
when they fall ill and lie alone in their home,
begin to fear they might die alone, unseen by anyone,
and walk out to the park, shaking with fever.

---

30. At the time the poem was written, catalogue shopping was hardly known in Japan.
It is assumed that this poem describes Ōba's observation of life in Alaska.

Shiraishi Kazuko
(Born 1931)

Born and brought up in Vancouver but taken back to Japan before the Pacific War, Shiraishi, at age seventeen, was discovered by the modernist Kitazono Katsue (1902–1978), who founded the artists' group VOU. Her initial influences were Miró, Dali, Jean Cocteau's *Orpheus*, and Albert Camus' *The Stranger*. She published her first book of poems, *Tamago no furu Machi* (*Town Where Eggs Fall*), in 1951, while a university student.

She soon became uncomfortable with Kitazono's "modernist rhetoric," which did not allow her to express "the rough postwar reality and sentiments" and by the early 1960s was more than ready for the jazz and Beat poetry that poured into Japan, she wrote in an essay on herself. In particular, John Coltrane's manner of expression—conveyed in his remark that he could find out what he wanted to express only after playing solo for an hour or more—mesmerized her. The results were "My Tokyo" and *Seinaru Inja no Kisetsu* (*The Season of the Sacred Lecher*), a book-length sequence of seven "chapters" that appeared in 1970 and earned her the Mr. H. Prize. Among other influences during the period were Nishiwaki Junzaburō (a surrealist absorbed in "Oriental nothingness" in his late years), Yoshioka Minoru (creator of "a demonic arena" by blending spirit and sensibility), Tomioka Taeko (chatty tone), Dylan Thomas ("Twenty-Four Years"), and Henry Miller (*Tropic of Cancer*).

With *Arawareru Monotachi o shite* (*Let Those Who Emerge . . .*), in 1996, she won the Yomiuri Literary Prize and Takami Jun Prize, and with *Fuyū-suru Haha, Toshi* (*Drifting Mother, the City*), in 2003, the Tsuchii Bansui Prize.

My Tokyo

like the Shakyamuni
almost seated in this city
I am now   being conceived of October's tedium

my dear girlfriend who walks about nude
in a New York loft
hysterically   vivaciously
you'll again   cling to Masuo's neck
and beg for kisses
I want to tear that skinny coquettish white nakedness
off from its frame   and *touch* it
it will be   very white   chalk white
a sea of desolate solids   also

Shiraishi Kazuko reading with Kenneth Rexroth

it must be a waterfall of plaster dirt
that falls in flakes when you touch it
I can see
the fat pants of the Italian who puts you in a laundry bag and carries it on his
    shoulder to a washing place
the cans of cheap beer he *treats* you to
lie empty in the street-level bar   and like rats
cry   squealing
that's America   America's *hungry*

my closemouthed   October
this concrete grumpiness
prowls *My Tokyo*
the *bothersome* phony tears and brown-nosing of phony mankind
that runs around aimlessly   overflow
from the jukebox   and then
turn into giant shoals of sardines   emit evil smells
and flow toward artistic poetic thoughts   usual
academic autumn

to all
that   saying bye-bye
I enter   as I haven't done for a long time
my inner canal
also   infiltrate my inner city
at this city's entrance   at summer's end
I met a single individual
Amenhotep (ancient Egyptian king)
he's a nameless youth   a modern bus conductor
a butcher   racer   poet   revolutionary   something else
he's all the rains   something that isn't all   also ancient   five thousand
     years ago
Egypt
its king   the eagle that is its amulet   the intestines of newly born crocodiles
     that turn into its food
infant's brains
unguents for the rites   pliant dresses of hatred   time
that which is the parts of these   and their whole

I held hands   with a moment of the man   Amenhotep
who became   visible and invisible   in this chaos
and plunged   into a season of personal performances
about that time
there was the sound of a subway running   at the bottom of my city my womb
     also   on the stage
drums and bass sounding   Sandra started to dance
Sandra who's all in black isn't Salome
a beautiful lesbian black   middle class
a gentle   lascivious housewife   a go-go dancer
a black Santa Maria who turned her husband
into a pale shark   a castrated Don Juan

my starting to take the subway
that was my first encounter with Henry Miller
the toilet   newspapers   old letters   chairs   milk
in every piece of furniture and food   I saw
his drinking water   cell   rag-like
life
I'm still   a regular user   of the subway
I love the subway   almost as long as
coitus   my subway
is no longer iron   a soft flesh shape
an illusion of civilization   a cradle of thought   now

in this city   the subway is
the innermost   stomach of meditation
on its ulcer   mankind that settled in the city
was clinging   somewhat half asleep half awake   incessantly
spitting out foam from its mouth   not words
not roars   not pleadings   neither smiles
nor words requesting love   nor satisfaction   nor battles
but   foam

at Club "So What"
one o'clock at night   Max Roach beats his drums
why is he   *handsome*
why do his drums appeal to me *lyrically*
also an awfully fierce rain of sounds at a technical extreme
there the people were stunned   steamrolled
the small cosmos of his music   beat up
the spawning of people's do-nothing-ness

My Tokyo
this city   almost
is our   womb
I stood   at its gate
with Amenhotep   and we kissed
then   the rain began   then
almost through the duration of or linkage   we died or mated
dying for five thousand years   and being born for five thousand years
yawning for five thousand years   and continuing to laugh for five thousand
    years   that should be more than love

everything   frogs   eggs   jam   a piece of
blue sky   lined paper   records   flies
"Let's hit the sheets"
that's our city's password
someone   in solitude   hit them with a dead cat
someone   too *handsome* a man
smashed up the mirror   grabbed with all his strength the penis of himself who
    was on the other side   and fainted
also   someone   incessantly afraid
of his feeble brain and body   eating catnip
wailing   squatted on the sheets
two young leopards   these men
quietly hold each other   in the deep woods of yearning
those beautiful monkey women   in each other's secret room

were casting rainbows of caresses   like morning glow

about that time
my personal performances continued   rapidly sullenly
from October to December   during which time
I was in a spider's web of aphasia   acute ecstasy   idiotic philosophizing
where my many selves became the spider's prey
uttered sloppy cries   and were captivated
one   of my selves
escaped   took the subway   and tried still
to do some music
this may not be love   it may merely be
season's greetings
but
something was musicked
my own self   painted
on to the already new melody   I heard
myself slapping my tail with the ferocity of a crocodile of hatred
but who is it   getting thrashed   by this tail
who is this soul being called into this music

Ah
at the terminal I see Joe who's turned into a ghost
already run over by a roller of sex
and has turned into   gray and a shadow
given up even by the last drop of the storage of life
and driven into a lazy desert   is he reddish brown iron sand
entwined by a viper roller
the limbs of his will gradually taken by a spider   already
rusting on the side of the delayed time   he's now
about to lower the last curtain

while I   also
am stirring my hot will   into the ashes
to clearly bury   my city

cutting through   layers of fogs of premonitions
I faintly heard God's pain
it   *suddenly* turned into a fiery pain
now   for the first time
I see God's entirety striking as lightning   and in the roar
becoming hot right next to me   and being there
almost like eternity   it's *momentary*

half ill and wounded   *lying*   this
in the guise of a feeble traveler

my city is
now   far in the distance
has already turned into a stranger's face
its concrete head   drooping
sleeping   an aimless sleep

From *The Season of the Sacred Lecher*

From *Chapter I*

‡

human beings are bored of
being very human beings

Human beings want   to be wolves
want to be weeds
want to be outlaws
want to put themselves at the mercy of   outlaws' whims
and destroy themselves
both men and women *leg*[31] the drama
in which they want to be very   rapidly destroyed

everyone   hurries toward death
wants   very much   to go to die
and so   most
want to bear children
and next
regret
sorrow that they've gotten old
and want to get old very impatiently
mankind doesn't want eternity.
all want to be destroyed
   they don't want to be lives
want to be romans

---

31. Apparently-African American slang for sexual intercourse.

or rather   roses
worms
to be trampled upon like worms
‡

what's called death isn't sweet
and
dithyramb is sweet
your living isn't sweet
and
your existence   your *soul*-raining landscape
is sweet
I'm not sweet
and
we are sweet
because
we are a decision
are a *romanesque* of decision
human beings with the name of will
by the way
the invisible   American dream
that carries it
isn't sweet
the American dream
arranges   with the same number
the space between the living and the dead

From *Chapter II*

- - -
a faint laugh (*smile*)
unbearable   gentleness
like a gauzy moon
it hangs above my aching chest   my soul
blurred
it becomes an aching landscape   a good spice   and smarts
you draw
a full   smile
from the bottom of the well
and give it to me
I   wordless

drink this   black death
like a poison

- - - - -

no longer   sorrowing over sorrows   I
make my transparent body
brighten   the color of blood
and put even sorrows   on the pleasure plate
the dog Ulysses sniffing
comes to turn inside out the flesh in my backyard
I begin quietly   to music
a mist rises   deep in the woods of my soul the flesh
thousands of   obscene sacred eyes
noses   lips   hands and feet   hair
part the skirts of these woods
and like purling streams
flow toward me

From *Chapter VI*

my honey man
I'll go on a trip of "It's delicious"
with   myself
now you aren't a "sweet tooth" but a "sweet spoon"
I lower myself a little   before
life's real   or   serious abyss
make the spoon brim with
a poison of honey (honey is poison isn't it)
and let it flow from lips   to throat
from throat into chest
from chest down toward the deep well
now,
there's nothing   saner
than all these   insanities

Let Those Who Emerge . . .

In the darkness   I strain my eyes
and gradually   I get used to it   and see where I am.
Above the dust   her crouched butt the color of the peach
the queen   crouched   looks toward me.
Mixed in the purling stream   released   from her crotch

a powerful sound of water   follows.
An ancient flush toilet   is there.
The queen crouched forward   her butt thrust backward a little
is faintly visible   the rest invisible.
An auditory hallucination perhaps   I heard the sound   of water
but with it   several thousand years   passed
leaving only
dry dust   and the remains of what was once an outfall.
Outside it's above 100 degrees. Out in it
pure-white flowers   descend to cover me.
Over the ancient site   white lives   turn into momentary
timelessness   and continue to bloom.   But fortunately
they have   no language.
They have only a fierce instinct for proliferation   and innocently
evilly?   continue to bloom.

I hear about   the things I saw in the darkness
a few minutes ago.
Next to the ancient flush toilet   is the queen's room.
Outside it is a courtyard   which is sun drenched.
From there she sometimes looks out to the outside world.
But the queen   mostly   looks at the blue dolphins
painted in the upper part of her living room.
It is freedom.   Dolphins   friendly
playfully sing.   She can hear them   the queen believes
when she's asleep   like a mermaid.
In her dreams   she mates with dolphins.   Her cries of ecstasy
are weird   her attendants think.
The dolphins still swim pleasantly   in the painting
in the upper part of the wall   but both her face
and her sensual butt   have faded
leaving only
the remains of an ancient flush toilet   several thousand years old   dusty and dry.

Amid white flowers   I find   myself.
Nonspeaking lives   spanning   several thousand years!
But   I   walk covered with white flowers   along the King's Road,
the road   from which the King is gone and is now an obsolete word
to the west.
To the west is a town. In the park at its entrance a dubious photographer
with a large black box installed   an invention dated but not to be imagined several
    thousand years ago
takes pictures of young foreign lovers.
While waiting for a sheet of printing paper to come out of the box   which the

photographer then tints
for about thirty minutes they eat ice cream in the shade of a tree.

Next to the people eating salads made of tomato and cucumber and onion
drenched in olive oil which also have goat cheese and oregano
I drink coffee.
When you say, "Greek coffee!"   and drink this Turkish coffee
both hatreds and betrayals   seem extremely
piteously childlike.
But because of them   people died   were killed
for over several thousand years.   What is the King's Road
but the Blood's Road   the Road of Conspiracy and Scheming?
Yet
the sky is blue   and the white flowers have already been extraordinarily
    abloom.
In the dust of an ancient flush toilet
the phantom of the butt the color of the peach   of someone once a queen now
    visible now invisible
becomes a gleaming fruit   receives baptism
from the eyes of desire and lust and of flesh   and though now several thousand
    years have passed
it doesn't appear faded   it doesn't appear aged.
When I strain my eyes   no in the darkness I almost close my eyes
there are those who emerge   powerfully
bits of soil clinging to their fingers   but their fingerprints surely
surely . . . match my memory.
Let those who emerge   emerge.

Takarabe Toriko
(Born 1933)

Soon after Toriko was born, in Niigata, the Takarabe family emigrated to Manchuria—or Manchukuo, as it was called as a state established in the previous year by Japan. Following the Soviet invasion of Manchukuo and Japan's defeat, in August 1945, all 320,000 Japanese immigrants became refugees. In the ensuing chaos and deprivation, 80,000 would perish, among them Toriko's father and three-year-old sister. (Before his death her father had her hair cropped to make her look like a boy to prevent rape and kidnapping.) It took thirteen months for the remaining family to make it back to Japan. In 1981 she went to visit the city where she grew up for the first time since the war. Her two novellas, collected in *Tenpu, Meifu* (*Fertile Land, Inferno*), in 2005, are careful reconstructions of her childhood in Manchuria and herself as a sudden refugee.

Takarabe published her first book of poems, *Watashi ga Kodomo datta Koro* (*When I was a Child*), in 1965. Among the books of poems she published subsequently, *Saiyūki* (*Journey to the West*), in 1984, won the Chikyū prize; *Chūtei Gentō Hen* (*Magic Lantern in the Courtyard*), in 1992, the Hanatsubaki prize; and *Uyū no Hito* (*Nonexistent Person*), in 1998, the Hagiwara Sakutarō prize. She translates modern Chinese poems.

The Death I Always See

—to a small younger sister who died as a refugee

My sister wearing sky-blue clothes
appears, disappears in a grass bush,
sister holding a face-like peony,
no, she's falling below the bridge;
at the bottom of that distant, deep valley stream
I stay awake,
I'm awake so I can catch her in my arms.
A blue wound
runs through my arms.

Enclosed by running wildfire
my sister and I are no longer there.
The loud weeping in the *baomi*[32] forest,
that isn't me.
I wake,
and notice
I've abandoned my sister
in dream's giant maw;

---

32. Corn.

I no longer can go back,
no longer can.

But run, run,
each time I run, the wound grows bigger,
tears apart peony-color,
and I die, die, many times.
Each time I die,
sister loses herself in a grass bush with a bird's nest,
sister's swallowed up
in the rapids of the Tangwang-he.[33]

And I abruptly wake,
can't go back, between the dreams where weeping persists,
that single gunshot, I don't want to hear it.

Daybreak Dream

In Blagoveshchensk,[34]
yes, in Blagovesh! Father said,
large Russian breasts weighed down on your daybreak dream.
Father drinks liquor in a *tochka*.[35]
That dot on the map is now
the color of a dream that's withered while standing.
Nothing blows but the wind.

My dead sister who keeps being chased by a heart-shaped beast
is unhappy.
But my heart's poetic leap
is very happy
until I hug her pale blue naked body on a snowy plain.

Also I am
a simply abstract
tusk of conically frozen tears.
In Blagoveshchensk, toward daybreak,
in that imagined place to the north,
I freeze, all my limbs cramped up.

---

33. A river in the province of Heilongjiang that flows into the Songhua River (Manchurian: Sungari), which in turn flows into the Heilongjiang (Amur River).
34. A Soviet (Russian) city on the Amur River, directly north of Harbin (Haerhpin).
35. Russian for "pillbox" or "blockhouse." It also means "dot."

Decisive winter there:
freeze the morning's waking of low blood pressure,
freeze the foods that rot,
freeze solid the amorous yearnings in infanthood,
for the nurturing of the thermometer.

Under the leaden sky,
my sister was about to be blown away,
astride a dream's dream.
The good-for-nothing icons
that sit, their bloody *rubashkas*[36] on,
try to jump up,
wobble, and finally fall.

When all dreams, while crushing,
warmly mate toward daybreak,
and I, still freezing,
they shout, each pointing,
Put out the dream's fire!
On the bank of Blagovesh where I never slept
ice flowers bloom, beautifully.

Talk of Horses

A woman eating gruel at the end of the village
also talks of horses.
A child who likes colored juice also talks of horses.
Far away, in a pond,
a man holding a stone in his arms never stops talking of horses.
Listen to my talk of horses.
A horse that has chewed tobacco in the straw doesn't stop struggling.
Horses neigh deeply, deeply between today and tomorrow.
A horse's full moon.
Because the villagers want talk of horses,
the horses stand erect as a cliff.
Because a rainbow of horses hangs over the roof the TV stops working.
Because villagers want talk of horses,
from one end of the tobacco field surges a flood of horses' afterbirths.
Their riots year in year out
never stop politely surprising the villagers.

---

36. Traditional Russian jackets.

(Can you imagine that cliché?)
They hang sheets from high windows and shout:
We want to talk of horses!
I wanted to talk of horses.
Just one talk of horses.
Then
from a paddy ridge flaming horses gallop out.
They are finally truly surprised
that they themselves are horse-shaped.
The awestruck villagers
make a dam of red manes.
Now let's talk of horses!

About Forms

On June 14, JAL's DC-8 carrying 86 passengers crashed in Jaitpur, a village
27 kilometers southeast of New Delhi. Bodies and broken parts of the aircraft
were scattered widely in the farmland on the bank of the Jumna River, which
flows at the edge of the village. Grotesquely contorted bodies, seats still with
humans tied to them, a white girl holding a doll, flames. Ambulances rushed
to the scene through dust on the riverbed which was so dry that the sand buried
the cars up to the hubcaps. . . . Family members of the passengers left for the
crash site on JAL's special plane at 10 a.m., on the 15th, which is expected to
arrive in New Delhi at midnight.

(Excerpted from a newspaper report)

Translator's addition: The aircraft made a landing error in a sandstorm. Among the
passengers was Takarabe's brother Tetsurō, who was on his way to Tehran to take
up a business post. He was thirty-six years old.

A corner of an old park by the hotel had a yogi.
A sandstorm had made the lotuses in the mud bloom;
his bones and skin
coiled around his lukewarm innards and rigid meditation.
He wouldn't touch salt
and seemed to wait single-mindedly for the colors to turn limpid.
A human body should go on drying up like that, I thought.
Facing a *jamun* tree,[37]

---

37. Indigenous to India, it has a lovely purple-black fruit about the size of a large berry.
It ripens around April–May.

it should go on drying up,
without reading written words,
without picking up meanings,
simply hoping not to return to being human.

But it's different in Maulana Azat.
Even a yogi's shadow acquires a raw smell.
Bouquets of *pure* lotus flowers,
ominous bats,
unfortunate flesh (though there is no such thing),
words become stereotypical,
things are swiftly carried from form to protyle.
But the philosophy
that protyle is plastic
earns me neither bread nor flower petals.

Maulana Azat abounds with *unfortunate* deaths.
An *ominous* stench strikes me down.
The voice *Don't touch* forces me back to being human; I walk without falling
and read the wooden plaques on the coffins.

>Male? In charred state
>Female: with false teeth, charred
>Small man: only half?
>Male about 30 years old with fragment of striped shirt
>Male: with remnant of dark hair; upper implant
>Female: blonde, ring with JCS
>Male: fat body, with capped teeth
>White female: golden necklace
>Male: about 180 centimeters tall, no head
>Male: 175 centimeters, Hitsujiya jacket
>Male? extremely charred.

They certainly seem to convey forms.
What form,
I find myself thinking.

I try to touch you with white gloves,
try to pull up the body that ought to be there, and I can't touch you.
Souls aren't written on wooden plaques, they say,
by color, weight, age, male, Oriental. . .
The question of soul. . .

Abruptly there's a voice near my brow:
"Do you believe in something formless?" it says.
"No, never.
It would be odd for a soul not to have a form."

Trees and cows that pass before my eyes wear nimbuses.
Soul and form, violently collapsed,
are seeping into the red sand.
I was *sad* and wouldn't accept anything,
but I could have been *sad* and accepted everything.
Red mud smeared on his body,
a yogi stands on his head and his form grows transparent.
Letting a mantra rise like steam,
trying single-mindedly to rot
in total red.

Yellow Catfish

Once the sky sprinkled with loess
and the great muddy river were shut in,
a town formed.
That was the pattern (a pattern doesn't make a poem).
Peering out the guesthouse window at invisible heaven and earth,
not really meaning to see anything all day,
a large catfish, thrown up on the riverbank,
seems roasting in swirls of yellow.
When the yellow sand that left Mongolia yesterday falls,
the yellow sand that left Mongolia a millennium ago also falls.
This ancient parallelism makes a maelstrom.
North of the street the midwife's house where Confucius was born still exists.
That's really nothing.
The role of a poet who struggles for eternity
becomes so dry she can hardly bat her eyes.
She has cup after cup of oolong tea.
Each time she goes to throw away the leaves in her teacup,
she tiptoes over the carpet notable for its bumpiness.
She fell once.
After all, it's curling up, historically, in four corners.
She's got to be cautious.

The Tanghulu Vendor

—Grandmother talked

Above the plain the Galaxy, head reared,
plays the flute in the dark universe tonight,
yet you can't hear it.
There must have been a word here
but everyone's forgotten it.
(You've been looking for it ever since.)
Even so the loess went on striking people's thin eardrums,
ceaselessly making a noise like rustling silk.
The night you were born a cold wind was blowing.
The large river that had rolled in grains of sand,
while tensing up at the hint of ice,
went on flowing north darkly.

The withered branches of weeping willows on the bank were swaying violently.
In my house at a street corner the river water
had amply enwrapped my little girl's little womb.
In her womb were you, an infant,
pricking up your ears.
The voice that came through the wind
was blown apart in the wind
and when the fragments reassembled,
they reached your ear as
tang-hu-lu . . . tanfūrū. . . .

You remember,
that was your father's voice,
the strong, throaty voice tinged with sadness,
the voice of a Shandong man in large cotton-padded pants.
What's wrapped in frozen molasses are scarlet haws.
Skewered like jewels and gleaming,
and those skewers, many stuck into reed bundles,
carrying them on his shoulders to sell them, he walks about,
runny nose freezing in cold wind.
That's your hometown.
Tang-hu-lu. . . .
Tanfūrū. . . .
Between the low rumbles of the river,
tanfūrū . . . prolonging the tail-end,
caressing the womb with a faint lantern lit in it, passing by.

(When I heard a tanghulu vendor's call as a child
I somehow thought of the other world.
I thought it was the voices of dragon kings afloat midair
or a voice that would take my soul away.
I have no father.)

You can't eat them without coating them with molasses,
those sour, puckery, medicinal seeds, poisonous seeds,
those scarlet seeds like planets ready to collapse,
you were chewing on them in the womb,
your face contorted,
a bitter, wrinkled, little face.
You took a breath,
swallowed the puckery haws,
then cried aloud
when you were born. You did.

Posterity

Does it mean as faint as the sound of the moment a lotus flower opens
or as faint as its scent?
You He, "Faint Lotus," she faintly opens her mouth,
she quietly nudges the warm fragrance out of her scarlet lips.
She called herself You He the Layman.[38]
One of her lines goes,
"At Lake Tai's bottom a grass carp sighs aggrieved."[39]
—A few of her poems are found in *The Anthology of Song Poetry*.[40]
She must have had a difficult grass carp
hidden in the stagnant depths of her heart.
The fish would occasionally come around the willowy bend
and rap her heart with his cool fins.

One long spring evening,
at the door of her room, she a prostitute, there is a tiff.
The overgrown lotuses blocked my boat,
says a young man outside the door.
A butterfly, a bee, comes to a flower however faint its scent may be,
she argues and refuses to open her door.

---

38. Sanskrit, *grhaspati*: a man who trains in Buddhism without taking tonsure.
39. Tai Hu: One of China's five great lakes, it lies 110 miles west of Shanghai.
40. An anthology of poems of the Song Dynasty (960–1280), originally compiled in 1666.

Before the usual hubbub in the gay quarters
above which an amorphous spring moon climbs,
bouncers' tough arms thwack the young man out the gate.
Another day, another commotion in her chamber,
and the young man finally throws himself into the lake, or so they say.
Unable to swim through her stagnant depths,
entangled in the weeds,
heart eaten by the carp's greedy grief perhaps,
he floats up one day.

"Outside my tower a thousand threads
droop from willows, spring about to leave.
A merciless rain scatters the blossoms,
turns the garden into a carpet of petals."
This beautiful poem on regrets over departing spring is hers, too.
Now, far beyond dust and dirt,
it blurs like a willow at the start of spring.
Only written things open their mouths, is the way of the world.
Besides it's up to the reader's fickle mind.
Her legacies: making a talented young man kill himself
and writing some fragile poems, is all.

But You He the Layman was a man, one theory goes.
—Or so says a note to *The Anthology of Song Poetry*.
Hailing from Huzhou, he passed the government test young.
Well, then, the poem on departing spring may be about sadness after licentious
    conduct.
You begin to see a totally different, decadent air.
Whose heart was it, then,
that the grass carp sighing aggrieved ate out of grief?
In the lake water spring days fermented,
I thought I saw fish scales quickly hide,
I thought I saw a gleam, but whose posterity was that?

Field Notes

                                                            —*At Bahutun*, Jilin

During grammar school summer vacation Father and I traveled together,
a distant past that barely exists,
to a small village called Kitsurin-shō Hako-ton[41]—

———————

41. Japanese pronunciation of Jilin-sheng Bahutun.

to a small village called Bahutun—
Father made Mother crop my short hair
until a lonely boy with a crewcut was born.
And we went to that remote place
where marriages were still said to be traded
to gather ethnic information.
Two men traveling,
we creakily rowed a dugout
and crossed the Songhuajiang.

It was a village with beautiful willows.
On the riverbank made of the water's smell
a crowd of villagers watched a parent and child of a different race.
After many questions and answers
Father wrote in his notebook something like this:

> "We can say the dugout, which appears crude, is one ethnic tool unique to the Manchurian tribe. At present they make them out of elm; two *mujiang*, 'wood craftsmen,' require eight months to build one, dedicating themselves to it. The cost is about ¥200 each. You can use it for about four years. The daily income from one is about ¥30."

Seeing me squat on the riverbank, my back turned, and urinate,
an ancient man of the village understood what I actually was and pleaded with
   Father:
I sincerely hope to have this girl as my son's bride.
Gold or silver, silk, donkey, you may ask for anything you want.
If the price is right, I'll be happy to sell her, Father said calmly.
He handed out cigarettes to the villagers and, with the ancient man, walked down
   to the water's edge where the sun glistened.
In accordance with tradition they started negotiating by counting narrow willow
   leaves.
"During the winter they use green peas and such. For negotiations they use things
   that can't be divided."
Father came back, alone, with willow leaves clinging to the tip of his shoulder
   and back.
He priced you at ¥1,000. Will you become a woman for ¥1,000?
What do you say? he said, laughing.
Was it also part of his effort to gather ethnic information? I can't say.
It's in a distant past that barely exists.
Lest villagers kidnap his daughter priced at ¥1,000,
Father hurried her along. We had to hurry.
We walked and walked, turning back to look at the corner of a white, plastered
   roof.

A cool scent of blood drifted from Father.
You're a boy, Father said to me.
You *are* a boy.
I lit the cigarette Father held in his mouth.
On the riverbank the dugout was bobbing.
When I jumped into it with a boy's deliberate cleverness,
the waves on the bank where evening shadows were encroaching
sneered . . . *byon byon byon.*

The Water and Mongolia

When I drink water, I wouldn't think of the sea.
I just stand in my kitchen,
looking up at the dirty blue ventilator.

I wouldn't feel, in my mind or on my back,
estuaries, inlets, or roaring waves in the distance.
I wouldn't think
that in the Mongolian grassland that resembles a sea,
in a *pao* in its midst,
there, too, is a TV. I wouldn't think
that almost all of the human body is made of water.
I wouldn't think the soul is made of water.

When I drink water
a sheep runs down my windpipe
like a brush of pianissimo.
At that moment my healed flesh
will give itself a tremble.
But when the water passes down my throat,
I wouldn't think of a Mongolian man following his sheep.

When you drink water, you wouldn't think of
a Mongolian man, either.
You wouldn't think
that simply because the sound of your throat echoes,
the Mongolian man, in his long sheepskin boots,
walks down to the water's edge, in large strides.

Walk, walk, to where the water shines.
When a wind blows across the withered grassland along the water's edge,
the grass bends, flowing low, flowing low, just like sheep

asleep.
The withered grass rebels against the wind and stirs,
that quick, soft leap
of that stirring, moving sound! No, you wouldn't think of such a thing,
when the water passes down your throat.

Simply from a transparent glass
you drink water single-mindedly.
That's of course what you do.

Bessho Makiko
(Born 1934)

Born to an old family of Shimane, Bessho studied social work at college and published her first book of poems, *Shinayakana Nichijō (Resilient Dailiness)*, in 1982, followed by *Akebono-zō wa Yuki o Mitaka (Did the Akebono Elephant See the Snow?)* in 1987 and *Nemuri no Katachi (The Shape of Sleep)* in 1992. An active member of a renku group, she has distinguished herself with studies of women haikai poets during the Edo period, among them *Bashō ni hirakareta Haikai no Josei-shi (History of Women in the Haikai Bashō Pioneered)* in 1989 and *Kotoba o Te ni shita Shisei no Onnatachi (Townswomen Who Got Hold of Words)* in 1992. The latter comes with a chronological list of women's haikai books. Bessho believes that the hokku/haiku is a one-line poem.

Water

You listen to its sound far inside the deep fern night. Neither filling up to overflow nor spurting, it drips without interruption.

It's the sound of the dreams of women who, while asleep, head toward coagulation again on the shore where the one who keeps running along the path of the fire he stole from Heaven refuses to return.

With a dark pipe laid down from the primordial place of water, there's the night's faucet that doesn't stop dripping.

Bottle

The water is dazzled. In the first light of daybreak, a cold flame, rising, circling in many layers, has formed a tower.

From its thin neck narrowed toward awakening to its shoulders, all regrets slide down and shatter. Clear through the bubbles of memories, a distant hollow begins to ring.

Hermetic, resplendent meaninglessness! Words lack their solubility, time has lost its specific gravity.

O, what kind of day will look good when inserted in the lips of regeneration the water has dreamed?

Mirror

Ever since it rose to its feet, the water has had to endure its position as a form of will that accommodates all, rejects all.

The outline of time that brilliantly goes on receding, the sadness that flows down perpendicularly, to attest to the place that reflects, that never can reflect.

Because of its crime of always showing an incarnation, the water can no longer generate waves.

Far inside the white light that overflows, who can measure the water depth of darkness?

Each morning, a woman drenched wet turns into a thin sheet of shadow and goes on drying.

The Skylight

Many layers of dust
with wave patterns chiseled into them
shone rainbow-colored at sunset
in the skylight of our earthen storehouse.
From there,
I could see a road like a yellow snake
climbing up to the watershed
beyond the deeply cut valley.
What was I waiting for?

I'm listening to my older sister's flutey voice
calling to me
in the distance (in a different habitat).
My heels touch the moist tatami. Mold smells.
The oblong box's butterfly lock and the ring-shaped lantern hanger
squeakily whisper to each other.
From under the shining ivy covering the white wall
a gecko slips across the beach
with his cute feet.
Below my eyes a cliff with a village of camellias, blue scales.

Why that skylight?

My elbows sprinkled
with rust peeled off the iron grille
I kept waiting for something
that would run down, light-footed, toward me,
on the snake twisting, crawling beyond the unknown.
All good fortune, happiness, and joys
were to come from there

(In red clothes and festive clogs)
On a summer evening the sun never seemed to set,
sitting on the shore of vague childhood,
I merely heard the faint sound of wings
of something passing by.

Turning on a heavy, box-shaped flashlight,
I climbed down the staircase like someone sinful,
relieved that I hadn't seen it after all,
afraid that I'd end up seeing it some day.

Waterless Month[42]

In Waterless Month I fire a heavy harquebus
    Trees' words that can't be exhausted,
    demented, scatter away in a green storm.
    Ophelia
    turns into a white sala blossom
    and drops onto a Nebukawa rock.[43]

Forerunner monsoon: mother also has a crying mole[44]
    Will a thousand-needles[45] do?
    In a river that's a black satin sash
    a man who loves matchsticks
    has lost sight of the other shore.
    The amniotic fluid is the temperature of the summer sea.

The giant salamander[46] comes with legs: the loveliness
    The magician roasted with pine needles
    has been sealed in his magic words.
    The fox can no longer escape.
    The whole family and its ilk depart on a balloon trip
    from the roof.

---

42. In this poem and the next, the first line of each stanza is written in the haiku form.
43. Pyroxene andesite. Called Nebukawa-ishi, because Nebukawa, in Odawara, has a famous quarry of this rock, which is often used for monuments.
44. A pigmented nevus that is supposed to be the result of too much crying.
45. A piece of cloth with a thousand needle stitches by a thousand different women made as a good-luck charm for a soldier going to the front.
46. *Hanzaki,* also *ōsanshōuo* (*Megalobatrachus japonicus*): the largest salamander in the world, which lives in Japan; it grows to be five feet long.

Death-prone: cherry blossoms in the clouded sky peach-sensuous
  I sold my soul.
  Because I bought a shadow with the money
  I remain on my feet in the pitch-dark.
  I, who resemble me,
  forever awake.

The Iwami Fudoki

Winter showers then it clears up: the *Iwami Fudoki*[47]
  The wind being stared at by a stone.
  From the dark gray-steel sky
  hangs like a string an occasional deflection.
  Because the sasanqua spilled white blood
  the soil began to tremble
  and ended up swallowing the eyes of the stone.

Snow pregnant gives birth to a tree-searer this holiday
  On the edge lies a giant clarinet.
  The wind-instrument music swiftly runs away.
  Ducking under a hedge of withered trifoliate oranges,
  to Oppel's shack, to the dead horse's stable,
  holding resilient whips,
  cheerful deities come to strike.

Hanging an anglerfish as is at the tip of a hoe
  The sea: a dark green arpeggio.
  The horizon lacks 130 degrees.
  Boats holding up naked bulbs on poles
  fell vertically into the star-gate
  came back, having caught eyeless cosmic creatures.
  A ring of lives circulating between the atmospheric strata.

---

47. Iwami is an old name of the western end of today's Shimane. Bessho plays on the literal meanings of the two Chinese characters for the word, *iwa*, "stone," and *mi*, "look" or "stare." *Fudoki* refers to any of the regional reports compiled by government order in 713. The *Iwami Fudoki*, however, is a fragment describing the poet Kakinomoto no Hitomaro, which is believed to be a document faked during the Kamakura Period. Here Bessho uses the term more loosely to mean something like a report on the Iwami region.

On Clothes Doubled trees the sound of water ringing
    On a moonlit night the dead rise.
    Gen'ichi who turned into a hazel and Misa who turned into a willow
    lay their shadows on each other in a golden grassland.
    The grains and such quietly begin to go mad.
    At the pain of looking it solidifies:
    the stone, the will to inspect.

Koyanagi Reiko

(Born 1935)

Born in Tokyo, Koyanagi opened a gallery in Nihonbashi in 1966 and published her first book of poems, *Mieteiru Mono* (*Visible Things*), that year. For her sixth book, *Yomi no Usagi* (*Rabbit of the Netherworld*), published in 1989, she won the Poets' Club prize. It is an attempt to recollect her wartime days, toward the end of which she almost died of tuberculosis, and their aftermath. In 1988, she started publication of the Mujinkan (Dreamer's Pavilion) series of art books, as well as books of poems. Among the artists she has published in the series are Frida Kahlo, Richard Dadd, Mendelssohn, Jean Delville, and Richard Oelze.

An Ode to Ravel

1

I loved music above anything else. It was because of small pieces for the piano such as "A Doll's Dreams" and "Silver Waves." Probably you don't know them. Even my eight-year-old daughter can play them, so they're easy. At the grammar school I attended, there were a couple of classmates who played the piano well. It was during the war, but these girls wore velvety one-piece dresses or dresses embroidered with beads, and during the class-day season, they would play for us the pieces I mentioned above. Wearing *mompe*-pants that were washed too often and with no special skill, I could only stare at those rich young ladies on the stage, holding my breath. I loved, like flowers, the music they played, the way they appeared while they played it, and every fluttering petal of their small conversations. They would never deign to speak to me, as I trembled with yearning for them. Soon I decided to write about such beautiful things in my novel. It was going to be a beautiful novel full of love. Even during the days when air raids became fierce, on bright afternoons these girls would gather in the music room and play. Unable even to be part of those who surrounded them, I would sit outside the window of the music room and enjoy the sound of the piano I heard through it. At such times, music was even more beautiful. Those were the days when you couldn't even get a loaf of *pain coupé* easily, but music seemed to drown out such sad dailiness and lure me into the fields, to the sea. I was to write some day. About those things that lured me, that never stopped making me tremble. Then I was to go away, to travel. Out of the framework of dailiness, to some place like a hometown where everything was clear and limpid!

2

I was less a mother than a demon.
I thoroughly despaired of my daughter who was merely beautiful but had no
    talent whatsoever with the piano.
"Go kill yourself, idiot!" I screamed once a day.
This became famous among my neighbors.
Some nights I was driven to think it would truly be *better* for her to kill
    herself.
The famous teacher who'd been giving her lessons since she was four years
    old is, like me, a demon when it comes to the piano.
My dimwit daughter, with no place to escape to, grew thin between the two of
    us and often became ill before she was eight. To hell with the piano—with
    that expression on her face, she's playing "An Angel's Voice."
It's a gentle, pure piece, and I'd like you to listen to it one of these days.
Please come play with us and listen to it for her.

3

Incidentally, these two phenomena have nothing to do with Ravel. Ravel's is
music that flowed into me during a different time, through a different route,
and fascinated me. About his origins, you can buy, for example, a record of
Gaspard de la nuit, and read about them on the back of its jacket, so I won't
write about them here. Also, if you have a small player, his music will overflow
the record and come inside you like water. It is assuredly more beautiful than
whatever words of praise I might be able to say. So I won't write about it.
    What was it that I was going to write?
    Was there anything I was to write—about Ravel, the piano, and many
other sundry topics?
    Why in the world did Ravel make music?

4

Ravel loved his fatherland, France,
but today there's no country I love.
There's of course nothing like a hometown.
This is extremely awkward to write,
but I have no home or family I love.
I don't travel.
Those beautiful young ladies
couldn't have possibly become even third-class pianists,
and I mutter, Serves them right,
as I listen to Le Tombeau de Couperin.
To be with its sound, which is too beautiful,
I understand just one thing.
There's nothing worth believing in,

and we've even lost a fantasy land
to which we can travel.
Ravel, most likely,
didn't love his fatherland
as he listened to this tribute to the war dead.
Let alone his friend killed in battle.
Can't you see
the large, nihilistic eyes
hanging at the end of the sound
that goes away like water?
—You didn't have a single day
you loved,
or did you?

Winter Journey

Late at night, snow, February:
Arrived at a town at the end of a wheat field.
Went to an inn named Helmet.
With the fire in the kitchen turned off,
 had a late supper of bacon and cold potatoes.
On a wall of the lobby hung Rembrandt's *Knight*,
a painting about size six.
In the thin light of a night lamp I looked at it, eyes almost touching it;
a metal plaque on the frame said in very small letters: Copy.
Facing *Knight*, on a darker wall, was a portrait of a lady.
She wore a violet dress with many creases and held a parasol in her hand.
Behind her spread a lake,
its shore, the trees, as desolate as the woman's face.
—Is the painter of that painting *famous*? In terrible English that almost didn't
   make it as English
I asked one of the waiters.
Both the painter and the woman painted
were already nameless.
The painting had no title.
Even the reason it was placed on this wall of the inn
was now unknown.
I walked past the hard doors
behind which strangers slept.
February, late at night,
the hall gradually
made turns into a dream

of someone I could not tell who.
In time to turn into no one,
I fold my red hands,
my red legs,
and sleep, in the snow.

From *Rabbit of the Netherworld*

—Tablecloth

I should also talk about Rabbit early on. Though it's an odd rabbit that I became friendly with when I was five or six years old. He was white—though, well, rabbits are mostly white—and was perched at the left edge of the tablecloth. The cloth was light green, probably representing a grass field. The flowers, which were red and blue, were terribly simple. At the center of the cloth was a plain two-storied house. The first floor had a kitchen and a dining room. The second floor was a tiny room for a girl. Somehow I knew that was the way it was.

The appearance of both flowers and clouds there was pleasant. The air was clean and dry. Above all, things that are incredible now, such as love, filled the windows and oven as if they were real.

In this design only red-eyed Rabbit looking sideways was inauspicious.

—Well, all I do is eat chickweed, you know. He often said that, but that was hardly enough of an excuse. First, he had a distinct shadow. When none of the things there, even the house or the trees, cast a shadow. His shadow at times looked like a deep hole. Or, in the poor light at night, it looked like the large face of a man. Father was laughing. The saurel broiled with salt had turned into a head and bones. The night meal was finished. A great many night meals were finished like that. The cloth grew dirty, and I don't remember when, but it was cut into small squares. It turned into rags for wiping shoes. Under where the cloth used to be, there were three orange crates lined up side by side—a distant memory. Because they formed the dining table of my house. Anyway, as a result, Rabbit ceased to be. From then on he would only occasionally show up in this world, looking sideways. I had decided to say my own good night to him only when I heard someone laughing in some distant corner.

—I

In the moist darkness I asked.

"Father. What are the mathematical formulas you're thinking of meant to express?"

—I can't explain them to a grade-school child, Father replied.

"But you can say they express, for example, something pointless or express something that's important to you but not so important to Mother, or a different degree of importance to each. Or that the same rabbit has been turned into a silver plate in the country beyond. Express such things with equations, see."

Father seemed startled, speechless. But at once he regained his usual calm voice.

—They're totally different things, he replied.

"You are trembling like this in the air-raid shelter but can still be thinking of something other than death, can't you?" I probably asked something like that. Maybe in very different words.

—Whether you think about it or not, death comes to you as it pleases, Father said. My formulas will remain forever in the dark unless I think about them. That's all, you see. Except you can't say all of them are good once you drag them out of the dark, the way this world is. There are those beautifully asleep in the dark.

"Aren't you afraid of dying?"

—I am. I am terribly afraid. But I am even more afraid of your dying. When I'm in mathematics, I can sometimes forget—that I must keep you alive. I can even say now forgetting that may be the happiest thing for me.

—Summer

How we reached Valley of Winds after that, my memory isn't certain. Somewhere at a station I was given a riceball the size of a child's head. Somehow only the memories of food are vivid.

Be that as it may, in an old house in a valley where the sounds of wind never ceased, our entire clan was to spend the summer. Uncles and an aunt died during the summer, one after another. About to be counted among the dead, I simply went on sleeping, Rabbit and I holding each other. The high fever, suppuration, and malnutrition bore a swamp-like hole in my body, and the hole kept expanding.

That old summer, though, already held in its deep chest many a new summer that was soon to come around. It had a faint, blue smell. And the many new summers would always hold this old summer in their chests as they came around to me feverishly, passionately.

—Rabbit's Story

Look. That's the storehouse where you and your father live. In the old days it had stacks of brass braziers and boxes in it. They were all given up for the war effort. They may have turned into guns and things somewhere. Now the second floor has the two of you, and below, it's full of hay and mulberry leaves, you see.

The detached quarter to the east is where your youngest aunt lies in bed.
She's been sick for a long time now. She mayn't last until August.

Your grandmother is sleeping with her daughter—

So that *she* may call someone when her suffering begins. Not your blood-related grandmother. Your real grandmother is asleep in the ground on the hill at back. She died very long ago, right after giving birth to your father.

And that is the main house. A surprise, isn't it, a whole group of thirty uncles and aunts and cousins are living there. In the attics are silkworms asleep. A large loom, too; and two horses in the stable. There by the oven where a stew with pumpkin is being cooked, you see Okiki-san. The same Okiki-san like gray smoke.

In the evening it began to rain.

Okiki-san wove in the attic all night long.

The big family slept listening to the clank-clank sound in their dreams. It was at such a time that bad news was quietly stepping toward Valley of Winds.

—The Coffin on the Moonlit Night

On moonlit nights they were especially busy.
Stepping on pearlworts, crossing the river,
Aunt and others with their white hands would come.
They formed a circle in the yard to the east.
They chatted among themselves like reeds.

On moonlit nights the job of the aunt and others was to make boxes.
The yard would fill with the noise of saws cutting cedar boards.
40 centimeters, 60 centimeters, 180 centimeters.
Hurry, hurry, Aunt and others whispered among themselves.
Before the moon goes away, you see.
40 centimeters, 60 centimeters, hurry, please.
It was very hard to make square boxes with any accuracy in the moonlight.
The white hands of Aunt and others, fifty to sixty of them, would sough as
    they swayed like pampas grass.
The moon, round and disfigured, was walking toward the cedar wood.

In the midst of the yard, boxes lay hazy as dreams.
Nails, please, one said; Wait, another one said.
Listen, isn't 180 centimeters too long?
It isn't, the person in the detached quarter is tall, you know.
Oh, I thought; someone in the distance said.
—I thought this box was for the child lying in the storehouse.
Aunt and others held the nails in their mouths, soughing, swaying,
    as the moon, turned into a tiny face, floated beyond the wood.

About the box in the moonlit night, it's also difficult to tell you accurately.
It was like the other moon shining in the moonlight,
as in a pool of water.
As the nails were hammered in, the box swayed, turned gray, acquiring in
   no time the hue of the ground.
Aunt and others swayed, acquiring the hue of the ground, saying, Hurry,
   hurry.
As the moon rose,
I've been running, all night, toward the box,
but still can't get there.
That's why I still can't tell you
the story inside the box.

—Dark Valley

Small Aunt had begun to rot. What shall I do? Her coffin wasn't ready in time. Not a single person in Valley of Winds could procure boards and nails. Aunt and others with white hands who rose up from the depths of the earth every night had grown bored of coffin making long before. All they did was to swarm all over the yard like pampas grass and sing to themselves vainly, restlessly.
   —Go to Dark Valley to dump it.
Dark Valley is a nice place.

Small Aunt had begun to rot. What shall I do? The day of Japan's defeat was just around the corner. No one knew it. Everybody just walked around the corpse. There were no boards or nails. What shall I do? Only the golden hair of the sun in its abundance kept turning round Valley of Winds.

The small coffin for me was carried out of the storehouse. Someone thought of putting Aunt in it. It was a coffin Father had made for me by taking apart an orange crate—such an awful thing that today even a cat would hesitate to lie in it. Even now, when I'm past forty, I can remember the box accurately. On the day of my death I'd like at least my heart to be put in it. It's something Father made, bloodying his fingers. It's the essence of the clumsy mind of the one I loved the most.

The coffin was too small for small Aunt. What shall I do? They bent her legs, twisted her neck, but still couldn't lay her in it. The moon rose. What shall I do now? White hands crawled out of the earth in countless numbers and Aunt and others began to make merry.
   —Cut off her legs, cut off her arms.
   —Go to Dark Valley, after cutting off her legs, cutting off her arms.

Firewood was piled up on a carriage. Aunt wrapped in a sheet was placed on it. Father pulling the cart, the whole clan walked to Dark Valley. In that region, the custom required that the corpses of those who died of infectious diseases be burnt in Dark Valley, cattle and pigs included. Aunt and others with white hands rising up from the bottom of the night gradually increased in number as they drifted like mist around the cart. When we passed a schoolhouse, its bulletin board had the latest war news pasted on it. The village had few radios, so everyone read it in the moonlight in hushed voices.

—In the said attack the enemy appears to have used a new type of bomb.

. . .

After that we all fell silent and, hand in hand, went down to Dark Valley. Small Aunt herself went down alone, with her quiet footfall, into an even deeper darkness.

Every night we ate a light stew with leaves of sweet potato in it. Every night Small Aunt came with the moon. In a sailor suit, looking down, she would slowly walk toward the schoolhouse. The whole family would stop moving their chopsticks, looking at her as she walked away. Since she no longer had a body, skinny rabbits, skinny frogs, bats, winged insects, and other late-night things swam through her, toward the western sky. About that time the moonlit nights began to show a faint suggestion of rotting.

—August 15, 1945

Late at night Father came back to the room in the storehouse. In those days his job, from morning to night, was to catch frogs in the swamp to add to the food for the whole clan. We cooked those small white fragments of flesh with sweet-potato leaves and ate them.

"Tomorrow at twelve, I'll be going to the mayor's house," Father said, near my pillow. The village had few radios with good reception. The custom therefore was for the villagers to gather at the mayor's house in order to listen to important broadcasts.

"They say there's going to be a very, very important talk, from His Majesty," Father said to me in a voice so low it was almost inaudible, as he wiped sweat off my brow.

"We're losing the war."

August 15. My fever was high. After Father left for the mayor's house, the darkness of the storehouse filled with mysterious beings: Okiki-san, my small aunt, my great-grandfather who had only one arm. The small man who sold winds made me hold a pinch of autumn wind. Everyone sang in unison, "Good night, good night." That was the end of the war that I, still young, faced.

Tomioka Taeko
(Born 1935)

"A native of Osaka, resident of Tokyo, and visitor to New York, she has the big city dweller's savvy and refusal to be awed by affectation or cant. Her sense of humor abets her in this cool, unillusioned approach, not a shrill or satirical humor but an air of wry amusement that permeates her view of herself and others and helps to make both endurable"—so wrote Burton Watson when a selection of Tomioka's poems in English translation, *See You Soon*, appeared in 1973.

Tomioka debuted with a book of poems called *Henrei* (*Courtesy in Return*), in 1957, when she was a student. About the time her complete poems appeared, in 1973, she was moving away from poetry to other genres, including novels and criticism. Until about the early 1980s she would dismiss feminists as "nonprofessional," but she has more recently been a formidable critic of distortions created by male-centered viewpoints.

Let Me Tell You About Myself

Because both Dad and Mom
Even the old midwife
In fact every single prophet
Bet that I'd be a boy
I tore out of the placenta determinedly a girl

Then
Because everybody praised it
I became a boy
Then
Because everybody praised it
I became a girl
Then
Because everybody bullied me
I became a boy

When I came of age
Because my sweetheart was a boy
I had to be a girl
Then
Because everybody except my sweetheart
Talked about how I had become a girl
I became a boy to everybody

Except my sweetheart
Because I regretted being special to my sweetheart
I became a boy
Then because he said he wouldn't sleep with me
I became a girl

Meanwhile several centuries passed
This time
The poor started a bloody revolution
And were being bossed around by a slice of bread
Therefore I became a medieval church
Saying love is the thing
I visited back alleys distributing old clothes and balls of rice

Meanwhile several centuries passed
This time
God's kingdom had come
And the rich and poor were great friends
So I hopped in a private helicopter
And scattered agitation leaflets

Meanwhile several centuries passed
This time
The bloody revolutionaries
Were kneeling before a rusted cross
I saw a fire of order in the disorder
So in the pub and in the den
Byron Musset
Villon Baudelaire
Hemingway girls in black pants
And I played cards drank
Talked nostalgically
About things like the libertines peculiar to
The country in the East called Japan
And mainly
Made fun of things like
Simultaneity of love

Because both Dad and Mom
Even the old midwife
In fact everybody said I was a child prodigy
I was a cretin
Because everybody said I was a fool

I became an intellectual and set up a residence somewhere in the rear
I didn't know what to do with my energy
When the rumor became widespread
That I was an intellectual somewhere in the rear
I began to walk out in the front
The walk I walked
Was the same as my Dad and Mom's
I the pervert was confused
Was tormented for the pervert's reputation was at stake
And so
I became a good solid girl
I became a boy to my sweetheart
And wouldn't allow him to complain

Still Life

Your story is finished.
By the way, today,
what did you have for a snack?
Yesterday your mother said,
I wish I was dead.
You took her hand,
went out, walked around,
viewed a river the color of sand,
viewed a landscape with a river in it.
They call the willow the tree of tears in France,
said Bonnard's woman once.
Yesterday you said,
Mom, when did you give birth to me?
Your mother said,
I never gave birth to any living thing.

Night

On nights I don't drink whiskey I drink hot water.
A female friend calls me.
I have nothing to talk about and stutter.
I call a male friend.
The male friend is talking, stuttering.
Most of my friends
I haven't seen for ten whole years.

Like old people perhaps the thing is to talk about the old days.
Better say
we're no longer friends with anyone.
No one talks ill of others
anymore.
No one gossips about others
anymore.
No one goes about bragging
anymore.
There's no metaphor, no adjective, no decoration, no exaggeration.
You have only to utter a voice.
Except, since you're a human being,
you can't *r a r g h* like an animal,
so you talk about something.
You have only to utter a voice and hear a voice
and notice that some human being you knew somewhere
is still breathing.
If the person's dead you have only to keep silent.
The phone rings, you pick up the receiver,
then there's no voice,
that's the best.
Even if you think of making a call,
since the person's already dead,
you can't dial.
Again the phone rings.
I pick up the receiver, hoping
that I'll hear nothing—

Kimura Nobuko
(Born 1936)

Born and brought up in a farming village in Ibaraki, Kimura attracted attention with poems that mix folkloric and dream elements. "A poem is born, not so much because I make one," she once said. "It's just that something spurts out of me and hurriedly presses me into writing it down." She started publishing her poems in her twenties and came up with her first book in 1971. Five books followed. Since the 1980s she has also published books of poems for children. A housewife since her marriage, she has remained independent of any poetry group.

Over There

I'm walking along when from the other side grandmother comes by and asks where
    are you going
so I say I'm going to see myself over there
and she says you'll run into horrible trouble if you become too friendly with the
    other one.
I say the other one seems gentler and more beautiful
and she says that's the trouble.
She says that's because the other one has makeup on.
Don't you smell my rouge?
Shall we try to see if you are really me? she'll say.
Shall we try to see if we exactly fit each other? she'll say.
Saying things like that, she intends to suck you in and become the real thing, she
    says.
You better watch out, she says and turns to walk away, and her back is glitteringly
    wet.
Giggle giggle giggle grandmother herself must have seen herself over there.
Smell rouge?
Exactly fit each other?
When I still don't know anything about the one over there and I'm going to her
    for the first time?

Into a Dream

Tonight I dress up in white and go into someone's dream.
Because I don't know who that someone is, I'm all the more excited,
so on top of dressing up in white, I use rouge before going.
While using rouge, I suddenly wonder

what if I went into father's dream tonight.
Father would be confused by my dress.
He'd be entangled by mother's obsessions that go beyond me, and get mad.
That would be fun, too,
but it would also be fun to flicker in that boy's dream.
But I never go to anyone I have such thoughts about,
and wondering if in a dream of someone unexpected
I'm going to be beautiful or mad,
I carefully retie my sash and go to sleep.

Clattering Sound

As even the smoke that incinerated father disappeared
my inside became empty
and I heard only the clattering sound of sadness going up and down.
Clatter, clatter.
Had both hating and loving been incinerated along with father's body?
Clatter, clatter.
I have turned into a clattering sound.

The Riverbed

I was preparing to pick up mother's scattered bones and the moon was pale.
Why are you on a riverbed like this? I asked,
and she laughed and said, The mother you know is not the only me.
I was about to put them in my kimono chest,
and she said, I no longer want to go back there,
leave me as I am.

The Night

Just when I was about to fall asleep
there was noise from the direction of the kitchen
and as I thought it was the noise of a knife stirring
I imagined myself taking it up and stabbing someone in the throat during the night
    and became wide awake.
I put the knife deep in the cupboard and tried to sleep
but then I thought I was the only one who knew it was in such a deep place
and I became even more wide awake.

When I Die

On the day of my funeral I want fine rain to fall.
I want you to hold an aquamarine umbrella over my coffin.
And I want all the mourners to use the same umbrellas.
That way everyone will understand me in their hearts,
all will become innocent for me.
(This being sentimentality)
On the day of my funeral it will be clear and windy.
I just hate winds.
Outside there will be cheery mourners loudly gossiping about me,
and the procession will take the same road mother's and grandmother's did.
(This being nostalgia)
On the day of my funeral rain won't fall,
they won't take that road.
Like the day I became a bride I'll be taken along an unknown road, full of anxiety.

When I die, throw me in the sea, I said.
Which sea do you prefer, my child asked.
There's only one sea, so it doesn't matter where,
anywhere you want to go will be fine, I said.
Summer would be nice, I could have some fun,
I could pick up tons of seashells before coming home, she said.

Mundaneness

I tore a man apart with my teeth and, soaking wet with the blood,
with the blood as my light, wandered about in my dream,
but when I awoke
mundaneness was as solid as a tough silk fabric.
With the same exasperation that I had as a child wanting to know the outside of
     the universe,
I am now yearning for the outside of the mundane.
Sometimes I become almost deranged with the desire to tear apart the mundane
     with my teeth.
Does the mundane appear as a man in my dreams because I am a woman?
So I may step outside the man finally tonight,
I formulate a magic spell on my pillow before making morning preparations.

Mother

When he turned twenty-five, the man pledged to his mother, From today on I'll
    look after you, Mama.
When he put her on his back, there was cushiony sensuality
and she was still too heavy for him.
Seems a little too hard for you still, his mother said triumphantly and from behind
    him wiped his sweat with a white handkerchief.
From then on, every morning,
singing with a voice that regained youthfulness, she makes up lightly
and puts her hands around him from behind.
As if troubled, he turns to look at her face.
She smiles like a girl,
winks, invokes a spell, and disappears,
only her weight clinging to his back even more persistently.
The man, uneasy about his mother's warmth,
works all day like a boy, his cheeks flushed.
At night, when he comes home,
his mother gets off his back,
regains the gentleness of being a little old,
and makes a warm meal for him.

She sometimes sings a lullaby in the room next to where he lies.
Listening to it,
the man gradually enters into a sleep
in which he sees a slender, young mother.

Suddenly he awakens, the daytime weight on his back beginning to hurt:
there in the pitch-darkness
the old mother, the daytime mother, and the mother in his dream
are struggling in a sticky triangle, wielding obsessions,
their hair wild.

A Negative of Spring

Spring sings,
sings into the depths of my wounds.
Thin rain is falling on a goat's back.
In my spine
the consciousness of the age of water revives:
elves playing, letting their knees knock each other;
a gardener puffing into flowers to make them balloon;

infant calls of a goat surfeited with grass;
a friend, accompanying a boy,
brings the cookies she made herself;
the excitement of fingers scooping up fresh cream.

Blue mold growing inside,
the family in a copper pot becomes ever more reticent:
a boy goes on polishing some amorphous triangle;
an older sister stares all day at a just imported fruit she bought.

Aged sisters are eating late-spring oysters.
At the other end of the telephone,
someone says:
We're conducting a survey of ladies of ages 19 to 39, and I'm wondering. . .
She isn't here.
When do you expect her back, ma'am?
To hell with them!

I remove my ears and plant them in the garden.
The rain goes on falling on them, too.
I hear a young fox playing the trumpet.
He must have seen that I love festivals.

Illness

A friend's come to visit,
I'm thinking,
and mother goes out
and is saying,
She's seeped into paper
and can no longer come out, you see.
A terrible thing to say, I think, and touch my face,
and there's nothing on it.
I go to a mirror
and a brownish sheet of paper has a faint smudge
that looks like my portrait,
and it appears to be me.
What a disastrous thing to happen to me, I'm thinking,
as I stare at the mirror,
and the picture, undulating, is disappearing.
Unthinkingly I rub it with both hands
and the hands are also disappearing along with it.

Mother brings in my friend.
Look at her.
She was sucked in by that old paper.
These days her color is gradually fading
and sooner or later will disappear. That's her illness, you see.
Her voice saying this
is also gradually
fading.

The Salmon

I thought I heard a voice, so went out,
and at the entrance a large bear stood.
What can I do for you, I asked,
and he said, Would you buy a salmon from me?
I've just caught it myself, you see.
The bear looked very much like my father,
and I was thinking, It's just a salmon,
I shouldn't mind buying it,
but what can I do with such a large, live salmon?
when the bear said,
I'll just leave it here,
please do whatever you like with it, ma'am,
and left, without taking any money for it.
The salmon said,
Please treat me nicely.
By treat me nicely
does he mean, Eat me as you please, I wondered,
and said, I like salmon broiled with butter,
and he looked scared.
At dinnertime I broiled salted salmon and offered it to the salmon,
and he ate it, looking unperturbed.

I deliberately kept feeding salted salmon
to the salmon who was utterly useless
but whom I now was in no position to eat,
yet the salmon lived on nonchalantly.
One such day
the bear came again,
this time bringing an even larger salmon.

The Staircase

I go home,
and rats are running all over the place.
In the oven lies the cat who's been with us since the old days.

On the wall to the north
hang a bull's head and a goat's.
Also there hangs the head of myself as a girl.

On the earthen floor my younger siblings are having a meal.
Only this place is as quiet as an old Western painting.
I open the kitchen cabinet and there's a staircase.

I go down the staircase.
I go down and down but the staircase continues.
I gradually become hungry.

I step off the staircase and there's an earthen floor
and my younger siblings are having a meal.
I open the kitchen cabinet and there's a staircase.

I go down the staircase.
I become even more hungry.
I go down and down but the staircase continues.

The Hands

Hands stretched from behind my back
are trying to grab my breasts away.
The hands, which are far plumper than my breasts,
are twisting, twisting them.
Stop that, I want to say, but my voice doesn't come out.
The strength to brush the hands away is gone, too.
It sure has to be that woman.

Your hubby, I tell you,
was walking with a young woman,
says an acquaintance I see on the street.
You couldn't have,
he died more than half a year . . . while I'm saying that,
a young woman pops up.

Don't bother us anymore.
The two of us, we're doing just fine.
You think I'm lying, just come see us,
she says, and tries to pull me away.
You, stop all this nonsense,
I have nothing to do with all that,
I brush her aside,
and there is no more of the woman
nor the acquaintance.

These are the hands of
that woman.
They're still doing it
as if twisting off a fruit.

Nagashima Minako
(Born 1943)

Nagashima began writing poems after she started taking an adult education course when she was close to forty. She published her first book of poems, *Hyōtan, Hechima* (*Gourd, Snake Gourd*), in 1986, when she was forty-three; it chronicles her daily family life; so does her second, *Shitsugo* (*Loss of Speech*), in 1991. Her third book, *Kurama Tengu* (*The Kurama Goblin*), published in 1995, is a collection of poems about her younger days. Her fourth, *Ampan Nikki* (*The Bean-Filled Bun Diary*), in 1998, describes her life with a husband, who was older by a quarter century, reduced to idiocy by a stroke. The book won the Oguma Hideo Prize. Her fifth, *Chotto tabesugi* (*You've Eaten a Bit Too Much*), appeared in 2000.

Since graduating from the Japan College of Social Work, Nagashima has continued to work at schools for the handicapped.

Landscape

My hubby has a pustule on his ass.
I put him on all fours
and apply a medicine that makes it erupt.

He's so defenseless.
He's got one dent,
bags that limply hang,
fuzzy things growing on them.
How simple, how comical.
A man's backside that's so desolate.

For fun I caress his bags from behind.
Hubby jumps!

Marks

The children I'm assigned to take care of
don't remember even my name
no matter how many years they stay with me.
They get promoted and that's it.
I leave no marks
on them.
It's that simple.

The marks the children have left on me:
The spine that has grown round as I've kept holding them;
the skill of feeding myself while feeding two of them;
proper manners during a wake;
how to conduct dialogue through the skin.

Among the relics in a cave in Iraq
that are two hundred thousand years old
they've found the bones of an old man
born multiple-handicapped, I'm told.
That he was able to live to a ripe old age
in a world of game hunting
tells us humans knew courtesy,
though they had monkey-like faces,
though they didn't have enough clothes or food.

Both those who assist
and those who are assisted
are small dots
that have cropped up on the earth.
Both those children and I
erase our memories
as we are put in small pots.

The Girl Who Turned into Tea

I looked into her face and she was like a wax doll.
Mouth slightly open,
she was lightly made up.

Her parents, sitting side by side, kept their eyes down.
Incense-burning done,
they nevertheless came firmly to thank me.
The sutra recitation went on.
Only adults went before her to burn incense, one after another.

If you work for a school for the handicapped,
a mourning dress is a must, they said.
But death is part of dailiness,
so should manners be at the farewell.
Nevertheless she came back to me
several days later, as tea.

Some came back as towels.[48]
When such things pile up in my house
I give them to a bazaar.
Each finds its home,
tea or towel.

When my turn comes, I'll use ice cream,
so it may melt away,
not to be used again.

Love

I thought of sleeping.
The man next to me, face turned this way,
is snoring comfortably.
Because he's asleep with his mouth open,
the smell comes.
Human innards smell rotten.
Fried chicken, salad, strawberries just eaten
change the moment they go down the throat.
Where and how do they change?
I'd like to stick my hand into his throat
and pull the single tube out of his body
for verification.
Where and how did we,
me and my man, change?
I'd like to pull in the core of our consciousness
for verification.

We go on rotting on the futon.
Both meat and fruit
are the most delicious when they begin to rot.
We're in the best moment to be eaten.

Do I love this man who comes with innards?
I ask myself.
At least the core of love
doesn't exist in the innards.
I turn his face away gently
lest I wake him.

---

48. In Japan (and in some other countries, no doubt), funeral participants receive a gift
from the chief mourner as a token of thanks.

At Midnight

The breathing next to me
suddenly cries out.
Pulled by an invisible hand,
he struggles, moans.
I get up,
kill my eyes,
turn into an ear.
He's already
stepped into
another world.
He's so close yet so distant.
If his voice stops
and he's dragged
to the other side,
that will be the end of one story.
For now
I don't want the story
to end,
so I call him back
to this world.
Then
holding each other
we sleep till morning.

A Silverfish

Out of the book where I wake and get up,
I prepare breakfast and go to work.
For the rest I follow the story line.
I know the outline.

The girl under a streetlight reading
went on turning the pages,
her dreams expanding.
Her life was in a place never imagined.
A man appeared
in accordance with stage directions.
She wept, she was joyous.
In accordance with the story line,

there was a parting,
there was another encounter.
As she kept turning the pages,
the characters increased,
the protagonist changed.

No matter which book I open,
a man and a woman are sure to step forth.
I begin to see the end of this story line, too,
so I get out of the book.
I awake and find myself in another book.
To be continued.

After the Last Train Left

There's a long line for taxis.
I estimate I'll be kept waiting for thirty minutes,
switch my mind to waiting, and stand in line.
I go home because he's waiting.
I keep close to the man in his waiting posture.
If he isn't waiting, where shall I go?
Unless you settle down, you can't eat.
This economic system is part of our history.
Because my own smell I've left in my room is also part of our history
and human beings make history,
I have no choice but to go home,
even if no one is waiting for me.

The tired faces in the line
are each withdrawn into their own minds,
chasing things amorphous.
Only their bodies are turned in the same direction.
Do they return to natural forms in peaceful places
and modestly make history?
The houses are already asleep.
To be not asleep, so late at night,
and stand in line
goes against nature.
We are beings who do what goes against nature
and want to go back to nature.

Falling Apart

We've rebuilt the house we lived in for twenty years.
They build a house with the idea of destroying it, they say.
Do we build a home expecting it to fall apart?
It went on falling apart,
with father, mother, and infant child.
The home is a nurturing place.
   Leave me alone, the child says
   and goes out today, too.
When man and woman are paired,
do they want something to nurture?
As childless couples love dogs and cats?

I've been destroying it, too,
living in a house I've let fall apart.
My parents live in a distant house,
just the two of them growing many plants.

I, having run out of things to nurture,
nurture myself.
Look, even something as deep and cold as this has grown, too.

Once in a while I get together with my child
and drinking coffee in the kitchen
idly talk about his future.
That's how we remain linked
under the same roof.

Borscht

I went to have an abortion,
ate borscht, and came home.
A single ball of meat lay in it.

The child I aborted:
a sea horse.

I feel neither good nor bad.
I am neither cold nor hot.
My body readily gets pregnant.

That I abandoned one, nobody knows.
As if nothing has happened, I go to work.
Work finished,
I go to see him, bleeding.

I go up the stairs to his apartment. A duplicate key.
The futon floats in the water.
Both he and I are impatient even with breathing.
My body readily gets pregnant.
A number of sea horses
drift in the room.

Chewing Gum

I'd feel better, my child says,
if you had a lover to play with.
He thinks he's already taking care of me.

A body that came out from between my thighs.
Without ado
I make him carry me piggyback.
The masculine smell of his sweat hits my nose.

Heavy, ain't I? I say. No, you aren't, he says,
pretending even as he reddens.
    Well, then, I say, and entwine
his body with my arms and legs.

Where are you going? I ask.
I'm going to throw you away, he says.
I've been waiting for this day.[49]

If my child throws me away, that's fine with me.
No mountain, though. I'd be too lonesome.
In the middle of a town, is my request.
On my child's back
I touch up my lips with Chanel no. 42.
Which town is best?
Noisily chewing gum,
I look about like an out-of-towner.

---

49. Refers to the legendary custom of throwing away or abandoning old people to reduce the demand for food. See p. 191f.

Ōnishi Kimiyo
(Born 1947)

Ōnishi, who was born in Aichi, has published two books: *Shida* (*Ferns*), in 1973, and *Henji* (*Reply*), in 1985. Commenting on the title poem of her second book in her anthology of modern Japanese women poets, Shinkawa Kazue wrote: "To be sure, each woman has something scary in her, but not everyone can express it. . . . Take this bathroom scene: everyone does small chores like washing her undies and such while taking a bath, but most stay at that stage, their imagination not going as far as pulling out their intestines and washing them. You can't do anything like that without having 'another perspective' that allows you to calmly objectify yourself." A Japanese bathroom has a space where you wash your body before immersing yourself in the tub next to it brimming with hot water.

Love

The thunder I'd heard rumbling in the distance in the evening turned into rain late at night. Grandfather had brought a metal tub into the semi-dark closet and was wiping Grandmother's body. Grandmother, who was small, was quiet as an infant girl, eyes modestly closed. In time I heard the noise of the rain-doors being put up and the voice of Grandfather saying goodnight mixing in the rain. The next day, Grandmother was laid on her bed, her pillow on the north side, face turned west. Time has passed since, and now I cannot remember, I don't know why, Grandmother's face, in that room, in that spot. Instead, I remember only the face of Grandfather who was seated by the futon, legs neatly tucked in. What was it that had sustained a man and woman who, grown old, had lost things like lust? I remember only the face of Grandfather who, bearing up with something dark and large gripped in his palms, stubbornly refused to join those taking Grandmother to her burial ground.

The Landscape Behind You

I can't help thinking about it
when I'm talking to someone,
when I'm working:
what the landscape behind me
is like.
There, in a world different from a moment ago,
several sober eyes
may be staring at
my defenseless back.

But when I turn to look,
what's behind me is always
a commonplace, regular space:
a traffic signal perhaps,
a row of gray office desks perhaps.
People are crossing the street,
I hear someone
typing.

Grave

On a slow incline,
in a surprisingly bright
place is her grave.

She grew rice, raised silkworms,
and in the meantime brought up children.
That's the sort of life she had.
And here it is,
her grave.
Died at age seventy-four.
It has no special offering.
A chipped rice bowl
is half buried in the soil.

A woman's grave
must be like this:
linked in some way
to those alive
and yet
utterly forgotten.

The Sleep of the Fish Family

The man
came back
with the face of a fish.

As he lay on a tatami,
arms and legs outstretched,
his arms turned into fins,

his legs into a short tail,
himself
into a fish.
Soon he fell asleep.

After I pulled over him
a soft water blanket,
I don't know what giant fish
swallowed us:
man, wife, and child
were asleep,
their beds side by side,
in the belly of a big fish.

Reply

Is anything wrong?
Because the woman's bathing was taking unusually long,
the man called out
to the bathroom.

Beyond the bathroom's
frosted glass
the woman raised her face a little.

Having washed her neck,
having washed her navel,
having washed her asshole,
she'd gone on,
pulled out her own intestines,
and was washing them.
In the soap bubbles
her intestines were snaking
like an independent living thing.

Holding them by one end,
Oh, nothing is wrong,
was
the woman's reply.

The Room

Outside the window light snow occasionally flickered.
The woman's sitting on the floor, legs tucked sideways, massaging her breasts
  with one hand.
In a minute I'll make tea for you,
she says, but she has no intention of doing that whatsoever.
In the park off the main street, dead leaves of poplars are rustling.
There was no news today, so the newspaper wasn't published. . .
We should have a day like this once in a while, shouldn't we?
She's still massaging her flat breasts.
Behind her, in a painting pinned aslant on the wall, a fish has been looking at her
  back for some time now.

A Winter Day

Morning, I awoke, and my pillow was wet.
I had absolutely no memory of having seen a sad dream, but there was the
  sense that part of a dream was caught somewhere, unable to be completely
  awake.
In the back alley a motorcycle delivering newspapers passed; after a while,
  the noise of milk bottles jostling each other came from the same alley.
  Then, someone who looked like an office worker walked by and away,
  the collar of his coat turned up.
On a chair my child's books were left out. Deep inside the cabinet the lid of
  a cookie box was ajar.
A stranger asked me the way, in some house there was the sound of music,
  and close to noon, a piece of direct mail came in my child's name.

Happiness

My eyes can't see,
the woman said.
I can't,
oh what's gonna happen to me?
I can't see.

The man's heart thumped.
Then, flustered,
he said,

Hush.
You'll wake up everyone.
But
I turned off the light,
yes.

The woman was asleep
again.
Between her lips
you could see her white teeth.

That was all.
But the man couldn't go back to sleep
for quite a while.

Tropical Nights

The man grabbed her breasts and pulled them as if opening doors. Then,
   a surprise, her breasts, like doors, opened up, and inside was a vacant,
   deep hole. The moment he peered in, he tripped forward and, in that position, dropped way down into the darkness. It happened in a breathless
   second.
After a while,
she went down to the watering hole.
There was no wind, so even if you stayed still, the sweat poured out. She'd
   had nights like this for many days now. She poured water in a dirty cup
   and downed it in one gulp.
That done, she completely forgot about the man who a while ago had dropped
   away into her.

Isaka Yōko
(Born 1949)

Isaka's first book of poems, *Chōrei* (*Morning Gathering*), published when she was thirty, attracted attention with some candid descriptions of high school life. The "morning gathering" here refers to the pre-class Monday congregation of all the faculty and students on the school ground, at which the principal gives an exhortation, followed by calisthenics. Her third book, *GIGI*, in 1982, won the Mr. H. Prize.

Uniform

I slowly walk up the slope.
Shaking off the light reflecting on its body
a car passes by me
and the hem of my skirt is disturbed.
Incidents where my hand accidentally touches
a stranger's
are so common
I become cautious even about my bashfulness.
The uniform forbids the changing of skin color
so every girl
is as beautiful as a ghost.
I try to prevent my body from unwinding
sternly with my eyes as I go to school.
Until a classmate points it out
during a recess
I can't even perceive
a streak of semen clinging to
the inside of a box pleat.

Orphan

When I woke,
there was no pain.
In the clean room
a futon was laid out next to me, too,
but there was no sign that someone had slept on it.
At the entrance lingered
several nursing interns.
In what shape was I,

having lost consciousness from an anesthetic shot,
carried up that narrow, steep staircase?
Placed on an operating table, I spread my legs,
when one of them,
eyeing that spot,
made a gesture of suddenly avoiding it.

Near the ticket gate of Mimamiguchi
a smattering of people suddenly come into the building
from the sunlight outside.
They're eating bread with finger marks on it,
grab pink, white milk bottles placed in a row at the vendor's,
and readily expose
their defenseless throats.
Please start counting, I'm told,
slowly, loudly, "One,"
lying in the darkness,
above me lying,
a vessel my height is floating
I begin to identify, "Two."
Floating just a little,
my memory begins to peel away,
and the vessel and I overlay each other and, each time I breathe, slip out of place,
    "Three"
Four, five, six. . . .

A healthy boy
in shorts,
both hands out of the pockets,
rises to his feet vertically from me as I lie.
I don't even understand the means to love.
The axis of a clump of grass
He throws a softball at a fence made of concrete blocks.
It's too far
for it to bounce back to me.
It's been exactly ten years,
so it was you, I think.
I didn't even know your sex
but you began to grow after you died
in a shadowless field.
I lie still in the darkness.
Unable to budge,
I feel with my entire body the orphan chasing a ball.

Marriage

I feel I was wedded to myself
long before
I was wedded to you.
I was about to die, writhing
between my easily bored, boring heart
and the indirect speech I exchanged with others.
I simply wanted to make time
dense
but it was a race with the number of brain cells that die 100,000 a day,
and I was able to capture it,
though only rarely,
on mornings that my head was relatively clear,
like a dace that throws itself or its tail up.
It became my pleasure, too.
That you should be absorbed in me,
who is and isn't me,
that, to you,
must be an affront, I think.
You began to appear in my dreams often
to accuse me
and, abandoning me because I couldn't really feel you
except in shallow dreams,
disappeared from my dreams.
Unaware that the real you had set out on a journey long ago,
I then repeatedly saw
a dream of loss.
I can no longer remember your face,
just as I have never seen my own face
in my dreams.
But I remember your dear name.
Thinking that a name can't possibly
take its shape in a dream,
I then became absorbed
only in writing down words.
In a dream I fell into a deserted labyrinth.

Kamakura Sayumi
(Born 1953)

Kamakura started writing haiku while a college student. She joined a haiku group but eventually left it. She did that, she explained, because haiku composed for group sessions "aim only to win sympathy and praise at the moment and to gain points," that they are made "only for those present at such sessions, even though the author might think they express her heart," and that they are "non-risky haiku that make everyone feel with relief, 'I've seen that kind before'" because they are products of "calculated imitation of others and oneself."

Kamakura published her first book of haiku, *Jun* (*Moisture*), in 1984; her second, *Mizu no Jūjika* (*The Cross of Water*), in 1987; and her third, *Tenmado kara* (*From the Skylight*), in 1992. The third collection is unusual in Japanese haiku, as it chronicles falling in love, getting married, giving birth to a child, and being anxious about the marriage.

Under burning sun out of my shadow a wingbeat

A wind rushes through a moment's darkness white iris

Daytime nap till the inside of my womb's dyed green

Their beak still wet the birds now up in the clouds

Father dead a stone goes over a spring river

A May wind already rushing toward the sea

The swimsuit on, my soles forget everything

Now I'd bathe in falling blossoms till my cheeks burn

Jacket hung on a branch I call up February clouds

My hair endlessly streaming out this is also spring

In the end I couldn't hear the sound of dew that fell

Today having learned the name of a tree I wait for birds

A summer hat left hanging on a nail the absence

If you want to doubt you've seen a firefly you can

Resembling a dream not possibly mine a cicada shell

The autumn parasol I shift at each whiff of breeze

Resembling the pain of a nail cut too deep water freezes

Her voice robbed by the moonlight a white cat

His breath on my ear I listen to a cicada shower

Falsity called husband and wife I burn the toast slightly

A girl hugging her breasts her summer faintly bitter

Being infants raindrops crouch on the ground

His back crowded out of the sun as he walks

Unable to say love bare hands bare feet hug a mirror

For the Galaxy deep in your eyes one-sided love

Love is smoke stardust-resembling smoke

Toward him toward him heaven's azure avalanches

From a precipice I peer into my own dreams

A camellia falls folding her vagina in the midst of day

Plucking flowers faint female fever since primordial times

Tearing apart a pomegranate's skin's adrift is it

Made love to a closed gentian opens clumsily

No virgin I receive snow glistening with my tongue

Blizzard night bite me starting with my right earlobe

Icicles ice columns with ecstasy I'm bound up tight

The female body a cape that bounces off the light

In my womb a dream a beast a beautiful camellia

Big with child the peony stamens are coarse

In conception I'm dazzled by an elephant's yawn

A lullaby goes to the darkness at my uterus's base

His arse was laughing even before his birth

Spurt out this mother's bone-colored milk

Supporting my divorce wish forest's silence

The withered-grass jealousy bubbling is boiled down

Stuck with mother of milk and honey a failed bomb

Ah skylark if you don't sing I'm sure to faint

Cherry O cherry my place has grown tattered now

I'll go see a cherry blizzard that flies toward tomorrow

Come mist the mother and child lean on mist

Up the crack between husband and wife soap bubbles rise

In the field I can't fly up from the grass is sweet

Seeking rainbow-colored scales a snake swims

After crying her heart out the sunflower stands erect

A tree and a swallowtail play in the distance small

Stepping on a wind lightly I'll set out for the sea

The Galaxy wound around my ankles I wish to grow old

Migrate birds before the light grows bitter

Rushing who is it that's making plums bloom?

Night with a blurred moon nails seem to grow crackling

Abe Hinako
(Born 1953)

"Born in Samarkand, Uzbekistan," Abe once said of her life, "I moved south through China during the Cultural Revolution and reached Japan toward the end of the 60s. I wrote my first book of poems, *Shokumin-shi no Chikei* [*Topography of a Colonial City*], in 1989, to show how much I had achieved in my study of the Japanese language in the ensuing twenty years."

Actually, Abe was born in Tokyo and has worked as a proofreader since graduating from high school. Her first book won the Rekitei New Face prize. Her second, *Tenga-na Ikidōri* (*Elegant Fury*), appeared in 1994, and her third, *Umiyōbi no Onna-tachi* (*Women on Seaday*), in 2001, won the Takami Jun Prize. On the occasion of receiving the second prize, she wrote: "At the time of *The Topography of a Colonial City*, which was an attempt to create my own receptacles for poetry, I asked myself, with each piece, 'Is this a poem, is this not a poem?' In *Elegant Fury* which followed, my task was to fill the receptacles for poetry with criticism, and I dreamed of 'criticism that is poetry, poetry that is criticism.' And this time, in *Women on Seaday*, I think I poured all my strength into presenting a record of a soul as poetry." So what was the soul like? "It was a soul trying to step out of suffering to go somewhere, a soul trying to find a way out of the dead-end of love." The last three in the selection below are from *Women on Seaday*.

Garden Party

Even though a strong spring wind occasionally brought sand and dust from the direction of the sea, the regular garden party held in the garden on the landfill was proceeding without any mishap, until that lady rushed in.

On the small stage with a tent hastily built to block the sun for the band-playing that was to start at noon, students from language schools invited by the city authorities were taking turns, gathering and lining up for commemorative photographs.

On the tables set out here and there, food was beginning to appear. Hors d'oeuvres made of spring vegetables, lentil soup, and, piled up high on large plates, a fricassee of that disgusting arthropod. Its long legs removed, the arthropod reminds you of the egg capsule of a certain seashell, or it looks like a red pepper or even resembles a gladiolus; yet in fact it is neither an oceanic creature nor something grown in a field, but a new species of insect that evolved on the landfill, now widely bred in city households, in glass tubes packed with vegetable waste that are as tall as you are—an indeterminate protein source.

The next item that the chef himself brought out was a dessert based on a new idea, entitled "Mr. Lamb Was Supposed to Take Care of Me, but While He

Abe Hinako

Was Necking and Petting That Woman, My Illness Became Seriously Worse."
Two or three extravagantly large grapes were set right next to the maraschino-
flavored ice cream that Madame Bovary adored. Then, immediately after silver
plates with Gruyère cheese and figs were brought in, that lady, accompanied
by a dog, tumbled in, her chiffon scarf fluttering after her.

No, she wasn't *accompanied*. A large, ferocious electric dog burst in,
dragging her in slacks, along with a tiny poodle, at the end of his thick chain,
kicking up swirls of dust, panting heavily. The metallic beast, shining black,
had a bamboo broom stuck into his anus. The size of a calf perhaps, like
a wounded rhino, he dashed into anybody in sight, overturning chairs and
tables, throwing the whole place into chaos, with all the people running in
all directions, trampling on mountains of food.

Many people were struck and fell bleeding. That day my father, driven
up against the brick wall surrounding the garden, and pressed between the
belly of the electric dog and the wall, finally died. Some of his own broken
ribs stabbed his heart. While his bones were crushing noisily, I, tottering in a
storm of cherry blossoms, maneuvered to place myself in front of the snout
of the steel dog and fearfully caressed his fluffy nose, which I had always
wanted to touch at least once.

Beggars of Love

Miss Charlene, Miss Shirley, Miss Shelley,[50] the three sisters with splendid cheeks[51]—
Imagine that the lover each had called by a different name
was one and the same man!
During the summer that suspicion deepened and each continued to fathom the others' minds,
utterly contrary to their chatting full of smiles
their hearts went on going far from one another with the eccentricity of a comet.
<Could it be that I'm paying for having made toys of men once upon a time when I was in a house of learning?>wondered Charlene.
<How could I, who received this century's highest education in espionage, have been so readily duped!> wondered Shirley.
<What fun is there in keeping my older sisters company, believers of Harlequin Romances?> wondered Shelley.
Well, suppose the three then had decided to work together to chastise the man,
this would have made a sophisticated *conte* enjoyable to tell,
but the actual development of the matter was quite different.

Though they feigned cool nonchalance, the three sisters were boorish at heart
and chose a thorny path where they'd fight one another with silent savagery without letting on.
Five, ten, fifteen months passed since the astonishing fact had come to light,
but they talked about the man as if each were talking about a different person as they'd done in the past.
<This fall will see the publication of X's dissertation, *The Saliva of the Lotus: Lascivious Art Ten Years After Its Pollution*> Miss Charlene would say.
<Well, I can ask Y to take it up in the witty column he writes for a review magazine> Miss Shirley would say.
<About those armchair immoralists who thrive in every polluted area, Z has also written a thoughtful essay> Miss Shelley would say.
Desperately hiding their hearts torn a thousand ways, they cheerfully chattered among themselves.
Because each one had no choice but to be cautious,
their subjects were largely limited to the man's achievements;
topics linked to sexual intercourse were shirked.

---

50. The names given the three women are *Uikyō* (fennel), *Yakkyō* (cartridge), and *Rakkyō* (shallot). All unlikely names for women (or, for that matter, men), they are played upon elsewhere for similarity in sound.

51. *Hōkyō* (ample cheeks, i.e., beautiful).

Theirs were the sort of afternoon conversations that might have readily offered
  samples for "the counter transference of expression that is structured to avoid
  certain contents" (Cuckoo Books).[52]
Yet behind their facade they were now worried where the others were going to
  visit—something of no concern whatsoever in the past—
and the three sisters' system of mutual speculation was strengthened from day to
  day.
Their anxiety and melancholy intensified as their memorandums of love
  increased.
<So, I see, he took Shirley when he went to make a round of the tunnels of Ap-
  palachian coal mines>thought Miss Charlene.
<Hmm, the tomboy he talked about who fell off a horse in the Carpathian Mountains
  has got to be Shelley> thought Shirley.
<Stupid to ask Charlene to the Dalmatian seacoast, she can't even swim!> thought
  Shelley.
And so most of the man's lies were transparent
but since no one pursued him on the matter, lies were in fact not lies,
counterfeit bills unabashedly continued to circulate.

Perhaps it's about time to retell the story from the man's side,
but this lady-killer had no shades of depth to be talked about.
Since none of the three sisters revealed to him that his identity was known to all
  (assuming, of course, that he had anything like identity),
he could believe he was behaving cleverly dealing with the sisters;
also, even if all were known,
what difference would it make?
A man who at age twenty sent a telegram, "AM EXHAUSTED WITH LOVE AFFAIRS,"
  couldn't possibly have had only three lovers.
<If they cause any trouble, I'll just throw them all out and try a different part of
  town>
was his principle of conduct, which, you see, was thoroughly heartless but
  lucid.
Now, if you are tenderhearted readers, you stop to wonder at this point:
Why were these three sisters, who, even though they may have been somewhat
  lacking in delicacy, were all charming,
why were they attached so long to such a shameless bastard?
What about him attracted them so?
To solve this puzzle, which the three sisters themselves would in the end wonder
  about many times,

52. The poet's own note: Alludes to the Japanese expression "cuckoo's cry," which
means "deserted," "not popular" as in reference to a bookstore.

the answer can only be bare-bones (you can only be bare-bones when you try to
talk about the man):

This man, as it were, was a wolf erotically charged and let loose on an impotent
city.

Adventuresome women are complete suckers when it comes to an agile, erotically
loaded animal.

<If things get messy, I'll just throw out every one of them and go to a different
front>

was the boast of the man, who wouldn't look twice at the plate he had breakfast
from.

Was he a lecher because he was an agile discarder of memories or was he an agile
discarder of memories because he was a lecher?

About this there's debate.

Anyhow, he was both an outlandish memory discarder and a record-breaking
lecher.

In an impotent city where 90% of its males had degenerated as a result of the
environmental pollution caused by quasi-hormone matter,

in an impotent city where even young adults had to depend on such rejuvenative
prescriptions as Hundred-Whip Wine and Snake Bones,

this man's mechanical existentiality which enabled him to arouse himself in only
three seconds, without any manipulation or secret method,

and repeat the act of love without a second's rest

was an irresistible attraction to the three sisters and other lovers (though this
may be something too lowly to talk about).

Furthermore, he was perfectly aware of the kinetics of the magnetic field of
sexual love

while at the same time, because he gave no more value to his congenital sexual
drive than to his strong legs,

he didn't seem to pride himself on it.

In short, his pragmatic ways attracted women all the more.

<I've gone too far to turn back>

was an excuse common to the three sisters (although of course it was muttered in
a voiceless voice).

<With one man of her crew alive, / What put to sea with seventy-five>[53]

was the thought common to the three sisters (although of course the degree of
confidence was in inverse proportion to the order of age).

This arrogant and insolent group of three was resolved not to give up to the
bitter end

and none of them would raise a white flag.

---

53. From a pirates' song in Robert Louis Stevenson's *Treasure Island*.

Five, ten, fifteen years passed while they battled one another underwater,
but, wonder of wonders, the beauty of the three sisters with splendid cheeks
never faded
while the man's sexual energy only increased.
In consequence the situation appeared to be dragged into a new stage.
These days not only did the man exercise his directorial power lest the three of
them bump into one another
but also the sisters themselves adjusted their schedules lest they invade one another.
No, that wasn't the only thing. They devised an illusionism that allowed them not
to be in one another's presence even when they actually were
and to take off and put on their robes of flesh as occasion required.
If such perversion were known to the man on the street,
society would curse them in foulest language:
What lowly ambitions! The lowliest sisters without a suggestion of fortitude to
protect women's honor!
Even with the Holy Mother's compassion it would be (logically) impossible to
defend the three sisters.
For, now, in the man's dance hall
here was Miss Charlene, there Miss Shirley, over there Miss Shelley,
in addition to Miss Charlotte, Miss Cherry, Miss Chiquita, Miss Chelsea, Miss
Charlie, Miss Chocolate, Miss Cher,[54]
the women of The Love Brigade dancing profusely perspiring.
According to the man's cold-eyed observation,
screw dancing, where no one wins or loses, trained the members of the brigade to
the highest degree possible
so that tributes of the age most outstanding in sentiment and beauty
were brought to the man year in, year out.
By the time fifty years passed, then a hundred years, and a hundred and fifty years,
after The Love Brigade was formed,
the man was showing off his riches more ostentatiously than ever before,
whereas the women, who, dragged by abstract thoughts, dashed toward the whirlpool world where everything was relativized,
became poorer than ever.
Their dresses torn, their dancing shoes tattered and worn,
they became poor and poorer on the whirlpool fuse,
even though that kind of poverty was what the women had seriously desired.
(W O R N / A N D / T O R N / B U T / S O / E N N O B L E D)
The three sisters went on dancing imagining their own elegant self-portraits,

---

54. *Kukkyō* (sturdy), *Haikyō* (apostasy), *Yōkyō* (fake insanity), *Henkyō* (borderline),
Zekkyō (scream), *Hakyō* (divorce), *Zankyō* (resonance).

although no matter how carefully you looked with your mind's eye, their seedy
appearances were merely seedy. . . .

"Beggars of love"
society calls them;
calling them that, despises and pities them.
Ah, but the meanness of the millionaires who've established themselves in the
spectator seats!
The greed and avarice of the elegant husbands and wives!
And so, today, too, another one,
Miss Sharon,[55] who's sick and tired of her parents' parsimony,
determinedly jumps into the whirlwind of screw dancing.
"Beggars of love"
society calls these women;
calling them that, despises and fears them.

The Future Belongs to Olenka[56]

No matter how tightly she held herself Olenka ended up being loved.
Invitations to rendezvous came down like showers of stars,
filling her morocco notebook with figures and initials.
When she walked in rhythmic steps down the street lined with date palms
would-be lovers with midsummer bouquets waited under the trees,
from the streetcar that leisurely meandered as it passed
admirers clinging to it like clusters of bells threw hibiscus to her,
which Olenka smiling beautifully picked up to adorn her hair.
Men who never gave flowers to their wives and lovers
rushed to flower shops or sneaked into flower gardens
and made bouquets to present to Olenka.
Why was only Olenka popular?
Was it because of her breasts that protruded in shapely fashion?
(She always wore a skintight camisole which was extremely thin.)
Was it because of her wasp waist?
(She sometimes went out without undies.)
Was it because of her upper lip that was provocatively turned up?
(Hers were lips more gluttonous than anybody else's, for good food, for chattering,
    for kissing.)
Was it because of her soft flesh that seemed to suck onto your palms?
(Hers was amber-hued soft flesh that made anyone ten years younger just by
    touching it.)

---

55. *Nekkyō* (fervor).
56. The name of the protagonist in Chekhov's story *Darling*.

Was it because of her laughter that popped and rolled?
(We hear there were gents who tickled her side just to hear that happen.)
Was it because of her bedroom ways that included fancy stunts?
(Her lower half, we're told, was of a malleable structure that had no trouble doing
    splits.)
Her cool crescent eyebrows, her marshmallow upper arms, her funny bowlegs,
oh, once you start counting them, there'll be no end.
Olenka burst with an abundance of charms.
This explains why
the adventurer now aged and rotting,
the bird-catcher adrift with winds,
the agitator the chirper in a bird's language,
the guard of the Museum of Sexual Revolution,
the pugilist the conqueror of beds,
the orchard owner worried about his impotence,
the cornet player of the Kumquat Orchestra,
the partisan with pomegranate grenades,
the artisan obsessed with making counterfeit money,
the metalsmith who scrapes his own golden brain and uses it,
the chief carpenter who advocates the use of the Golden Pound Cake Method,
the surgeon who golden-sections corpses with trembling hands,
the stage director who's hot manipulating women every which way,
the tattooist who tattoos zodiacal beasts on women's buttocks,
the miner who digs diamonds holding a top-shell lamp,
the baker who bakes "brilliant-cut" brioche,
all sought love with Olenka,
all went out with Olenka.
That is, the Olenka who held herself tight
was an Olenka who accepted all requests unselectively
and the Olenka who was courageous, never cowed by anybody she came across.
Be it someone's gentle, older husband,
be it someone's brainy fiancé,
Olenka returned the love received by doubling, tripling it.
Be it with an old man on his sickbed, or with a street boy who'd run away from
    school,
or with a nouveau riche on the stock exchange, or with a starvation artist in a
    slum,
Olenka made love very quickly indeed.
Nondiscrimination, no-limits, inexhaustibility, all-encompassingness was Olenka's
    attitude.
No-hesitation, no-secrets, no-personal-feelings, perfect-disclosure was Olenka's
    principle.

Incidentally, Olenka has a husband who is an admirable character,
of the type who, because he's deeply in love with his wife, says,
"She can do no wrong."
Understanding very well how busy Olenka is and brimming with goodwill,
he grows potted plants for the wife who comes home only once in a while,
plucks the lute to welcome her back.
Meanwhile, her lovers, whose numbers continued to grow,
remained in an uncomplaining posture whether their share came around or not,
waiting for a tryst with Olenka like loyal dogs,
while dashing about dedicatedly checking out a restaurant or a villa for rent.
So years and months passed while her husband and lovers shared joys and sorrows
    so elegantly
and for Olenka the borderline between marriage and affairs that didn't have any
    meaning for her in the first place
grew ever more ambiguous, ever more faint.
Now for her husband and her lovers, too, the borderline was a thin line,
which, like a thinning surgical mark, they could barely see no matter how they
    stared.
That may well have been the case, but how did the situation look to the women
    involved?
How did they deal with this difficulty?
The women who found themselves sharing their husbands and lovers with
    Olenka
were at first upset, dispirited, or agonized,
but—who'd have expected this?—as soon as they lost on the average half a pound
    and thereby improved their feminine looks
they gallantly recovered and returned to their daily lives.
"She was too powerful; it isn't that I lost" was their excuse.
No matter how their men showered Olenka with gift flowers,
they remained their wives or fiancées.
Men might go far afield in Olenka's convertible,
but wouldn't let go their companionship with their women,
so what was wrong with it?
The uncertainties of the nights their men might or might not be with them were
    great indeed,
but once they were used to them, they'd wake up the next morning bright, refreshed,
they'd feel like dancing, body lighter by the equivalent of a single heart.
All this is to say that no one resented Olenka.
Furthermore, if Olenka hadn't existed,
how monotonous, tasteless, and dry their lives would have been!
Although neither men nor women would say this,
when they indulged in the act of love with Olenka's image wedged between them,
they savored all the subtleties there were in this life.

That is, the Olenka who was an all-out response to any solicitation
was an Olenka who put up with excessive use without a peep,
an Olenka who was exploited by both masters and mistresses.
But, you see, no matter how exploited or devoured, Olenka would never wear out,
she'd simply laugh off the exploitation by masters and mistresses, laughing, laughing;
Olenka was bursting with such health.
That being the case, what was wrong with it?

"All girls are Olenkas" is the trend.
This joyful trend, which was gradually taking shape deeply, secretly, for several
     years,
has budded all at once this summer and the world is abloom with Olenkas.
The large Olenka driving a Citroen to a resort,
the medium Olenka walking back and forth on main street in sprightly steps,
the small Olenka skillfully riding a unicycle in the school yard of a branch school
     in the mountains—
the girls' names are all Olenka
and they have no shadow right under the strong sun.
How in the world have the Olenkas who continue to multiply
from today to tomorrow turned themselves into Olenkas?
How long do they intend to be Olenkas?
Even when the abundance of charm and health rots and drops away one after
     another,
will Olenkas continue to be Olenkas?
People ask thus,
but the shadowless women cheerfully laugh and laugh, unable to stop.
Not giving a damn about contradictions in terms,
crossing the Rubicon a hundred, a thousand times, they go afar
(something we, idle talkers, couldn't do even once).
Olenkas who return the love received by doubling, tripling it,
Olenkas who make love very quickly indeed,
Olenkas who openly step on the tiger's tail,
the future belongs to Olenka!

Nagami Atsuko
(1955–1985)

After college, Nagami worked for a trade association, quit it in a year to work for a publisher, and after several months became a freelancer. She began writing poems when twenty and at twenty-five published her first book of poems, *Ishigaki no aru Fūkei* (*A Landscape with a Stone Wall*). From 1982 to 1984 she published three more books of poems. At the end of 1984 she had a major operation under the pretext of an ulcer, when it was, in fact, untreatable cancer. She died ten months later. Her fifth book, published posthumously in 1986, mostly consisted of poems written while she was ill. She wrote her last poem, "Descending to 'Hell Valley' in the Nippara Stalactite Cave," while receiving intravenous treatment.

A River

After an evening shower
I must have stepped over a dream
somewhere:
in a spotlighted garden
a river flowed.

At the edge of the garden
I took a boat out on the river
to the farthest end
of my endless afternoon sleep.

The fragrant smell of flowers
comes at each joint of a wind.
Lured by them,
I apply scissors
to your favorite flowers.
Innumerable petals
shatter and fall, one after another,
and sink below the water.

At night, I'm certain,
wonderful flower gardens will be there, on and on,
over the bottom of the river.

After the dream
you come across the river
and enter the garden.

Perhaps you were violently tossed about by the water:
your hands and feet still gleam
with fish scales.

Party[57]

The people who'd been transported
by an elevator
gather under a light.
Even those who've turned into memorial tablets
and those taken away to the crematory
are holding clean plates as if nothing had happened.
Hi—someone taps me on the shoulder.
Startled, I peer into his face.

The woman
who this morning, in an operating room,
had her blood completely sucked away
is already carrying on on a chair in a far corner.
Now, down to
her slip
she's moving the knees of a big man nearby
back and forth like a swing.
Do it!
Get it over with!
Rolling horny words like a lollipop
in her mouth,
she looks at me
perilously, acutely.

A man, aroused, is shaking his brand-new head
at the center of the hall.
I grab someone
who is a man or a woman
I can't tell.
It's so funny, tears come out.
In the darkness of my buttocks
a male prostitute's penis is stuck.
Seems someone's trying to suppress giggles.

---

57. When she wrote this, she had "discovered" Henry Miller.

Arms of excited men
are offered to the *party*
and instantly
twist around her hips.
Jealous, I am,
I cut down
their arms one after another
the instant I get to them.
Someone's recording all this
with an 8-millimeter camera.

All this bizarre behavior in the light's glare
is like a devil leaping back and forth
between the wall and the ceiling.
I throw out the bouquet
and ride a man who's stunned and can't think.

The Apartment

The road that leads from the park
to the apartment
makes a slow detour.
The keys hanging from my waist
I exhale my breath
forward.
Like a memory rolling up in the wind,
I haven't turned to look
for a long time.

A car comes into the garage.
Once, here,
I was almost run over.
My scream then
still runs about inside me.
Son-of-a-bitch!
You dragged the man out by the collar.
Every time his head jerked away,
the face was a totally different man's.
Desperately clinging
to your arm
I'm standing on a precipice.
The wind that blows up from straight below

like a giant's tongue
sharply rolls in every part of my body.
The driver's cap
is like a beast leaping away from peak to peak.
The fearful thought turning away,
this thrill—
I've now left far behind
the hands of father
who ran after me.

With a key like a crooked finger
I open the door of the apartment.
The sound of scooping out the water fills the air,
under the light
splashes flying everywhere.
The person now out of the bathroom
will try to sink me
tonight, again.
A man I made a vow with in my former life perhaps,
but I can't remember his face.
He'll transform himself into body temperature
and invade the depths of my body, I think, and resist.
I kick
as if to tear the bottom of a dream
and go on shrinking, sensation fragmented.

In the distance
the sound of a car stopping.
The back of the man chiseling an unseen position
is trembling.
Is father now right around the corner
to get me?

A Regressing Woman's Face

You turn into water in the depth of your body,
that sexual memory falls like a waterfall.
My brain becomes soppy wet
and grows soft, it's summer.
Tearing apart the blade-like light,
woman, you slowly ooze out of the folds of the brain.
I let a coquettish voice, a fishing line,

into the telephone
and pull up a man's actual voice
but the form of her man who is a woman is already beginning to move.
Like a hirsute
independent organism it goes through the semitropical zone,
crossing Third Street under the signal, on foot.
Ahead, a planet inclines,
and at the bottom of the darkening brain she opens her thighs,
the obscene gesture provocative.
Woman, whom I want to possess,
my desire dashes over the horizon of my bestial imagination
and wants to take complete possession of her.
Now, her ripe buttocks split like a pomegranate tremble.
I caress the swelling of their bones.
My fingers make a round of the moist land,
her pubic hair entangling them.
We repeat our sexual intercourse.
The penis that flickers in our darkness
where we ride over the soft waves of muscles,
the plantlike shadow that grows between her thighs
superimposes itself forlornly on the planet.
I have electric spasms.
Whipped by a voice
my throat extends like a rubber hose
to the extending planet's end
carrying the regressed woman's face.

Come, I'll set fire
to your lust.
Scalding fleshy voices boil up in this town
and yet, she tramples upon
and tortures those men's faces
that crawl up the suggestive words,
her tiny face not ceasing to overlap painfully with mine.
She casually throws the harvested men's flesh
on the table and leaves.
Her nose, which sniffs out the quotidian odor,
gleams, you see.
Swimming in a man's closed field of vision
I am a body that goes on distorting itself,
I am the moist intestines.
The women's faces reflected in the windows of the metropolis
are all pupas.

When they turn into butterflies
fluttering their bloody wings
they dance down into the valley of sexual dreams, that savage noise!
I hoodwink her
and pluck the soft wings off her.
Her secretions extend to me
and we regress while warming each other:
this, our final joy.
I no longer
love men.

Descending to "Hell Valley" in the Nippara Stalactite Cave

That day as the demarcation point
my condition suddenly worsened.

Toward daybreak, deep in my throat pain as if that part were being tightened.
Spit out the saliva accumulated in mouth.
Caressing stomach,
eyes wander out the whitening window.

August, we drove a rent-a-car from Sengoku
and weaving through the sunlight on Okutama (with Inoue-san)
reached the Nippara Stalactite Cave.
Admissions:
Adults: ¥500; Students: ¥350; Children: ¥250.
Hours:
From 8 AM to 5 PM.

On a meandering path
we advance as if being sucked in.
From both left and right stalactites press upon us in their mysterious forms;
we walk, making our bodies small, low.

All night long, a dull stomach pain continues.
Toss and turn many times
and try to drive my body into the hole of sleep,
but pulled back by the pain,
can only moan;
cross the dreamless night, dozing.

Because cold air fills the cave

the temperature for thinking rapidly goes down.
The memory
that I once had come through a narrow dark path
seems to throb faintly in the depths of my brain,
but I have no fear.
Only instinct vaguely illuminates my interior.
The soft feet of a fetus
crawl toward the depth of a hole, rubbing the wet path.

Underbelly swells,
belly bloated as if a stillborn possessed it.
Stomach and intestines hurt as if pulled and twisted.
Can't even raise my body.
Move slowly, body bent forward.

Underground water drips down the walls of the stalactite cave,
making puddles near our feet.
Past "The Latticed Ceiling" and "The Garboard Rock,"
we look up to "The Ceiling Unknown."
We can't see where the vacant hole ends
that is made in a fissure between stalactites piling one upon another.
As I stare and stare,
I realize that I've come to a point of no return.
My feet no longer have the marks
of shackles,
but several hundred years ago I was a man
confined in an underground prison like this, I feel.

Shit has stopped coming out and I take a laxative every day.
At eight in the morning sit on the toilet
and repeatedly let out mushy molten shit for about an hour.
A great quantity of toilet paper is consumed
and the waste water is flushed downstairs like waterfalls.

We cross "The River Styx" and descend to "Hell Valley."
The face of Inoue-san who is looking down upon me as I stand in a deep part of
    the underground
becomes that of a man I don't know.
Wedged between stalactites
this is
my final place—
that memory
lies quietly at the base of my brain.

Now these memories are like dark, cold rocks.
Whatever I look up at
all lies
far in the distance.

September, enter the gate of the Health Recovery Institute, which is in Osaka.
The name of the disease that had been desperately hidden from me is revealed.
Relapse and metastasis, most likely that's about it.
They try bone-cracking shiatsu and a milk hunger cure.
But neither agrees with body and condition quickly worsens.

Night, the stomach violently hurts periodically
and I can't sleep.
Repeatedly vomit gastric juice and blood, and vomiting,
can't stop shitting.

Next day, return to Tokyo by the Bullet Train.

Cheon Mihye
(Born 1955)

Born in Tokyo to Korean parents (her father went to Japan as a teenager, following Japan's annexation of Korea in 1910; her mother was born there), Cheon Mihye (Zen Mie in Japanese pronunciation) attended Korean schools in Tokyo, serving as manager of the soccer team in high school, and studied at Ehwa Women's University, in Seoul, in the mid-1970s. She began writing poems in the 1980s when she learned of a poetry writing workshop run by Arakawa Yōji, and published her first book *Urimal* (*Mother Tongue*) in 1995. Cheon became a naturalized Japanese citizen after giving birth to her first son, in 1987. She works as an instructor of Korean (most recently for the Tokyo Metropolitan Police) and a translator (of poems, children's books, and movie subtitles).

Portrait of Cheon Mihye by Kim Bak-Sung

Urimal

Just speak *our language*.
It's Japanese. *Our language*,
urimal, is that a foreign language?
The more I think about it the more mixed up I get.
The *hwagyo* (overseas Chinese) in the *haew oejidogyosusil* (Office of the Professor
    for Overseas Guidance) was
surely, surely, Chinese.

Money, money, money, they exchanged their language for money,
the language of their Motherland. By exchanging it for money
they stayed alive here, the Issei,[58] their hardships, the tab on those
has come to us.
We're compared with *jaemigyopo* (our American compatriots).
Your *urimal* is no good.
You've forgotten the *urimal*. So you taunt us,
but you, people of our Fatherland!
    Would you think this way,
    that Japanese is just a *dialect*?
"Don't forget it even when you're out there in an alien land,"
so says our Fatherland, but
"You people of our Fatherland, do not forget, either,"
that Issei were too busy trying to stay alive.
What can we Nisei, Sansei,[59] do?
We were given *everything* we wanted,
we were brought up with far, far
greater material abundance than you in the Fatherland.
Do we have the right
to speak our language?

The Fatherland I hadn't seen was wonderful.
But the moment I touched the *hwangto*,[60] the *gap*,
"I've come to hate my Fatherland!"
I've seen many of my friends say that

---

58. In this case, Korean migrants to Japan. The term is normally applied to the Japanese
who immigrated to the United States. After Japan annexed Korea, in 1910, sizable migration
occurred between the two countries.
    59. Children and grandchildren of immigrants.
    60. Korean for "our earth," "our land." The two Chinese characters for the word, *huang-
tu,* mean, in Chinese, "the place of our ancestral origins." It also means "loess" and "netherworld."

and go back.
Where does the *gap* come from?
What on earth is it?

You go down to the *sijang* (market) and touch the "sensitivity."[61]
I seem different somehow.
"*Ilboneseo gosaeng haeskkuna* (You must have had a difficult time of it in Japan)"
an *ajumma* (auntie) gently says to me.
"It's not me but my *abeoji* (father) and others who had a difficult time of it"—these
   words remain stuck in my throat.
She can tell I'm from Japan.
I spoke *urimal*
but accented (poor mother tongue!).
Out of nostalgia perhaps,
an *ajeossi* (uncle) speaks to me proudly,
"*I am peri kut at Shapaniz*,"
Well! If it comes to this,
people of my Fatherland!
I can't just leave it with that.
I don't know how to haggle, but the *ajumma* said,
"*Ssage haejulkke* (I'll make it cheap for you)"
and made it truly cheap,
something I hadn't even imagined.
But "sensitivity" was also found in Japan.

> "Perhaps because I studied Korean a little bit, when I see girls in black *chima
> jeogoro*[62] from Korean schools on a Tokyo train, I am tempted to get close to
> them. That's because I'd like to hear the language coming out of their mouths.
> But my expectations are, as I anticipate, betrayed 100%. What they use is
> Japanese and their topics are bound to be 'The Checkers,'[63] 'The Shibugaki
> Unit,'[64] or 'Kyonkyon.'[65] They'd never imagine there are Japanese who are
> disappointed to hear them." (Yoshioka Tadao, *Seoul Rhapsody*)

There's a reality I hadn't known,
there's the *urimal* that doesn't become the reality,
there's the reality that uri have lost our mal.

---

61. *Jeong* (Chinese: *qing*). Like its Japanese counterpart, *jō* (*nasake*), the Korean word is thought to convey an attitude or sentiment unique to the Korean people.
62. Traditional Korean dress consisting of a short jacket (*jeogoro*) and a long, flowing skirt (*chima*).
63. A seven-man rock band hailing from Kurume, Japan.
64. a group made up of three singing boys.
65. Nickname of the popular singer Koizumi Kyōko.

The Consultation Corner[66]

Beyond the plywood wall
I couldn't see her face
but saw her voice (of a woman, of Asia).
Someone from the Philippines? or a *Chinese*?
Doesn't seem like a *Korean*.
I have an occasional glimpse of the way
she's having difficulty with the language.
The next-door officer is loud-voiced.
His condescending gestures leak out.
With her difficult language
is she becoming a human being of this country?
Can she? Does she want to?
Who decides to give her Japanese nationality
after examination of so many papers?
The privacy of the naturalization consultation corner
is just a single sheet of plywood.
"There should be no problem for you."
This officer is a quiet, pleasant person,
so I'm lucky.
My uncle who was condemned as a traitor[67]—
did he also engage in a conversation that isn't like a conversation
between plywood walls?
A friend in Seoul
was surprised
that my nationality was still
Hanguk, and asked.
"Why are you hung up on it?"
So did every single person I met.
"Japan is different from America."
We may be a Sansei or a Yonsei,[68]
but we are not born Japanese.[69]
Reason for naturalization is just one word:
"Marriage."

---

66. An indirect reference to the Naturalization Application Section, Ministry of Justice.
67. Some Korean residents of Japan condemn as traitors those of Korean ancestry who take Japanese citizenship.
68. Great grandchild of immigrants.
69. That is, birth in Japan doesn't mean automatic citizenship.

That alone can't fill this paper with ink.
It's dazzlingly white as if to say, "Write something more,"
so: "Expecting to give birth."
My officer, whose face seems to say, "Well, this is too . . . ,"
continuing to talk in a friendly manner,
scribbles, adding things.
What should I have written here?
Are you saying, sir, there was a correct answer
that would have satisfied you?
Could that Asian woman naturalize?
(Her reason for naturalization was the same as mine, I think.)
And could she get hold of happiness?

An Omnibus on "Laugh"

1. Pastscape
   Why laugh?
   I always, always, smiled, in Seoul, and in Tokyo.
   It was what I did, was part of me.
   I'd catch someone's eye and, before greeting her,
   I'd smile.
   "*Wae, useo*? (Why laugh?)"
   she'd ask, nonplussed.
   Come to think of it, the women didn't smile much.
   In Seoul, which was like an alien country,
   I couldn't speak the language well
   so I had no choice but to smile,
   to mask my embarrassment by smiling.
   Two or three years passed
   and I'd *assimilated* myself with the women who didn't smile unless
       necessary,
   had become a woman no longer winsome.

2. Futurescape
   If I said this to her
   she'd probably be offended
   and beginning tomorrow wouldn't speak to me again.
   So your son is in the Self-Defense Forces.
   Now he's a soldier and you must be worried.
   (*He might kill or be killed.*)
   "No, he's not a soldier. He's a member of the Self-Defense Forces.
   It's not like in the past, it's peaceful now. (*Smile*)

There's nothing to worry about"[70]
She said and laughed it off.
    I managed only a confused smile.
    They're a good employer for learning skills, they say,
    but if any of my sons wanted to join them, I'd absolutely oppose.

3. Presentscape
    "With us, our son's called by his real name, Kim-kun, at school.
    No one taunts him *Chōsenjin,*[71] as in the past, I tell you.
    It's all changed. There're no kids now at Japanese schools
    who make fun of us as *Chōsenjin,* I say,"
said a classmate of mine.
Because I married a Japanese
my son is Japanese.
"Your mother is a *Chōsenjin,* I've heard,"
S-kun laughed, saying that,
my son said, nonplussed.
(Laughed, laughed, truly?)
Why did he laugh?

What Am I, "I" of When I Write a Poem[72]

I am a Zainichi. When I say that,
where is my feeling?

I am a Zainichi. When I say that,
why is it that my voice becomes so small?

---

70. Reflects the poet's experience in Seoul, where the military presence was daily felt as they drilled in case of an attack from the North. There is also an amorphous sense among the Japanese that the Self-Defense Forces—land, air, and maritime—are not really "military," not like the former army and navy in Japan anyway, and that therefore no one joining them turns into a soldier, an old-style *gunjin.*
  71. Korean.
  72. This poem is based on the fact that there is no commonly accepted word in Korea or Japan that corresponds to the English word *Korea,* which is derived from *Goryeo,* the name of the dynasty that lasted from 918 to 1392. At the risk of simplifying the matter, so-called North Korea is referred to in Korean as *Joseon* (in Japanese, *Chōsen*) because of its official name, *Joseon Minjujueui Gonghwaguk,* and so-called South Korea or simply Korea is referred to as *Hanguk* (in Japanese, *Kankoku*) because of its official name, *Taehanminguk.* One result of this in Japan is that those of Korean descent who maintain allegiance to the North are called *Jeseonin* (in Japanese, *Chōsenjin*) and those who maintain allegiance to the South are called *Hangukuin* (in Japanese, *Kankokujin*). To avoid political entanglement, those of Korean descent in Japan adopted for themselves the Japanese term *Zainichi,* which simply means "being in Japan." In recent years, *Korian* and *Korean Japanese* have been gaining currency in some quarters.

I'm a Joseon person, didn't you know?
I am a Hanguk person, didn't you know?
Why is it that there's a difference in saying the two?
I am a Zainichi. When I have said that,
people's reactions have been so multifarious it's funny.
One heard it with a pitying look.
One insistently told me, I don't mind it at all.
And yet she said, I'll absolutely keep that secret.
One apologized, I'm sorry.
One said, What's that?
One said, So someday you're going back.
One said, That's terrific.
One said, Many show business people are from *over there*, aren't they?[73]
One said, Why do you live in Japan?
One said, When did you come to Japan?
And there've been many who wanted to hear more about it.

One expected stories of how I've been oppressed,
wanted to hear how I've been bullied,
asked me to explain in detail the kinds of discrimination I've had,
because someone else's misfortune has a taste of honey.
and she tasted a sense of superiority.
One casually said, You are, I see,
but simply ignored me when we passed each other the next day.
One lightheartedly dismissed it, Don't worry about it, no one will notice unless
    you say that.
One whispered to me, You better not tell that to anybody else.

Lately Hanguk is flooding here.
Hanguk cuisines, travel programs, TV dramas, movies.
They say it's a Hanguk boom.
But if I say I'm Hanguk, too,
some say, Nooo! You must be a Zainichi,
(implying, You are no Hanguk person, are you?)
reminding me that I am a Zainichi.
When I say I'm a Joseon person,

---

73. There are Zainichi in all fields, of course, but those in show business, by the nature of
their profession, tend to attract a great deal of attention, especially when popular performers make a "coming out" announcement, as the immensely popular singer Wada Akiko—a
Japanese name—did, in 2005.

some boast, The happy groups are famous,[74] I know some of them,
laughing, but you can't be one of the defectors from the North, can you?
I can't speak the language, I can't eat kimchi.
Do they call someone like me a Zainichi?

Nothing is going to happen in any specific way,
I can't say my whole life is Zainichi,
I have naturalized but am not a Japanese,
but that doesn't mean I am a Hanguk person when I go to Hanguk,
but even so, if someone asks me of which nationality are you,
I'm after all a Hanguk person,
I haven't had many painful thoughts or bitter experiences,
I've been friends with only those who are friendly to me,
I've lived, moving in easier, more nonchalant directions,
that's the only way I've been able to live,
it's been serious so I've hidden my serious face,
it's been sad so I've put away my tears.

That's how I should write "here," right?
when I write a poem like this,
which may be the only time I am a Zainichi,
it may be that my feeling exists only "here."

---

74. Some scandal sheets occasionally suggest that some of the more attractive young
women in North Korea are forced to work as sexual entertainers, hence "happy groups."

Hirata Toshiko
(Born 1955)

Hirata debuted in 1984 with *Rakkyō no Ongaeshi* (*Shallot Returning a Favor*), which won the Modern Poetry New Face prize. Her 1993 book, *Omoroi Fūfu* (*Funny Couple*), is a candid autobiographical account of her life with an incompatible husband. Her 1997 book of poems, *Terminal*, was a runner-up for the Takami Jun prize.

Recent Photos, Photos of the Dead

Because I'm greedy by nature, I can't let you escape. That you want to get out, I noticed long ago. Also, that you drench me with enmity when I turn back to you, and that you thrust your pale arm forward. That's all the more reason I don't want to let you go. I want to keep you under my control, a loose rope tied to you. I want to feed you evil-smelling wine and ham and keep you shut up here all your life. You will serve me every night with your unbathed, dirty body. Rub my arms and legs with tears in your eyes. Caress me with your nailless fingers. I won't free you. I won't put you behind the iron door. Decay here in a leisurely manner.

Your emaciating body. Your eyes are muddy, you cough horribly, your skin is coarse. You don't talk, you don't eat, you don't act. You can't even stand erect on your own. Bones stand out on your scrawny body. Medicine has no effect on you. Do you spit it out secretly? Your condition worsens day by day. Your end may be unexpectedly close.

I want to be in touch with you. I want to be always in touch with you. With your thin, flat chest, your shoulders, your slender neck. Not to mate, but I want to be holding you. I want to feel human temperature. If you die, your body temperature will be lost. To be in touch with a dead body is pleasant at first. But one gets tired of it in no time, before the day darkens. A dead body is a boring creature. You'll be no good once you die. You may die if you revive at once. But I won't tolerate your remaining dead. Are you hoping to die? Your hope won't be fulfilled. I won't let you die. And yet you go on emaciating. You only sleep, inert.

Do you have an older twin brother? Do you have in this world an older twin brother whose limbs are far skinnier, lips thinner, and whose hair is brown—that is, one with an advanced likeness to you? If you do, call his name wordlessly. Tell him to come here within three days and do the transition work against that day. Teach him the rituals of this room. This will be your last assignment. You can't die before you finish it. I won't tolerate a wishy-washy transition.

Get to it with that in mind.

Sleep forever if you do it to perfection.

If you don't have an older twin brother, you won't be allowed to die. I'll call your name many times. I'll even go to the Netherworld to call your name. Wake up and love me. Hold me tight with arms that seem ready to snap. You must stay here until your old, one-eyed mother gives birth to an aphasiac older brother.

This Room One Night

towel
this pliant cloth with no definitive shape
towel
this breath in which verblike echoes flow
towel
this costume to wrap a naked body with that calls forth winds
having it placed near me
like a handmaid
shampoo
this froth that exposes the past
shampoo
the poison that clings to you like scaly dust
shampoo
the detective who has known too much
I haven't talked to him
today
bathtub
this useless safe house
bathtub
a coffin cheaper than a paint box
bathtub
a one-woman skiff not knowing whereto
absent-mindedly
I lay myself in it
razor
this elite fang hiding in the darkness
razor
a laconic brother with a criminal record
razor
a refreshing beverage for the summer
wrist
a sunny table
wrist
a perch for an emerald bird

wrist
a plate for emotions
a woman's
face
quietly
pressed
against it
light
this busy-body accountant
light
citizen with no pleasures to talk about
light
a frivolous slow-witted companion
is illuminating
unmoved
like the goods
in the show window
this room
one night

A Woman's Life or Nakayama Atsuko

The wound on Nakayama Atsuko's right arm was made by her
real mother, Shizu, 42, who slashed at her one spring evening
when her honorable self was three. Trying to avoid Shizu, who
still came after her, brandishing a Bizen Osafune,[75] she fell off the
verandah of the main house, with a thud.
The wound on Nakayama Atsuko's head is the one made when
she hit a corner of the stepping stone as she fell.

The butterfly on Nakayama Atsuko's thigh was tattooed by her
stepfather, Sadazō, 51, one summer evening when her honorable
self was ten. Sadazō, who tended to become wild when drunk, sent
her mother to a distant sake store and schemed to do something
with his daughter's thigh.
The wound above Nakayama Atsuko's eye was made when,
shaking off her stepfather's hands and running, she bumped into a
pillar.

---

75. Osafune is the name of a town in Bizen Province (today's Okayama). The town
produced excellent swordsmiths for many generations. As a result, Bizen Osafune became
synonymous with a sword of superior make.

The burn on Nakayama Atsuko's belly was made by her brother, Sadaichi, 16, one autumn evening when her honorable self was fourteen. Sadaichi, who excelled academically, was given free rein at home. He savagely mistreated his sister, who was not blood-related, and once splashed boiling water on her belly.
The wound on Nakayama Atsuko's calf was made by a dog that bit her when she ran away, without even putting on simple clogs, and stepped on his tail.

The wound on Nakayama Atsuko's left shoulder was made by a cousin of the same age, Sachihiko, one winter evening when her honorable self was eighteen. Knife in hand, he importuned her for sex and cut her, along with her clothes.
Nakayama Atsuko doesn't have one small finger because she lost it in slapping the knife away.

The mark on Nakayama Atsuko's neck was made by her husband, Masayoshi, 39, who tried to strangle her one summer evening when her honorable self was twenty-eight. The country was in a depression and the company he ran went bankrupt. In despair, he attempted double suicide.
The vertical wrinkles between Nakayama Atsuko's eyebrows were chiseled into her flesh as she writhed.

The wound on Nakayama Atsuko's back was made one autumn evening when her honorable self, 35, fell down the staircase. Trying to get to the telephone under the staircase, she slipped, and the impact on her back left her breathless.
Nakayama Atsuko's sprained ankle resulted from her landing on the floor.

Nakayama Atsuko is missing a front tooth because her stepsister, Akiko, 32, struck her one winter evening when her honorable self was 39. She stepped in to mediate Akiko's quarrel with her husband, and Akiko, blood rushing to her head, hit her.
For a moment the world turned white for Nakayama Atsuko, but the couple's quarrel ended without any other damage.

The dent on Nakayama Atsuko's head was made by her oldest son, Hideki, 16, one spring evening when her honorable self was forty-five. A problem child, Hideki approached her from behind with a baseball bat. His first blow struck her on the side. His second managed to graze her head.

Two of Nakayama Atsuko's ribs were broken in the first blow.

Nakayama Atsuko's crooked nose was made one summer evening when her honorable self, 51, grappled with a burglar. He'd come into the newly built house without taking his shoes off, and that gave her extra strength. She valiantly put up a fight and subdued him.
The entrance of Nakayama Atsuko's house is decorated with a letter of commendation from the police.

Nakayama Atsuko's arms become numb,
Nakayama Atsuko suffers pain in her hips,
Nakayama Atsuko has a crooked spine,
Nakayama Atsuko's fingers tremble,
Nakayama Atsuko's life continues.

Itō Hiromi
(Born 1955)

Born in Tokyo, Itō studied Japanese at Aoyama University. Since publishing her first book of poems, in 1978, she has been productive, bringing out books of poems, essays, and novellas. Two things characterize her poems: straightforward references to various body parts and bodily functions and shamanistic use of plain language. Invited as a writer-in-residence by the University of California in San Diego, in 1990, she has since alternated her residence in that city and Kumamoto.

The Sexual Life of Savages

*Rorschach[76]

"This is a female sex organ, isn't it?"
I was asked.
"It looks like the line connecting the female sex organ and the anus,"
I replied.
"And there should really be above this a hole from which the piss comes out."
"But I wonder if such a line exists."
"Yes, it does,"
I replied.
"There is a similar line between my navel and my sex organ."
"That's different."
"But they are about the same color."
"Well, then, what is the line for, I wonder, the line connecting the female sex organ
     and the anus."
I couldn't answer this question.
"See, there's nothing that isn't necessary."
"But, then, how about pubic hair and armpit hair?
"How about doughy earwax and the underarm odor resulting from it?
"I'm told that if your earwax is doughy, you are 90% likely to have a strong
     underarm odor.
"How about slimy blue snot?"
"All those things that are dear to me with which I always want to fiddle are not
     necessary and can only be thrown away.
"There are even those who don't have such things."
"Let me say this is really a female sex organ."
"But to me it only looks like the line connecting the female sex organ and the anus."

---

76. The asterisk is part of the original subtitle. The poem's title is taken from the anthropologist Bronislaw Kasper Malinowski's book with the same title.

Itō Hiromi

"Let me tell you it *is* a female sex organ."
"But I am more fascinated by the line connecting the female sex organ and the
    anus."
"Let me tell you it *is* a female sex organ."
"But I find the line connecting the female sex organ and the anus more pleasant."
"Let me tell you it *is* a female sex organ, and its entirety links up with a male sex
    organ.
"The portion you insist is a female sex organ is the clitoris.
"That's where you get a pleasant sensation.
"You are somewhat biased toward the anus,
"you are embarrassed,
"you are, let's say, about the female sex organ,
"you are, let's say, somewhat repressed about the female sex organ,
"when you were small,
"did you have anorexia,
"or did you have bulimia,
"do you menstruate?"
"I am a pregnant woman."
"Are you having sex?"

"I am.
"But my stomach moves.
"Even while we're doing this, it's hiccupping.
"Its regular stimulation of my intestines bothers me.
"I have confirmed that all children are turds
"and that they are born like turds."

Harakiri[77]

Cherry blossoms are falling.
I once went to see the disembowelment maniac Mr. O and asked,
What kind of person,
among movie actors, for example, which one
would you like to see disembowel himself?
At this, Mr. O said,
Hmm, well, you see,
I've never thought about that.
He crossed his arms on his chest,
looked upward,
gave another groan,
Hmm,
and said,
I'd say Oki Masaya. [78]
Because I liked his face for a long time,
since before he jumped off the Keiō Plaza, since before his death.
As a result I can instantly
conjure up his face when he disembowels himself.
Oki Masaya, I see. How,
in what way,
I asked,
while imagining in my mind
Oki Masaya disemboweling himself in a white costume, in Asano Takuminokami's
    situation.[79]

---

77. Itō says this poem includes quotations and ideas from Mr. Maebashi's words in *BILLY BOY*, a Japanese magazine devoted to perverse acts.

78. A popular action star and singer (1952–1983) who committed suicide by jumping off the roof of the brand-new, 47-story Keiō Plaza Hotel, in Tokyo.

79. Asano Takuminokami Naganori (1667–1701) was a daimyo who was ordered to disembowel himself for assaulting and wounding a fellow daimyo during a ceremony in the shogunate castle of Edo. The shogunate handling of the matter was thought unfair because of the prevailing judicial principle that the parties involved in a quarrel were equally to blame and led to the famous vendetta by forty-seven samurai almost two years later on Kira Kōzukenosuke Yoshinaka, the daimyo who had provoked Asano to attempt to kill him.

And Mr. O said,
I'd say it has to be a naked, standing disembowelment.
Well, then, in what kind of place,
I pressed further.
Hmm, I'd say a graveyard.
With cherry blossoms falling,
I'd say a graveyard, where cherry blossoms are falling.
By naked, you mean totally naked?
No, of course he has a loincloth.
A loincloth that closely clings to all the erogenous zones,
the penis, the perineum, the anus.
Cherry blossoms are falling.
The graveyard has wooden tablets rising helter-skelter.
Ah yes, this is somewhat grotesque. Well, anyway, this ought to be enough.
Well, then, sir, would you like to see Oki Masaya suffer a lot before he dies, or,
I pressed further.
When it comes to that, I would see him in prolonged agony before he dies.
Because it would have to be an exact copy of myself,
said Mr. O.
And after that, he changed into a white loincloth
and did a standing disembowelment.
He thinks disembowelment should be beautiful.
He thinks disembowelment has got to be male aesthetic.
He thinks cherry blossoms.
He thinks cherry blossoms in full bloom.
He thinks cherry blossoms in full bloom should fall.
He thinks he'd like to die while he's beautiful after all.
He will be sixty years old in several years.
He thinks when it comes to disembowelment it's Asano Takuminokami.
He thinks Mishima Yukio beat him to it.[80]
He thinks wooden tablets in a graveyard.
He thinks
cherry blossoms for disembowelment.
Ah yes, this is grotesque, somewhat, he said.
He thinks cherry blossoms are for the Way of the Warrior.
I neglected to ask if his ancestors were samurai.
He thinks that through discipline pain becomes pleasure.
That's why I'm disciplining myself, he said.
(Frigging)

---

80. The internationally renowned writer Mishima Yukio (1925–1970) chose to die by
disembowelment and beheading at the height of his career.

The ultimate would be to be able to disembowel myself face to face with a
    woman.
(Frigging)
Samurai
(Frigging)
Ah yes,
(Frigging)
Cherry
(Frigging)
Cherry blossoms fall
(Frigging)
Grotesque, isn't it

Shamanic[81]

my dear uncle in his black formal outfit knelt on the white cloth (the virgin's
    path)
took my dear aunt's hand wept loudly
my dear aunt (a virgin) who was marrying my dear uncle, in her bridal wear
had come down with a cold
and was incessantly sniffling
just two weeks earlier
my dear uncle had fulfilled his life's wish of masturbating
without anybody helping him
since then he had masturbated, alone,
to the very day of the ceremony
done it till now and will do it from now on, too, he said
my dear uncle, onto the next step to take on a new task
he would give birth to a child
but he would not do it
it wasn't that he was conscious of the desire
to give birth
giving birth to a child, if someone was to give birth
my dear aunt would give birth
she would become pregnant
she would do the delivery
my dear uncle would ejaculate

---

81. Itō notes that this poem includes quotations and ideas from Umezu Kazuo's *Watashi
wa Shingo* (*My Name Is Shingo*). Umezu Kazuo (born 1936) is a popular comic artist famous for "horror comics." *Watashi wa Shingo* is a panoramic tale of love in seven volumes
featuring a girl and a boy in sixth grade.

proliferation procreation.
"Done it till now and will do it from now on, too," my dear uncle said
"From now on, too, so it won't get in the way of my work," my dear aunt said
for a long time after that my dear uncle and aunt
prospered
    father, older brother, younger brother. . .
    when they no longer could work. . .
    the Chinese character. . .
    for man. . .
    surfaced. . .
    on the softest spot of my shoulder. . .
please wait, I'll deliver the message first, mother said
will you wait, I'll deliver the message first, mother said
wait, I'll deliver the message first, mother said
stay there, I'll deliver the message first, mother said
don't move, stay there, I'll deliver the message first, mother said
at grandfather's death, mother kept collapsing crying from the wake to the memo-
    rial service, to the crematorium
kept crying and collapsed
collapsed and kept crying
such ostentatious lament struck me as eccentric
neither older aunt nor younger aunts nor grandmother lamented as much as mother
    did
people did the drinking and eating
people drank and ate
mother drank sake and ate vegetables and things cooked together
next to the people were gifts piled high
and when those funeral rites were finished
and the people and mother returned to normal life
a deity possessed grandmother for the first time in a long while
her husband who couldn't work, numerous young sons and daughters
now sons and daughters
grandmother yawned
had a trance
wait, stay there, I'll deliver the message first, mother said
don't move in that spot, I'll deliver the message first, grandmother said
    on the day before an air raid. . .
    that electric pole. . .
    burned up in a flash. . .
    only I. . .
    and mother. . .
    saw it. . .
they say. . .

this place has a whole lot of pregnant people, they're terribly conspicuous,
said a woman, who had had her wedding ceremony last week and just arrived in
    this place
she's experienced sexual intercourse for some years
but not once
has she gotten pregnant
hasn't experienced pregnancy for twenty-nine years
the area around us is nicknamed a child-bearing village, I hear
she told us as a story she heard from her husband she has sexual intercourse with
    every night
three are very common, there are four and five
just the other day, the fifth child was born
to so-and-so, I hear
here you have to give birth to one child after another
here you end up having to give birth to one child after another
grandmother kept giving birth
to one child exactly every two years
from when she was twenty-eight years old to forty-four
a total of nine children
the father of the first three and the father of the next six are different
and the first child and the next one didn't make it
the fourth one did make it
but died early
the other children lived on
but they all grew old
and now a third is about to die
will die
    the electric pole. . .
    that showed me and mother. . .
    the way it burned up. . .
    in the air raid the following day. . .
    it accurately. . .
    burned up and collapsed. . .
    they say. . .
    the man was me. . .
    they say. . .
    father and older brother and younger brother who couldn't work. . .
    older sister and younger sisters and mother. . .
    all depended upon me. . .
    they say. . .
you keep waiting, don't move, I'll deliver the message first, mother said
the rainy season will be over
the wind will stop completely

stay still, I'll deliver the message first, mother said
stay there, I'll deliver the message first, mother said
the wind stops completely
stay still, I'll deliver the message first, grandmother said
I was. . .
the man. . .
they say. . .
I was. . .
the man. . .
they say. . .

Park Kyong-Mi
(Born 1956)

Born to Korean parents in Tokyo, Park studied English at Tokyo Metropolitan University and has translated Gertrude Stein (*The World Is Round, Geography and Plays*). She published her first book of poems, *Suupu* (*Soup*), in 1980 and her second, *Sono Ko* (*That Girl*), in 2003. She began studying Korean in her late teens and became increasingly attracted to various manifestations of traditional Korean culture, such as weaving, lute playing, and dancing. She describes such interests in many of her short essays collected in *Itsumo Tori ga Tondeiru* (*Birds Are Always Flying*), published in 2004, but rarely touches on her interactions with things Korean in her poems, at least not overtly; the first one of the three translated below, which is about the traditional Korean dress called in Japanese *chima chogori* (*chima jeogoro*, in Korean) is one of the exceptions. Her poems are often characterized by disjunctive use of language as well as disjunction with the surroundings or circumstances she describes.

Chima Chogori

There, I sensed a *chima* waver
(there's a person in *chima chogori*).
In the dusty space in an underground path in Shinjuku
where people were coming and going randomly
the *chima*, having inhaled a great deal of air, had ballooned.
Though for a very brief while I stared at it.
Though for a very long while I stopped walking
and made sure of the profile of the person
who passed by smartly
in the crowd.

It was an indigo
chima chogori.

The white collar
showed the nape of her neck sharply,
the chest of the
chima chogori brimmed with breath,
had something that moved,
had something that bounced,
which *as it was untied*
started to spill,
started to melt,
its warm, painful core remaining as it was,

its fragrance *in my memory* beautiful,
it was a feeling I had as I looked,
seemed like a very brief while,
seemed like a very long while,
and so I remembered.

Just looking at the words Korean dress *I'd get mad*
I'd look askance at any Japanese who said chima chogori are wonderful
I wouldn't walk with my grandmother in her chima chogori[82]

The indigo
chima chogori
for a very long while
finding it interesting, mouth agape

You are always me

A Cat Comes Carrying Her Cat Baby in Her Mouth
(Still, still continuing)[83]

Yes, let's pull the curtain shut.
Yes, it will embarrass me.
All of me watched.
Oh, no, I don't like it, I'm in my muslin nightgown
worn out, shiny.
Your shiny bald pate.
I caressed it for you.
Your joke.
Can see through it.
Your excretion.
It's about time.
I can see it.
Find it.
I can see it.
Find it.
I squatted in the toilet
and it found me. I pulled the door of the window and I saw the ground, like that. The
sun was shining on it, or was it? I wonder. The toilet is at the back of the house, it's

---

82. In one of her essays (in *Itsumo Tori ga Tondeiru,* p. 15), Park recalls her paternal grandmother's visit from Jeju Island in the early 1970s and recoiling from her dress as something "Korean" and alien.

83. One in a sequence of poems with the same title, hence the parenthetical addition.

somewhat dark, even during daytime. Large leaves coming out of a stout stalk, just at my eye level. They were thick leaves and the leaf veins looked as though they were carved into them. I being small, I stared, concentrating. Because, you see, I sensed something. Because, you see, oh, oh, it was a large caterpillar. Whaaaaat's that? It was glued to the back of a leaf, I swallowed my saliva. The sound of my own pee surrounding, surrounding, surrounding me, I had to stay still.

The caterpillar was brocade,

the leaf yellow-green,

the flower in a pink tassel brilliant,

yes. It was midsummer, wasn't it? No matter how hot it was, it was chilly in the toilet in the old days, you know. Even the smell of the dark earth pushed up against you. It was different from the smell that enveloped you even when you pinched your nose. Different. That was the smell of You're watched, you're watched. Spooky. I don't like that. The caterpillar started to move, shaking its head a bit. Yes, it was moving. It was gaining momentum. It was crunching, crunching on the leaf. When I was making the sound of peeing! What a scene!

Where a round

hole was made

only the leaf veins remained, brittlely,

I held my breath, stared,

then

there was the sound of water

then

I turned the faucet and let the water run. You've got to wash your hands after you pee. The water exploded on the tin sink, going down, exploding. Splatter, splatter, it began like a miniature gong or a drum, and then, suddenly, suddenly, it's like someone crying, waaaah, waaaah! A baby? My kid brother? Waaaah, waaaah, waaaah, waaaah! Doesn't stop crying! It is somebody! He wants to pee! You must take care of him, quick! Mo-other!

I called

and called

but mother didn't come.

I wonder if I'll come to witness your last moments.

Routines are tough.

A snow-white cloth is cruel

on something that's turned sour.

In the first place the starch is too strong, too hard to absorb.

So I have this hidden with me.

It's what you forgot.

It's a handkerchief, I've washed it many times.

How often has it gone through the water?

I will gently wipe the soil off you with it.

Now you need to worry no more.

Now you can just wait.
Look, it touches your skin so softly.
I've done this to survive
quietly, patiently, leisurely.

A Cat Comes Carrying Her Cat Baby in Her Mouth: VI

Stay in good health
Stay in good health
Stay in good health

I'd like you to stop that now. You say that too many times I think I won't be able to
see you anymore. That's it. That's where my big brother and I differ in our thinking.
I wonder if you could stop saying "Stay in good health." Don't you think, sister?

I don't regret it
I don't go back
From when, you say,
From when, you say

How can I tell you that? Today I'd like to take a bus, I'd like to walk the Ginza to my
heart's content, I'd like to buy a shortcake there, and I may have made a promise to meet
someone, oh, no. Had I said all this to you before? Am I repeating myself? Yes, I am repeating myself. All this happened a long, long time ago. I was simply longing for you.

See that? Floating up there in the sky
is my big brother who didn't return from the South Seas.
He let a balloon go in the sky and that was it. Where's he now?
'Cause we got along with each other very well.
I wanted to talk with him once again.
I wanted to have a leisurely talk with him.
Yes, yes.
I am selfish,
I can enjoy a whole shortcake all by myself,
and, yes, it is expensive. It's special, you know.
Feel free to share it with me, please.
Yes, you do it as you usually do.
First, you slice it straight,
and cut it apart crosswise.
On the tea table the horns of the milky white cream's reflected aglow, it enchants
me. Held between the stages of sponge cake are the cream and slices of strawberry,
held repeatedly, it's marvelous. It must be putting its soft cheek against the slippery

skin of the white porcelain. So puffy. I'd like to use that, the fork, dexterously, but I'm conscious of that person's eyes and my hand trembles. I bring it to my mouth hastily and both the cream and strawberry fall and I scoop them up again. Each time I put the fork into it, the stages of the sponge cake fall apart. The bright red of the strawberry seeps lightly into the cream and dyes it. It's sweet-sour, isn't it? Our forks clink, clink, is that because they are hitting the plate? No, no, it's just that the clock on the post struck. Almost simultaneously with him, I look up at it, the clock on the post. It tick-tocks and it's past eight o'clock. It's sweet-sour, isn't it?

Tick-tock.
What do you think?
You're lying to me.
What do you think?
Things like a sixth sense don't work.
What do you think?
You're so hasty.
Where are you going?
My clog-thong may be loose, I said,
but did he hear that? I wonder.
Oh, he's already gone now.
If you make it to nine thirty-five, it will be all right.

Mizuhara Shion
(Born 1959)

Born in Yokohama, Mizuhara studied French literature at Waseda University. After receiving an MA, in 1986, she joined a tanka-writing group simply called Tanka. Her first book of tanka, *Bianca*, in 1988, won the Modern Tanka Poets Society prize; her third, fourth, and seventh books also won prizes. A dedicated student of Nō and kabuki, she uses interlinear spaces, punctuation, and other devices while maintaining the monolinear format. The following selections are made from her first three books: *Bianca*, *Utaura* (*Fortunetelling by Tanka*), published in 1992, and *Marōdo* (*Visitor*), in 1997.

Am I an animal able to distinguish beams of light like music this moonlit night eyes closed

When the two hands pass each other by there's a moment of hesitation the soul of the clock

Throat white the one eating May needlefish is the vessel that sent me out into this world

In love with the term wind burial these evening moments I grow light little by little

I miss the youth who in his own eyes can see like a transparent cathedral a musical score

With permission I'd like to bear children who tinkle to each other like glass • seashells • clocks

In June the morning when the narcissi do not bloom, the word elephant terrifies me

Does any man grow thin on poetry? The trail a crawling snail leaves more beautiful than a river

The one who's no more is a pure-white bridge: as I tread on it it sways as if still pulsating

Loneliness because it is a persimmon tree it wears many green leaves even while I bathe

Aren't the ginkgo leaves falling yellow my children? As they shine and dance my breasts ache

One of the terrifying dreams bush clover standing upright   I can no longer see you

The sadness like tuning forks in the water must have become extreme a cloud bears a child

When you recall to your mind the depth of the kiss skylark skylark may you loathe the sky

Noonday when the snow strikes the snow   as whose heart shall I regard a bunch of grapes?

The winter thistle ought to stab heaven my lover with arms sticking out at unlikely angles

In the midst of trees' powerlessness   the sky's powerlessness I see a cloud's operating table

In the darkness of my eyelids I closed in your embrace I see a quarry I see the mother of stone

Crow looking down upon me atop a lightning rod is the chrysanthemum far bluer?

Jangling the keys to the clouds   the keys to the lake   you have forbidden me a small death

You who have changed space into the shape of a horse   when I'm not even a gentle saddle

Outside my hesitation of saying "Yes" and saying "No" pasania leaves waver and waver

My breasts wrapped in silk feeling refreshed communicate with a black bag lying on the road

In a dream in which everything that shines is a snake someone caught for arson cries gleaming

There's a fountain at the back of a dark green suit of someone who danced a desert deity

Koike Masayo
(Born 1959)

Born in Tokyo, Koike studied international relations at Tsuda College and worked as
an editor of law books and magazines until 1998, when she became a freelancer. She
published her first book of poems, *Mizu no Machi kara Arukidashite* (*Beginning to Walk
from a Water Town*), in 1988. Her third book, *Eien ni Konai Basu* (*The Bus That Just
Doesn't Come*), published in 1997, won the Hanatsubaki prize.

The Bus That Just Doesn't Come

Morning, I wait for the bus.
Azaleas are in bloom.
The prefectural bus is very slow to come.
Those waiting increase to three, to four.
The bus in May is very slow to come.
Our heads tilted in unison toward its direction,
four people, five. Eight-twenty.
Then, finally, it comes.
From beyond the bridge a fragment of green
quickly balloons, turns into a bus, running.
The eyes tense in waiting relax with relief,
five, six people move close to the curb where the bus stops.
Six, seven people get on, heads hanging down.
It's a mystery that something you've kept waiting for should come
Because it's my job to wait for something that never comes.
After getting on board I notice:
a woman who didn't walk up to the bus fast enough
and must be waiting, still alone.
Emerging from beyond the bridge,
it was something like hope.
Her skirt with muddy spots curled up by the wind,
she sees the bus go away, it gets cloudy, it gets sunny,
and in today's morning, too, toward the sky
chimneys of the dusty town stretch up.
Torn away from them,
we are simply,
meekly,
carried toward the
next bright stop.

Penis from Heaven[84]

The woman hesitatingly touches with her hand
the center of the man's crotch spread wide.
The man is large,
the hair on his head thinning.
The woman is schizophrenic,
the owner of a beautiful soul.

"How've you been able to avoid men so long?"
She's the kind of woman likely to be asked a question like that
on her wedding bed,

(Come, look at it)
(Touch it)

He speaks no such
words
but being gentle thinks them,
looking at his cock and the woman
alternately, that was good.
I'm talking about a movie.
I don't think there's a scene more beautiful.
There's no scene more gentle.
One day
there was something painful
and I was depressed that day
for some reason
in a very natural move
that scene revived
in me

(Come, look at it)
(Touch it)

That moment
instead of the woman's hand reaching out
a hand reached out from inside me
and my fingers touched something very warm.
The human crotch

---

84. The original title is in English. This poem refers to Lars von Trier's 1996 movie
Breaking the Waves.

which is semi-dark, deeper than any other place,
and he had spread his crotch wide
like that.
What kind of a man is he?
The human experience
in the movie
revived in me
that moment
and warmed me, who was crushed,
from the center.

"Through marriage (with me), don't you think everything (about her) has blossomed?"

The hand that quietly reached out from inside me
and the image of
the tactile sense of touching a warm penis—
these, gracelike gentlenesses,
where on earth did they come from?

For example:
like the impudent, black earth
that in spring suddenly emerges from under the snow;
for example,
like fresh water that has just boiled.
But
no simile could reach it.
It was
the core of life
itself.

The Most Sensual Room

One wall of the bathroom of Jay's apartment has a cat's footprints. Absence
is something like that. To leave evidence. I see it. By rolling the world back.
The way the cat ran up the wall and escaped out of the window. The wind that
came in just as the cat left knocked down everything it touched by reversing
time, from the small past in which the cat had disappeared, toward the present. The wind, having substantially disturbed the proper position of a light
letter on the desk, has now passed by. And it is no longer here. Jay and I are
contained in the room. And yet, the room feels vacant, somehow. Am I here?
Clearly exist here? I am passing through it. I will become absent.

From the open window I hear the sounds of the neighbor's house. Why
aren't you finishing your homework? The noise of plates. Would you come

here and help me a bit? The noise of plates. What did you do with that? The
noise of a washing machine. The soft ringing of a telephone. Hello, hello?
Hello, hello? The beep signaling that the washing machine finished its work.
We don't know the faces of our neighbors. Nonetheless, they come in. Like
a flood. Our neighbors' daily routines, into this vacant room.

Jay and I turn on music. A brief conversation. Sexual intercourse. Laughter.
The sound of slapping flesh. Two people cursing each other. These noises,
too, slowly go out. Toward our neighbor's house. Unobtrusively, directly. We
languidly blend with one another, with voices alone. On the ground separating us ivy leaves overgrow.

The Sunday morning when I leave Jay's room. There is Jay's room where
I no longer am. I don't leave a single footprint, but my invisible fingerprints
are imprinted everywhere. Nights, I think of the room. I peer out of the window. I see the absences of myself and the cat. Jay is a man who is part of that
room. His long body tightly coiled into hardness, he, the penis of the room,
is quietly asleep. I stretch my hand and touch the room. The wall is soft. I
push the room harder, and the room goes out of the room. The room that
contains nothing, except Jay, at first with some bounce, like a soap bubble,
goes out of the hard room, slowly.

Ombra Mai Fu[85]

Because we deeply loved each other we married
wasn't the case.
Both he and I, in those days, too, were so alone it hurt.

Let's live together.
I'll be your ally.
If a human being has one assured ally,
he can live.
You, who are like a saucy younger brother with beautiful eyes!

It may not necessarily be that we had to be made for each other.
Nevertheless, somewhere deep in my heart,
it was as if one reason, like a raindrop,
had suddenly dropped on me, and with that swiftness,
I decided to make a go of it.

How can one choose, choose a human being?
Such a terrible, impudent thing!

---

85. A line from the aria in Act I, Scene 1, of Handel's opera *Serse*. The stanza reads,
"Ombra mai fu / di vegetabile / cara ed amabile, / soave piu!" (Never was the shade / of
any plant / sweeter, dearer / more agreeable!).

In the event, I'd bump into someone, like an accident.
Ombra mai fu (My dear tree shade!)

An old couple walking side by side
was the most beautiful scene I ever saw in this world, said
Greta Garbo, and died.
For blindingly long months and years to live close to
a man, to a woman, what all that means,
I couldn't imagine at the time.

One morning
a bird, its large wings spread,
alighted on my chest.
Shocked, I jumped up awake:
it was no bird, but my man's heavy right arm.
At the time I was at least thinking quietly
it was the first morning of this kind.
Ombra mai fu (My dear tree shade!)

Awake, and my man was by my side.
I touched him, and he was warm.
And he was exceptionally poor.

Lifetime

At the tip of a wildly stretching aloe leaf
a drop of water is shining this morning.
It rained toward daybreak, I can tell.
How long has it stayed like that,
trembling?
As I look at it,
inside me
something quietly collects into dew.
Taking care
not to shake it off,
keeping still
I look at the shining tip of the leaf
and virtually everything in my lifetime
rotates in the drop of water
and in an instant congeals.
Before it drops to the ground,
how long will it endure like that?

Mayuzumi Madoka
(Born 1962)

Mayuzumi Madoka hit haiku stardom in 1994 with her book *B-men no Natsu (Summer on Side B)*, which describes an illicit love affair—an affair "both parties knew would have only a brief life," as the poet put it in her afterword. The book won a Kadokawa prize. She published her second book of haiku, *Hana-goromo (The Flower Robe)*, in 1997. Among her other books is *Ra • Ra • Ra "Oku no Hosomichi" (La • La • La "Narrow Road to the Interior")*, an account of her visits to some of the places Bashō went to see during his famous journey.

Her book-length sequence describing a love affair in haiku may be radical in conception, but Mayuzumi is traditionalist in two respects: she uses a season word (*kigo*) in each piece and generally maintains the 5-7-5 syllable format, unlineated, with no punctuation. It is notable that some of the French translations, by Laurence Boulting, accompanying some of the pieces in her 1999 collection, *Kuchizuke (Kisses)*, are done in one line.

Once a "kimono queen" and immensely popular in various media, Mayuzumi is said to have touched off the current haiku boom in Japan. She publishes the monthly *Tokyo Hepburn* as head of a women-only haiku society she founded.

from *B-men no Natsu (Summer on Side B)*

Crossing many a spring river a friend marries

Plum scent on the border of I like you I don't like you

Vernal thunder[86] comes with a slight male scent

Someone's given me a spring I don't know how

A vernal breaker[87] collapses without climaxing

Vernal thunder I am pregnant in my dream

A tortoise cries[88] when I'm in a yoga posture

---

86. *Shunrai*: in a haiku view of things, spring thunder is supposed to last briefly but invite premonitions by disturbing the vernal peace.
87. *Shuntō*: breakers in spring are supposed to be peaceful.
88. *Kamenaku*: a seasonal word for spring whose "humor" lies in the assumption that tortoises cry.

Mayuzumi Madoka

Wanting to see wanting to see him I step on thin ice

I love winds I love oxeye daisies I love *you*

Blossom cold[89] my high heels hurt me easily

On Mother's Day I end up making mother cry

Mannequins whisper to each other in blurred moonlight

Birds into a cloud[90] someone I shouldn't fall in love with

My earrings remain cold at a spring festival

---

89. *Hanabie:* a sudden drop in temperature during the climatically unstable season of cherry blossoms.

90. *Torikumo*: any of the migrating birds—geese, ducks, thrushes—that come to Japan in the autumn and fly back north as spring wanes.

Amaryllis doesn't have any proper Japanese name

The shepherd arrives in advance at the summer resort

Before I know it I'm selecting a swimsuit with his eyes

Love has begun with the perfume switched[91]

The stars are cool the mystery of you being here

He names it right the perfume's called "Mitsuko"

"Ordinary" hating this word I wash my hair[92]

Stockings taken off leg-shape the summer's come

Distant thunder I'm in love even in my dream

Back to the starting point this argument a tropical fish

A hermit crab leaves her abode a star in love[93]

Thinking of something else distant fireworks

The scent of perfume's left after we part

A sparkler in hand she still hasn't experienced a kiss

Being kept waiting forever in the evening glow[94]

More than an older brother less than a lover shaved ice[95]

---

91. *Kōsui:* A season word for summer because, at least in Japan, the use of deodorant becomes more common during the summer. This piece consists of seventeen syllables but does not scan: *Koi wa hajimatteiru kōsui o kaete.*

92. *Kami arau:* an act indicative of summer because you tend to wash your hair more often during that season.

93. *Hoshi no koi:* summer on account of the reference to the Star Festival or Tanabata, on July 7. Technically, this has another season word, *yadokari,* "hermit crab," which indicates spring.

94. *Yūyake:* indicative of summer because the evening glow is supposed to be particularly attractive during that season.

95. *Kakikōri:* a summer snack.

The first date a white parasol for the first time

Distant fireworks that's a word of farewell I think

Summer missed I press a seashell to my ear

Love ended I throw a pebble to a September sea

Autumn shower I buy a fish that has no scales

Unable to say farewell a dragonfly[96]

An autumn mosquito eats an unexpected spot

An autumn wind begins on a day without an outline

The autumn wind turns a page of my heart

I pick nuts while keeping my lover waiting

In a muffler I'm loved and I'm unhappy

from *Hana-goromo (The Flower Robe)*

Spring waves love also has the moment to retreat

Blossom cold I broil fish slenderer than my fingers

This flower robe[97] I have someone I'd like to go to see

Blossom cold he makes my mouth shut with his lips

I cut my hair spring melancholy this sweet thing

I almost touch him and wake from a spring dream

Still warm in the next room my flower robe

---

96. *Akitsu*: an ancient name of the dragonfly, which, like most other insects, is indicative of autumn.
97. *Hanagoromo*: a kimono worn for cherry-blossom viewing.

The go-between arrives late under peach blossoms

Your hand stays in my lap this flower fatigue[98]

Complimented the bush-warbler calls once again

A flower night his reply has a slight falsity

A firefly comes close to my window so do you

Stopping by hydrangeas I've wet my chest

I'll never see him again I'm washing my hair

Birds migrate this pot forever remains unsold

So eager to erase my footprints autumn waves

Thinking of you shooting stars fly[99] randomly

A shooting star the two of us go back to our talk

Autumn wind in a place like this you hold me close

In snow country the bright scarlet of rental boots

With a stranger I remain watching swans[100]

I ring the bell and come home in a winter shower

The winter Galaxy I want to see him when I can't

I keep trudging on fallen leaves till the promised time

Winter waves their blueness keeps people away

I walk past winter colors winter sounds

---

98. *Hanazukare*: fatigue felt after viewing cherry blossoms, which entails crowds eating, drinking, and making merry.

99. *Tobu hoshi*: shooting stars are indicative of early autumn.

100. *Hakuchō*: as migrant birds, swans are indicative of winter.

from *Kuchizuke (Kisses)*

Forgetting the word I just looked up it's warm

Frogs croak as I get off in an unknown town

The promise on a distant day the wheat still turns green

Accompanying an autumn butterfly I've crossed a traffic light

Following an autumn wind following you I alight in Paris[101]

With an autumn rose held behind him he welcomes me[102]

With tickets for different destinations the night is long

In autumn wind we part without either volunteering

The snow falls on a bench where I was once with you

---

101. Boulting: *Poursuivant le vent d'automne et en chasse de mon amant, j'arrivai à Paris.*

102. Boulting: *Se tenant caché la rose d'automne en arrière de lui, il n'attendait.*

Tawara Machi
(Born 1962)

Tawara hit tanka stardom with her first book, *Salad Kinenbi* (*The Salad Anniversary*), in 1987, which sold an unprecedented 2.6 million copies. The book describes a love affair in a lighthearted manner, without angst. It was preceded a year earlier by a selection of thirty-two pieces in a magazine, which won the Kadokawa Tanka Prize and which forms the first part of *Salad Kinenbi*. The book went on to win the Gendai Kajin Kyōkai (Association of Modern Tanka Poets) Prize. Two complete English translations of the book followed.

Her second book, *Toretate no Tanka desu* (*These Are Freshly Picked Tanka*), in 1989, is notable for including a number of lineated tanka, though Tawara notes that she had to break up those tanka into lines for "layout" reasons; they were serialized in a monthly with photographs by Asai Shimpei. *Kaze no Tenohira* (*The Wind's Palm*) appeared in 1991. Her 1997 collection, *Chocolate Kakumei* (*The Chocolate Revolution*), which apparently describes a series of affairs, also became a best seller. The following selections are made from all her books.

With the gentle gestures of waves rolling in and out I wouldn't mind when you
　　say farewell

After a silence you are selecting the words that hesitation I find myself enjoying

The way your left hand is fumbling for my fingers one by one may well be a sign
　　of love

"Call me again" "Just wait for me" always always you say your love in the impera-
　　tive mood

Raindrops start falling down I look up and in that posture suddenly, I want your
　　lips

Having someone who remembers me at midnight with that happiness I pick up
　　the phone

"I don't really care" says he and not knowing don't care for what I find myself
　　nodding

Since I stopped waiting for you a glorious Saturday or a rainy Tuesday has been
　　the same

The 300-yen sand-eel sushi I eat with you this deliciousness you know is what's
　　called love

"I'll just hang out till 30," you say what kind of scenery prop I wonder am I to you?

Knowing full well a man who thinks only of me is no good I still want you to do just that

I watch with you a love scene filling the screen the lead actor acting just like you

Having told me Marry a good *fellow* this *fellow* who won't take me as a wife kisses me

Because you said, "This tastes good," July the 6th has become The Salad Anniversary

"Good night," I've said to you and so tonight the telephone won't need to ring again I think

The memory of being loved somehow transparent I'm always alone I'm alone all the time

Enveloped in many layers of your love
I'll become an apple in an apple pie

Waiting for you by the poolside
glistening
I line up words into a single vertical line[103]

Clearly in haste
he hangs up late at night
maybe an affair that needs excuses

"I have many people I love" I reply
and as I reply I'm lonesome suddenly somehow

Asleep fumbling my hair your gentle fingers in your dream too do you make love to me

Like chocolate melting we embrace each other in a sauna hut my flesh against your flesh

---

103. A statement in which a tanka poet makes it clear that the tanka is conceived and composed as a one-line poem.

I too have a secret I tell myself this afternoon as I paint my fingernails pearl-
white

The day that starts with being loved resembles a sea in which you became tired
of swimming

Plucking your hairline with my fingers the instrument that is you begins to fill
with strength

Being loved like a peach its juice sucked I think I was female in my previous life
as well

Because you do things like giving me too gentle a kiss I end up noticing you are
lying

You're making love to a woman like a doll tonight you better become a doll
yourself

"Don't cry" I'm told and for the first time I realize it is for myself that I'm crying
now

I'd like to think it's the beginning but it may be the end tonight I let myself be
loved

"It turns out I'm getting married" "Not turns out but you decided to marry didn't
you?"

Once we've decided we'll no longer meet I feel happy and talk about the weather
tomorrow

Thinking of the period soon to come I swim on my back seeing a night flight fly
away

A single membrane between us we love each other your rationality sometimes
desolates me

"Love triumphs!" sings the youth   What will happen I wonder when love battles
love

Hayashi Amari
(Born 1963)

Hayashi debuted in 1986 with a book of tanka, *Mars☆ Angel*, which contained some startlingly graphic descriptions of sexual acts—an approach she has maintained in her later collections. She writes her tanka in two lines, saying she has too much to say in a single line. The tanka poet, critic, and anthologist Okai Takashi has noted that she adheres to that format "with some stubbornness," even though she "can't possibly be unaware of the way modern tanka are written"—in a monolinear form, mostly without punctuation. Her tanka are often hypersyllabic and sometimes hardly scan. A Christian, she teaches Sunday school. She also reviews theater.

The following selection is from *Mars☆ Angel* and her 1998 book, *Bedside*. She published several books in between.

The sibilant sound of his swooshing off his tie in a flash
    his neck begins to emit heat

After talking gleefully about your wife with whitish eyes
    are you going to hold me

"*I love you*" "*I like you*" such cliché lines
    —even without them I let him strip me

The FUCK during menstruation is hot
    with wonder the two of us end up staring at a sea of blood

Because there's no absolute contraceptive
    when my heart's apart by a petal I don't mate

Something coming into me bit by bit from behind
    I can't identify it but love the sensation

Connected with my lover
    nonetheless can feel nothing anywhere this anxiety

His hand first reaching my sex
    sorrow suddenly intensifies this autumn dusk

The man starts stripping upon arrival in the room
    and I feel something has gone wrong

Sex as a solution of a conflict
   my body can't follow it this unhappiness

I want to be relaxed   simply sniffing the scent
   things like sex organs forgotten completely

The moment by chance I said it hurt
   your penis wilted small so gentle of you

What is it they're looking for
   your fingers are slow inquiringly

Even in a bed like a continuation of a dream
   strands of hair remain as fact

His palms gently touching my breasts
   as if looking for some help

Little by little I open my thighs
   making myself fluffy empty I go on receiving him

The sweetness spreading throughout my hips
   the moment I think I can put up with everything

An amorphous darkness, a slimy darkness,
   a blinding darkness, an assaulting darkness

Parting slowly my raised thighs you kiss me
   I feel I once gave birth to you

His is an arm
   that gives me five minutes of white deep sleep

The moment he enters he gives a deep sigh "Ah"
   I have no wings to wrap him with

Now I must get on a wave   I let two ripples pass
   the large wave, here it comes

Kamiyama Himeyo
(Born 1963)

One of the minority who lineate haiku, Kamiyama won two prizes, in 1983 and in 1992, before publishing her first book of haiku, *Chi no Rizumu* (*Blood's Rhythm*), in 1996. Her second, *Taiyōshin* (*The Sun God*), appeared in 1998. Her third, *Yakobu no Kaidan* (*Jacob's Ladder*), in 2001, was reissued as a paperback edition, by a different publisher, in 2003. The pieces in this collection are cast horizontally, rather than vertically (as is normally done); they also come with roman transliterations that render her lineations even more radical than in Japanese. Her fourth, *Mishō-on/Shiji no Mori* (*Resentment Before Birth / Forest of Stillborns*), came out in 2003.

Kamiyama explains that she lineates haiku to release them from the monolinear form into a spatial world—to "regenerate" them in the world of calligrams and concrete poems. Despite lineation and varied spacing, she mostly uses seventeen syllables and often employs seasonal indicators. She also writes one-line haiku.

The right wind and
    the left wind meet
        a green temple

*

Its color stolen
      by Cézanne
           white hydrangea

*

A white peach's peel horizontal
          daytime moon

*

Distant thunder the blue blood vessel tenses up

*

Love • love • love
    love raised to nth power tonight   ends

*

Conspiring a day's scenery a camellia drops

*

DNA
     no matter what
           the bull's tongue is thick

*

Carti-
     lage   cooked
               col-
                    laps-
                       es
     in spring darkness

*

The seated female body wanders through the night of primary hues

*

<Violating the sun>
     Nietzsche's
             smile

*

On a summer day
     in a summer sea
             <the Sun God>

*

To endure it
     ● ● ● single-mindedly ● ● ●

  the summer's lightning rod

*

Having gotten ill
  midnight's
    silver needle

*

The newborn's first cry
    has a deep valley
holy May

*

Turning into an emphatic
    lightning's
 door to wisdom

*

Burning noon
 a lattice of flesh
     (look)
   the seventh ward

*

The love letter
    ends
 in a single line
     busy farming season

*

Beginning
  with
    the
      womb
a circu-
  lar deficiency

*

Turning into a globe a larva's white darkness

Hachikai Mimi
(Born 1974)

Born in Kanagawa, Hachikai studied ancient Japanese literature at Waseda University. Her first book of poems, *Ima nimo uruotteiku Jinchi* (*The Position That's Being Moistened Even Now*), published when she was a graduate student, won the Nakahara Chūya prize. All the poems translated below, except the first, come from her second book, *Kū Mono wa Kuwareru Yoru* (*The Night Those Who Eat Get Eaten*), in 2005, which won the Geijutsu Senshō Shinjin prize. She also has a collection of mini-essays, *Kujaku no Hane no Me ga Miteru* (*The Eyes on a Peacock's Feathers Are Watching*), 2004, in which she says, "When you are about to write a poem, the time and space an instant before the words come out are dense. Tightly packed. Quick, if you can, you think. But once you put it down in words, there's something that falls between words and never comes up. Sometimes it's something you deliberately throw away in an instant, sometimes it's something you drop without meaning to that never comes back." She often alludes to classical Japanese literature and engages in wordplay.

The Position That's Being Moistened Even Now

That abandoned house surrounded by a violence of summer grass, when we found
    it—
there's no one living in it, and so we hesitate
to step in, but, look, the sliding door at the entrance is open the size of my fist.
We end up overwhelmed. Dust creaky,
pieces of the earthen wall that peeled off, needless to say, snowy cobwebs.
But in the sink by the window that sections off the green-blue sky

    The faucet, why, is alive,
    I turn it off but it doesn't stop at all,
    a column of water, like an icicle,
    keeps standing

Oh, I see, it's drawn from a spring,
tapping on the windowpane from outside the building, so
she tells me. Then, we open some heavy stuff,
a cardboard box, and, inside, it has a great many ocarinas,
mouthpieces missing. *Where did they go, leaving all this?*
Along a brook, watercress, a brook, long, *cresson*, people gone
in any case

    Marks of digging indigo
    fill the wall, like icons,
    fill it up, about to come unhinged

Hachikai Mimi

Situated by the water this house is becoming a plant it's already
of that kind, has this kind of breathing, this kind of breathing
(Hope she won't step on it)
That instant, just as I'd expected, she, without noticing it, easily
stepped on a torn piece of a musical score that lay there.
Gray and gold notes scattered.

I'm Mongoloid, You See

Was slurping it
hands holding the rim
drank it up   held it
over the fire   roasted it   well
without thinking lifted it
between teeth   soon
the meat separated   silently
from the bone
at noon with no one el   se
I was chewing

the deer the woman[104]

downwind body hidden waiting for a prey
ankles washed by the waves in the reeds
warm mud   a water strider flits   a cloud goes out of shape
pushing an invisible wall with her snout   a deer
carries on her back a box on which stars fall frost falls
her body horizontally   a deer
I enter the deer's inside the deerskin's
inside   stay there   and will run
tomorrow I'll choose an arrow choose a bullet and will be in flight
when   a flute sounds hewwwy
(they call it making a kill)
(I call it catching it in my arms)
dragged to the end of the creaturely stream
the sweat on a peach collects underground   this is my new heaven and earth
a creature lies at the end of her life
above her back   the summer revives   the sound of grass
a flute sounds   hewwwy   hewwwy
inside the structure I choose an arrow choose a bullet and gallop

This Crab[105]

This crab   where is it from   a hundred relays away Sagami's
carapace[106]   touching the heels that are lying down pincers of passage are
two   the island shadow   drinks the fore and aft behavior and swells   rises
to its feet captures roasts and devours it   throws its shell in the boat detours
the fragments of seaweed   the distance I gain is read in advance   and
abandoned amid the waves   here where are we?

---

104. Most lines of this poem consist of 5-7-5- or 7-7-syllable units, giving a feeling of an attempted renga or an assemblage of haiku.

105. The original of this poem vaguely suggests the common modern printing format of chōka, with spaces between syllabically separable phrases. The poem is characterized by a casual admixture of classical phrasings and modern colloquialisms.

106. The first three phrases are from the opening of Emperor Ōjin's song wooing Princess Yakawae, recorded in the *Kojiki*. *Momotsutau*, here given as "a hundred relays away," is a makura-kotoba that usually modifies words other than Sagami. For a translation of this song, see Donald Philippi, trans., *Kojiki*, pp. 277–78; for another, Hiroaki Sato and Burton Watson, trans., *From the Country of Eight Islands*, pp. 7–8.

This deer   where is it from   the blue-clay-is-good[107] Nara Park   tracing back any number of generations   going over the lawn   walking
over the lawn   eating thin round cookies   she drops things from her
arse   steps on them herself   antlers   cross them   lunge into each
other with antlers   they drop off   drop again and grow branches glow
again   gripped   targeted   they stop sparrows lodge flies   what they're
doing   I begin not to understand

The bear   where is it from   of-the-three-chestnuts[108] the Middle Mountain
bear   the person I've met for the first time in two years mutters   the bear
liver truly works wonders   a relative goes out to shoot them   the liver's
valuable I tell you   there's only a little bit you can get you swallow it and
it immediately begins to work   on my fingers under the table   I hurriedly
begin to count   the bears I'm intimate with   four   five   six   look
someone I don't know   is pressing his face against the window

> The following poem alludes to a folktale commonly found in the Northeast
> region, "Salmon Ōsuke and Kosuke." On the 15th of Frost Month fishermen
> used to take the day off because that day every year the giant salmon Ōsuke and
> Kosuke (Big John and Little John), followed by a large school, returned to the
> river calling out, "Here we come up, Ōsuke and Kosuke!" The wealthiest man
> of the village, once deciding that not fishing that day was a waste of time and
> much loss of income to him, forced the fishermen to fish that day. The fishermen
> caught nothing no matter how hard they tried. That night an old silvery woman
> appeared in front of the wealthy man, thanked him for his hard work, and
> quietly walked into the river. Then there was that familiar call, "Here we come
> up, Ōsuke and Kosuke!" and a great school of salmon appeared. Hearing that
> call, the wealthy man died.

The Night Those Who Eat Get Eaten

Don't make   any sound   tonight
Don't make any sound   whatsoever
Back to back   our empty torsos elongated
We lie down   we don't sleep together
With our wet eyeballs reflecting each other's figures   in them

---

107. *Aoniyoshi*, "the blue clay is good," is a makura-kotoba for Nara. Nara Park is full of
tame deer. In the fall those with fine antlers are rounded up and their antlers are sawed off.
108. *Mitsuguri no*, "of the three chestnuts," is a makura-kotoba that appears in Ōjin song
mentioned in footnote 106; it modifies "middle."

Back to back   the sound of the river   rising we listen
The night you don't do it   is the night I don't let you do it
Don't make   any sound   this evening
Don't make any sound   whatsoever
The souls burning and falling glow one after another aslant
Endlessly resisting the law of the liquid   calling
Scales   peel off   paste themselves   on the rock skin
Those that rise up from the bottom of the river are all uprooted
Those uprooted   pushed into the flow
Pebbles tremble   chase after the shadows   breathing with gills
Red and red   they rise
Dedicating to them silent court cases   without hesitation
Voice suppressed   stabbed by the moon
Inside the nightwear into which we are rolled

    I'll be dead if I hear this
    What do you mean by "this"
    Here we come up   Ōsuke   and Kosuke

I haven't forgotten   they're coming up
Synchronizing their breathing they come up slithering on the riverbed
The smell of the water seeping into the abyss of their scales
Gets beaten up from inside just when
A thought moves into the center:
The pale white migration that takes away the legs has been all
For this evening   to fold
Pushed to the river rapids   I can't   breathe
Someone I don't know   coming heavily on top of me
I want to say this but below me too   is   someone I don't know
I have   something to say even though
I have no choice but to gulp   it the gills that don't collect
Distance me   and I multiply
And after I'm filled   I fade away
The acts that pile up   are close to
What was poured into my ear once   when I was asleep
Covered by scales covered by sounds
The riverlight swallows   down everything without leaving anything
Heavily envelops riverbed and   houses

    I'll be dead if I hear this
    By "this"   what do you mean
    Here we pass   Ōsuke   and Kosuke
    Don't make   any sound   tonight

Don't make any sound
Whatsoever

The Surrender Flag No One Can See

If it's an emergency meal   some still left   if it's fried oysters   still
The announced friction   passed by hurriedly   and nothing happened wasn't
     it nice?
So soon   it's spring   spying what's on the ground   out of the bottoms of the
     holes persistently dug
Spying   mauve   multiplying   mausoleum   mauling
Mikado's miracle-rings the night I pick 'em up and go home   there's even a
     man who's quicker

Tonight   I'm getting familiarized   I know how to
Damage   here and there   if so   drawing   on the rocks   deeply
The number of deployments   piling them up and burning them spreading
     them   again   the remote control

click   in monochrome half a century ago chased   zigzag to the island's
cliff   off which I a woman jump   or about to
I   don't even   think of the surrender flag she (on the island)
in the cold   sky a flower falling   flutter-flutter[109]

When this mist clears,   when it clears up clean   I'll hold these children in
     my arms
And cross over to the coast to the left   a remnant of last evening   fried oysters
In the remote microwave oven   puff   they burst with self restraint and then
For the first time, or pretending that's the case   we
Don't know   simply   straightforwardly
Stab at them
With brand-new chopsticks

The next (and last) poem alludes to "the Miwayama legend," Miwayama or Mount
Miwa being the most sacred mountain in Nara, 467 meters (1,540 feet) high. As
the *Kojiki* tells it: "The reason we know this person called Ōtataneko is a deity's
child is that Princess Ikutamayori was beautiful in form. There was a man who

---

109. Refers to Suicide Cliff or Banzai Cliff on the Island of Saipan. See note to Ishigaki
Rin's "Cliff," p. 342.

was incomparable in figure and dignity, and he suddenly appeared [to her] at midnight. Accordingly, they admired each other, made love, and stayed together [every night]. In no time whatever, the maiden became pregnant. Therefore, her father and mother thought it strange that she was pregnant and asked her, saying, 'You became pregnant by yourself. How did you become pregnant without a husband?' And she replied, saying, 'There's a beautiful man. I don't even know his clan name, but every night he came and stayed with me, and I became pregnant by myself.' In consequence, her father and mother wanted to know who the person was and instructed her, saying, 'Scatter red clay in front of your bed. Thread spooled hemp yarn to a needle and stab the needle into the hem of his robe.' Accordingly, she did as told and [her parents] looked early the next morning: The hemp attached to the needle went out through the keyhole on the door, leaving only three spools [*miwa*] of hemp. Therefore, they knew how the yarn went out of the keyhole and followed it as it went, and they came to Mount Miwa, where the yarn stopped in front of the shrine for the deity. Accordingly, they knew the man was the deity's child. Accordingly, because there were three spools of yarn left, they named the place Miwa." The deity in question is Ōmononushi, a collaborator in nation creation of Ōkuninushi, otherwise known as the Deity of Eight Thousand Spears. See p. 3.

Mount Miwa

I don't overlook hereditary reed shoots[110]   to thin considerations   I go
on burying all thereabouts   with precision go on burying them   in spring
to the eye[111]   I grow up nonchalantly   the everlasting[112] sky   avoiding
the reed shoots   recedes into heavenly distance

> My breast-sagging[113]
> mother asked me you see
> Who is   your partner   so
> I told her you know.
> Come night   there's a man
> opens the side door   and comes in I   said.
> 'Cause
> that's the truth.

---

110. *Ashikabi.* At the beginning of the *Kojiki*, where the formation of the land is described, is this sentence: "The name of the deity that came to be out of matters that sprouted and arose like reed shoots was Umashi-ashikabi-hikoji-no-kami." The name means "fine reed-shoot male deity."

111. *Me mo haru*: an old punning phrase, which also means "as far as the eye can see."

112. *Hisakata no*, "everlasting," is a makura-kotoba that modifies "light," "sky," etc.

113. *Tarachine no*, "breast-sagging," is a makura-kotoba that modifies "mother."

Even a daughter of ours like that   seems to have someone who comes to see
her   night after night   I think I and father   wanted to   know who it
was   a bud of curiosity   followed madder-illumined[114] days   stretching
its stem   I   we   not pruning   it

The parents brought their heads together   each differently shaped   for
consultation   and told her this   scatter red clay in front of your bed
thread to the needle   thread through its eye   stab it somewhere in the
man's robe   stab in the back alley behind your eyelid   secretly unknown
unnoticed   do that

>My breast-sagging
>mother told me
>stab a needle   into his clothes
>where the thread goes   stretching
>then   you'll know   who the fellow is
>though I feel bad about it   I also want to   know
>until this minute   I couldn't
>I can't say why
>speak out and ask till daybreak

On moonless nights
he melts it melts it   until it loses its shape
early bloom in a greenhouse   in this early bloom   breathing   cloud
those in a greenhouse   each becomes
its own egg   becomes its own cocoon   hold each other by the side
warm each other and crush each other to death
pine needles   each on its branch
drips turn reflecting all
break on the ground

From the needle   stabbed into the hem of his robe   the thread
stretches   the thread grows   dragged through the dark night   without
getting entangled   daybreak dew drops and wets
cutting down one-side leaves and stalks   and runs and runs the thread
     runs

The keyhole
threading through it the thin thread that I follow as it goes on and on

---

114. *Akane-sasu*, "madder-illumined," is a makura-kotoba that modifies "day" and other
similar words.

slowly slowly slowly slowly rising   that is
Mount Miwa   the Shrine of Miwa   where sake is sweet[115]
and then   we knew
our daughter   her father   and I knew

Miwa's mountainside   pressed into the eye   imprinted
here yes it continues   bloody reeds   reed plains[116]
the hereditary stem   recedes   stands still   sways back
all the bells   clanged   destroy
the woman I gave birth to with no color in her face
obediently closes her clam
utters no words
clanged   destroy

---

115. *Umasake no,* "where sake is sweet," is a makura-kotoba that modifies Miwa because Miwa also means "divine sake."

116. *Ashihara no kuni,* "country of reed plains," was one of the ancient names for Japan.

Japanese Verse Forms and Poetic Terms

Chōka: "Long song." Also called *nagauta*. A poem consisting of three or more combinations of 5-7-syllable units, it often ends with an extra 7-syllable unit and an envoi of one or more tanka. Some of the greatest poems during the *Man'yōshū* era (the seventh to the eighth century) were composed in this form. The form did not prosper for long, however. After the editors of the *Kokinshū*, in the early tenth century, chose the *tanka* as the almost exclusive poetic vehicle in Japanese, the vitality of *chōka* began to wane. Later, the combination of syllabic units switched to 7-5, with a not infrequent insertion of an extra syllabic unit. The 7-5- or 7-7-syllable combination survived in the verse sections of narratives and plays well into the Meiji era.

Fūryū: *Fengliu,* "the flow of the wind," in Chinese. Originally, the Chinese ideal of worldly pleasure deriving from the lute, poetry, wine, and women of entertainment; later, an inclination for things that are not mundane or quotidian, as well as for activities that nurture or reflect such inclinations: poetry, painting, music, calligraphy, drinking tea in a ramshackle hut, and so forth. *Fūga,* "wind elegance," and *fūkyō,* "wind madness," mean similar things, with *fūkyō* coming close to "poetic dementia."

Haibun: "*Haikai* prose." A genre that grew out of the tradition of combining prose interspersed with *tanka,* it is prose heightened with the *haikai* spirit, often including a *hokku* or two. Matsuo Bashō (1644–1694) was the first to use the term. The best *haibun* may come close to what Baudelaire called *poème en prose.* In Japan, haibun withered as *zuihitsu,* "essays," gained popularity in the twentieth century. But in the United States, it has gained popularity in recent decades.

Haikai: A broad term for an unorthodox approach to poetry, especially *renga,* "unorthodox" here meaning "not court-dictated." It is often translated as "humorous" or "comic," and it certainly carries those elements; but in its core it means employing daily language, as opposed to "poetic diction," and choosing plebeian ideas and topics for the subjects. During certain periods, *haikai* was also a shorthand for *haikai no renga.*

Haikai no renga: *Renga* composed in a *haikai* spirit. In Bashō's day, the standard length became 36 units, called *kasen,* "poetic saints," in honor of the practice that Fujiwara no Kintō (966–1041) started of selecting thirty-six outstanding poets. In later periods, it became even shorter.

Haiku: In its classical formation, it consists of 5-7-5 syllables. The form is the direct descendent of the *hokku,* with one classical rule requiring the inclusion of a *kigo,* or seasonal word. No doubt the most popular verse form in the world today, it is usually understood to be a tercet; but in Japan it is regarded as a one-line poem by the majority of *haiku* practitioners and commentators. At the same time, since Bashō's day, some have ignored syllable count and, since the early twentieth century, *kigo.* In recent decades, some have even employed lineation. The term *haiku* gained currency only in the early twentieth century. It is often used retroactively to designate *hokku*—though not in this anthology.

Hokku: "Opening unit," so called because it was the verse unit with which to start a renga sequence. Composed in 5-7-5 syllables, it was required to indicate the circumstances of the renga session, including the season. It was also required to be congratulatory of the occasion or salutatory in tone. Another, "stand alone," requirement eventually led to its true independence as a verse form in the seventeenth century.

Hyakunin Isshu: An anthology of one hundred poets, each represented by a single *tanka.* Thought to have come into being when Fujiwara no Tameie slightly revised the *Hyakunin Shūka (Superior Poems by One Hundred Poets),* a similar compilation by his father, Teika, which was made up of one hundred and one poets, each represented by a single *tanka.* Valued as the anthology of anthologies by the Nijō School of poets, the *Hyakunin Isshu* was later turned into a game.

Hyakushu-uta: A set of one hundred *tanka,* consisting of sections on spring, summer, autumn, winter, love, and miscellany.

Imperial anthology: An anthology of verse compiled at the command of an emperor. The first such anthology was of *kanshi,* or verse in classical Chinese, in 751. The *Kokinshū,* in the early tenth century, is the first imperial anthology of Japanese poetry. A total of twenty-one imperial anthologies of Japanese verse were compiled, the last one in 1439, the last four actually assembled at the command of a shogun.

Kana-shi: "Verse in Japanese syllabary." Often rhyming verses in various syllabic arrangements and lines, which Kagami Shikō (1665–1731) and his circle of poets created. Also called *washi.*

Kanshi: Verse composed in classical Chinese, in accordance with classical Chinese prosody.

Kasen: A sequence of *haikai no renga* with thirty-six links.

Kidai: "Seasonal topic," also known as *kigo,* "seasonal word." Its origins date from the practice of composing poems on proposed topics, which was learned from the Chinese. It developed with the notion of *hon'i*—that each phenomenon or concept has an essential attribute (for example, that *harusame,* "spring rain," is always soft, fine, and quiet, never hard, torrential, and noisy)—and became an integral part of the poetics of *renga*. But by the early nineteenth century as many as six thousand *kidai* or *kigo* were listed, and today the number reaches fifteen thousand or more. Thus one can argue that the designation has become more or less meaningless, although only about eight hundred are said to be committed to memory for actual use.

Kigo: "Seasonal word." See *kidai*.

Kikōbun: "Travel diary." Often interspersed with *hokku*.

Koshiore: "Broken at the hip." Deprecatory term for *tanka*.

Kyōka: "Mad song." Satirical poem in *tanka* form.

Maeku-zuke: See *senryū*.

Makura-kotoba: "Pillow word." Consisting of five syllables or less, it modifies the word that follows by association in meaning or sound. Comparable to the epithets in Homeric poetry.

Renga: "Linked song." A sequence alternating 5-7-5 and 7-7 syllables up to fifty times, a total of one hundred syllabic units, usually composed by a group. Other than the influence of the Chinese practice of linking short stanzas together, called *lianju,* the idea of linking 5-7-5- and 7-7-syllable units came into being as a result of the tendency of the *tanka* to break into two sections, the 5-7-5-syllable "upper" hemistich and the 7-7-syllable "lower" hemistich. At first, a renga was simply a statement made in either 5-7-5 or 7-7 syllables followed by a response made in 7-7 or 5-7-5 syllables, composed by two persons. But as the "chaining" of alternating units became longer, the standard was eventually set at one hundred, beginning with 5-7-5 and ending with 7-7. Basically a parlor game for multiple participants, the renga had as its core rule what Earl Miner, the first American scholar to study the form closely, termed *disjunction*: any two consecutive units must make sense but three may not. In the end, the *renga* developed extraordinarily complex rules.

Renku: "Linked units." Another name for the *haikai no renga* of thirty-six units. Though it did not gain currency until the early twentieth century, the term is often used retroactively, though not in this anthology.

Senryū: "River willow." Satirical verse in *haiku* form, *senryū* grew out of practice renga sessions in which verses were composed to "follow" a given unit. Known as *maeku-zuke,* "follow-up to the preceding unit," the practice sessions in time became an independent game and, during the time of the *haikai* judge Karai Senryū (1718–1790), immensely popular, hence the eponymous name. Originally, *senryū* dealt with human and social affairs—rather than natural and seasonal phenomena—in a knowing or wry manner. Today the distinction between *haiku* and *senryū* is often hard to detect.

Shi: "Verse." Originally Chinese (*shi*), *shi* is a blanket term for poetry, though in common usage it means "free verse" and denotes poems that are not *tanka*, *renga (renku)*, or *hokku (haiku)*.

Tanka: "Short song." In its classical formation, it consists of 5-7-5-7-7 syllables. Dating from as early as the sixth century, it may be described as the oldest poetic form in continuous use in the world. Most modern *tanka* writers regard the verse as a one-line form. (For a speculation on how the view may have evolved, see the introduction.) In the twentieth century, Ishikawa Takuboku (1885–1912), following the example of Toki Aika (1885–1980), famously broke it up into three lines and Shaku Chōkū (Orikuchi Shinobu as an ethnologist, 1887–1953) made a variety of experiments with the form, but lineated *tanka* have not attracted a sizable number of followers; some estimate the share of lineators to be 5 percent of the tanka population. Some, Toki among them, have also ignored syllable count, at times composing very long "short songs" that can't be scanned. One recent tendency is to blur the distinctions between syllabic units.

Uta: "Song." Usually tanka; broadly includes *chōka*.

Uta-makura: "Poetic pillow." Usually a place name, it functions to evoke a certain image or create a certain association.

Uta-monogatari: "Poetic tales." Short, episodic stories sprinkled with *tanka*.

Waka: "Japanese song." Originally verse written in Japanese, as opposed to *kanshi*, which is verse written in Chinese. Narrowly, *tanka*. See *uta*.

Waki: 7-7-syllable verse that serves as the second unit in a *renga* sequence. It "seconds" the *hokku*.

Washi: "Japanese verse." See *kana-shi*.

Bibliography

Anthologies

Virtually all publishers are in Tokyo. It is common practice in Japan for publishers to compile without indicating the responsible editor or editorial coordinator. The first seven items are typical of such anthologies.

Gendai Haiku Zenshū. 6 vols. Tachikaze Shobō, 1977–78. A large collection of modern haiku poets, each with a substantial selection.

Gendai Kajin Bunko. 30 vols. Kakubunsha, 1981–88. A selection of modern tanka poets, each volume dedicated to a single poet. The series begins with the avant-garde classicist (if such a thing is possible) Tsukamoto Kunio (1920–2005). The last five volumes are collections of essays on modern tanka.

Gendai Kashū. Chikuma Shobō, 1973. Vol. 94 in the publisher's series of modern Japanese literature. The selection of twenty tanka poets begins with Onoe Saishū (1876–1956) and ends with Kagoshima Juzō (1898–1982). None of the twenty is a woman. Cited here to show how idiosyncratic an anthology selection can be.

Gendai Kushū. Chikuma Shobō, 1973. Vol. 95 in the Chikuma series mentioned in the preceding entry. The selection of thirty-six poets begins with Naitō Meisetsu (1847–1926) and ends with Ogiwara Seisensui (1884–1976). Five are women: Hoshino Tatsuko (1903–1984), Mitsuhashi Takajo (1899–1972), Hashimoto Takako (1899–1963), Hosomi Ayako (1907–1987), and Nozawa Setsuko (1920–1995).

Gendaishi Bunko. Shichōsha, 1968–. A famous series of poets who did notable work in postwar Japan. Each volume is dedicated to a single poet, the first volume a selection of poems of Tamura Ryūichi (1923–1998). At the time of this writing, the latest volume is number 184. *Nihon Gendai-shi Bunko,* published by Doyō Bijutsu Shuppan Hanbai, is one of the competitors.

Joryū Tanka. Kawade Shobō Shinsha, 1988. One in a series of *bungei tokuhon,* "literary arts readers," this anthology covers women tanka poets from ancient to modern times.

Nihon Shijin Zenshū. 34 vols. Shinchōsha, 1967–69. Begins with Shimazaki Tōson (1872–1943) and ends with two volumes dedicated to selections of poets in the Shōwa era.

*

Abe Kimio and Asō Isoji, eds. *Kinsei Haiku Haibun Shū.* Iwanami Shoten, 1964. A collection of hokku and haibun from the Edo period. Hereafter ABE.

Ariyoshi Tamotsu, ed. *Hyakunin Isshu.* Kōdansha, 1983. There are a great many annotated editions of the canonical anthology, originally compiled by Fujiwara no Teika (1162–1241). This edition is fully annotated but accessible. One unusual edition is *Hyakunin Isshu Hitoyo Gatari,* edited by Ozaki Masayoshi (1755–1827), Furukawa Hisashi, Iwanami Shoten, 1972; it comes with anecdotes, legendary or otherwise, about each poet. Another is the winter 1972 edition of the magazine *Taiyō;* sumptuously illustrated with paintings by Kōrin, Tan'yū, and others, the special issue has the anthology as famously interpreted by Andō Tsuguo (1919–2002).

Asō Naoko, ed. *Josei-tachi no Gendaishi.* Godō Shoin, 2004. A selection of one hundred living poets, a poem each, with a number of poems chosen for their political content.

Bessho Makiko. *Bashō ni hirakareta Haikai no Josei-shi.* Origin Shuppan Center, 1989. Not an anthology but a study that illuminates how the haikai poet Matsuo Bashō (1644–1694) enabled women to become involved in haikai writing.

————. *Kotoba o Te ni shita Shisei no Onna-tachi.* Origin Shuppan Center, 1993. Not an anthology but an original study of women haikai poets during the Edo period, which introduces four lesser known but important figures.

Fujimoto Kazue, ed. *Go-Shūi Waka Shū.* 4 vols. Kōdansha, 1983. The closely annotated fourth imperial anthology of Japanese poetry.

Fukushima Riko, ed. *Joryū.* Vol. 3 of *Edo Kanshi Sen.* Iwanami Shoten, 1995. Selections of kanshi by three women: Ema Saikō, Hara Saihin, and Yanagawa Kōran. Hereafter FUKUSHIMA.

Furutani Chishin, comp. *Edo Jidai Joryū Bungaku Zenshū.* 4 vols. Nihon Tosho Center, 1979. A reprint of the pioneering collection of women's writing during the Edo period, originally compiled in 1918. Vol. 4 is dedicated to tanka, hokku, and kyōka, topped by the tanka collection *Ōji Shū* by Inoue Tsūjo (1660–1738), who was acclaimed to be "the most outstanding woman writer since Princess Uchiko." All the tanka poets are included in Nagasawa's compendium (which see). The haikai poets included are Shūshiki, Sonome, Chigetsu, Sute-jo, Chiyo-ni, Kasame, and Tayo-jo. Nihon Tosho Center started to publish a new edition of these four volumes in 2001. Hereafter FURUTANI.

Hisamatsu Sen'ichi, Aoki Takako et al., eds. *Heian Kamakura Shikashū.* Iwanami Shoten, 1964. Four of the seven poets selected are women: Izumi Shikibu, Princess Shikishi, Kenreimon'in Ukyō no Daibu, and Lord Shuzei's Daughter. Hereafter HISAMATSU AND AOKI.

Hisamatsu Sen'ichi and Imoto Nōichi, eds. *Koten Haibungaku Taikei.* 16 vols. Shūeisha, 1970–72. A large compendium of Edo haikai. Hereafter HAIBUNGAKU.

Ijichi Tetsuo, ed. *Renga Shū.* Iwanami Shoten, 1960.

Isogai Jirō and Kuroko Kazuo, eds. *Zainichi Bungaku Zenshū,* Vols. 17–18, *Shiika Shū.* Bensei Shuppan, 2006. An 18-volume compilation of literature by Japanese residents of Korean descent. Vol. 17 includes tanka.

Itō Kei et al., eds. *Chūsei Waka Shū: Muramachi Hen.* Iwanami Shoten, 1990.

Kado Reiko. *Edo Joryū Bungaku no Hakken.* Fujiwara Shoten, 1998. Not an anthology but a study of women's literature during the Edo period that started with the question: Didn't women write during the period from Murasaki Shikibu to the Meiji era? Hereafter KADO.

Kaneko Kinjirō, ed. *Tsukuba Shū no Kenkyū.* Kazama Shobō, 1965. A close study of the anthology of renga *Tsukuba Shū,* which Nijō Yoshimoto compiled in 1356.

———— et al., eds. *Renga Haikai Shū.* Shōgakukan, 1974.

Katagiri Yōichi, ed. *Gosen Waka Shū.* Iwanami Shoten, 1990. The second imperial anthology of Japanese poetry.

Katano Tatsurō and Matsuno Yōichi, eds. *Senzai Waka Shū.* Iwanami Shoten, 1993. The seventh imperial anthology of Japanese poetry.

Kawamura Teruo, Kashiwagi Yoshio, and Kudō Shigenori, eds. *Kin'yō Waka Shū, Shiika Waka Shū.* Iwanami Shoten, 1989. The fifth and sixth imperial anthologies of Japanese poetry.

Kira Sueo, ed. *Haika Kijin Dan, Zoku Haika Kijin Dan* by Takeuchi Gengen'ichi and Takeuchi Seisei, published in 1816. Iwanami Shoten, 1987. Descriptions of haikai poets as eccentrics.

Kojima Noriyuki, ed. *Kaifūsō, Bunka Shūrei Shū, Honchō Monzui.* Iwanami Shoten, 1964.

————, ed. *Kokufū Ankoku Jidai no Bungaku.* Haniwa Shobō, 1976. A collection of early kanshi, annotated.

————, ed. *Ōchō Kanshi Sen.* Iwanami Shoten, 1987. A collection of early kanshi, annotated.

Kojima Noriyuki and Arai Eizō, eds. *Kokin Waka Shū.* Iwanami Shoten, 1989. The first imperial anthology of Japanese poetry. There are a great many annotated editions.

Kojima Noriyuki, Kinoshita Masatoshi, and Satake Akihiro, eds. *Man'yōshū.* 4 vols. Shōgakukan, 1971–75.

Komachiya Teruhiko, ed. *Shūi Waka Shū.* Iwanami Shoten, 1990. The third imperial anthology of Japanese poetry.

Kubota Jun and Hirata Yoshinobu, eds. *Go-Shūi Waka Shū.* Iwanami Shoten, 1994. The fourth imperial anthology of Japanese poetry.

Kurano Kenji and Takeda Yūkichi, eds. *Kojiki, Norito.* Iwanami Shoten, 1958.

Kuriyama Riichi et al., eds. *Kinsei Haiku Haibun Shū.* Shōgakukan, 1972. A collection of hokku and haibun during the Edo period. Hereafter KURIYAMA.

Kusogami Noboru, ed. *Nishi-Honganji Sanjūroku-nin Shū Seisei.* Kazawa Shobō, 1982 (new edition). An anthology of thirty-six poets selected by Fujiwara no Kintō, who were later called "poetic saints."

Mizuhara Shūōshi, Katō Shūson, and Yamakoto Kenkichi, eds. *Nihon Dai-Saijiki.* Kōdansha, 1983. Lists about 15,000 kigo. The number of hokku or haiku assembled may easily go beyond 100,000.

Morita Susumu and Sagawa Aki, eds. *Zainichi Korian Shi-senshū: 1916-nen~2004-nen.* Doyō Bijutsusha, 2005. A large collection of poems by people of Korean ancestry living in Japan.

Morita Yōko, ed. *Renku Saisai.* Kadokawa Shoten, 1994. Renga (renku) composition has become popular in the past three decades, and this is just one of many collections.

Nagasawa Mitsu, ed. *Nyonin Waka Taikei.* 4 vols. Kazama Shobō, 1962–1972. A meticulous compendium of chōka and tanka composed by women from the earliest times to the end of the Edo period. The fourth volume is dedicated to studies, with a chronology. Hereafter NAGASAWA.

Nagata Yōichi, ed. *"Dōjidai" to shite no Josei Tanka.* Kawade Shobō Shinsha, 1992. A convenient survey of "contemporary" women tanka poets, with a chronology of developments since the beginning of the Meiji era. It contains discussions and comments by non-tanka poets.

Okai Takashi, ed. *Gendai Hyakunin Isshu.* Asahi Shinbusha, 1991. An anthology of one hundred postwar tanka poets, each represented by a single poem. Thirty-four poets are women.

Ozawa Masao et al., eds. *Fukuro Zōshi Chūshaku.* 2 vols. Haniwa Shobō, 1974–76. Closely annotated.

Sakamoto Tadao, ed. *Tanka, Haiku, Senryū 101 Nen: 1892–1992.* Shinchōsha, 1993. A panoramic survey of three genres of verse, each of the 101 years represented by one tanka, one haiku, and one senryū poet, each one with twenty pieces.

Sakamoto Tarō et al., eds. *Nihon Shoki.* 2 vols. Iwanami Shoten, 1965–67.

Shiba Keiko. *Aizu-han no Onna-tachi.* Kōbunsha, 1994. Not an anthology but a study of ten women in the samurai class in Aizu from the early Edo period to the Meiji era. It shows how women studied and acted in that fiefdom.

Shinkawa Kazue, ed. *Onna-tachi no Mei-shishū.* Shichōsha, 1992. A selection of sixteen modern women poets.

————, ed. *Zoku Onna-tachi no Mei-shishū.* Shichōsha, 1992. A sequel to the previous volume, it also includes sixteen modern women poets.

Shinkawa Kazue and Yoshihara Sachiko, eds. *Nijisseiki Josei Shishū.* The Winter 1993 special issue of the magazine *La Mer,* this anthology includes 126 women poets of the twentieth century, each represented by a single poem.

Taira Sōsei, ed. *Ryōran Josei Senryū.* Midori Shobō, 1997. An anthology of women's senryū, with commentary on individual poets, each represented by a selection of twenty pieces.

Takagi Ichinosuke, Gomi Tomohide, and Ōno Susumu, eds. *Man'yōshū.* 4 vols. Iwanami Shoten, 1957–62.

Takagi Ichinosuke and Hisamatsu Sen'ichi, eds. *Kinsei Waka Shū.* Iwanami Shoten, 1966. The Ryōkan section includes tanka of the nun Teishin (1798–1872).

Takahashi Mutsuo, ed. *Hyakuin Ikku.* Chūō Kōron Sha, 1999. Idiosyncratic anthology of one hundred haiku writers, male and female, each represented by a single piece, going back to the *Kojiki.* Only fifteen of them are women, but Takahashi says more than half of them would be women if the coverage were limited to modern times.

Takano Kimihiko, ed. *Gendai no Tanka.* Kōdansha, 1991. A substantial anthology of 105 tanka poets since the Meiji era, of which thirty-eight are women.

Tanaka Yutaka and Akase Shingo, eds. *Shin-Kokin Waka Shū.* Iwanami Shoten, 1992. The eighth imperial anthology of Japanese poetry. There are many annotated editions.

Taniyama Shigeru et al., eds. *Shinpen Kokka Taikan.* 2 vols. Kadokawa Shoten, 1983. A compilation of the twenty-one imperial anthologies.

Tsuchihashi Yutaka and Konishi Jin'ichi, eds. *Kodai Kayō Shū.* Iwanami Shoten, 1957. An anthology of ancient "songs" from the *Kojiki, Nihon Shoki,* and a number of other sources.

Uda Kiyoko and Kuroda Momoko, eds. *Joryū Haiku Shūsei.* Rippū Shobō, 1999. A collection of modern women's haiku, it contains about 12,000 haiku by eighty-one haiku poets. Hereafter UDA.

Ueno Sachiko, comp. *Josei Haiku no Sekai.* 3rd ed. Iwanami Shoten, 1998. Discusses twelve woman hokku and haiku writers, from Den Sute-jo (1633–1698) to Hosomi Ayako (1907–1997). Here cited as representative of this type of survey.

Yamada Katsuhiko, ed. *Sugita Hisajo to Hashimoto Takako: Futari no Bijo no Monogatari.* Bokuyōsha, 1989. A large collection of the two women haiku poets' writings, along with essays on them and reproductions of original editions.

Yamada Yoshio et al., eds. *Konjaku Monogatari Shū.* 5 vols. Iwanami Shoten, 1959–63. There are several other editions of this ancient anthology.

Yazaki Ai, ed. *Renku Renren.* Chikuma Shobō, 1992. A playful introduction to modern renga (renku) composition with a selection.

Individual Poets

In this section, books are listed by the poet. Since poets before the mid-nineteenth century tend to be anthologized and annotated with other poets, cross-references are made. Commentaries, which are common with them, are also included.

Before the Mid-Nineteenth Century

Abutsu, the Nun. Fukuda Hideichi et al., eds. *Chūsei Nikki Kikō Shū.* Iwanami Shoten, 1990. Includes *Utatane* and *Izaiyoi Nikki.*

———. Morimoto Motoko, ed. *Izyoi Nikki, Yoru no Tsuru.* Kōdansha, 1979.

———. Tsugita Kasumi, ed. *Utatane.* Kōdansha, 1978.

Akazome Emon. Sekine Keiko et al., eds. *Akazome Emon Shū Zenshaku.* Kazama Shobō, 1997.

Arii Shokyū. Ōuchi Hatsuo, Iino Matsuko, and Abe Ōju, eds. *Kohakuan Shokyū-ni Zenshū.* Izumi Shoin, 1986. The text of *Akikaze no Ki* is also included in vol. 14 of HAIBUNGAKU.

Den Sute-jo. See ABE, FURUTANI, KURIYAMA, and NAGASAWA.

Eifukumon'in. Higuchi Yoshimaro et al., eds. *Chūsei Waka Shū: Kamakura Hen.* Iwanami Shoten, 1991. Includes a paired set of two hundred tanka by Eifukumon'in.

———. Nishino Taeko. *Shirasu no Tsuki.* Kokubunsha, 1984. Commentary on a selection of her poems. Includes commentary on Hino Meishi's diary *Takemuki ga Ki.*

———. Takenishi Hiroko. *Shikishi Naishinnō, Eifukumon'in.* Chikuma Shobō, 1972. Commentary on Eifukumon'in's life and poetry.

Ema Saikō. Kado Reiko, ed. *Ema Saikō Shishū: "Shōmu Ikō."* 2 vols. Rev. ed. Kyūko Shoin, 1994. See also FUKUSHIMA and KADO.

Furukawa Kasame. See vol. 4 of FURUTANI.

Hara Saihin. See FUKUSHIMA and KADO.

Inoue Tsūjo. Inoue Tsūjo Zenshū Shūtei Iinkai (committee), ed. *Inoue Tsūjo Zenshū.* Kagawa-kenritsu Marugame Kōtō Gakkō Dōsōkai, 1973.

Ise. Sekine Yoshiko and Yamashita Michiyo, eds. *Ise Shū Zenshaku.* Kazama Shobō, 1996. Also see various imperial anthologies.

Izumi Shikibu. Komatsu Tomi et al., eds. *Izumi Shikibu Shū Zenshaku: Zokushū Hen.* Kasama Shoin, 1977. Close annotation of what is commonly known as the *zoku,* "sequel," edition of Izumi's tanka.

———. Shimizu Fumio, ed. *Izumi Shikibu Shū, Izumi Shikibu Zokushū.* Iwanami Shoten, 1983. Minimally annotated, this volume includes all tanka attributed to Izumi Shikibu. Also see HISAMATSU AND AOKI, as well as various imperial anthologies.

Kaga no Chiyo-ni. See ABE, FURUTANI, KURIYAMA, and vol. 13 of HAIBUNGAKU.

Kamei Shōkin. See KADO.

Kawai Chigetsu. See ABE, KURIYAMA, and vol. 9 of HAIBUNGAKU.

Kenreimon'in Ukyō no Daibu. See HISAMATSU AND AOKI.

———. Hisamatsu Sen'ichi and Kubota Jun, eds. *Kenreimon'in Ukyō no Daibu Shū.* Iwanami Shoten, 1978. The book, sparsely annotated, comes with tales about Taira nobles.

———. Nakamura Shin'ichirō, commentary. *Kenreimon'in Ukyō no Daibu.* Chikuma Shobō, 1972. An attractive book in which Nakamura tells us that Ukyō no Daibu was popular during the Second World War, and no wonder: she describes the anguish of a woman whose lover is taken away by war.

Korenaga. See Kojima, *Ōchō Kanshi Sen.*

Michitsuna's Mother. Hasegawa Masaharu et al., eds. *Tosa Nikki, Kagerō Nikki, Murasaki Shikibu Nikki, Sarashina Nikki.* Iwanami Shoten, 1989.

———. Kakimoto Tsutomu, ed. *Kagerō Nikki.* Kadokawa Shoten, 1967.

———. Suzuki Tomotarō et al., eds. *Tosa Nikki, Kagerō Nikki, Izumi Shikibu Nikki, Sarashina Nikki.* Iwanami Shoten, 1957.

———. Uemura Etsuko, ed. *Kagerō Nikki.* 3 vols. Kōdansha, 1978.

Murasaki Shikibu. Hasegawa Masaharu et al., eds. *Tosa Nikki, Kagerō Nikki, Murasaki Shikibu Nikki, Sarashina Nikki.* Iwanami Shoten, 1989. Includes Murasaki's *kashū,* tanka collection, fully annotated.

———. Namba Hiroshi, ed. *Murasaki Shikibu Shū.* Iwanami Shoten, 1973. This paperback edition has only minimum annotation.

Nozawa Ukō-ni. See vol. 8 of HAIBUNGAKU.

Ogawa Shōfū. See vol. 8 of HAIBUNGAKU.

Ono no Komachi. See various imperial anthologies and Kusogami's compilation.

Ōtomo, Princess. See Kojima's *Ōchō Kanshi Sen.*

Rikei-ni. See vol. 1 of FURUTANI.

Sagami. Takeuchi Harue, Hayashi Maria, and Yoshida Misuzu, eds. *Sagami Shū Zenshaku.* Kazama Shobō, 1991. See also various imperial anthologies.

Sakuma Tachieko. Unpublished but available from Hiroaki Sato, hironan@ix.netcom.com.

Shiba Sonome. See ABE, FURUTANI, KURIYAMA, and vol. 8 of HAIBUNGAKU.

Shikishi, Princess. Nishiki Hitoshi, ed. *Shikishi Naishinnō Zen-kashū*. (Rev. ed.). Ōfūsha, 1988. All the tanka attributed to Princess Shikishi—399 of them—are included and annotated. See also HISAMATSU AND AOKI.

Shōshō no Naishi. See Ijichi's *Renga Shū* and Kaneko's *Tsukuba Shū no Kenkyū*.

Tagami Kikusha. Ueno Sachiko, ed. *Tagami Kikusha Zenshū*. 2 vols. Izumi Shoin, 2000.

Takahashi Gyokushō. See KADO.

Ta-ni-guchi Den-jo. See Katsumine Fufū, ed. *Keishū Haika Zenshū*. Shūeikaku, 1922. I have seen only Den-jo's section, courtesy of Bessho Makiko. See also Bessho's *Kotaba o Te ni shita Shisei no Onna-tachi,* which is listed elsewhere.

Uchiko (Uchishi), Princess. See Kojima's *Kokufū Ankoku Jidai no Bungaku* and *Ōchō Kanshi Sen.*

Yanagawa Kōran. See FUKUSHIMA.

After the Mid-Nineteenth Century

Abe Hinako. *Umiyōbi no Onna-tachi*. Shoshi Yamada, 2001.

———. *Shokuminchi no Chikei*. Shichigatsudō, 1989.

———. *Tenga na Ikidōri*. Shoshi Yamada, 1994.

Bessho Makiko. *Akebono-zō wa Yuki o mitaka*. Kaibisha, 1987.

———. *Nemuri no Katachi*. Kashinsha, 1992.

———. *Shinayakana Nichijō*. Mugi Shobō, 1982.

Cheon Mihye. *Urimal*. Shiyōsha, 1995.

Fujiki Kyoko. See UDA.

Fujita Fumie. *Fujita Fumie Shishū: Yoru no Koe*. Fūtōsha, 1991. A reprint, with the addition of three essays by three writers, of her first and only book of poems, published in 1933.

Fukao Sumako. *Madame • X no Haru: Fukao Sumako Sakuhin Shō*. Ozawa Shoten, 1988. A small sampling of her poems, short stories, and essays.

Hachikai Mimi. *Ima nimo uruotteiku Jinchi*. Shiyōsha, 1999.

———. *Kū mono wa kuwareru Yoru*. Shichōsha, 2005.

Hayashi Amari. *Bedside*. Shinchōsha, 1997. The paperback edition of the book, published in the same year, includes other tanka.

———. *Girlish*. Shūeisha, 1999.

———. *Mars ☆ Angel: Hayashi Amari Kashū*. Chūsekisha, 1986.

Hayashi Fumiko. *Hayashi Fumiko Shishū*. Shichōsha, 1984. Complete poems.

———. *Hōrōki*. Shinchōsha, 1996. The novel that made Fumiko famous.

Hirata Toshiko. *Atlantis wa Mizu-kusai*. Shoshi Yamada, 1987.

———. *Omoroi Fūfu*. Shichōsha. 1993.

———. *Rakkyō no Ongaeshi*. Shichōsha, 1984.

———. *Terminal*. Shichōsha, 1997.

———. *Yogoto futoru Onna*. Shichōsha, 1991.

Hiratsuka Raichō. Kobayashi Tomie and Yoneda Sayoko, eds. *Hiratsuka Raichō Hyōron-shū*. Iwanami Shoten, 1987; a collection of high-powered essays by the founder of *Seitō (Bluestockings)* magazine. Also, Horiba Kiyoko, ed. *"Seitō" Josei Kaihō Ronshū*. Iwanami Shoten, 1991; a collection of essays by members of the Seitō group.

Ibaragi Noriko. *Ibaragi Noriko Shishū*. Shichōsha, 1969. Vol. 20 in *Gendaishi Bunko*.

———. *Sunshi*. Kashinsha, 1982.

———. *Yorikakarazu*. Chikuma Shobō, 1999.

Iijima Haruko. *Bōbō*. Kadokawa Shoten, 1996.

———. *Iijima Haruko Shū*. Bokuyōsha, 1987. Installment in a series of books, each with the poet's own explications of one hundred haiku.

———. *Iijima Haruko Shū*. Kashinsha, 1994.

Imahashi Ai. *Ōkyaku no Hiza.* Hokumeisha, 2003.

————. A set of one hundred tanka in the inauguration issue of the magazine *Tanka Wave,* summer 2002, issued by Hokumeisha. The set won the publisher's prize.

Isaka Yōko. *Chi ni ochireba sumu.* Shichōsha, 1991.

————. *Chōrei.* Shiyōsha, 1979.

————. *GIGI.* Shichōsha, 1982.

————. *Isaka Yōko Shishū.* Shichōsha, 1988. Vol. 92 in *Gendaishi Bunko.*

————. *Nemuru Aozora.* Chūsekisha, 1984. One in the publisher's series of modern women poets.

————. *Violin-zoku.* Shichōsha, 1987.

Ishigaki Rin. *Ishigaki Rin Bunko.* 4 vols. Kaōsha, 1987–88.

————. *Ishigaki Rin Shishū.* Shichōsha, 1971. Vol. 41 in *Gendaishi Bunko.*

Itami Kimiko. *Garuda.* Gendai Haiku Kyōkai, 1983.

————. *Itami Kimiko Kushū.* France-dō, 1993.

————. *Shijin no Ie.* Chūsekisha, 2001. Not a collection of haiku but a collection of essays on haiku poets, including herself. One essay discusses the use of spacing in haiku and another the difference between shi and haiku.

————. *Unga to Suisen: Cannal and Daffodil.* Shun'yōdō, 1999.

Itō Hiromi. *Itō Hiromi Shishū.* Shichōsha, 1988. Vol. 94 in *Gendaishi Bunko.*

————. *Kawara Arekusa.* Shichōsha, 2005.

————. *Territory Ron I.* Shichōsha, 1987. With photographs by Araki Nobuyoshi and Kikuchi Nobuyoshi.

————. *Territory Ron II.* Shichōsha, 1985.

————. *Watashi wa Anju Himeko de aru.* Shichōsha, 1993.

Itō Hiromi and Ueno Chizuko. *Noro to Saniwa.* Heibonsha, 1991. Itō's poems paired with Ueno's essays.

Kamakura Sayumi. *Kamakura Sayumi Kushū.* Sunagoya Shobō, 1998.

Kamiyama Himeyo. *Chi no Rhythm.* Gendai Haiku Kyōkai Seinen-bu, 1996.

————. *Jacob no Kaidan: Jacob's Ladder.* Sōbunsha, 2001.

————. *Taiyōshin.* Self-published, 1998.

Kaneko Misuzu. *Kaneko Misuzu Zenshū.* 3 vols. JULA Shuppan Kyoku, 1984.

Katase Hiroko. Takahashi Mutsuo, ed. *Katase Hiroko Shishū: 1957–1997.* Shoshi Yamada, 1997.

Kikuchi Toshiko. See Shinkawa, *Zoku Onna-tachi no Mei-shishū.*

Kimura Nobuko. *Deteitta.* Kyōiku Shuppan Center, 1986. Poems for children.

————. *Himeguri.* Shichōsha, 1996.

————. *Jikanwari ni nai Jikan.* Kado Sōbō, 1983. Poems for children.

————. *Kadoki.* Hakuteisha, 1987.

————. *Kari Kari.* Kado Shobō, 1985.

————. *Kimura Nobuko Shishū.* Gingasha, 1971.

————. *Kotchi mo muite yo.* Kado Sōbō, 1993. Poems for children.

————. *Mō Daijōbu dakara.* Dai-Nihon Tosho, 2000. Poems for children.

————. *Onna Moji.* Shikaisha, 1979.

————. *Tegamitte Te no Kamisama?* Kado Sōbō, 1990. Poems for children.

————. *Watashi to iu Matsuri.* Kashinsha, 1982.

Koike Masayo. *Eien ni Konai Basu.* Shichōsha, 1997.

————. *Mottomo Kannōtekina Heya,* Shoshi Yamada, 1999.

Koike Sumiyo. *Gazoku.* Roppō Shuppansha, 1991.

————. *Umezono.* Shichōsha, 2002.

Koyanagi Reiko. *Ashi no Sato kara.* Kashinsha, 1976.

————. *Kodomo no Ryōbun.* Kashinsha, 1997.

————. *Kumogaoka Densetsu.* Shichōsha, 1993.

————. *Mieteiru Mono.* Gendaishi Kōbō, 1966.

————. *Obasan no Ie.* Komagome Shobō, 1980.

————. *Takanna Chijō.* Gendaishi Kōbō, 1969.

————. *Tsukiyo no Shigoto.* Kashinsha, 1983.

————. *Yomi no Usagi.* Kashinsha, 1989.

Matsuda Tokiko. *Matsuda Tokiko Zenshū.* Miraisha, 1985.

Mayuzumi Madoka. *B-men no Natsu.* Kadokawa Shoten, 1994.

————. *Hanagoromo.* PHP Kenkyūsho, 1997.

————. *Koko ni Anata no iru Fushigi.* PHP, 1999. A collection of short essays, each ending with a haiku.

————. *Kuchizuke.* Kadokawa Haruki Jimusho, 1999.

————. *Kyoto no Koi.* PHP Kenkyūsho. 2001.

————. *Ra • Ra • Ra "Oku no Hosomichi."* Kōbunsha, 1998. An account with haiku of her visits to some of the places Bashō went to during his famous journey to the interior.

Michiko, Empress. *Seoto.* Daitō Shuppansha, 1997. A selection of tanka from 1959 to 1995.

Mizuhara Shion. *Hoshi no Nikutai.* Shinya Sōsho Sha, 1995. Selections of essays and tanka.

————. *Marōdo.* Kawade Shobō Shinsha, 1997.

Nagami Atsuko. *Nagami Atsuko Zenshū.* Shichōsha, 1991. Complete poems, essays, letters, and diary.

Nagase Kiyoko. *Akegata ni kuru Hito yo.* Shichōsha, 1987.

————. *Nagase Kiyoko Shishū.* Shichōsha, 1990.

Nagashima Minako. *Anpan Nikki.* Mujinkan, 1997.

————. *Chotto Tabesugi.* Mujinkan, 2000.

————. *Hyōtan Hechima.* Seijisha, 1985.

————. *Kurama Tengu.* Mujinkan, 1995.

————. *Shitsugo.* Seijisha, 1991.

Nakajō Fumiko. *Nakajō Fumiko Kashū.* Kokubunsha, 1981.

Nakayama Mickey (Miki). *Atlantis no Ei.* Murasaki no Kai, 1997.

Nomura Hatsuko. Hirayama Yoshiaki, ed. *Kogane-mori.*Okinawa-ken Kawa-kai Henshū Iinkai, 1995. An anthology of tanka compiled to commemorate the fiftieth anniversary of the end of the Second World War.

Ogawa Anna. *Banka Kōgenshi.* Bunkyō Shobō, 1995.

————. *Sono Toki Jūmin wa.* Midori Bijutsu Insatsu Kabushiki Kaisha Shuppanbu, 2000. This book focuses on the struggle to block the building of a power plant in the estuary of the Fuji River; in addition to essays and such, it contains a small selection of poems.

Okamoto Kanoko. *Okamoto Kanoko Zenshū XI.* Chikuma Shobō, 1994. This volume contains all the 4,409 tanka left by Kanoko.

Ōnishi Kimiyo. *Henji.* Urawa, Saitama: Sakitama Shuppankai, 1985.

————. *Shida.* Nagoya: Shikōsha, 1973.

Ōniwa Minako. *Sabita Kotoba.* Kōdansha, 1971.

Park Kyong-Mi. *Neko ga Nekoko o kuwaete yattekuru.* Shoshi Yamada, 2006.

————. *Sono Ko.* Shoshi Yamada, 2003.

————. *Suupu.* Shiyōsha, 1980.

Sagawa Chika. *Sagawa Chika Zen-shishū.* Shinkaisha, 1983.

Satō Sachiko. *Ishimure.* Yayoi Shobō, 1980.

Shinkawa Kazue. *Hanebashi.* Kashinsha, 1990.

————. *Haru to onai Doshi.* Kashinsha, 1991.

————. *Hatahatato Page ga mekure . . .* Kashinsha, 1999.

————. *Kesa no hi ni.* Kashinsha, 1997.

————. *Kore wa kore wa.* Reifū Shobō, 2000. With Nomiyama Gyōji's paintings.

————. *Shinkawa Kazue Bunko.* 5 vols. Kashinsha, 1988–89.

————. *Shinkawa Kazue Shishū.* Shichōsha, 1975. Vol. 64 in *Gendaishi Bunko.*

————. *Shinkawa Kazue Zen-shishū.* Kashinsha, 2000. Includes all the poems published up to the end of 1999.

————. *Ushio no Niwa kara.* Kashinsha, 1993. An exchange of poems with Kajima Shōzō.

————. *Watashi o tabanenai de.* XYLO, 1996. With Itō Keiji's paintings.

————. *Yottsu no Mado.* Shigetsusha, 1988. Limited edition of fifty-eight copies.

————. *Zoku Shinkawa Kazue Shishū.* Shichōsha, 1995. Vol. 132 in *Gendaishi Bunko.*

Shiraishi Kazuko. *Arawareru Mono-tachi o shite.* Shoshi Yamada, 1996.

————. *Furenama, furemon, furumun.* Shoshi Yamada, 1988.

————. *Hirahira, hakobarete yuku Mono.* Shoshi Yamada, 1992.

————. *Kuroi Hitsuji no Monogatari: Personal Poetry History.* Jinmon Shoin, 1996. Not a collection of poems but a selection of essays that throw light on Shiraishi's struggle to remain true to herself as a poet.

————. *Sazoku.* Shoshi Yamada, 1982.

————. *Shinsen Shiraishi Kazuko Shishū.* Shichōsha, 1978. Vol. 113 in *Gendaishi Bunko.*

————. *Shiraishi Kazuko Shishū.* Shichōsha, 1969. Vol. 28 in *Gendaishi Bunko.*

Tada Chimako. *Fū o kiru Hito.* Shoshi Yamada, 2004. Her last collection, this book comes with a description of her memorial service and a complete collection of the haiku she wrote while ill. The same haiku were published later under the title *Kaze no Katami* as a not-for-sale publication.

————. *Hafuribi.* Ozawa Shoten, 1986.

————. *Kawa no Hotori ni.* Shoshi Yamada, 1998.

————. *Nagai Kawa no aru Kuni.* Shoshi Yamada, 2001.

————. *Tada Chimako Shishū.* Shichōsha, 1972. Vol. 50 in *Gendaishi Bunko.*

————. *Teihon: Tada Chimako Shishū.* Sakoya Shobō, 1994. The "definitive," complete poems up to the time of publication.

Takarabe Toriko. *Monochro Kronos.* Sinchōsa, 2002.

————. *Mōsui suru Onna-shijin no Hibi.* Shoshi Yanada, 2006.

————. *Takarabe Toriko Shishū.* Shichōsha, 1997. Vol. 145 in *Gendaishi Bunko.*

————. *Uyū no Hito.* Shichōsha, 1998.

Takeuchi Rie. *Takeuchi Rie Sakuhin Shū.* Origin Shuppan Center, 1990. Contains all the poems, short stories, and essays collected by Rie's son Tatsurō.

Tawara Machi. *Chocolate Kakumei.* Kawade Shobō Shinsha, 1997.

————. *Kaze no Tenohira.* Kawade Shobō Shinsha, 1994.

————. *Sarada Kinenbi.* Kawade Shobō Shinsha, 1987.

————. *Toretate no Tanka desu.* Kadokawa Shoten, 1989.

Tokizane Shinko. *Kaze no Madobe de.* Asahi Shimbunsha, 1997. Sixth installment of the annual series of compilations-cum-commentary of Tokizane's senryū group, Shinko-za. The series began in 1991.

————. *Kirakira nayamu.* Kōdansha, 1996. Not a collection of Tokizane's senryū but a selection from her advice columns à la Ann Landers, with occasional insertion of her senryū and a small selection of senryū published in the magazine she edits.

Tomioka Taeko. *Tomioka Taeko Shishū.* Shichōsha, 1968. Vol. 15 in *Gendaishi Bunko.*

————. *Tomioka Taeko Shishū.* Shichōsha, 1973. Complete poems. After the publication of this book, Tomioka wrote a set of ten poems, which were published in a magazine, and quit writing poems altogether.

Yosano Akiko. *Midaregami.* Kadokawa Shoten, 1956. A reproduction of the original with typographical and orthographic errors corrected in the endnotes, this edition comes with a collection of tanka written during the same period but not included in the famous book. *Midaregami* is also available in a number of other editions and anthologies.

————. *Teihon Yosano Akiko Zenshū.* Kōdansha, 1980. Vols. 9 and 10 include her shi.

————, ed. *Yosano Akiko Kashū.* Iwanami Shoten, 1943. This poet's own selection famously includes only fourteen pieces from *Midaregami.*

Index of Poets

About the Translator

A leading translator of Japanese poetry into English, Hiroaki Sato has won, with Burton Watson, the PEN American translation prize for *From the Country of Eight Islands: An Anthology of Japanese Poetry* (Doubleday Anchor, 1981; reprint, Columbia University Press, 1986). He has also won the Japan–United States Friendship Commission's prize for *Breeze Through Bamboo: Kanshi of Ema Saikō* (Columbia University Press, 1997). Among his recent books are *Miyazawa Kenji: Selections* (University of California Press, 2007), which is part of the UCP's Poets for the Millennium series, and *The Modern Fable: Poems of Nishiwaki Junzaburō* (Green Integer, 2007). He writes a monthly column, "The View from New York," for *The Japan Times*.